LOGICAL FRAMEWORKS

LOGICAL FRAMEWORKS

Edited by

Gérard Huet
Directeur de Recherche, INRIA-Rocquencourt

G. Plotkin
Professor of Theoretical Computer Science,
University of Edinburgh

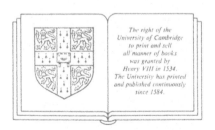

The right of the
University of Cambridge
to print and sell
all manner of books
was granted by
Henry VIII in 1534.
The University has printed
and published continuously
since 1584.

CAMBRIDGE UNIVERSITY PRESS
Cambridge
New York   Port Chester
Melbourne   Sydney

CAMBRIDGE UNIVERSITY PRESS
Cambridge, New York, Melbourne, Madrid, Cape Town,
Singapore, São Paulo, Delhi, Tokyo, Mexico City

Cambridge University Press
The Edinburgh Building, Cambridge CB2 8RU, UK

Published in the United States of America by Cambridge University Press, New York

www.cambridge.org
Information on this title: www.cambridge.org/9780521413008

First published 1991

A catalogue record for this publication is available from the British Library

ISBN 978-0-521-41300-8 Hardback

CONTENTS

Preface

This book is a collection of papers presented at the first annual Workshop held under the auspices of the ESPRIT Basic Research Action 3245, "Logical Frameworks: Design, Implementation and Experiment". It took place at Sophia-Antipolis, France from the 7th to the 11th of May, 1990. Seventy-four people attended the Workshop: one from Japan, six from the United States, and the rest from Europe.

We thank the European Community for the funding which made the Workshop possible. We also thank Gilles Kahn who, with the help of the Service des Relations Extérieures of INRIA, performed a most excellent job of organisation. Finally, we thank the following researchers who acted as referees: R. Constable, T. Coquand, N.G. deBruijn, P. de Groote, V. Donzeau-Gouge, G. Dowek, P. Dybjer, A. Felty, L. Hallnäs, R. Harper, L. Helmink, F. Honsell, Z. Luo, N. Mendler, C. Paulin, L. Paulson, R. Pollack, D. Pym, F. Rouaix, P. Schröder-Heister, A. Smaill, and B. Werner.

We cannot resist saying a word or two about how these proceedings came into being. Immediately after the Workshop, participants were invited to contribute papers by electronic mail, as LaTeX sources. One of us (Huet) then collected the papers together, largely unedited, and the result was "published electronically" by making the collection a file available worldwide by ftp (a remote file transfer protocol). This seems to have been somewhat of a success, at least in terms of numbers of copies circulated, and perhaps had merit in terms of rapid and widespread availability of recent work. Having done this, we then followed a more conventional route, inviting contributors to submit papers for the present volume.

G. Huet, INRIA, Rocquencourt
G. Plotkin, Edinburgh University

Introduction

This book contains a collection of papers concerned with logical frameworks. Such frameworks arise in a number of ways when considering the relationship between logic and computation, and indeed the general structure of logical formalisms. In particular, in Computer Science, there is interest in the representation and organization of mathematical knowledge on the computer, and in obtaining computational assistance with its derivation. One would especially like to implement program logics and prove programs correct. Again, there is direct computational content in various logical formalisms, particularly constructive ones. Finally, such issues provoke interest in re-examining purely logical questions.

Logical frameworks arise in two distinct but related senses. First, very many logics are of interest in Computer Science, and great repetition of effort is involved in implementing each. It would therefore be helpful to create a single framework, a kind of meta-logic, which is itself implementable and in which the logics of interest can be represented. Putting the two together there results an implementation of any represented logic.

In the second sense, one chooses a particular "universal" logic which is strong enough to do all that is required, and sticks to it. For example, one might choose a set theory, and do mathematics within that. Both approaches have much in common. Even within a fixed logic there is the need for a descriptive apparatus for particular mathematical theories, notations, derived rules and so on. Providing such is rather similar to providing a framework in the first sense.

There is however a deeper relationship which provides the essential conceptual basis of the work presented here. It arises from the question of the computational content of logic. An important answer was given by Curry, Howard and de Bruijn and developed by Martin-Löf. They provided the "propositions-as-types" interpretation. Associated is the interpretation of proofs as inhabitants of these types. Types and their inhabitants — and so propositions and proofs — are presented syntactically by a variety of terms. There are judgements of inhabitation and equality (rather than of truth, as in logic). The whole forms a typed λ-calculus or type theory. This provides a very versatile tool. For example, terms of the type theories can be directly evaluated, thereby providing a functional programming language. If a constructive theory is chosen as a universal logic then proofs of existence yield terms of the type theory witnessing the existential; these terms are programs in the functional language.

Such methods have already been proposed in mathematical logic as the so-called realisability interpretations. The recent development of functional programming languages in Computer Science enables one to make these translations from proofs to programs more direct, and to start designing realistic programming environments built around proof systems.

Working on the meta-level, the syntax of a logic can be thought of as being given by the types of its terms and formulas. Then to each judgement in the logic there is associated the type of proofs of the judgement. Rules of the logic are given by λ-abstractions, which are terms of higher functional type. One can then try to find a type theory rich enough to express all these types for a wide variety of logics.

The connections that arise can be quite surprising. For example, searching for a proof of a proposition amounts to searching for a term of a given type. On the one hand, this ties up directly with proof theory. On the other, allowing free variables in the types and fixing a search strategy results in a logic programming language. Thus there is an intimate relationship between logic programming and type theory.

We have organized the papers into a variety of themes illustrating some of the ideas sketched above. The first theme concerns choices of *frameworks* for (a variety of) logics. In the first of the papers, Aczel, Carlisle and Mendler treat LTC, the Logical Theory of Constructions, which is in fact based on a type-free calculus. One of the main ideas employed is to treat the notions of proposition and truth as fundamental and use them to explain the notions of type and elementhood.

The next paper is by de Bruijn, a pioneer in the field, who headed the Automath project at Eindhoven University from about 1968 to 1988. Automath is a typed λ-calculus, where the types are themselves λ-terms. There is thus no need for a separate syntax for the types: the λ-abstraction operator functions as a product operator, producing dependent types (these are the types of functions where the type of the result of the function can depend on its argument). In his paper, de Bruijn argues that frameworks of strong logical complexity may not be necessary, since they may be encoded in weaker frameworks which are easier to implement and understand. He discusses various design issues for such weak frameworks, drawing from the Automath experience.

The last paper in this theme builds on the syntactical structure underlying Automath proofs, the Λ formalism of Nederpelt. In the paper, de Groote adds context operators to a non-extensional version of Λ in order to represent mathematical theories, including definitions and lemmas. The resulting system is reminiscent of de Bruijn's own ΛΔ, but definitional equalities are handled separately from β-conversion.

The second theme concerns experience with *implementations* of type theories. The first paper, by Basin and Kaufmann, makes an extensive comparison between two popular proof systems: the Boyer-Moore theorem prover and the Nuprl Proof Development System. A non-trivial combinatorial theorem, due to Ramsey, is used to test the two systems. Such comparisons are very valuable in helping a potential user assess the relative merits of systems as regards ease of axiomatization, help in automating proof search, proof length, proof replay time, user interaction time and so on.

The next paper, by Helmink and Ahn, describes an implementation, under development at Philips Research Laboratories, of Generalised Type Systems, one of the current family of logical frameworks. This Constructor proof system uses a systematic goal-directed proof procedure, reminiscent of logic programming. The paper discusses the completeness of this procedure. Finally, the paper by Pfenning on Elf relates to the Edinburgh Logical Framework, LF, which is based on a type theory with dependent types. Pfenning's idea is to unify logic definition in the style of LF with logic programming in the style of λProlog. The paper presents the design and preliminary implementation of Elf.

The third theme is concerned with *representing formal systems* in others. An important example of this is representing a logic in a logical framework. The first paper, by Burstall and Honsell examines how to encode operational semantics definitions of programming languages in LF. This natural deduction treatment is appropriate to the rigourous treatment of binding operators in programming languages. The paper by Felty presents a translation of LF into the fragment of higher-order logic implemented in λProlog. This translation exactly encodes the consequence relation of LF, and so logics defined in LF can be implemented in λProlog.

The fourth theme is concerned with issues of the *type theories* themselves. The paper by Coquand proves the decidability of βη-conversion (and related properties) for a typed λ-calculus with dependent function space types and a single universe. The key to the proof is an extension of the method of logical relations to the case of dependent types. Results of this kind had previously proved exceedingly difficult to obtain by more direct syntactic methods.

The paper by Dybjer gives a presentation of Martin-Löf's type theory including rules for a large class of inductive constructions in type theory.

It also gives a set-theoretic interpretation of the resulting type theory. The inductive rules comprise schemata for inductive sets and families of sets (or types) and also for primitive recursive functions and families of functions over the sets and families.

The fifth theme is that of *proofs and computations*, where one exploits the view of proofs as terms of a type-theory. The first paper, by Pym and Wallen, discusses the problem of automating proof search in the λΠ-calculus, the type theory of LF. Various presentations of the λΠ-calculus are given, progressively easing the problem of automation of proof search, while preserving provability.

The next paper, by Constable and Murthy, discusses the constructive content of classical proofs. A refinement of the double negation interpretation of classical logic, Friedman's A-translation, is presented as a proof transformation procedure in the Nuprl system, and explained by means of a problem inspired by Higman's lemma. The relationship with continuation-passing style in programming languages is briefly discussed.

The last theme, of *logical issues*, considers naturally arising logical questions. The paper by Hallnäs presents a model theory for partial inductive definitions First, Aczel's rule-sets (essentially) receive a logical interpretation in terms of a sequent calculus. This approach is then extended to definitions where rules may have arrows in their conditions. Finally, partial inductive definitions are treated by means of simple definitions via a kind of Curry-Howard interpretation.

Finally, Schröder-Heister builds on a distinction of Gentzen for sequent-style systems of logic, where structural connectives (such as the comma) and inference schemas (such as contraction) form a framework for logical inference schemas (such as ∨-introduction). He presents a variety of structural frameworks, and discusses how elimination schemas reflect the introduction schemas via general structural principles.

FRAMEWORKS

Two frameworks of theories and their implementation in Isabelle

Peter Aczel   David P. Carlisle   Nax Mendler

Computer Science Department
Manchester University
Manchester, M13 9PL

Abstract

In this paper we describe a version of the LTC (Logical Theory of Constructions) framework, three Martin-Löf type theories and interpretations of the type theories in the corresponding LTC theories.* Then we discuss the implementation of the above in the generic theorem prover Isabelle. An earlier version of the LTC framework was described by Aczel and Mendler in [15].

1 Introduction

In [15] the notion of an open-ended framework of deductive interpreted languages is formulated, and in particular an example is given of a hierarchy of languages L_i in the LTC framework. In the first part of this three part paper, sections 2 to 4, we review this hierarchy of languages and then discuss some issues concerning the framework, which lead to another hierarchy of languages, LTC_0, LTC_1, LTC_ω. In the second part, sections 5 and 6, we give three type theories, TT_0, TT_1 and TT_ω, and their interpretations in

---

*This work has been partially supported by both SERC grant No. GR/E29861 and the ESPRIT Basic Research Action 'Logical Frameworks'. The paper combines two talks,[4] and [16], that were presented at the Antibes workshop.

the corresponding LTC language. In the final part, sections 7 to 9, we document the implementation of the LTC hierarchy in the generic theorem prover, Isabelle, developed by Larry Paulson at Cambridge [19, 20]. We also describe a programme for verifying, in Isabelle, the interpretations of the type theories TT_0, TT_1 and TT_ω.

The basic LTC framework is one that runs parallel to the ITT framework. ITT stands for "Intuitionistic Theory of Types", see [13, 14]. It is a particular language from the latter framework that has been implemented in the Cornell Nuprl System, [8]. The basic LTC framework is intended to be, at the informal level, the framework of ideas that were used by Per Martin-Löf in his semantical explanations for ITT in [13]. Those explanations seem to treat the notions of proposition and truth as fundamental and use them to explain the notions of type and elementhood as used in ITT. This is, of course, going in the reverse direction to that which occurs when ITT is used, when the propositions as types idea is applied so as to represent the logical notions as notions of type theory.

The LTC framework has its technical origins in the first-order theory of combinators of [1]. An investigation of the models was first undertaken in [2] and a revised notion of model is considered in [3], which is closely related to the approach of [5]. The version of the LTC in [15] was essentially based on this revised notion of model. A formulation of an LTC language may be found in the dissertation [21], which also gives an account of the translation of the early version of ITT, [12], into the LTC language. In [22] may be found a translation of the later version of an ITT language into an LTC language. A description of the LTC approach that is oriented more towards computer science may be found in [9].

The unifying theme behind variant versions of the LTC framework is the idea to focus on a universe of objects which include both the data values of a lazy functional programming notation and also the propositions of an internal reflection of logic (for those LTC languages that are rich enough to include a reflection of logic). When interpreting a type theory in an LTC theory the types are represented as certain kinds of partial equivalence relations on this universe.

In connection with the internal reflection of logic there is a truth predicate T, which expresses, of an object of the universe that is a proposition, that the proposition is true. In some approaches, such as that of [22], this predicate is only meaningfully applicable to objects that are propositions. This leads to formulations that involve a non-standard formalisation, where the rules of formula formation are mixed up with the rules of deduction. In particular there may be a rule that allows the formation of a formula $T(a)$ provided that a formula $P(a)$ has been deduced, where P is a predicate expressing that an object of the universe is a proposition. In the present paper, as in [15], we have kept to a simpler, more standard kind of formalisation that involves a mild extension of the predicate calculus. So for us, when an *LTC* theory has a truth predicate *T* it is one that is applicable to all objects of the universe.

The functional programming notation that we use comes from *ITT*, but here, of course, it is untyped. In some versions of the *LTC* framework the universe of objects forms the domain of values for a denotational semantics of the programming notation, so that, in particular, the universe forms a model of the lambda calculus. In [15] an alternative approach, reviewed in section 2 here, was taken in which programs of the programming notation were themselves represented as objects of the universe and an operational semantics for the programming language was explicitly expressed by an *evaluation* relation, $\leadsto$, on the universe. This has led to the focus on certain kinds of term models as standard interpretations of *LTC* theories. In these term models the equality relation on the universe is decidable. In the present paper we have experimented with a compromise between the two approaches, which might be called the *denotational* and *operational* approaches. The idea is to separate out two aspects of functional computation, the *purely recursive* from the remaining *control* aspects. In the compromise we deal with the purely recursive aspect in a denotational way; i.e. purely recursive definitions are treated as equalities. But the remaining control aspects of functional computation; i.e. *discrimination* between distinct canonical forms and *selection* of the components of a canonical value, are treated operationally using the explicit evaluation relation as before. Term models are still used as standard interpretations of *LTC* theories, but now the purely recursive definitions can be used in the identification of terms. It seems to be an open problem, which may be rather dificult, to determine whether or not equality in the term models is still decidable. Nevertheless, as with the other two approaches, a Church-Rosser theorem may be proved, which ensures that the term models are well-behaved.

A minor advantage of this compromise approach is that it gives a pleasing regular pattern to the operational semantics. But it is unclear, at present, what more significant advantages it may have over the purely operational approach. We have focused on it in this paper because it seems to be a new idea that we believe merits further investigation.

In focussing on the *LTC* framework we are pursuing the idea that the notions of proposition and truth are, after all, the fundamental ones for logic and that the logical notions are the fundamental ones for a deductive system for mathematics. According to this idea, although the notion of type is also essential for mathematics and computer science it is less fundamental conceptually.

2   The *LTC* framework and the languages L_i.

In [15] an attempt was made to make precise the general notion of a framework of deductive interpreted languages, each such language being a triple (σ, T, I) consisting of a signature σ, a theory T for σ and an interpretation I of σ that models T. We will not review that here. To some extent that notion of a framework is better captured using the notions of institution and general logic. See for example [17]. But more is needed to adequately capture the intended notion of a conceptual framework of ideas, such as that of the *ITT* framework, that determines notions of signature, theory and standard interpretation.

The increasing hierarchy of four languages L_i for $i = 1, \ldots, 4$ was originally defined in [15]. In keeping with the notion of framework presented there each language L_i has the form (σ_i, T_i, I_i), as above. Here we shall give a description of the basic framework and then go on to describe the languages L_i, ignoring for the most part in each case the, not to be implemented, interpretation component I_i of the language.

The basic LTC framework

As presented in [15], the signatures of the *LTC* frameworks are taken over from the theory of arities as used by Per Martin-Löf in [14] and the Gothenburg group in [18]. This is essentially a simply-typed lambda calculus with two atomic types, ι for terms and o for formulae, but now types are called arities and the notation for abstraction and application avoids any explicit symbols such as λ for abstraction or Ap for application. We use the following *currying* abbreviation.

$$[\alpha_1, \alpha_2, \ldots, \alpha_n] \longrightarrow \alpha \quad \equiv \quad \alpha_1 \to (\alpha_2 \to \cdots (\alpha_n \to \alpha) \cdots)$$

So an arity $[\alpha_1, \ldots, \alpha_n] \longrightarrow \alpha$ is the arity of n-place function expressions having arguments of arities $\alpha_1, \ldots, \alpha_n$ and a value of arity α. A signature will be made up of a set of constant symbols, taken from a fixed sufficiently large set, each symbol being of some arity. Expressions are built up in the usual way from these constants and the variables using abstraction and application. If b is an expression of arity β and x is a variable of arity α then we will write $(x)b$ for the expression of arity $\alpha \to \beta$ obtained by abstraction on the variable x. Also if f is an expression of arity $\alpha \to \beta$ and a is an expression of arity α then we write $f(a)$ for the expression of arity β obtained by function application. Obvious notational conventions will be adopted for repeated abstractions and repeated applications. Interconvertible expressions will be identified, so that in particular the notion of a bound occurrence of a variable no longer makes sense. To indicate expression e is of arity α, we write $e : \alpha$.

Each arity has a *level*, with the atomic arities having level 0 and the arity $\alpha \to \beta$ has level $max(l + 1, k)$, where l, k are the levels of α, β respectively. For most purposes only symbols having an arity of level ≤ 2 are needed. The languages L_i only have such symbols.

Every LTC signature will include a standard signature σ_0 for intuitionistic first-order logic having the following connectives and first-order quantifiers.

$$\bot \; : \; o \qquad\qquad\qquad = \; : \; [\iota, \iota] \longrightarrow o$$
$$\wedge, \vee, \supset \; : \; [o, o] \longrightarrow o \qquad \forall, \exists \; : \; (\iota \to o) \to o$$

In addition to $\forall$ and $\exists$ we will also need in LTC_0 the quantifiers $\forall^1, \exists^1$ of arity $((\iota \to \iota) \to o) \to o$ that quantify 1-place function variables of level 1. The usual infix notation for binary connectives and equality will be used. Also the usual notation for quantifiers will be used, so that, for example, we write $\forall x \phi$ for $\forall((x)\phi)$. The above connectives and quantifiers are called the *logical symbols*, the remaining symbols of a signature being *non-logical*. As in ordinary first-order logic the non-logical symbols are of two kinds, function symbols and predicate symbols. We say a symbol $F : [\alpha_1, \ldots, \alpha_n] \longrightarrow \iota$ is a *function* symbol and a symbol $F : [\alpha_1, \ldots, \alpha_n] \longrightarrow o$ is a *predicate* symbol. In each case we assume that the arities $\alpha_1, \ldots, \alpha_n$ are *elementary*; i.e. they only involve the ground arity ι and not o. The individual terms and the formulae of the language can be inductively generated in more or less the standard way as in the predicate calculus, using the function symbols to build up terms and the predicate symbols to form atomic formulae. Formulae are then built up from the atomic formulae using the logical symbols.

When using a basic formal theory with a signature of primitive symbols it is often convenient to work with extension signatures obtained by adding new defined symbols, adding their defining axioms to the axioms of the basic theory. Such *definitional* extensions of the basic theory are inessential in the sense that the new symbols can always be systematically eliminated. For this reason it is natural to partition the symbols of a signature into the *primitive* symbols and the *defined* symbols, where a defining axiom is associated with each defined symbol. There is no need to have defined symbols in the basic languages and there are none in the languages L_i. But in our formulation of the languages LTC_i we have experimented with the use of a development of the concept of a definitional extension by allowing recursive definitions of function symbols. The definitions are no longer deductively inessential.

Each theory for a given signature will include a standard system T_0 of schematic axioms and rules for the intuitionistic predicate calculus with equality. In addition to the usual rules for equality there are special rules for equality that express that the primitive function symbols of the signature should denote injective functions with pairwise disjoint ranges. We certainly do not want such rules for the defined symbols.

There are two kinds of special equality rules.

$$(SE1) \qquad \frac{c(f_1, \ldots, f_n) = c(g_1, \ldots, g_n)}{f_i(a_1, \ldots, a_{k_i}) = g_i(a_1, \ldots, a_{k_i})}$$

$$(SE2) \qquad \frac{c(f_1, \ldots, f_n) = d(h_1, \ldots, h_m)}{\perp}$$

where c is an n-place primitive function symbol of arity $(\alpha_1 \cdots \alpha_n)$, $1 \leq i \leq n$, f_j, g_j are terms of arity α_j for $1 \leq j \leq n$ and $a_1, \ldots, a_{k_i}$ are terms of the appropriate arity. Also d is a primitive function symbol of arity $(\beta_1 \cdots \beta_m)$ distinct from c and h_j is a term of arity β_j for $1 \leq j \leq m$.

The motivation for having these special equality rules is that they are correct for the LTC interpretations, which are always certain kinds of term models. In these models each elementary arity is interpreted as a suitable equivalence class of closed terms, involving function symbols from a signature that may be an extension of the signature being interpreted.

$$\textit{The language } L_1 = (\sigma_1, T_1, -).$$

This language is a first-order version of the Peano axioms for the natural numbers. The symbols of σ_1 consist of the logical symbols of σ_0 plus the primitive symbols $0 : \iota$, $S : \iota \rightarrow \iota$ and $N : \iota \rightarrow o$. Two of the Peano axioms are already captured by the special equality rules for $0, S$.

$$\frac{S(a) = S(b)}{a = b} \qquad\qquad \frac{S(a) = 0}{\perp}$$

The remaining three Peano axioms need to be added explicitly to get the theory T_1.

$$\frac{}{N(0)} \qquad \frac{N(a)}{N(S(a))} \qquad \frac{\phi(0) \quad \forall x(\phi(x) \supset \phi(S(x)))}{N(a) \supset \phi(a)}$$

The language L_1 is still very weak as there is as yet no way to express addition and multiplication of natural numbers.

The language $L_2 = (\sigma_2, T_2, -)$.

L_2 extends L_1 by incorporating a simple functional programming notation with an explicit operational semantics. In the interpretation of L_2 the *values* of the programming language will be the objects of arity ι that are in *canonical form*. Such objects will be elements of the term model for L_2 whose outermost primitive function symbol has been stipulated to be *canonical*. The primitive function symbols that are stipulated to be non-canonical will be the control constructs of the programming language. The function symbols in σ_2 are $0, S$ from L_1 plus the following.

$$
\begin{array}{rcl}
\lambda &:& (\iota \to \iota) \to \iota \\
\langle\_,\_\rangle &:& [\iota, \iota] \longrightarrow \iota \\
Inl, Inr &:& \iota \to \iota
\end{array}
\qquad
\begin{array}{rcl}
Ap &:& [\iota, \iota] \longrightarrow \iota \\
Spread &:& [\iota, [\iota, \iota] \longrightarrow \iota] \longrightarrow \iota \\
Decide &:& [\iota, \iota \to \iota, \iota \to \iota] \longrightarrow \iota \\
Ind &:& [\iota, \iota, \iota \to \iota] \longrightarrow \iota
\end{array}
$$

Each primitive function symbol of L_2 is stipulated to be canonical or non-canonical. Symbols 0, S, from L_1, and those in the above left-hand column are canonical, while the symbols in the right-hand column are non-canonical. As with the quantifiers we can write $\lambda x a$ for $\lambda((x)a)$.

The operational semantics for lazy evaluation of the expressions of the programming language is captured by using the predicate symbol $\_ \leadsto \_ : [\iota, \iota] \longrightarrow o$. This is intended to express the relation of evaluation to canonical form. A term of arity ι is *canonical*, i.e. is in canonical form, if its outermost function symbol is a primitive canonical symbol. The theory T_2 is obtained from T_1 by adding the following evaluation rules for the control constructs.

$$
(\leadsto 1) \quad \frac{}{c \leadsto c} \qquad\qquad (\leadsto 2) \quad \frac{a \leadsto c \qquad d \leadsto e}{k(a) \leadsto e}
$$

Where in $(\leadsto 1)$, c is required to be canonical, and in $(\leadsto 2)$, (c, d, k) is required to be a *computation triple*, a triple of the forms listed in the following table. Note that the first column of the table lists all the canonical forms.

The Computation Triples of L_2.

c	d	k
$\lambda(f)$	$f(b)$	$(x)Ap(x,b)$
$\langle b_1, b_2 \rangle$	$h(b_1, b_2)$	$(x)Spread(x,h)$
$Inl(b)$	$f(b)$	$(x)Decide(x,f,g)$
$Inr(b)$	$g(b)$	$(x)Decide(x,f,g)$
0	b	$(x)Ind(x,b,h)$
$S(c)$	$h(c, Ind(c,b,h))$	$(x)Ind(x,b,h)$

In the interpretation of L_2 the evaluation relation is inductively defined using the above two rules as the clauses of the inductive definition. It follows that the following two rules are also correct. Although they are not in L_2 we shall have them in the language LTC_0.

$$(\leadsto 3) \quad \frac{a \leadsto e_1 \quad a \leadsto e_2}{e_1 = e_2} \qquad (\leadsto 4) \quad \frac{a \leadsto c \quad k(a) \leadsto e}{d \leadsto e}$$

In $(\leadsto 4)$, (c,d,k) is required to be a computation triple.

The language $L_3 = (\sigma_3, T_3, -)$.

The language L_3 can be viewed as a metalanguage for L_2, as it involves an internal representation of the semantics of L_2. To do this the signature σ_3 includes two new primitive predicate symbols P_1 and T of arity $\iota \to o$. Also σ_3 includes a new canonical primitive function symbol corresponding to each of the logical symbols and predicate symbols of L_2. These new function symbols will be indicated by placing a dot over the symbol they correspond to. The new rules of T_3 express in a fairly straightforward way a semantics for L_2, when the predicate symbol P_1 is used to internally represent the *propositions* of L_2 and the predicate symbol T is used to represent the *true* propositions of L_2. For each dotted symbol there is a *proposition formation rule* and also a rule giving the *truth conditions* for a proposition formed using the symbol. We can present the new rules of T_3 in a systematic way by associating with each individual term c of L_3 formulae Φ_c^1 and Ψ_c as detailed below. The new rules for c are

$$\frac{e \rightsquigarrow c \quad \Phi_c^1}{P_1(e)} \qquad\qquad \frac{e \rightsquigarrow c \quad \Phi_c^1}{T(e) \Leftrightarrow \Psi_c}$$

Here we use $\phi \Leftrightarrow \psi$ to abbreviate the formula $(\phi \supset \psi) \wedge (\psi \supset \phi)$. The formulae Φ_c^1 and Ψ_c are specified in the following table, where we use $\top$ to abbreviate $(\bot \supset \bot)$.

c	Φ_c^1	Ψ_c
$(a\dot{=}b)$	$\top$	$(a = b)$
$\dot{N}(a)$	$\top$	$N(a)$
$(a\dot{\rightsquigarrow}b)$	$\top$	$(a \rightsquigarrow b)$
$\dot{\bot}$	$\top$	$\bot$
$(a\dot{\wedge}b)$	$P_1(a) \wedge P_1(b)$	$T(a) \wedge T(b)$
$(a\dot{\vee}b)$	$P_1(a) \wedge P_1(b)$	$T(a) \vee T(b)$
$(a\dot{\supset}b)$	$P_1(a) \wedge (T(a) \supset P_1(b))$	$T(a) \supset T(b)$
$\dot{\forall}(f)$	$\forall x P_1(f(x))$	$\forall x T(f(x))$
$\dot{\exists}(f)$	$\forall x P_1(f(x))$	$\exists x T(f(x))$

The language $L_4 = (\sigma_4, T_4, -)$.

The language L_3 was obtained by a process of reflection on the language L_2. This process can be repeated to obtain a metalanguage for L_3, a metalanguage for that language and so on. The language L_4 is a language incorporating the result of repeating the reflection process any finite number of times. So there is now a hierarchy of predicate symbols P_i for $i = 1, 2, \ldots$ with P_{i+1} being used to internally represent the propositions of the sublanguage of L_4 that only involves the predicate symbols $P_1, \ldots, P_i$. There need to be dotted function symbols $\dot{P}_i$ corresponding to these predicate symbols. The rules of T_4 are obtained by adding to the rules of T_2 the following rules for $i = 1, 2, \ldots$

$$\frac{e \rightsquigarrow c \quad \Phi^i_c}{P_i(e)} \qquad \frac{e \rightsquigarrow c \quad \Phi^i_c}{T(e) \Leftrightarrow \Psi_c} \qquad \frac{P_j(e)}{P_i(e)} \ (j < i)$$

Here Φ^i_c is defined like Φ^1_c using P_i instead of P_1, except that there is the following additional row in the table defining the formulae Φ^i_c and Ψ_c.

c	Φ^i_c	Ψ_c
$\dot{P}_j(a)$ (with $j < i$)	$\top$	$P_j(a)$

There is no need to add a primitive functional symbol $\dot{T}_i$ to internally represent the true propositions of L_i, because if one defines $\dot{T}_i(a)$ as $\dot{P}_i(a) \wedge (\dot{P}_i(a) \supset a)$, then $P_{i+1}(\dot{T}_i(a))$ holds and $T(\dot{T}_i(a))$ is equivalent to $P_i(a) \wedge T(a)$.

3   Term models, recursion extensions of theories and full evaluation for natural numbers

In this section we focus on some issues that are relevent to an understanding of the *LTC* framework as presently conceived. A suitable notion of term model is basic to the interpretations of the *LTC* languages and this is discussed below. But because the defined and primitive symbols are treated differently in term models we start by reviewing the familiar notion of a *definitional extension*. We also formulate a generalisation, the notion of a *recursion extension*. Finally we look at the distinction between *numerals* and *natural numbers* that exists in the context of a lazy evaluation relation and also formulate the additional notion of full evaluation that seems to be needed for the natural numbers.

Definitional Extensions

The notion of a *definitional extension* of a theory is a familiar one that makes sense for many logics. The idea is to extend a theory by adding to it new defined symbols with their defining axioms. The new theory should be an inessential extension in the sense that the defined symbols can always be systematically eliminated. The formulation of this notion for *LTC* theories is straightforward.

We assume given an LTC signature σ and theory T for it. A definitional extension for the theory is obtained by adding some new defined symbols to the signature and for each new symbol F a new axiom is added to the theory, called the *defining axiom* for the symbol. If F is a function symbol of arity $[\alpha_1, \ldots \alpha_n] \longrightarrow \iota$ then the defining axiom has the form

$$F(x_1, \ldots, x_n) = e$$

where $x_1, \ldots, x_n$ is a non-repeating list of variables of arities $\alpha_1, \ldots \alpha_n$ and e is an term of arity ι of the old theory whose free variables are among $x_1, \ldots, x_n$.

If F is a symbol of arity $[\alpha_1, \ldots \alpha_n] \longrightarrow o$ then e should be a formula whose free variables are among $x_1, \ldots, x_n$ and equality should be replaced by logical equivalence, $\Leftrightarrow$.

Definitional extensions are deductively inessential in the sense that all defined symbols can in principle be eliminated from terms and formulae in a systematic way using the definitions. It follows that a definitional extension is conservative over the original theory; i.e. any theorem of the new theory that is expressed in the old signature will already be a theorem of the old theory.

Definitional extensions are also semantically inessential in the sense that any model of the old theory will have a unique enlargement to the new theory. The enlargement is defined by interpreting each new symbol in the model in the obvious way using the interpretation of the right hand side of its definition. It may be as well to emphasise that the LTC framework is based on an extension of first-order logic in that the function and predicate symbols are allowed to be variable binding. Nevertheless the notion of definitional extension works as in the more familiar first-order case.

Term Models

The notion of a term model for a theory makes sense for many logics and is often useful. The general idea is that the elements of a term model are terms or something like terms. Often they are equivalence class of terms under a suitable equivalence relation.

In the LTC framework a notion of term model will play an essential role, as only term models of a particular kind will be allowed as interpretations. Given an LTC signature σ, by a *term model for σ* we mean something obtained in the following way. Take a signature σ' obtained from σ by adding new function symbols. For each elementary arity α (i.e. one not involving the ground arity o) let T_α be the set of closed terms of σ' of arity α. Let $\{\equiv_\alpha\}_\alpha$ be the family of equivalence relations $\equiv_\alpha$ on T_α that forms a congruence with respect to the function symbols of σ' generated by using the α, β and η rules of the theory of arities and the defining equations for the defined symbols of σ'. Let A_α be the set of equivalence classes $[t]$ of the terms t of T_α relative to the equivalence relation $\equiv_\alpha$. Each function symbol F of σ of arity $[\alpha_1, \ldots, \alpha_n] \longrightarrow \iota$ now has an interpretation as the unique function

$$[[F]] : A_{\alpha_1} \times \cdots \times A_{\alpha_n} \longrightarrow A_\iota$$

such that for $t_1 \in T_{\alpha_1}, \ldots, t_n \in T_{\alpha_n}$

$$[[F]]([t_1], \ldots, [t_n]) = [F(t_1, \ldots, t_n)].$$

The specification of a term model for σ is now completed by interpreting each primitive predicate symbol F of σ of arity $[\alpha_1, \ldots, \alpha_n] \longrightarrow o$ as a relation $[[F]] \subseteq A_{\alpha_1} \times \cdots \times A_{\alpha_n}$. Such a term model for σ gives rise to a semantics for the formulae of σ in the usual way. The quantifiers $\forall, \exists$ are interpreted to range over A_ι and the quantifiers $\forall^1, \exists^1$ are interpreted to range over $A_{\iota \to \iota}$. The correctness of the special equality rules can be obtained as a consequence of the standard Church-Rosser result that is available for the theory of arities with additional rewrite rules given by the explicit definitions for the defined symbols. The defined predicate symbols need to be given that interpretation that makes their defining axioms come out true. Of course the truth of the defining axioms for the defined function symbols has been built in to the notion of term model.

Recursion Extensions and their term models

Here we wish to consider a generalisation of the notion of a definitional extension, which we will use in the language LTC_0. In the LTC framework there is a clear separation between those aspects that are to do with definitions and the resulting notion of definitional equality and those aspects that are to do with the computation triples and the resulting evaluation relation. These aspects are conflated in the type free lambda calculus and in the original notion of Frege structure [2] that was used as the first idea for the interpretations of something like the LTC framework [22]. By our use of explicit evaluation relations over term models we keep these aspects separate. Our idea here is to compromise between the two approaches by allowing definitions to be recursive and only leaving discrimination/selection to be represented in the computation triples. Take the example of the non-canonical primitive function symbol Ind of the language L_2. It is used to capture primitive recursion on the natural numbers, a computational notion. We can analyse primitive recursion into the two separate components of recursion and discrimination/selection and move the recursion component to the definitional aspect, keeping only the discrimination/selection features of computation to be captured with the computation triples. To do this we now take *Ind* to be a defined symbol with recursive defining equation

$$Ind(c, b, h) \quad = \quad DecideNat(c, b, (x)h(x, Ind(x, b, h)))$$

Here *DecideNat* is to be a new non-canonical primitive function symbol used in the following computation triples.

c	d	k
0	b	$(x)DecideNat(x, b, g)$
$S(c)$	$g(c)$	$(x)DecideNat(x, b, g)$

These replace the old computation triples for the primitive function symbols $0, S$ that used *Ind*. The symbol *DecideNat* is purely a discriminator/selector as are the other non-canonical function symbols of L_2: Ap, *Spread* and *Decide*. The idea for this kind of separation of recursion from discrimination/selection came from a reading of [10] although they do not distinguish between equality and evaluation in the way we do.

Let us now describe the general notion of a *recursion extension* of a theory. This notion will generalise the notion of a definitional extension. Although no longer necessarily always an inessential extension it turns out that a recursion extension will still have a reasonable notion of term model. A recursion extension is a new theory obtained from an old one by adding new defined function symbols to the signature and for each defined symbol, F, a new defining axiom

$$F(x_1, \ldots, x_n) = e$$

as in the case of a definitional extension except that now the term e is a term of the new signature (so that it may contain F itself) whose free variables are among $x_1, \ldots, x_n$.

In the previous subsection we gave the definition of the notion of a term model for a signature where the defining axioms for the defined symbols were always non-recursive. That definition will still carry over to the more general situation where we allow recursive defining axioms for the defined function symbols as above. Fortunately the Church-Rosser theorem that we had before will extend to a Church-Rosser theorem here, even though the reduction relation will now no longer be strongly normalising as it was before. We hope to discuss this elsewhere. Because we still have a Church-Rosser theorem the special equality rules will hold as before.

We have made one change to the table of computation triples. The triples involving *Ind* were replaced by those involving *DecideNat*. With this change the computation triples are formed in a pretty uniform way. Only the triple for the canonical primitive function symbol λ departs slightly from a very clear-cut pattern. The canonical primitive function symbols form into subsets of related symbols. While λ and $\langle\_,\_\rangle$ are on their own *Inl, Inr* are related and so are $0, S$. With each maximal set

$$\{c_1, \ldots, c_m\}$$

of related canonical primitive function symbols there is associated a non-canonical primitive function symbol Δ and computation triples given in the following table

c	d	k
$c_1(f_{11}, \ldots, f_{1n_1})$	$h_1(f_{11}, \ldots, f_{1n_1})$	$(x)\Delta(x, h_1, \ldots, h_m)$
$\vdots$	$\vdots$	$\vdots$
$c_m(f_{m1}, \ldots, f_{mn_1})$	$h_m(f_{m1}, \ldots, f_{mn_1})$	$(x)\Delta(x, h_1, \ldots, h_m)$

The three symbols that play the role of Δ for the three sets $\{\langle\_,\_\rangle\}$, $\{Inl, Inr\}$ and $\{0, S\}$ are, of course, *Spread, Decide* and *DecideNat*. To get a computation triple for λ to fit the pattern we need a non-canonical primitive function symbol *Pa* and the computation triple

c	d	k
$\lambda(f)$	$h(f)$	$(x)Pa(x, h)$

The symbol *Ap* can now be introduced as a defined function symbol with definition

$$Ap(x, b) \;=\; Pa(x, (f)f(b))$$

Note that *Pa* is a symbol of arity $[\iota, (\iota \to \iota) \to \iota] \longrightarrow \iota$, an arity of level 3.

The above groupings of canonical primitive function symbols has its origin in the groups of canonical function symbols associated with each form of type. There seems to be no reason why a new non-canonical constructor Δ with computation triples as above could not be associated with any set $\{c_1, \ldots, c_m\}$ of canonical primitive function symbols.

Natural numbers and their full evaluation

The predicate N of the language L_1 expresses the property of being a *numeral* in unary notation; i.e. being one of $0, S(0), S(S(0)), \ldots$. This notion of numeral is inadequate for computational purposes in the *LTC* framework. We need a notion of *natural number* which will guarantee, for example, that $plus(a, b)$ will be a natural number whenever a, b are. Here *plus* is defined in terms of *Ind* so as to have the following evaluation rules.

$$(plus1) \quad \frac{a \rightsquigarrow c \qquad b \rightsquigarrow 0}{plus(a, b) \rightsquigarrow c} \qquad\qquad (plus2) \quad \frac{b \rightsquigarrow S(c)}{plus(a, b) \rightsquigarrow S(plus(a, c))}$$

It will not do to define a natural number to be an object that evaluates to a numeral. This is because our notion of evaluation is lazy and objects are only evaluated to outermost canonical form. For example $plus(S(0), S(0))$ evaluates to $S(plus(S(0), 0))$ which is not a numeral. The correct definition is that a natural number is an object that is inductively generated by the rules (*Nat1*) and (*Nat2*) below. The rule (*Nat3*) is the principle of mathematical induction for this notion of natural number.

$$(Nat1) \quad \frac{a \rightsquigarrow 0}{Nat(a)} \qquad\qquad (Nat2) \quad \frac{a \rightsquigarrow S(b) \qquad Nat(b)}{Nat(a)}$$

$$(Nat3) \quad \frac{\forall x(x \rightsquigarrow 0 \supset \phi(x)) \qquad \forall x, y(x \rightsquigarrow S(y) \,\&\, \phi(y) \;\supset\; \phi(x))}{Nat(a) \supset \phi(a)}$$

Every natural number should have a full evaluation to a numeral. But it is not clear if this notion of full natural number evaluation can be expressed in L_2 even when *Nat* and its rules have been added. So we want a relation $\rightsquigarrow\!\!\!\!\rightarrow$ to express this notion of full evaluation. Its rules are

$$(\rightsquigarrow\!\!\!\!\rightarrow 1) \quad \frac{a \rightsquigarrow 0}{a \rightsquigarrow\!\!\!\!\rightarrow 0} \qquad\qquad (\rightsquigarrow\!\!\!\!\rightarrow 2) \quad \frac{a \rightsquigarrow S(b) \qquad b \rightsquigarrow\!\!\!\!\rightarrow c}{a \rightsquigarrow\!\!\!\!\rightarrow S(c)}$$

$$(\rightsquigarrow\!\!\!\!\rightarrow 3) \quad \frac{\begin{array}{c}\forall x(x \rightsquigarrow 0 \supset \phi(x, 0)), \\ \forall x, y, z(x \rightsquigarrow S(y) \,\&\, \phi(y, z) \;\supset\; \phi(x, S(z)))\end{array}}{(a \rightsquigarrow\!\!\!\!\rightarrow b) \supset \phi(a, b)} \dagger$$

---

†Ocassionally, for typographical reasons, premises in rules will be listed vertically instead of horizontally.

The first two rules give the clauses for the inductive definition of the full evaluation relation and the final rule expresses proof by induction following the inductive definition. Using these rules we can derive the rules for N and Nat when these have defining axioms

$$N(x) \quad \Leftrightarrow \quad x \rightsquigarrow x$$
$$Nat(x) \quad \Leftrightarrow \quad \exists n(x \rightsquigarrow n)$$

We can also define the relation $EqNat$ of natural number equality by

$$EqNat(x,y) \quad \Leftrightarrow \quad \exists n(x \rightsquigarrow n \wedge y \rightsquigarrow n)$$

This is used in defining the type of natural numbers. So we shall take the rules for $\rightsquigarrow$ as primitive in LTC_0 and use the above definitions of N and Nat.

4   The Languages LTC_0, LTC_1 and LTC_ω.

In this section we describe the three languages. Our description can be brief as these languages are only slightly different to the languages L_2, L_3 and L_4 of [15] and section 2, and the points of difference have been discussed in the previous section.

The LTC_0 theory uses a natural deduction style axiomatisation of intuitionistic logic with equality for the first-order logical symbols $\bot, =, \supset, \wedge, \vee, \forall, \exists$ and the second-order quantifiers $\forall^1, \exists^1$ of arity $((\iota \rightarrow \iota) \rightarrow o) \rightarrow o$ that quantify 1-place functions from individuals to individuals. The non-logical symbols are made up of

Function Symbols

- Canonical primitive: $0, S, \lambda, \langle \_, \_ \rangle, Inl, Inr$
- Non-canonical primitive: $DecideNat, Pa, Spread, Decide$
- Defined: Ap, Ind

Predicate Symbols

- Primitive: $\rightsquigarrow, \rightsquigarrow$
- Defined: $N, Nat, EqNat$

The non-logical rules of LTC_0 consist of:

- The special equality axioms $(SE1), (SE2)$ for the primitive function symbols.

- The evaluation rules ($\leadsto$ 1), ($\leadsto$ 2), ($\leadsto$ 3) and ($\leadsto$ 4), using the computation triples tabled in section 2 except that the computation triples involving *Ind* and *Ap* are replaced by those involving *DecideNat* and *Pa* given section 3.

- The full evaluation rules ($\leadsto\!\leadsto$ 1), ($\leadsto\!\leadsto$ 2) and ($\leadsto\!\leadsto$ 3) of section 3.

- The defining axioms for the defined symbols *Ind*, *Ap*, *N*, *Nat*, *EqNat*, as presented in section 3.

The languages LTC_1 and LTC_ω are obtained from LTC_0 using exactly the same kind of internal reflection and its iteration that are used in the formation of L_3 and L_4 from L_2. Instead of the constructor $\dot{N}$ of L_3 there is now a constructor $\leadsto\!\leadsto$. Also there are new constructors $\dot{\forall}^1, \dot{\exists}^1$ reflecting the function quantifiers of LTC_0.

5   The type theories TT_0, TT_1 and TT_ω

We now present three Martin-Löf-style type theories [14, 8, 18]: TT_0, a type theory without type universes; TT_1, a type theory with one type universe; and TT_ω, a type theory with a cumulative hierarchy of type universes. We assume the reader is familiar with such type theories. See [8] or [18] for an introduction to Martin-Löf type theory. The style of type theory we are giving here has been called *polymorphic* because terms like $\lambda x\, \lambda y\, x$ have many types, rather than a unique type, as is the case in so-called *monomorphic* type theories. This polymorphism lets us write a simple rule for universe cumulativity where in a monomorphic type theory an explicit embedding function would have to be used.

After presenting the type theories, we give interpretations of each in the corresponding LTC theory of the previous section. The style of the proof rules for the type theories was chosen so that the interpretation of the rules could be easily expressed in a theorem prover like Isabelle [20], which is suited to implementing object logics expressed in a natural deduction style. In such a setting one can then formally verify the soundness of the interpretation.

In type theories, equality is problematic. Here we are not thinking of equality as definitional, as it is sometimes done. Instead, equality between types is taken to be extensional, and the equality on a type's members has a similar extensional flavor: for instance, in a Π type, terms representing functions are equal if they map equal terms in the domain to equal terms in the codomain.

The type theories we present here are expressed in the theory of arities of LTC except that now, in addition to the atomic arities ι for terms and

o for formulae, there is also the atomic arity τ for type expressions. There are only two basic forms of formulae: type equality, and term equality in a type:

$$\_ = \_ \quad : \quad [\tau, \tau] \longrightarrow o$$
$$\_ = \_ \in \_ \quad : \quad [\iota, \iota, \tau] \longrightarrow o$$

For convenience, we define abbreviations for their reflexive instances: A *Type* for $A = A$ and $a \in A$ for $a = a \in A$. The proof rules for each type theory will be given in a natural deduction style. Each judgment will assert a formula in the context of a list of assumptions, each assumption having the form

$$x = x' \in A$$

where x, x' are distinct variables of arity ι. For example, the rule for forming equal Π types is:

$$[x = x' \in A]$$
$$\vdots$$
$$\frac{A = A' \qquad B(x) = B'(x')}{\Pi(A, B) = \Pi(A', B')}$$

where x and x' are assumed to be new variables whose instances are bound in the right-hand subproof, and the hypothesis $x = x' \in A$ is discharged by this proof rule, as the brackets are meant to indicate. In the Isabelle presentation, this rule would be written:

$$(A = A') \supset (\bigwedge_{x, x'} (x = x' \in A) \supset (B(x) = B'(x'))) \supset \Pi(A, B) = \Pi(A', B')$$

Normally, type theories have assumptions in the form $x \in A$. Then the interpretation of, for example, $d(x, y, z) = d'(x, y, z) \in D(x, y, z)$ in the context $x \in A$, $y \in B(x)$, $z \in C(x, y)$ would be, roughly speaking,

$$[A](x, x') \wedge [B(x)](y, y') \wedge [C(x, y)](z, z') \supset$$
$$[D(x, y, z)]([d](x, y, z), [d'](x', y', z'))$$

where the double brackets indicate the interpretation of expressions. The thing to note is the substitution of primed variables for unprimed variables in d', for as many variables as there are assumptions. Such an interpretation, operating at the level of formulas-in-context, is not expressible within Isabelle. Thus, wishing to formalise all this within Isabelle, we revised the usual form of Martin-Löf type theory slightly.

Type theory TT_0

Our first type theory is a type theory without a type universe. TT_0 has the function symbols $\lambda, Ap, \langle\_,\_\rangle, Spread, Inl, Inr, Decide, 0, S, Ind$ as in the language L_2 and has in addition the function symbols $Any : \iota \to \iota$ and $True, Peano : \iota$. It also has the following list of type constructors.

$$\Pi \; : \; [\tau, \iota \to \tau] \longrightarrow \tau \qquad\qquad \Sigma \; : \; [\tau, \iota \to \tau] \longrightarrow \tau$$
$$\_+\_ \; : \; [\tau, \tau] \longrightarrow \tau \qquad\qquad I \; : \; [\tau, \iota, \iota] \longrightarrow \tau$$
$$Void \; : \; \tau \qquad\qquad Nat \; : \; \tau$$

The proof rules for TT_0 are the following.

General rules

$$\frac{a = a' \in A, \quad A\ Type}{a' = a \in A} \qquad\qquad \frac{A = A'}{A' = A}$$

$$\frac{a = a' \in A, \quad a' = a'' \in A, \quad A\ Type}{a = a'' \in A} \qquad \frac{A = A', \quad A' = A''}{A = A''}$$

$$\frac{a = a' \in A, \quad A = A'}{a = a' \in A'}$$

$$\frac{[x = x' \in A] \atop {\vdots \atop b(x) = b'(x') \in B(x) \quad a = a' \in A}}{b(a) = b'(a') \in B(a)} \qquad \frac{[x = x' \in A] \atop {\vdots \atop B(x) = B'(x') \quad a = a' \in A}}{B(a) = B'(a')}$$

Π *rules*

$$\frac{[x = x' \in A] \atop {\vdots \atop A = A' \quad B(x) = B'(x')}}{\Pi(A, B) = \Pi(A', B')} \qquad \frac{[x = x' \in A] \atop {\vdots \atop f(x) = f'(x') \in B(x)}}{\lambda(f) = \lambda(f') \in \Pi(A, B)}$$

$$\frac{c = c' \in \Pi(A, B) \quad a = a' \in A}{Ap(c, a) = Ap(c', a') \in B(a)} \qquad \frac{c = c' \in \Pi(A, B)}{c = \lambda((x)Ap(c', x)) \in \Pi(A, B)}$$

$$\Sigma \ rules$$

$$[x = x' \in A]$$
$$\vdots$$

$$\frac{A = A' \quad B(x) = B'(x')}{\Sigma(A,B) = \Sigma(A',B')} \qquad \frac{a = a' \in A, \quad b = b' \in B(a)}{\langle a,b \rangle = \langle a',b' \rangle \in \Sigma(A,B)}$$

$$\frac{\begin{array}{c} c = c' \in \Sigma(A,B) \\ [x = x' \in A, \ y = y' \in B(x)] \quad \cdots \quad f(x,y) = f'(x',y') \in C(\langle x,y \rangle) \\ [z = z' \in \Sigma(A,B)] \quad \cdots \quad C(z) = C(z') \end{array}}{Spread(c,f) = Spread(c',f') \in C(c)} \ddagger$$

$$+ \ rules$$

$$\frac{A = A', \quad B = B'}{A + B = A' + B'}$$

$$\frac{a = a' \in A}{Inl(a) = Inl(a') \in A + B} \qquad \frac{b = b' \in B}{Inr(b) = Inr(b') \in A + B}$$

$$\frac{\begin{array}{c} c = c' \in A + B \\ [x = x' \in A] \quad \cdots \quad f(x) = f'(x') \in C(Inl(x)) \\ [x = x' \in B] \quad \cdots \quad g(x) = g'(x') \in C(Inr(x)) \\ [z = z' \in A + B] \quad \cdots \quad C(z) = C(z') \end{array}}{Decide(c,f,g) = Decide(c',f',g') \in C(c)}$$

$$Void \ rules$$

$$\frac{}{Void \ Type} \qquad \frac{a = a' \in Void}{Any(a) = Any(a') \in A(a)}$$

---

‡ Again, for typographical reasons, premises in rules will be listed vertically instead of horizontally.

I rules

$$\frac{a = a' \in A, \quad b = b' \in A, \quad A = A'}{I(A,a,b) = I(A',a',b')} \qquad \frac{a = b \in A}{True = True \in I(A,a,b)}$$

$$\frac{c \in I(A,a,b), \quad c' \in I(A,a,b)}{c = c' \in I(A,a,b)} \qquad \frac{c = c' \in I(A,a,b)}{a = b \in A}$$

Nat rules

$$\frac{}{Nat\ Type} \qquad \frac{}{0 \in Nat} \qquad \frac{a = a' \in Nat}{S(a) = S(a') \in Nat} \qquad \frac{0 = S(0) \in Nat}{Peano \in Void}$$

$$\frac{\begin{array}{c} a = a' \in Nat \\ [x = x' \in Nat] \quad \cdots \quad A(x) = A(x') \\ b = b' \in A(0) \\ [x = x' \in Nat,\ y = y' \in A(x)] \quad \cdots \quad f(x,y) = f'(x',y') \in A(S(x)) \end{array}}{Ind(a,b,f) = Ind(a',b',f') \in A(a)}$$

The fourth rule is necessary in a type theory without a universe type, because such theories admit trivial models where all terms of a given type are equal. But even in a type theory with no universe types, we want to be able to prove zero is not equal to one.

Computation rules

The computation rules are gathered together here because they are all of the form: redex equals contractum in type if either one of them is in the type. These rules are easily shown. We have been influenced by the NuPrl [8] style of "direct computation" rules, which exploit the fact that the interpretation is by untyped terms. The more usual computational rules are also sound in our interpretations, so they could be substituted for these stronger rules. The computation rules are

$$\frac{d \in D}{k(c) = d \in D} \qquad \frac{k(c) \in D}{k(c) = d \in D},$$

where (c,d,k) is a computation triple of L_2, as given in section 2.

Type theory TT_1

We extend type theory TT_0 by adding a universe, a type whose elements are indices of other types, and which are mapped to types by the new constructor $itTy$. The function symbols of TT_1 are the ones of TT_0 plus the list:

$$\dot{\Pi} \;:\; [\iota, \iota \to \iota] \longrightarrow \iota \qquad\qquad \dot{\Sigma} \;:\; [\iota, \iota \to \iota] \longrightarrow \iota$$

$$\_\dot{+}\_ \;:\; [\iota, \iota] \longrightarrow \iota \qquad\qquad \dot{I} \;:\; [\iota, \iota, \iota] \longrightarrow \iota$$

$$\dot{Void} \;:\; \iota \qquad\qquad\qquad\qquad \dot{Nat} \;:\; \iota$$

The type constructors of TT_1 are the type constructors of TT_0 plus $U_1 : \tau$ and $Ty : \iota \to \tau$. The proof rules of TT_1 are the proof rules of TT_0 plus the following.

U_1 rules

$$\frac{}{U_1 \; Type} \qquad\qquad\qquad \frac{a = a' \in U_1}{Ty(a) = Ty(a')}$$

$$\frac{}{\dot{Void} \in U_1} \qquad\qquad\qquad \frac{}{Ty(\dot{Void}) = Void}$$

$$\frac{}{\dot{Nat} \in U_1} \qquad\qquad\qquad \frac{}{Ty(\dot{Nat}) = Nat}$$

$$\frac{a = a' \in U_1, \quad b = b' \in U_1}{a \dot{+} b = a' \dot{+} b' \in U_1} \qquad\qquad \frac{Ty(a \dot{+} b) \; Type}{Ty(a \dot{+} b) = Ty(a) + Ty(b)}$$

$$\frac{\begin{array}{c} a = a' \in U_1 \\ b = b' \in Ty(a) \\ c = c' \in Ty(a) \end{array}}{\dot{I}(a,b,c) = \dot{I}(a',b',c') \in U_1} \qquad\qquad \frac{Ty(\dot{I}(a,b,c)) \; Type}{Ty(\dot{I}(a,b,c)) = I(Ty(a),b,c)}$$

$$\frac{a = a' \in U_1 \qquad [x = x' \in Ty(a)] \;\;\cdots\;\; b(x) = b'(x') \in U_1}{\dot{\Pi}(a,b) = \dot{\Pi}(a',b') \in U_1} \qquad \frac{Ty(\dot{\Pi}(a,b)) \; Type}{Ty(\dot{\Pi}(a,b)) = \Pi(Ty(a), Ty \circ b)}$$

$$\frac{a = a' \in U_1 \qquad [x = x' \in Ty(a)] \;\;\cdots\;\; b(x) = b'(x') \in U_1}{\dot{\Sigma}(a,b) = \dot{\Sigma}(a',b') \in U_1} \qquad \frac{Ty(\dot{\Sigma}(a,b)) \; Type}{Ty(\dot{\Sigma}(a,b)) = \Sigma(Ty(a), Ty \circ b)}$$

Type theory TT_ω

Our final type theory has a cumulative hierarchy of universes. Let i, j vary over the numerals 1,2,3... The function symbols of TT_ω are the ones of TT_1 plus $\dot{U}_i : \iota$ for for $i = 1, 2, 3, \ldots$ The type constructors of TT_ω are the ones of TT_1 plus $U_i : \tau$ for $i = 2, 3, \ldots$. The proof rules of TT_ω are the proof rules of TT_1, now with the universe rules given for every level i, plus rules asserting that $\dot{U}_i$ is the reflection of

U_i and that the universes are cumulative:

Additional U_i rules

$$\frac{}{\dot{U}_i \in U_j} \; (i < j) \qquad \frac{}{Ty(\dot{U}_i) = U_i} \qquad \frac{a = a' \in U_i}{a = a' \in U_{i+1}}$$

6   The interpretation of the type theories in the *LTC* framework

We now show how to interpret each type theory in the corresponding *LTC* language. These interpretations are similar to the interpretations given by Jan Smith in [21, 22], and Stuart Allen in [5, 6]. In fact, our pattern of binding new variables in pairs in the proof rules gives an encoding of their notions of "true sequent."

In all three interpretations we interpret type expressions as binary predicates. This will induce an interpretation of the type theory rules as rules of the *LTC*, and one can show these are all derived rules, verifying the soundness of the interpretation.

In each interpretation, the judgments will be interpreted as follows. The judgment $A = A'$ will be interpreted as a formula asserting that the interpretations of A and A' are logically equivalent and are also partial equivalence relations on canonical values, that is, they are symmetric, transitive and relate only canonical values. Thus:

$$\begin{aligned}
[\![A = A']\!] \; \equiv \; & \forall u, u'([\![A]\!](u, u') \Leftrightarrow [\![A']\!](u, u')) \wedge \\
& \forall u, u'([\![A]\!](u, u') \supset [\![A]\!](u', u)) \wedge \\
& \forall u, u', u''([\![A]\!](u, u') \supset [\![A]\!](u', u'') \supset [\![A]\!](u, u'')) \wedge \\
& \forall u([\![A]\!](u, u) \supset u \rightsquigarrow u)
\end{aligned}$$

The judgment $a = a' \in A$ will be interpreted as the formula asserting that the interpretations of a and a' evaluate to values related by the interpretation of A. Thus:

$$[a = a' \in A] \quad \equiv \quad [a] = [a'] \ in \ [A]$$

where $\_ = \_ \ in \ \_$, of arity $[\iota, \iota, [\iota, \iota] \longrightarrow o] \longrightarrow o$, is defined as:

$$a = a' \ in \ A \quad \equiv \quad \exists u, u'(a \rightsquigarrow u \wedge a' \rightsquigarrow u' \wedge A(u, u'))$$

It is also convenient to extend the interpretation of types as binary predicates to an interpretation of families of types as ternary predicates. We define, for $B : \iota \to \tau$,

$$[B] \quad \equiv \quad (x)[B(x)]$$

Now we give the interpretation for each type theory in turn.

The interpretation of TT_0

The interpretation of type theory terms is easily done. All the function symbols except *True*, *Any* and *Peano* already appear as symbols of LTC_0, so interpret them by their namesakes. And for the remaining three, we define:

$$
\begin{aligned}
[True] &\equiv 0 \\
[Any] &\equiv (x)x \\
[Peano] &\equiv 0
\end{aligned}
$$

(One can check that *True* needs only to be a canonical term, and that since *Any* and *Peano* arise in only logically absurd situations, no properties are required of them.) The following are the interpretations of the type constructors.

$$
\begin{aligned}
[\Pi(A, B)](z, z') &\equiv \exists^1 f, f'(z = \lambda(f) \wedge z = \lambda(f') \ AND \\
&\qquad \forall x, x'(x = x' \ in \ [A] \supset f(x) = f'(x') \ in \ [B](x))) \\
[\Sigma(A, B)](z, z') &\equiv \exists a, a', b, b'(z = \langle a, b \rangle \wedge z' = \langle a', b' \rangle \wedge \\
&\qquad a = a' \ in \ [A] \wedge b = b' \ in \ [B](a)) \\
[A + A'](z, z') &\equiv \exists a, a'(z = Inl(a) \wedge z' = Inl(a') \wedge a = a' \ in \ [A] \vee \\
&\qquad z = Inr(a) \wedge z' = Inr(a') \wedge a = a' \ in \ [A']) \\
[I(A, a, b)](z, z') &\equiv z = [True] \wedge z' = [True] \wedge [a] = [b] \ in \ [A] \\
[Void](z, z') &\equiv \bot \\
[Nat](z, z') &\equiv z \rightsquigarrow z \wedge z' \rightsquigarrow z' \wedge EqNat(z, z')
\end{aligned}
$$

One can show that the interpretations of the proof rules of TT_0 are derived rules of LTC_0.

The interpretation of TT_1

We extend the previous interpretation to give an interpretation of TT_1 in LTC_1. In particular, we use the reflected notion of proposition and truth present in LTC_1 to interpret the universe type U_1.

In the same way as we extended the interpretation of types to families, it is handy to extend the interpretation of terms to families of terms by defining, for $b : \iota \to \iota$,

$$[\![b]\!] \equiv (x)[b(x)]$$

We interpret $Ty(a)$ as the binary predicate for which $[\![a]\!]$ is an internal representation.

$$[\![Ty(a)]\!](u, u') \equiv T([\![a]\!]uu')$$

We interpret U_1 as a binary predicate that holds between two canonical terms when they are both internal, binary propositional functions which are the internal representations of equal types.

$$[\![U_1]\!](z, z') \equiv z \rightsquigarrow z \wedge z' \rightsquigarrow z' \wedge \forall u, u'(P_1(zuu') \wedge P_1(z'uu')) \wedge$$
$$[\![Ty(z) = Ty(z')]\!]$$

We define the notational abbreviation $\_ = \_ \,\dot{\in}\, \_$ of arity $[\iota, \iota, \iota] \longrightarrow \iota$ by

$$a = a' \,\dot{\in}\, b \equiv \dot{\exists} u, u'(a \rightsquigarrow u \wedge a' \rightsquigarrow u' \wedge buu')$$

so that $T(a = a' \,\dot{\in}\, [\![b]\!]) \Leftrightarrow a = a'$ in $[\![Ty(b)]\!]$. We interpret the new type index constructors as the internal versions of the interpretations given to the corresponding type constructors.

$$[\![\dot{\Pi}(a, b)]\!] \equiv \lambda z, z'.\dot{\exists}^1 f, f'(z \doteq \lambda(f) \wedge z' \doteq \lambda(f') \wedge$$
$$\dot{\forall} x, x'(x = x' \,\dot{\in}\, [\![a]\!] \supset f(x) = f(x') \,\dot{\in}\, [\![b]\!](x)))$$

$$[\![\dot{\Sigma}(a, b)]\!] \equiv \lambda z, z'.\dot{\exists} u, u', v, v''(z \doteq \langle u, v \rangle \wedge z' \doteq \langle u', v' \rangle \wedge$$
$$u = u' \,\dot{\in}\, [\![a]\!] \wedge v = v' \,\dot{\in}\, [\![b]\!](u))$$

$$[\![a \dot{+} a']\!] \equiv \lambda z, z'.\dot{\exists} u, u'((z \doteq Inl(u) \wedge z' \doteq Inl(u') \wedge u = u' \,\dot{\in}\, [\![a]\!]) \dot{\vee}$$
$$(z \doteq Inr(u) \wedge z' \doteq Inr(u') \wedge u = u' \,\dot{\in}\, [\![a']\!]))$$

$$[\![\dot{I}(a, c, c')]\!] \equiv \lambda z, z'.z \doteq [\![True]\!] \wedge z' \doteq [\![True]\!] \wedge [\![c]\!] = [\![c']\!] \,\dot{\in}\, [\![a]\!]$$

$$[\![\dot{Void}]\!] \equiv \lambda z, z'.\dot{\bot}$$

$$[\![\dot{Nat}]\!] \equiv \lambda z, z'.z \rightsquigarrow z \wedge z' \rightsquigarrow z' \wedge \dot{\exists} u(z \rightsquigarrow u \wedge z' \rightsquigarrow u)$$

One can show that the interpretation of the proof rules of TT_1 are derived rules of LTC_1.

The interpretation of TT_ω

Finally, we extend the previous interpretation to give an interpretation of TT_ω in LTC_ω. First, we interpret U_i in the manner of the interpretation of U_1:

$$[U_i](z, z') \;\equiv\; z \rightsquigarrow z \land z' \rightsquigarrow z' \land \forall u, u'(P_i(zuu') \land P_i(z'uu')) \land$$
$$[Ty(z) = Ty(z')]$$

Then we interpret the type index $\dot{U}_i$ as the reflection of this:

$$[\dot{U}_i] \;\equiv\; \lambda z, z'.z \rightsquigarrow z \land z' \rightsquigarrow z' \land \dot{\forall} u, u'(\dot{P}_i(zuu') \land \dot{P}_i(z'uu')) \land_c$$
$$(z \dot{=}_{Ty} z')$$

where we define the notational abbreviations "conditional and" and "equal type indices" (both of arity $[\iota, \iota] \longrightarrow \iota$) as follows.

$$a \land_c a' \;\equiv\; a \land (a \supset a')$$
$$z \dot{=}_{Ty} z' \;\equiv\; \dot{\forall} u, u'(zuu' \Leftrightarrow z'uu') \land \dot{\forall} u, u'(zuu' \supset zu'u) \land$$
$$\dot{\forall} u, u', u''(zuu' \supset zu'u'' \supset zuu'') \land \dot{\forall} u(zuu \supset u \rightsquigarrow u)$$

Thus given $\forall u, u'(P_i(zuu') \land P_i(z'uu'))$, we have $T(z \dot{=}_{Ty} z') \Leftrightarrow [Ty(z) = Ty(z')]$. As before, one can show that the interpretation of the proof rules of TT_ω are derived rules of LTC_ω.

7   Isabelle

By a 'Generic Logic Proof Development System', we mean a system in which one expresses an *Object Logic* under consideration in a *Meta Logic*. The system then furnishes a proof development system for that logic i.e. mechanisms for deriving and storing rules and theorems of the object logic, matching rules to goals, and a programmable *Meta Language* in which one may write Tactics or Proof Strategies. In fact Isabelle uses Huet's higher-order unification algorithm rather than matching. There are now quite a few such systems, but Isabelle seems to be particularly well suited to the notion of a *Framework* developed in [15], which has similarities to the Isabelle notion of a *Theory* and its *extensions*.

The Meta Logic of Isabelle is a version of higher-order logic. The terms are those of the typed lambda calculus. Initially the only ground type is **prop** (**Aprop**). When implementing an object logic new ground types and constants may be added. There are also function types $\sigma \rightarrow \tau$ where σ and τ are types. Isabelle implements higher-order unification (i.e. unification up to α and β reduction) as the main mechanism for constructing proofs. Note that as unification rather than matching is used schematic variables appearing in a goal may be instantiated as well as those appearing in the rules. Usually one does not want schematic variables in the main goal as this may result in a proof of only a special case of the goal. Unification is mainly used in the instantiation of variables that have been introduced into subgoals produced by previous proof steps.

The framework has been implemented as a series of *extensions* to the standard Isabelle theory FOL which implements a natural deduction style intuitionistic First-Order Logic with equality.

8   The implementation of the *LTC* framework

In this section we give an outline of our Isabelle implementation of the languages LTC_0, LTC_1 and LTC_ω.

LTC0

This is an implementation of LTC_0. The Isabelle notation for specifying the types (arities) of constructors is similar to that of section 2. The declaration of the types of the constants of LTC0 is shown below.

```
Infixr("~>", [Aterm,Aterm]--->Aform, 60),
Infixr("~~>", [Aterm,Aterm]--->Aform, 60),
Delimfix("<_,_>", [Aterm,Aterm]--->Aterm, "Pair"),
Delimfix("0", Aterm, "0"),
Delimfix("S", Aterm-->Aterm, "S"),
. . .
(["Ind"], [Aterm, Aterm, [Aterm,Aterm]--->Aterm]--->Aterm),
(["Spread"], [Aterm, [Aterm,Aterm] ---> Aterm] ---> Aterm),
(["Decide"], [Aterm,(Aterm --> Aterm),(Aterm --> Aterm)]
            ---> Aterm),

(["Lambda"], (Aterm-->Aterm) --> Aterm),
(["Ap"], [Aterm,Aterm]--->Aterm),
(["Inl","Inr"], Aterm-->Aterm),
(["Pa"], [Aterm,(Aterm-->Aterm)-->Aterm]--->Aterm),
(["DecideNat"], [Aterm,Aterm,Aterm-->Aterm]--->Aterm),

(["N"], Aterm-->Aform),
(["Nat"], Aterm-->Aform)
```

Here `-->`, `--->` `Aterm` and `Aform` correspond to $\to$, $\longrightarrow$ ι, and o respectively.

The first five constants are declared using Isabelle's new mixfix syntax. This is used to declare the concrete syntax for a constant, if this is different from the normal, prefix application. Thus `~>` and `~~>` are infix operators, and the notation `<a,b>` is equivalent to `Pair(a,b)`.

The constants `O` and `S` are treated in a special way as the `LTCO` parser allows, for instance, either `#N3` or `S(S(S(0)))` as concrete syntax for the term $S(S(S(0)))$ of LTC_0. The details of this *parse translation* and its associated *print translation* will be omitted.

There is one further mixfix declaration:

```
Mixfix("LAM _. _",[id_list,Aterm]--->Aterm," LAM",[],10),
```

This is somewhat special as it does not result in a constant being defined in the abstract syntax for `LTCO`. The details of the parse translation will again be omitted, but this declaration allows `LAM x y. f(x,y)` as an alternative to `Lambda(%x.Lambda(%y.f(x,y)))`. The other constants of `LTCO` require no special syntax, they are listed with their types.

In Isabelle there is no difference between the representations of rules and theorems. Both are represented using the implication $\Rightarrow$ (`==>`) of Higher-O rder Logic. The rules are given in a textual form, together with a name. For instance we hav e the following rule.

```
"(a ~> Inr(b)) ==> (g(b) ~> e) ==> Decide(a,f,g) ~> e"
```

Note that in the 1990 version of Isabelle, the function mapping object-language truth values (*form*) to meta-language truth values (*prop*) is "invisible" (The parser applies the function `Trueprop` of type `Aform-->Aprop` when necessary). Because of this feature, one has to explicitly constrain terms to type *prop* if they appear in rules, by following the term with `$$prop`.

The above rule corresponds to the axiom

$$\frac{a \rightsquigarrow Inr(b) \quad g(b) \rightsquigarrow e}{Decide(a,f,g) \rightsquigarrow e}$$

of the language L_2, of [15]. In LTC_0, we wish to derive this rule from ($\rightsquigarrow$ 2) and the fact that $(inr(b), g(b), (x)Decide(x,f,g))$ is a computation triple. In order to express this fact in `LTCO`, we introduce a new constant `ALPHA` of type `[Aterm,Aterm,Aterm-->Aterm] ---> Aprop`. `ALPHA(c,d,k)` expresses at the meta level the fact that (c,d,k) is a computation triple.

Thus corresponding to ($\rightsquigarrow$ 1) and ($\rightsquigarrow$ 2) we have the following two axioms of `LTCO`

```
("A_canon", " ALPHA(c,d,k)$$prop ==>  c ~> c "),
("A_non_canon", "[|ALPHA(c,d,k)$$prop ; a~>c ; d~>e|]
               ==>  k(a) ~> e"),
```

The computation triple above is implemented as:

```
("A_inl", " ALPHA(Inl(b) ,g(b) ,%x. Decide(x,g,h))$$prop "),
```

The special inequality rules of the *LTC* are particularly awkward to implement. $SE1$ is reasonably straightforward, for each primitive function symbol we need to add rules such as

```
("inj_pair_1", "Pair(a,b) = Pair(a',b') ==> a = a'" ),
("inj_pair_2", "Pair(a,b) = Pair(a',b') ==> b = b'" ),
```

One way to implement $SE2$ would be to add, for each pair of distinct primitive function symbols, say S and λ an axiom of the form

```
("S_lam",    " S(a) = Lambda(f)  ==> False " ),
```

There are 10 primitive function symbols in the language LTC_0 and so there would be 45 rules like the one above. In any extension of the theory, when adding the nth primitive function symbol, $n - 1$ rules would have to be added. This is clearly not desirable, as even if the input of these axioms were automated, the proof tactics would have to search over an ever growing list of rules, just to prove an instance of the rule $SE2$.

Such considerations have lead us to introduce a new ground type, *token* into the meta theory, together with four new constants, with the following type declarations:

```
Delimfix("t0", Atoken, "t0"),
Delimfix("tS", Atoken-->Atoken, "tS"),
. . .
(["Token"], Aterm --> Atoken),
(["DiffToken"], [Atoken,Atoken]---> Aprop),
```

Parse translation functions let us write #T3 for the token $tS(tS(tS(t0)))$.
   $SE2$ may now be encoded as:

```
("token","[| a = b ; (DiffToken(Token(a),Token(b)))$$prop |]
         ==> False"),
```

Now, for each primitive function symbol, we only need to add one rule, such as

```
("E_S", "Token(S(b))  == #T6" ),
```

which assigns a unique token to each primitive function symbol.

The other axioms related to tokens are quite straightforward:

```
("tSS", "(DiffToken(a,b))$$prop ==>
        (DiffToken(tS(a),tS(b)))$$prop" ),
("tSZ", "(DiffToken(tS(a),t0))$$prop" ),
("tZS", "(DiffToken(t0,tS(a)))$$prop" ),
```

The constants *Ind* and *Ap* are defined by meta level equalities as discussed in section 3.3:

```
("ind_def", "Ind(c,b,h)==DecideNat(c,b,%x. h(x,Ind(x,b,h)))"),
("ap_def", "Ap(x,b) == Pa(x,%f. f(b))")
```

LTC1

`LTC1` is an Isabelle extension of `LTC0` corresponding to LTC_1. The main interest here concerns the introduction of a new meta-type, `Alevel`.

LTC_1 only has one predicate symbol P_1, to express a single level of internal propositions. LTC_ω has an infinite sequence of predicate symbols P_1, P_2, ... expressing an infinite hierarchy of levels of propositions. In the implementation `LTC1`, a constant `Prop` of type `Alevel --> Aterm --> Aform`, is introduced, rather than simply a constant `P1` of type `Aterm --> Aform`. In `LTC1` the type `Alevel` has only one constructor, `lev_one`.

Readers might expect the rules of `LTC1` to refer to `Prop(lev_one,a)`, however this would mean that the extension `LTCW`, corresponding to LTC_ω, would have to re-implement the rules for higher levels. In fact, the rules implemented for `LTC1` all involve a meta-variable `lev` ranging over the type `Alevel`. This does have the drawback that in some circumstances schematic variables ranging over `Alevel` are introduced during a proof. In the usual situation, where one is attempting to prove a theorem by working backwards from the goal which has been entered by the user, these schematic variables ranging over `Alevel` will be instantiated to `lev_one` before the proof is finished. In `LTCW` the type `Alevel` is augmented with a unary constructor `lev_S` denoting the successor function on the natural numbers. The parsing and printing functions are defined to so that, for example `lev_S(lev_S(lev_one)` is treated as `#L3`.

The names of the 'dotted' term forming versions of the logical symbols are formed by prepending a `D` or `.` as appropriate to the name of the symbol, e.g. `DForall` and `.--> `.

Thus corresponding to the pair of rules

$$\frac{e \rightsquigarrow a \dot{\wedge} b}{P_1(a)} \qquad \frac{e \rightsquigarrow a \dot{\wedge} b}{T(e) \Leftrightarrow T(a) \wedge T(b)}$$

of LTC_1, we have the following pair of rules in **LTC1**.

```
("Dconj_P", "[| e ~> (a .& b); Prop(lev)(a); Prop(lev)(b) |]
            ==> Prop(lev)(e)" ),
("Dconj_T", "[| e ~> (a .& b); Prop(lev)(a); Prop(lev)(b) |]
            ==> T(e) <-> (T(a) & T(b))" ),
```

In the present implementation, these rules are given as axioms. It would be possible to introduce a new meta-level predicate, **BETA**, corresponding to the table of triples (c, Φ_c^1, Ψ_c) in section 2, just as **ALPHA** coresponds to the table of computation triples in that section. These rules would then be derivable.

The rules for T are given in the same style as [15], but they are not well suited to Isabelle's proof style. The **LTC1** tactics use, instead, derived rules such as:

```
Dconj_T_elim
"[| T(e); e ~> (a .& b); Prop(lev)(a); Prop(lev)(b);
   (T(a) & T(b) ==> R)|]  ==> R"
```

```
Dconj_T_intr
"[| e ~> (a .& b); Prop(lev)(a); Prop(lev)(b);
   (T(a) & T(b)) |] ==> T(e)"
```

In [15] it is mentioned that in the theory for the language L_3, (or LTC_1) neither P_1 nor T can be internally defined, i.e. the following two theorems hold.

$$\neg \exists t. \forall x. P_1(Ap(t, x)) \wedge (T(Ap(t, x)) \Leftrightarrow T(x))$$

$$\neg \exists p. \forall x. P_1(Ap(p, x)) \wedge (T(Ap(p, x)) \Leftrightarrow P_1(x))$$

These may be viewed as analogues of Russell's paradox. We have developed a series of lemmas culminating in the following theorems of **LTC1**

```
"~(EX t. ALL x. Prop(#L1)(Ap(t,x)) & (T(Ap(t,x)) <-> T(x)))"
"~(EX p. ALL x. Prop(#L1)(Ap(p,x)) &
   (T(Ap(p,x)) <-> Prop(#L1)(x)))"
```

The above theorems demonstrate the way that Isabelle allows the concrete syntax of the object logic implemented to be very close to the concrete syntax normally used for that logic. (An earlier version of Isabelle allowed the better syntax P_1(a) for $P_1(a)$, it seems hard to do this for all levels with the 1990 version of Isabelle). <-> is defined by the Isabelle *definition* mechanism i.e. metalevel equality, FOL has the rule

```
("iff_def",  "P<->Q == (P-->Q) & (Q-->P)"),
```

EX, ALL and # are all delimiters which form part of Isabelle's system of *notation*, thus they may be considered as part of definitions which are always unfolded by the parser, and folded by the printer. *Definitions* such as that for <-> are not unfolded unless this is explicitly demanded, derived rules are proved, and then the defined constructor may be used in just the same way as the primitive ones. This ability to tailor the syntax to your requirements more than makes up for Isabelle's complete lack of a user interface. While the provision of some nicer fonts would improve the look of the output, these extra characters should be able to be *typed* in.

LTCW

LTCW is an Isabelle extension of LTC1 corresponding to LTC_ω. The implementation of Alevel is described above. We introduce a new constant, lev_S, of type Alevel-->Alevel. The rules given in LTC1 then immediately apply to all levels.

The expression forming version of P_i, $\dot{P_i}$, is treated in the same way as P_i. A constant DProp of type Alevel --> Aterm --> Aterm, is declared.

The only further complication arises from the implementation of the side condition $j < i$ on the rules

$$\frac{e \rightsquigarrow \dot{P_j}(a)}{P_i(e)} \quad \text{and} \quad \frac{P_j(e)}{P_i(e)}.$$

We introduce a new constant of type Alevel-->Alevel-->Apropnamed lower_lev. Note that Aprop is the type of meta-level truth values, not the object-level Aform. We then add a minimal set of axioms that allow us to deduce that one level is lower than another, namely:

```
("lower_S", "(lower_lev (j,i))$$prop ==>
             (lower_lev(lev_S(j) , lev_S(i)))$$prop"),
("lower_1", "(lower_lev(lev_one ,lev_S(i)))$$prop")
```

The remaining rules for LTC_ω may then be coded as:

```
("A_Dprop", "ALPHA(DProp(l,a), g(l,a),%x.DecideDP(x,g))
          $$prop"),
("E_Dprop", "Token(DProp(l,a)) == #T19" ),

("DPj_Pi", "(lower_lev(j,i))$$prop ==> e ~> DProp(j)(a)
          ==> Prop(i)(e)"),
("DP_T", "e ~> DProp(j)(a) ==> T(e) <-> (Prop(j)(a))"),
("Pj_Pi", "(lower_lev(j,i))$$prop ==> Prop(j)(a)
          ==> Prop(i)(a)"),
```

The first rule is mainly used to express the fact that the primitive function constants $\dot{P}_1$, $\dot{P}_2$ ... are canonical. The non canonical **DecideDP** is not used at present. The rule E_Dprop just assigns the token **#T19** to **Dprop** as described earlier. Note that this will not allow us to deduce $\neg(\dot{P}_1(a) = \dot{P}_2(a))$. An axiom capturing $SE2$ for different levels is required (but not currently implemented).

9   The type theories as Isabelle extensions of *LTC* theories

Isabelle theories **TT0**, **TT1** and **TTW**, corresponding to the type theories defined in section 2 have been implemented as extensions of the theories described above. These extensions only consist of declarations of new constants, and rules which are all meta-level equalities giving definitions for the new constants in terms of the *LTC*. The axioms of the type theories should then all be derivable within Isabelle. At present the derivation of all of the axioms has not been completed.

TT0

TT0 corresponds to the theory TT_0. It is built as an Isabelle extension of **LTC0**.

Types are interpreted as certain binary predicates. So they have the *LTC* arity $[\iota, \iota] \longrightarrow o$. As this occurs very often in the constant declarations below, the ML identifier **Atype** is bound to **Aterm-->Ate rm--Aform**. **Atype** does not refer to a new ground type *type* of the meta-language. Using this abbreviation has the advantage that these files could easily be converted to define a primitive Isabelle theory (not an extension of **FOL/LTC**) in which **Aterm**, **Atype** and **Aform** are three ground types corresponding to terms types and judgments in the Type Theory.

The constants are

```
Mixfix("<| _ ~= _ in _ |>", [Aterm,Aterm,Atype]--->Aform,...
```

```
Mixfix("<| _ ~= _ |>", [Atype,Atype]--->Aform,"EqType",...

Mixfix("PROD _:_. _", [SId,Atype,Atype]--->Atype,
      " PROD", [], 10),
Mixfix("SUM _:_. _", [SId,Atype,Atype]--->Atype,
      " SUM", [], 10),
Infixr("+", [Atype,Atype]--->Atype, 30)
. . .
(["NAT","void"], Atype ),
(["I"], [Atype,Aterm,Aterm] ---> Atype ),
(["true"], Aterm ),
(["any"], Aterm-->Aterm ),
(["Prod","Sum"], [Atype, Aterm-->Atype] ---> Atype )
```

PROD and SUM relate to Prod and Sum just as LAM relates to Lambda. In particular these declarations do not result in constants being defined in the abstract syntax of TT0

We will not give all the definitions here. But the definition of the judgement that two terms are equal in a type (written <| x ~= x' in X |> or equivalently EqElem(x,x',X)) is:

```
("eqelem_def", "<| x ~= x' in X |> == EX u u' .
              (x ~> u) & (x' ~> u') & X(u,u')"),
```

The definition of the type $X + Y$ is:

```
("plus_def", "(X + Y)(x,x') == EX a a'.
  ((x = Inl(a)) &(x' = Inl(a'))) & (<| a ~= a' in X |>)) |
  ((x = Inr(a)) &(x' = Inr(a'))) & (<| a ~= a' in Y |>))"),
```

TT1

TT1 is an Isabelle theory corresponding to the type theory TT_1. This has a natural interpretation in LTC_1. To build TT1, we need to use Isabelle's mechanism for *merging* theories. Two theories may be merged if any constants they have in common have the same type. In the merged theory, these constants are considered equal.

We first merge LTC1 and TT0. Here of course, the constants that the two theories have in common are all those constants that were defined in FOL or LTC0. We then extend this theory by adding new constants and meta level equalities relating to the Universe U_1, and term forming versions of the constants of TT0, to get the theory TT1.

```
Mixfix("<| _ ~= _ Din _ |>",[Aterm,Aterm,Aterm]--->Aterm,...
```

```
Mixfix("DPROD _:_. _", [SId,Aterm,Aterm]--->Aterm,...
Mixfix("DSUM _:_. _", [SId,Aterm,Aterm]--->Aterm, " DSUM",...
Infixr(".+", [Aterm,Aterm]--->Aterm, 30)
. . .
(["DNat","Dvoid"], Aterm ),
(["DI"], [Aterm,Aterm,Aterm] ---> Aterm ),
(["DProd","DSum"], [Aterm, Aterm-->Aterm] ---> Aterm ),

(["Univ"], Alevel --> Atype ),
(["Ty"], Aterm --> Atype )
```

A Typical definition is:

```
("dsum_def", "DSum(a,b) == LAM z z'.DEX u u' v v'.
  (z .= <u,v>) .& (z' .= <u',v'>) .&
  (<| u ~= u' Din A |>) .& (<| v ~= v' Din b(u) |>)")
```

The axioms of TT_1 should all be derivable in the LTC once these definitions have been unfolded, we have not currently attempted this within Isabelle.

TTW

The definition of TTW follows the same lines as that of TT1. First we merge LTCW and TT1, and then extend this theory with a constant DUniv of type Alevel-->Aterm, and a meta level equality expressing the translation of U_i into the LTC.

10   Conclusion

We have presented two series of theories. The first come from a series of three LTC languages that have been developed from the series of languages, L_i, of the LTC framework, first presented in [15]. The second is a series of type theories, parallel to the three new LTC theories. Connecting them are interpretations of each type theory in its corresponding logical theory. The type theories were designed to make this interpretation easily expressible in a theorem prover like Isabelle. We have implemented LTC_ω and TT_ω in Isabelle and should now be able to formally prove the soundness of the interpretation, as well as developing other theories within TT_ω and LTC_ω.

Bibliography

[1] Peter Aczel. The strength of Martin-Löf's type theory with one universe. In *The Proceedings of the Symposium on Mathematical Logic, Oulu, Report No. 2*, pages 1–32, Department of Philosophy, University of Helsinki, 1977.

[2] Peter Aczel. Frege structures and the notions of proposition, truth and set. In Keisler Barwise and Kunen, editors, *The Kleene Symposium*, pages 31–59. North Holland, 1980.

[3] Peter Aczel. Frege structures revisited. Notes and Abstracts from the workshop on Semantics of Programming Languages, Gothenburg. pp 5-14, August 1983.

[4] Peter Aczel and David Carlisle. The Theory of Constructions: A formal framework and its implementation. May 1990.

[5] S. F. Allen. A non-type-theoretic definition of Martin-Löf's types. In *Proceedings of the 1st Annual Symposium on Logic in Computer Science*, pages 215–221. IEEE, 1986.

[6] S.F. Allen. *A Non-type-theoretic semantics for a type-theoretic language*. PhD thesis, Cornell University, 1987.

[7] A. Avron, F. A. Honsell, and I. A. Mason. *Using typed lambda calculus to implement formal systems on a machine*. Technical Report ECS-LFCS-87-31, University of Edinburgh, 1986.

[8] R.L. Constable et al. *Implementing Mathematics with the NuPrl Proof Development System*. Prentice-Hall, 1986.

[9] Peter Dybjer. Program verification in a logical theory of constructions. In *Functional Programming Languages and Computer Architectures, Lecture Notes in Computer Science, Vol. No. 201*, Springer Verlag, 1985. Revised Version, Preprint June, 1986.

[10] Peter Dybjer and Herbert Sander. A functional programming approach to the specification and verification of concurrent systems. *Formal Aspects of Computing*, 1:303–319, 1989.

[11] R. Harper, F. A. Honsell, and G. Plotkin. A framework for defining logics. In *Proceedings of the 2nd Symposium on Logic in Computer Science*, pages 194–204, IEEE, 1986.

[12] P. Martin-Löf. An intuitionistic theory of types: predicative part. In H.E. Rose and J.C. Shepherdson, editors, *Logic Colloquium '73*, pages 73–118, 1973.

[13] P. Martin-Löf. Constructive mathematics and computer programming. In *6th International Congress for Logic, Methodology and Philosophy of Science*, North-Holland, 1982.

[14] P. Martin-Löf. Intuitionistic type theory. Notes by G. Sambin of a series of lectures given in Padua, June 1980, Bibliopolis, Napoli, 1984.

[15] N.P. Mendler and P. Aczel. The notion of a framework and a framework for the LTC. In *Proceedings of the 3rd Annual Symposium on Logic in Computer Science*, pages 392–399. IEEE, 1988.

[16] N.P.Mendler. A series of type theories and their interpretations in the logical theory of constructions. May 1990.

[17] J. Meseguer. General Logics. In the *Proceedings of Logic Colloquium '87*, edited by H.D. Ebbinghaus et al. North Holland, 1989.

[18] B. Nordström, K. Petersson, and J. Smith. *Programming in Martin-Löf's Type Theory*. Oxford University Press, 1990.

[19] Lawrence C. Paulson. The foundational of a generic theorem prover. Technical Report 130, University of Cambridge, 1988.

[20] Lawrence C. Paulson and Tobias Nipkow. Isabelle tutorial and user's manual. Technical Report 189, University of Cambridge, 1990.

[21] Jan Smith. *On the relation between a type theoretic and a logical formulation of the theory of constructions*. PhD thesis, Gothenburg University, 1978.

[22] Jan Smith. An interpretation of Martin-Löf's type theory in a type-free theory of propositions. *Journal of Symbolic Logic*, 49:730–753, 1984.

A plea for weaker frameworks

N.G. de Bruijn
Eindhoven University of Technology

Abstract

It is to be expected that logical frameworks will become more and more important in the near future, since they can set the stage for an integrated treatment of verification systems for large areas of the mathematical sciences (which may contain logic, mathematics, and mathematical constructions in general, such as computer software and even computer hardware). It seems that the moment has come to try to get to some kind of a unification of the various systems that have been proposed.

Over the years there has been the tendency to strengthen the frameworks by rules that enrich the notion of definitional equality, thus causing impurities in the backbones of those frameworks: the typed lambda calculi. In this paper a plea is made for the opposite direction: to expel those impurities from the framework, and to replace them by material in the books, where the role of definitional equality is taken over by (possibly strong) book equality.

1 Introduction

Verification systems

A verification system consists of

(i) a framework, to be called the *frame*, which defines how mathematical material (in the wide sense) can be written in the form of *books*, such that the correctness of those books is decidable by means of an algorithm (the *checker*),

(ii) a set of basic rules (*axioms*) that the user of the frame can proclaim in his books as a general basis for further work.

For several reasons (theoretical, practical, educational and sociological) it may be recommended to keep the frames as simple as possible and as weak as possible. A second recommendation is to prefer frames belonging to a hierarchy in which the various specima can be easily compared.

We shall restrict the discussion to frames that have typed lambda calculi as their backbone, an idea that is gaining field today, along with the rising popularity of the principle to treat proofs and similar constructions in exactly the same way as the more usual mathematical objects. The rules of the frame involve rules for handling lambda terms, lambda reductions, and rules about attaching a type to a term. The typing rules are strongly influenced by the notion of *definitional equality*. The latter notion is primarily based on the reductions of the lambda calculus.

The centerpiece of this paper is the typed lambda calculus $\Delta\Lambda$. It improves on the slightly simpler system Λ (Nederpelt) in a sense that is well suited for implementing definitions. Quite some attention will be given to relating members of the Automath family to $\Delta\Lambda$.

Verification systems which are not related to Automath in any way will not be discussed in this paper. Nevertheless the author believes that such systems could have similar profits from confrontation with $\Delta\Lambda$.

Strengthening the frame

Over the years there has been the tendency to put more and more power into frames, at the price of impurities of the typed lambda calculus. This already started with the early versions of Automath (AUT68 and AUT-QE, see [3], [6], [13]) which were very advanced for their time (around 1968) in the sense that the frames were light and that almost all logical and mathematical knowledge was to be developed in the books. Nevertheless there was the impurity of so-called type inclusion (see section 4). A proposal to get rid of it (see [11]) came too late for implementation in the Automath project).

Motives for strengthening

Let us list some of the motives one might consider for strengthening the frame.

(i) One has the idea that the rules of the frame can be handled automatically and that book material has to be produced essentially by hand. This explains that wherever one sees things that can be automated, one has the tendency to shift them from the book into the frame.

(ii) Mathematicians have been trained to base their work on as few axioms as possible, preferring strong axioms over lists of weaker ones. So much the nicer if one can shift axioms into the frame, where one does not see them any more!

(iii) Strengthening the frame can enlighten the burden of writing books.

(iv) It is natural to have the feeling that the way one thinks about mathematics and its implementation in a verification system should somehow be reflected in the frame.

In particular these points may mean that much of what is achieved by book equality (the kind of equality that is to be considered as a mathematical proposition and for which proofs have to be provided by the user of the system) can be shifted to definitional equality, which is based on reductions in the frame that can be handled automatically).

Candidates for admission into a frame

There are two kinds of candidates, innocent ones and others. The innocent ones are what one might call *syntactic sugar*. They deal with ways to abbreviate book material, usually in a way that corresponds to existing habits of mathematicians. One might decide to enrich the frame with rules for such forms of sugaring.

Under the heading of sugaring we have things like:

(i) Ways to handle finite strings of terms, and strings of applicators and abstractors (in the latter case we call them *telescopes*, see [17]) by means of a single identifier, just as if they were ordinary objects.

(ii) Ways to to omit pieces of input and output that can be retraced easily and uniquely by the checker.

(iii) In particular this may refer to ways to replace explicit proofs and similar constructions by hints.

Sugaring is innocent since it has no influence on the validity and the interpretation of the things we present in our verification system.

The other candidates are not necessarily innocent. They may stem from mathematical or logical insights, but once incorporated into the frame they may get applications for which they were not intended in the first place. We might even fear antinomies.

Unlike the situation in a law court, the accused is to be considered as guilty as long as its innocence has not been established. This may mean that strengthening the frame gives us quite some work, possibly of a model-theoretical nature.

The non-innocent ways to strengthen the frame all increase the number of valid definitional equalities and the number of valid typings. This does not necessarily mean increasing the number of derivable mathematical results, but it might. And some of these extensions (like (iv)) damage the purity of the typed lambda calculus backbone.

We mention

(iv) Rules for type inclusion, or, what amounts to the same thing, Π-rules (see section 4).

(v) The principle of *proof irrelevance* (cf. [13], [21]), declaring two proofs for one and the same proposition to be definitionally equal.

(vi) Shifting knowledge about natural numbers, induction and recursion into the frame.

A plea for weaker frames

When one uses arguments of economy in order to put more power into the frame, one forgets that it is neither very hard to put some automation in the task of writing books. We can invent abbreviational facilities that may result in automatic writing of parts of the books (parts that the user even does not need to see if he does not want to). In particular this may refer to handling trivial equalities like those we need when dealing with pairs and cartesian products. This need for automatic textwriting will turn up in many other situations too. It happens every now and then, when we want to economize on writing things that we consider as part of our subconcious thinking. It does not seem to be the right thing to enrich the frame at every occasion of that kind.

And needless to say the tendency to provide the frame with facilities that depend on local and personal preferences may lead to an undesirable variety of diverging frames.

Let us list a number of arguments for retreating to weaker frames.

(i) Weaker frames means fewer frames. We are still far from a general acceptance of typed lambda calulus verification systems in the scientific world, the mathematical world in particular. Maintaining a variety of competing but hardly compatible systems will not be very helpful in this respect. And it will neither be very helpful for establishing cooperation between the various groups handling verification systems.

(ii) Having to understand a verification system, one has to see the clear borderline between frame and books. The distinction is easy to understand if the frame contains everything that can not be treated in the books, and nothing else.

(iii) For many people a pure system of typed lambda calculus is already hard enough. Impurities make it harder.

(iv) As said before, the frame is not the only place where things can be done automatically. There are plenty of cases for automated or semi-automated book-writing anyway. Verification systems would hardly have a future if we would have to depend on doing all the tedious and dirty work by hand.

(v) There is no reason at all to let any kind of syntactic sugaring slip from the book into the frame. Sugaring is meant to make reading and writing easier, or better adapted to traditional notations, and that belongs entirely in the world of the book. The frame is supposed to be operated by machines which do not have the same ideas as humans if it comes to the question whether things are difficult or tedious to handle.

(vi) The pain of having to keep things book-equal that one would prefer to have definitionally equal can be somewhat relieved by the introduction of a third kind of equality: *strong book equality* (see section 6).

Hierarchy of frames

In section 1 it was recommended to limit the number of frames that we present to the world. But the world would certainly also appreciate seeing a clear hierarchical structure among the different frames we present. The hierarchical relation $F_1 \leq F_2$ should be the one that expresses that every book valid with respect to frame F_1 is also valid with respect to F_2.

The hierarchy need not necessarily be linear, but it would certainly be appreciated if the hierarchy contains a maximal element F_m with $F \leq F_m$ for all the F in the hierarchy.

The inequality $F_1 \leq F_2$ has to be kept more or less informal in the present discussion. After all, we have not given a mathematical definition of the notion "frame". We shall also use the notation $F_1 \leq F_2$ in cases where the notion of validity of a book with respect to a frame still needs some interpretation (like in the case of $\Delta\Lambda$, where the system itself does not say how a book has to be considered as a lambda term).

Implementability

An even more informal notion is the one of implementability. We write $F_1 \xrightarrow{i} F_2$ if F_1 can be *implemented* in F_2. By this we mean that the essence of what F_1 can do for us can also be done in the (weaker) system F_2, provided that the books written under F_2 start with a number of suitable axioms, and that we take it for granted that some of the definitional equalities in F_1 are to be replaced by book equalities.

We should not forget that $\overset{i}{\to}$ indicates a rather weak form of implementation; one might rather call it *mimicking*. Nevertheless it might give an idea about the strength of various systems, both in a theoretical and a practical sense.

Purity of lambda calculi

We shall be informal here, *not* start by saying what a typed lambda calculus is. We just stress the essential items for purity.

(i) Definitional equality ($\overset{d}{=}$) should be defined by means of β-reduction only. It would probably do no harm to admit η-reduction too, but it seems hardly worth while. We do not mention α-reduction since its role can be reduced to the level of syntactic sugaring; one can assume that the frame deals with namefree lambda calculus.

(ii) We should require full unicity of types. So assuming the typing $P : Q$ and the validity of R, we have $P : R$ if and only if $Q \overset{d}{=} R$.

(iii) We should require that both abstraction and application commute with typing. So with the usual notation

$$\frac{\Gamma, (x : A) \vdash P(x) : Q(x)}{\Gamma \vdash [x : A]P(x) : [x : A]Q(x)},$$

$$\frac{\Gamma \vdash P : Q \quad \Gamma \vdash \langle a \rangle Q}{\Gamma \vdash \langle a \rangle P : \langle a \rangle Q}.$$

Here we followed the Automath notation for abstraction and application. Abstractors are written like $[x : A]$, where x is the bound variable and A its type, and are written in front of the term they act on. Applicators are also written in front: $\langle a \rangle P$ describes what is interpreted as a function value, where P is the function and a the argument. And, as usually, Γ stands for any context, and $\Gamma, (x : A)$ is its extension by means of the declaration of the typed variable x.

The above rule for application is not sufficient for getting all cases of $\Gamma \vdash \langle a \rangle Q$. We have to add the rule

$$\frac{\Gamma \vdash a : A \quad \Gamma \vdash Q \overset{d}{=} [x : A]R(x)}{\Gamma \vdash \langle a \rangle Q}.$$

2   A proposal for a hierarchy of frames

We shall discuss three frames, forming a linear hierarchy:

$$\text{AUT-QE-NTI} \ \leq \ \Delta\Lambda \ \leq \ \Lambda\Sigma.$$

The first one, AUT-QE-NTI , was designed in 1978 as an Automath language without impurities. The other members of the Automath family can be implemented in it (in the sense of section 1,subsection Implementability (see [11])). In particular we have

$$\text{PAL} \ \leq \ \text{AUT68} \ \leq \ \text{AUT-QE} \ \xrightarrow{i} \ \text{AUT-QE-NTI},$$
$$\text{AUT}\Pi \ \xrightarrow{i} \ \text{AUT-QE-NTI}.$$

For PAL, AUT68 and AUT-QE we refer to [3], [6], [13].

$\Delta\Lambda$ was designed in 1985. It is very close to the system Λ for which Nederpelt proved strong normalization ([20]). That Λ was a reformulation of the system AUT-SL ([4]) which presented complete Automath books (with extremely liberal abstraction rules) in the form of a single line. In order to do that, all definitions of the book had to be eliminated first, and therefore AUT-SL had theoretical interest only. With $\Delta\Lambda$, however, this elimination of definitions is no longer necessary (see section 5).

$\Delta\Lambda$ is strong enough for implementation (in the sense of $\xrightarrow{i}$) of Barendregt's Generalized type systems (see [2]), which in particular contains the Coquand-Huet theory of constructions. It may be interesting to compare Barendregt's [2] with the much older note [7]. The essential differences are: (i) in [7] type inclusion (cf. section 4 below) was restricted to degree 1, and (ii) in [2] there is no place for the typical Automath feature of admitting more contexts than those for which it is allowed to abstract from.

In section 7 we shall devote some attention to the system $\Lambda\Sigma$, which is intended as a very substantial extension of typed lambda calculus. But at present it should be said that the relation $\Delta\Lambda \leq \Lambda\Sigma$ is rather a program for development of $\Lambda\Sigma$ than a fact.

3   The typed lambda calculus $\Delta\Lambda$

Syntax

The difference between $\Delta\Lambda$ and Nederpelt's Λ lies in the notion of correctness, not in the syntax.

Let us agree that what we really mean is the namefree version, and that the use of names of variables is syntactic sugar (both in the description as in the use of the syntax). A complete description was given in [15] by means of trees with reference arrows (arrows from the variables at end-points of the tree to the corresponding lambdas). That reference arrow system seems to be the easiest way to describe syntax and language theory. At the stage of implementation in a checker one might decide how to implement those arrows. One might use depth references, but if the implementation is in terms of a programming language with a pointer mechanism, one might use those pointers instead. For input and output of mathematical texts, however, there is much to be said for the syntactic sugar of named variables.

In order to avoid repeating the complete formal description given in [15] we give an informal one here, with the use of names of variables. In the first round of syntax description we formulate

(i) τ is a term.

(ii) A variable is a term.

(iii) If x is a variable, if P and Q are terms, where P does not contain x, then $[x : P]Q$ is a term.

(iv) If P and Q are terms, then $\langle P \rangle Q$ is a term.

In the second round we add the restriction that a term should not contain any free variables.

Every bound variable in a term has a unique type, obtained by agreeing that in (iii) all x occurring in Q get type P.

Every term has a terminating symbol on the extreme right. If that symbol is a τ we say that the term has degree 1, and we do not define the type of the term. If the terminating symbol of the term E is a variable x, we get the *type* of E (notation typ(E)) if we simply replace that terminal occurrence of x by the type of x.

And we define the *degree* of a term E recursively by the rule degree(E) = degree(typ(E)) + 1.

Correctness

Correctness of terms depends on the notions of typing and definitional equality.

Definitional equality in $\Delta\Lambda$ is defined by means of *mini-reductions*: local β-reductions and so-called AT-removals, instead of by the global β-reduction used in Λ. Local β-reduction means that some sub-term $\langle R \rangle [x : P]Q$ is transformed into $\langle R \rangle [x : P]Q^*$, where Q^* is obtained from Q upon replacing a single one of the occurrences of x by R. It can of course be done only if there is at least one occurrence of x in Q. If there are no occurrences of x in Q we allow AT-removal: we remove the AT-pair $\langle R \rangle [x : P]$, so $\langle R \rangle [x : P]Q$ turns into Q. (A few words to explain the "AT": in the metalanguage used in [15] the "A" refers to applicators ⟨ ⟩, and the "T" to typed abstractors [:].)

In the usual way we get the notion $\stackrel{\mathrm{d}}{=}$ of definitional equality by reflexive transitive symmetric closure of the set of mini-reductions.

For practical reasons it can be recommended to extend the set of mini-reductions by basing them on AT-*couples* instead of AT-pairs (see [15], section 4.3). As an example we mention that in $\langle R\rangle\langle Q\rangle\langle P\rangle[x:A][y:B][z:C]$ the $\langle R\rangle$ and $[z:C]$ form an AT-couple. Extending the notion of mini-reductions to AT-couples does not alter the notion of $\stackrel{\mathrm{d}}{=}$. This easily follows from the fact that applicators may jump to the right over an AT-pair, since

$$\langle Q\rangle\langle P\rangle[x:A]W \stackrel{\mathrm{d}}{=} \langle P\rangle[x:A]\langle Q\rangle W.$$

As we start from the term om the left, the Q does not contain x. Therefore definitional equality follows by full β-reduction applied to both sides.

Having the notion $\stackrel{\mathrm{d}}{=}$, we can get to the matter of correctness.

The essential point in the definition of correctness is in the situation of subterms of the form $\langle R\rangle P$. The usual conditions in typed lambda calculi, in particular in Nederpelt's Λ, are

(i) R and P are both correct,
(ii) in the finite sequence P, $\mathrm{typ}(P)$, $\mathrm{typ}(\mathrm{typ}(P))$, ... there is a term that is definitionally equal to a term of the form $[x:S]W$, with $\mathrm{typ}(R) \stackrel{\mathrm{d}}{=} S$.

If a term is correct in the sense of Λ then it is also correct in the sense of $\Delta\Lambda$, but the converse is not true. $\Delta\Lambda$ is more permissive concerning the applications $\langle R\rangle P$. In $\Delta\Lambda$ it is no longer required that P is correct all by itself: the correctness check may make use of the fact that $\langle R\rangle$ is in front of this P. An example is

$$[W:[t:\tau]\tau]\ [p:\tau]\ \langle p\rangle\ [u:\tau]\ [s:\langle p\rangle W]\ \langle s\rangle\ [x:\langle u\rangle W]\ \tau.$$

Correctness of the $\langle s\rangle[x:\langle u\rangle W]\tau$ at the end requires that $\langle p\rangle W$, the type of s, is definitionally equal to $\langle u\rangle W$. According to the rules of $\Delta\Lambda$ this is the case indeed, because of the pair $\langle p\rangle[u:\tau]$ earlier in the formula. Putting

$$R=p, \quad P=[u:\tau]\ [s:\langle p\rangle W]\ \langle s\rangle\ [x:\langle u\rangle W]\ \tau,$$

we see that R is correct in the context $[W:[t:\tau]\tau][p:\tau]$, but that P is not. So in that context $\langle R\rangle P$ is incorrect in the sense of Λ. In the sense of $\Delta\Lambda$ it is correct, and therefore this example shows that $\Delta\Lambda$ is more permissive than Λ.

We shall see in section 5 how this feature enables us to interpret an Automath book as a term in $\Delta\Lambda$. The algorithm for checking the correctness of the term is an efficient algorithm for checking the correctness of the whole book.

The fact that $\Delta\Lambda$ deviates from Λ is connected to the algorithmic nature of the definition of correctness in $\Delta\Lambda$. It processes a sub-term $\langle R \rangle P$ from left to right. By the time it gets to P it makes use of the fact that $\langle R \rangle$ had been there. The definition of correctness of $\Delta\Lambda$ as given in [15],section 5.3 * will not be repeated here. Instead of repeating that algorithmic definition we shall describe an algorithm that implements it.

Algorithm for checking correctness

From the algorithmic definition of correctness in $\Delta\Lambda$ we can get to an algorithm that checks whether a given string is a correct term.

The algorithm can be described in two rounds. In the first round the algorithm runs through the term from left to right, and for every applicator it produces a context and a pair of terms for which definitional equality in that context remains to be established. The second one of the pair is always the type of a third one, and therefore our definitional equality checking can also be called *type checking*.

The first round can be completed irrespective of whether all these definitional equalities can be established or not. And we mention that this first round runs practically in linear time.

In the second round the definitional equalities of the list have to be checked. This second round does not depend on typing any more. It can be interpreted in untyped lambda calculus, and it is a matter of practice to devise an efficient strategy. The questions are decidable because of the property of strong normalization in Λ, but it is certainly a poor strategy to try to establish $\overset{\mathrm{d}}{=}$ by evaluation of normal forms: these can be exceedingly long.

This way to split the algorithm into two rounds is mainly intended for better understanding and for theoretical purposes. When we have to deal with very large terms (like those that represent complete mathematics books) it may be more efficient to look into every definitional equality question as soon as it comes up.

The first round of the algorithm will be presented here in Pascal style, operating on terms represented as lambda trees of the kind described in

---

*That definition in [15] should be corrected: the phrase "if (R, ε, U) and (R, ε, P) represent" is to be read as "if (R, ε, K) and (R, ε, U) represent".

[15], section 2.5. The trees are binary trees, with a label attached to each vertex. The tree structure is described by means of the usual vertex-to-vertex functions father, leftson and rightson. The labels will be called "pointlabels", in order to avoid confusion with the Pascal notion **label**. The binary nodes of the tree carry pointlabels A or T (related to application and typed abstraction, respectively), and the endpoints have as pointlabel either the symbol τ or a vertex (which has to be a vertex with pointlabel T). Finally a lambda tree has to satisfy what we shall call the *reference condition*. It reads: if P and N are vertices, and if the pointlabel of P is N (whence P is an end-point and N is a binary node with pointlabel T), then P is either the rightson of N or a descendant (in the sense of leftsons and rightsons) of the rightson of N.

In [15] the relation between lambda term and lambda tree is described in detail. Here we give a short sketch. For every node in the lambda tree we can consider the subtree which has that node as its root, and that subtree will correspond to a term. First consider a binary node N. Let N_1 and N_2 be its leftson and rightson. Let P, P_1, P_2 be the lambda terms corresponding to these three points. Then we have $P = \langle P_1 \rangle P_2$ if N has pointlabel A, and $P = [x : P_1]P_2$ (where x is an appropriately chosen name for a bound variable) if N has pointlabel T. We also have to describe the terms corresponding to end-points of the lambda tree. If the pointlabel is τ, the corresponding term is just τ itself. If the pointlabel of such an end-point is a vertex N (whence N is a binary node with pointlabel T, then the term coresponding to the end-point is the variable introduced in the abstractor $[x : P_1]$ which corresponds to N.

We shall provide our lambda tree with an extra vertex **fakeroot** as father of the real root of the tree. The real root is the leftson of the fakeroot; the rightson of the fakeroot plays no role. This little trick will simplify the algorithm,

The type **lab** will be used in the program for typing the pointlabels, so a **lab** is either a vertex, or A, or T, or τ.

The execution of the program will list all cases where a typecheck has to be carried out. The procedure **task(ind:integer;u,v:vertex)** reports it has to be shown that the subtree rooted by the vertex u is equal (in the sense of β-equivalence interpreted in the context indicated by **ind**) to the subtree rooted by v.

What is called "context" here is not the usual notion of an abstractor string. Here it does not necessarily contain abstractors only. Apart from those, it can have pairs consisting of an applicator followed by an abstractor. This sequence of abstractors and applicators will be described by the array **context** from 0 to **ind**. Every entry in the array is a vertex, and that vertex is always the leftson of its father. Its father's pointlabel (either A or T) shows whether that entry is an applicator or an abstractor, in the following way. Let N be one of those entries, and let P be the lambda tree corresponding to N. Then N will be associated with the applicator $\langle P \rangle$ if N's father has pointlabel A, and with an abstractor $[: P]$ if N's father has pointlabel T.

The M in the program represents the number of vertices of the original tree.

One of the features of the program is that it avoids typechecking work that was done previously. The integer variable **status** takes care of that. It has value 0 if it gets to a binary node for the first time (before entering the left branch), value 1 if it gets there for the second time (after a non-stop trip from an endpoint to the first binary node that is approached from the side of the leftson), but when it has value 2 the left branch of the binary node is not searched at all. The effect is that for every A-node in the lambda tree we get exactly one call of the procedure **task**. Quite another matter is that we often want to apply the program to trees that contain a large amount of repetition themselves. Avoiding duplication of work in those cases is of cause a separate problem.

As usual, the **abort** will mean that the execution of the program is to be stopped. This happens when incorrectness is established already without any typechecking (example $\langle \tau \rangle \tau$).

After all these preparations we now give the program. It is assumed that the functions **father(v:vertex):vertex, leftson(v:vertex):vertex, rightson(v:vertex):vertex**, and **pointlabel(v:vertex):lab** describe a lambda tree, so in particular the program does *not* check the reference condition.

```
var ap1:array[0..M] of vertex;ap2:array[0..M] of integer;
    ap3:array[0..M] of boolean;context:array[0..M] of vertex;
    m,ind,status:integer;loc:vertex;ba:boolean;labloc:lab;

procedure P1;
   begin m:=m+1;ap1[m]:=loc;ap2[m]:=ind;
         ap3[m]:=true;loc:=leftson(loc);
   end;
procedure P2;
   begin case labloc of
           'A': begin m:=m+1;ap1[m]:=leftson(loc);
                      ap2[m]:=status;ap3[m]:=false
                end;
           'T': begin if (not ba) then
```

```
                  begin x:=ap1[m];m:=m-1;
                    if ap2[m]=1 then task(ind,x,leftson(loc));
                    ind:=ind+1;context[ind]:=x;
                  end;
                  ind:=ind+1;context[ind]:=leftson(loc)
               end;
           end {case labloc};
     loc:=rightson(loc);if status=1 then status:=0;
   end;
procedure P3;
   begin if labloc='tau' then abort
         else begin status:=2;loc:=leftson(labloc) end
   end;
procedure P4;
   begin loc:=ap1[m];ind:=ap2[m];m:=m-1;status:=1
   end;

begin loc:=fakeroot;m:=0;status:=0;ind:=-1;ap3[0]:=true;
   repeat
   labloc:=pointlabel(loc); ba:=ap3[m];
   if labloc='A' or labloc='T'
     then begin if status=0 then P1
                 else begin if (status=1) or (not ba) then P2
                              else P4
                       end
           end
     else begin if ba then P4 else P3 end
   until loc=fakeroot;
end.
```

4   Characteristics of Automath languages

Generalities

Without trying to explain much in detail, we just indicate a number of issues
in which Automath differs from some other verification systems based on
typed lambda calculi.

Automath books are written as sequences of lines: definitional lines
and primitive lines. Every line is written in a certain context, which is a

sequence of typed variables

$$(x_1 : A_1) \cdots (x_k : A_k),$$

where each A_j is a term that may contain the previous $x_1, \cdots, x_{j-1}$. As meta-notation for contexts we use symbols like Γ, and for conxtext extensions $\Gamma, (x : A)$. There is a notion of validity of contexts, a notion of validity of terms (lambda-typed lambda terms) inside a context (meta-notation $\Gamma \vdash P$), and a notion of validity of typings inside a context (meta-notation $\Gamma \vdash P : Q$).

A definitional line (in context Γ) has the form "$f := P : Q$", where f is a new identifier, and where $\Gamma \vdash P : Q$. A primitive line has the same form, but for the fact that the term P is replaced by the symbol PN (which is not considered as a term). PN is acronym for "primitive notion".

There is a fixed set of *basic* terms (like τ, type, prop) which are said to have *degree* 1. The degree of all further valid terms is found by the rule that if $P : Q$ then degree(P) = degree(Q) + 1. And if $f := P : Q$ (or $f := $ PN $: Q$) is a line then degree(f) = degree(Q) + 1. In Automath the degrees are restricted to the values 1, 2, 3, so in lines $f := P : Q$ or $f := $ PN $: Q$ the Q should have degree 1 or 2.

Abstractors and applicators are denoted as at the end of section 1.

Some of the Automath languages (AUT-QE , AUT-QE-NTI) admit *quasi-expressions*, which have the form of a sequence of abstractors followed by a basic term, like

$$[x_1 : A_1] \cdots [x_k : A_k] \text{ type}.$$

They are given degree 1.

Instantiation

Very typical for Automath is the fact that the rule for validity of contexts is more permissive than the rules for abstraction. Abstractors [x:type] are not allowed, but context extensions (x:type) are. A valid context Γ can be extended to a new valid context by any extension $\Gamma, (x : Q)$ provided that x is a new variable, that $\Gamma \vdash Q$ and that the degree of Q is 1 or 2. The requirements for abstraction can be more severe. Abstraction $[x : A]$ is restricted anyway to the case that A has degree 2, in AUT68 and in AUT-QE-NTI moreover by the condition that the type of A is a basic term. In PAL there are no abstractors at all.

In the Automath languages there are (like in standard mathematical language) two different devices for describing functional relationship, the *instantiation device* and the *lambda device*. The use of instantiation admits explicitly defined functions. If inside a context

$$\Gamma, \ (x_1 : A_1) \cdots (x_k : A_k)$$

we have a line $f := P : Q$ or $f := PN : Q$ then in any later line (in a context Γ_1 that at least starts with Γ), we can *instantiate* f by attaching a string of sub-terms, writing $f(B_1, \ldots, B_k)$. These B_j have to be typed (in the context Γ_1) by the things we get from the corresponding A_j if we replace the x_i's by the corresponding B_i's. It has to be mentionend that the instantiation device generates new definitional equalities by means of the δ-reduction, which is essentially nothing but replacing the defined identifier f by its definition P (in case the line was $f := P : Q$).

In cases where $[x_1 : A_1] \cdots [x_k : A_k]$ are admissible abstractors, the step from f to $f(B_1, \ldots, B_k)$ corresponds to the one from F (where F is obtained from $f(x_1, \ldots, x_k)$ by k-fold lambda abstraction) to the k-fold application $\langle B_k \rangle \cdots \langle B_1 \rangle F$.

In the instantiation device the notion of function is restricted to explicitly defined functions, so it cannot describe mathematics beyond the level of the 18-th century. Nevertheless the system of "proofs as objects" enables the lambda-free Automath language PAL to use the instantiation device for true mathematical reasoning.

But what the instantiation device cannot do is to let us talk about arbitrary functions, and to *say* in the language that a function obtained by the instantiation device is a function indeed. That is what we need the lambda calculus for. We might say that the lambda calculus internalizes instantiation.

Type inclusion

Type inclusion is the point where the Automath languages AUT68 and AUT-QE deviate from pure lambda calculus. Having type inclusion is equivalent to having Π-rules like those in Zucker's AUT-Π (see [21]) and in many other systems of typed lambda calculi. Actually one can say that the notations with Π serve as sign posts for places where type inclusion has been applied. The checker never needs those indications, since it is always directly retraceable where and how type inclusion has been applied. That retraceability was the main reason why such indications were omitted in the design of Automath.

The meta-language of Π-rules seems to be more generally accepted than the one of type inclusion, and the feature of type inclusion may have been one of the reasons why in the early days of Automath logicians were inclined to dislike it. Therefore it may be the right place here to give it some attention, not just to the formal rules but also to interpretations.

The original idea about using a notation Q : type was that it just served as an indication that Q had degree 2, what meant that Q could be used as a type for other terms, like in $P : Q$. There is an obvious analogy between the "real" typing $P : Q$ and the notation Q : type. They play the same role in the formation of contexts: by context extensions (Q : type) we can introduce type variables. And they play the same role in definitional lines: just like such lines can be used for defining new objects (of degree 3), they can be used for defining types (of degree 2). And primitive lines can be used for creating primitive types (of degree 2) just like they can be used for creating primitive objects (of degree 3). All this can be achieved without saying that type is a term; instead of considering Q : type as a relation between two terms, we consider the combination "; type" as a kind of predicate applied to Q.

In the light of this opinion about type one has to interpret the AUT68 rule

$$\frac{A : \text{type} \quad \Gamma, (x : A) \vdash Q(x) : \text{type}}{\Gamma \vdash [x : A]Q(x) : \text{type}}.$$

It just says that $[x : A]Q(x)$ is again a valid term of degree 2.

The next step is that sometimes we want to say more about $[x : A]Q(x)$ than that it has degree 2. We sometimes want to express about some term H of degree 2 that it behaves like a term that starts with the abstractor $[x : A]$. If we have some $a : A$ we may wish to form the application $\langle a \rangle H$, and if moreover we have some $f : H$ we may want to form $\langle a \rangle f$. In order to register those possibilities, the *mock typing* $H : [x : A]$type was invented, and that extended AUT68 into AUT-QE. Note that the acronym QE in AUT-QE stands for "quasi-expressions", clearly indicating that $[x : A]$type was not considered as a term. As before, the combination "; $[x : A]$type" was considered as a kind of predicate applied to H.

The mock typing $H : [x : A]$type just gave more information about H than just H : type. Of course we took the right in AUT-QE to pass from $H : [x : A]$type to H : type (but not the other way round). It can be interpreted as sacrifice of information. We can see it as applying an inclusion $[x : A]$type $\subset$ type, and to the step from $H : [x : A]$type to H : type was called *type inclusion*. It can also be applied repeatedly:

$$[x : A][y : B][z : C]\text{type} \subset [x : A][y : B]\text{type} \subset [x : A]\text{type} \subset \text{type}$$

(note that B may depend on x, and C on both x and y).

Once we start implementing AUT-QE in a lambda calculus like $\Delta\Lambda$ (cf.
section 6) we of course begin to consider all the quasi-expressions as lambda
terms, and the mock typings as typings of the typed lambda calculus, and
that means having impurities. The type inclusion rule conflicts with the
idea of unicity of types.

For dicussions where the type inclusion feature is compared to the usage
of Π in AUT-Π we refer to [18] and [10].

5   AUT-QE-NTI

The rules

The syntax of AUT-QE-NTI is the same as the one of AUT-QE. The main
difference is type inclusion: the acronym NTI stand for "no type inclusion".

AUT-QE-NTI handles quasi-expressions (see section 4). And all quasi-
expressions can be used for typing of variables in context extensions. The
general rule is that whenever Γ is a valid context, and $\Gamma \vdash Q$, where the
degree of Q is 1 or 2, then $\Gamma, (x : Q)$ (with a new variable x) is a valid
context. But where AUT-QE allows abstraction over all Q with degree 2,
AUT-QE-NTI restricts it to the case where $Q : B$, where B is a basic term
(like **type**, **prop**, or τ). So the abstraction rule is

$$\frac{\Gamma \vdash A : \mu, \quad \Gamma, (x : A) \vdash P(x) : Q(x)}{\Gamma \vdash [x : A]P(x) : [x : A]Q(x)} ,$$

where μ is one of the basic terms. The rules for application and instantiation
are the same as for AUT-QE.

In our further discussions about AUT-QE-NTI we shall ignore the possibility to have more than one basic term, and just formulate everything
for τ only.

AUT-QE-NTI books as terms in $\Delta\Lambda$

We shall explain here how a book written in AUT-QE-NTI can be transformed into a single term of $\Delta\Lambda$. The book consists of a finite sequence of
lines; some are primitive lines, others are definitional lines. Corresponding
to every primitive line we form a corresponding abstractor, and to every
definitional line we form a pair consisting of an applicator and an abstractor. We just concatenate these abstractors and applicator-abstractor pairs
in the order of the lines of the book, and we complete that sequence with
a τ. That concatenation will be the term that represents the whole book.

A thing that should be looked into first, is that $\Delta\Lambda$ does not handle
instantiation, and therefore the instantiations in the AUT-QE-NTI book

have to be remodelled to applications. In the last line of the example given below there is a (double) case of instantiation, and from that example it will be clear how the remodelling works in general.

In [5] a notational convention was explained that can be helpful here. If the identifier f is introduced in a context of length k, then the identifier $\textcircled{3}f$ will be used for what we get from f by abstracting over the last 3 pieces of the context, and the reader is suppposed to understand this without seeing a line where that new identifier $\textcircled{3}f$ was introduced. With this convention we can say that the instantiation $f(U, V, W)$ is definitionally equal to the application $\langle W \rangle \langle V \rangle \langle U \rangle \textcircled{3}f$.

We now describe how the abstractors and applicator-abstractor pairs are obtained from the book lines. In the case of a primitive line

$$(x_1 : A_1) \cdots (x_k : A_k) \vdash f := \text{PN} : Q$$

we create a new identifier F and take as the abstractor

$$[\, F \; : \; [x_1 : A_1] \cdots [x_k : A_k] Q \,];$$

in the case of a definitional line

$$(x_1 : A_1) \cdots (x_k : A_k) \vdash f := P : Q$$

we form the applicator-abstractor pair

$$\langle [x_1 : A_1] \cdots [x_k : A_k] P \rangle [\, F \; : \; [x_1 : A_1] \cdots [x_k : A_k] Q \,].$$

The new identifier F should not be confused with the old f (with the notation mentioned above it should be $\textcircled{3}f$), only if the context was empty there is no danger for such confusion.

We give a short example. Let the book be

	$\vdash A$	$:=$	PN	$: \tau$
	$\vdash c$	$:=$	PN	$: A$
	$\vdash f$	$:=$	$[y : A]c$	$: [y : A]A$
$(x : A)$	$\vdash g$	$:=$	$\langle x \rangle f$	$: A$
	$\vdash B$	$:=$	A	$: \tau$
$(z : \tau)$	$\vdash h$	$:=$	$g(g(c))$	$: B$

This book transforms into the following term in $\Delta \Lambda$:

$$[A : \tau]\,[c : A]\,\langle [y : A]c \rangle\,[f : [y : A]A]\,\langle [x : A]\langle x \rangle f \rangle\,[G : [x : A]A]$$

$$\langle A \rangle\,[B : \tau]\,\langle [z : \tau]\langle \langle c \rangle G \rangle G \rangle\,[H : [z : \tau]B]\,\tau.$$

Under this translation from a book in AUT-QE-NTI into a term in $\Delta\Lambda$ we see how essential the difference between $\Delta\Lambda$ and Λ (indicated in the subsection "Correctness" of section 3) is. If in an AUT-QE-NTI book we replace some definitional line $f := P : Q$ by the primitive line $f := \text{PN} : Q$, the rest of the book will often become incorrect, since the validity of the book might have depended on the definitional equality of f and P, which gets lost if we replace P by PN. But if in the definition of correctness in $\Delta\Lambda$ we would have insisted that correctness of $\langle R \rangle P$ requires correctness of P (see section 3), we would actually have required that the term in $\Delta\Lambda$ that corresponds to the AUT-QE-NTI book would remain correct after just omitting the applicator that carries the information about the definition of f, and that means the same thing as replacing the P by PN.

The example above demonstrates this for the pair $\langle A \rangle [B : \tau]$. If we would omit the $\langle A \rangle$, the type of $[z : \tau]\langle\langle c \rangle G \rangle G$ would no longer be $[z : \tau]B$.

In AUT-SL (see [4]) there was the standard convention that in an application $\langle R \rangle P$ both parts P and R were required to be correct, and that made it necessary to eliminate all definitions of the book (by means of δ-reductions) before the translation into a lambda-term could begin. For that reason AUT-SL could not be more than a way to streamline Automath language theory, whereas $\Delta\Lambda$ is more than that: it is also a practical tool for working with Automath, in particular for the checker.

It is not too easy to say exactly what kind of terms in $\Delta\Lambda$ correspond to an AUT-QE-NTI book according to our translation, since *inside* a line the notion of correctness has to handle the old requirement about correctness of $\langle R \rangle P$, i.e., it has to require the correctness of both R and P. Here we might recommend the Procrustes technique: if a feature of AUT-QE-NTI does not fit in the bed $\Delta\Lambda$ then we just *make* it fit by changing the definition of AUT-QE-NTI. What we gain is the facility of admitting abbreviations which are local inside a line, or even inside a part of a term in that line. But a more important gain is the simplicity of the properties of the result of the embedding.

6   Implementing AUT-QE in AUT-QE-NTI

Introduction

AUT-QE-NTI is definitely weaker than AUT-QE and also weaker than AUT68, just because of its purity. In order to let AUT-QE-NTI enjoy the blessings of type inclusion without actually having it, we can start our book with a set of axioms that mimic the effects of type inclusion. In that way we can say that we can implement AUT-QE and AUT68 in AUT-QE-NTI.

There are two prices we have to pay:

(i) applications of what corresponds to type inclusion have to be written in the book, by means of references to those axioms, with explicit statement of the terms that have to be substituted for the parameters in these axioms,

(ii) the definitional equalities generated by type inclusion have to be replaced by book equalities.

We can try to overcome these objections by (i) providing automatic text writing facilities that does all the dirty work for us, and (ii) by distinguishing two different kinds of book equalities, a strong and a weak one, where the strong one can enjoy the decidability that the definitional equality is supposed to have (see section 6).

The axioms for Π

We now get to the axioms that mimic the type inclusion. Since they of course also mimic the role of Π, we shall use the letter Π as an identifier. Actually there is a multitude of axioms for Π, since the axioms get two parameters σ and μ that stand for basic types (like **type** or **prop**). We could do with a single set of axioms if we would handle only one basic term, or if we would introduce a facility for creating basic terms (that can be done by opening the possibility of degree 0, with a single term $*$ in it, and letting $\mu : *$ mean: "Let μ be a basic term").

As a set of axioms for Π we present

$$
\begin{array}{lll}
(X : \sigma)(Q : [x : X]\mu) & \vdash \Pi_{\sigma\mu} \quad := \text{PN} & : \mu \\
(X : \sigma)(Q : [x : X]\mu)(u : \Pi_{\sigma\mu}) & \vdash Ax1_{\sigma\mu} := \text{PN} & : [x : X]\langle x \rangle Q \\
(X : \sigma)(Q : [x : X]\mu)(v : [x : X]\langle x \rangle Q) & \vdash Ax2_{\sigma\mu} := \text{PN} & : \Pi_{\sigma\mu}
\end{array}
$$

These $Ax1$ and $Ax2$ permit us to jump up and down from Q to $\Pi(X, Q)$, and that mimics the type inclusion feature without frustrating the typing rules of the lambda calculus.

We remark that in two cases we have used the "η-expansion" $[x : X]\langle x \rangle Q$ instead of Q itself. This deviates from [11], and is done here in order to avoid having to apply η-reduction in cases of multiple application of the axioms for Π.

If one wants to implement mathematics without ever having to use η-reduction, it probably suffices to pass at once to the η-expansion of Q in all those cases where $Q : [x : X]\mu$ and Q is *not* definitionally equal to a term starting with the abstractor $[x : X]$ (this happens in cases like the one above, where Q was introduced as a variable typed by $[x : X]\mu)$. This remark is similar to the observation by D. van Daalen, mentioned in the discussion on η-reduction in section 4.1.1 of [19].

We have to add equality axioms, expressing that we have (in abbreviated form)

$$Ax1(Ax2(v)) = v, \quad Ax2(Ax1(u)) = u.$$

The equality here will have to be book equality.

Axioms for Σ

Another set of axioms in AUT-QE-NTI can organize the operation Σ of AUT-Π. In the context X : **type**, Q : $[x : X]$**type** it postulates the type $\Sigma(X, Q)$, that can be imagined as being the type of all pairs p, q with $p : X$, $q : \langle p \rangle Q$. With the terminology of telescopes (see [17] it can be described as a type that enables us to replace the telescope $[x : X][y : \langle x \rangle Q]$ of length 2 by the telescope $[w : \Sigma(X, Q)]$ of length 1. Actually this set of primitives was used extensively in AUT68 under the name "OwnType" in order to treat sets (subtypes) as types.

By multiple application of Σ we can condense telescopes of length > 2 into length 1.

We can introduce Σ by means of the following axioms:

$$
\begin{array}{lll}
(X : \sigma)(Q : [x : X]\mu) & \vdash \Sigma_{\sigma\mu} := \text{PN} & : \mu \\
(X : \sigma)(Q : [x : X]\mu)(\varphi : \Sigma_{\sigma\mu}) & \vdash \text{proj1}_{\sigma\mu} := \text{PN} & : X \\
(X : \sigma)(Q : [x : X]\mu)(\varphi : \Sigma_{\sigma\mu}) & \vdash \text{proj2}_{\sigma\mu} := \text{PN} & : \langle \text{proj1}_{\sigma\mu} \rangle Q \\
(X : \sigma)(Q : [x : X]\mu)(t_1 : X)(t_2 : \langle t_1 \rangle Q) & \vdash \text{pair}_{\sigma\mu} := \text{PN} & : \Sigma_{\sigma\mu}
\end{array}
$$

We have to add equality axioms, expressing (with book equality) that

$$\text{proj}_1(\text{pair}(t_1, t_2)) = t_1, \quad \text{proj}_2(\text{pair}(t_1, t_2)) = t_2,$$

$$\text{pair}(\text{proj}_1(\varphi), \text{proj}_2(\varphi)) = \varphi.$$

Further axioms

Needless to say we want some more axioms for dealing with standard mathematics, in particular axioms about book equality (a survey of what we need in AUT-QE can be found in [19]).

A thing that one might also like to implement is *proof irrelevance*. Proof irrelevance has been proposed as a rule for making different proofs of one and the same proposition definitionally equal (connected with the fact that mathematicians have the opinion that objects do not really depend on proofs), but that means another impurity of the typed lambda calculus. In the vein of AUT-QE-NTI it of course requires some book axioms, and the equality involved in it is a serious candidate for strong book equality (see section 6).

A further candidate for being shifted from the frame to book axioms is the matter of admitting more than 3 degrees. It is to be expected that this feature can be mimicked efficiently by means of axioms over a frame that handles only 3 degrees.

Three kinds of equality

The systems we have considered all use two kinds of equality: *definitional equality* and *book equality*. Definitional equality is handled in the frame by means of the reductions of the language. In general we expect the languages to have the property that definitional equality is decidable, whence it need not be expressed in the books. And there is never an assumption or a negation of definitional equality. On the other hand, book equality is introduced as a notion in the book, and particular book equalities can be proved, disproved or assumed in the book. In general there is no decision procedure for establishing book equality.

The effect of replacing impurities of the lambda calculus by book material is that one will have to live with the administration of many rather trivial book equalities. Let us use the term *strong book equalities* for them. Wherever we shift rules for definitional equality to the book we get such strong equalities, and, conversely, these strong equalities will be considered by others as suitable candidates for putting more definitional equalities into the frame.

As candidates for such strong book equalities we mention the equality axioms for Π and Σ in section 6.

It seems reasonable to give the strong equalities a separate status among the book equalities, in particular since much of the administrative work with these strong book equalities can be automated.

Right now this matter of strong book equality it is not more than a suggestion. The author has not acquired substantial experience with this, and such experience would be necessary for finding out whether it will be sufficiently efficient on the long run.

In order to describe some suggestions we denote ordinary book equality by IS, and strong book equality by ISSt (for types) and ISSo (for objects). Ordinary book equality is defined on any type X; if $x : X, y : X$ then $\mathrm{IS}(X, x, y)$ is a proof class. Strong book equality can be expressed between types too: If X : **type**, Y : **type**, then $\mathrm{ISSt}(X,Y)$ is a proof class. Moreover, we can express strong book equality between objects belonging to different but strongly book equal types. If X : **type**, Y : **type**, $u : \mathrm{ISSt}(X,Y)$, $x : X$, $y : Y$ then we may have $\mathrm{ISSo}(X,Y,u,x,y)$. A book axiom will express that $\mathrm{ISSo}(X,X,v,x,y)$ (where v refers to the reflexivity axiom $\mathrm{ISSt}(X,X)$) implies ordinary book equality $\mathrm{IS}(X,x,y)$. And there have to be axioms for strong equality for function values $F(x)$ and $G(y)$ if we have strong equality between F and G as well as between x and y.

Quite something has to be done about the relation between book equality (weak or strong) and typing. We can have book equality between types. A common case is that there is a function F mapping type X into type Y, and that we have $p : X$, $q : X$, where p and q are book-equal. We of cause want to call the types $F(p)$ and $F(q)$ book-equal. But if $r : F(p)$, $s : F(q)$ then r and s cannot be compared by ordinary book equality, since they do not have the same type ($r : U$ implies $r : V$ only if U and V are definitionally equal, see section 1, subsection Purity of lambda calculi). If we do not like to extend the notion of book-equality to objects belonging to book-equal types, we will have to work with explicitly constructed bijections, which gives quite some irritating administration. But again, we can expect that such work can be efficiently automated.

We might also use strong equality for proof irrelevance. If P and Q are strongly book-equal proof classes, we may express the principle of irrelevance of proofs by postulating that whenever $p : P$ and $q : Q$ then the proofs p and q are strongly book-equal.

In [16] it was recommended to use the possibility to have two or more kinds of logic interwoven in one and the same book. In that case we have to introduce a different kind of proof classes for each kind of logic. Apart from assigning the type **prop** to a proof class, one might also handle **iprop** (for intuitionistic proofs) and **pprop** for positive (negation-free) proofs. It can be used like this: if p is some proposition then we can form Q with Q : **iprop**, and then $b : Q$ will mean that b is an intuitionistic proof for p. (In [16] it was recommended to use the word **prooftype** instead of the misleading word **prop**, and similarly **pprooftype** for negation-free logic.

In [16] this way of mixing various kinds of logic in one and the same book was recommended for treating constructions (like geometrical constructions). The idea is that we want to be able to say that something is a construction, but we do not want to allow to say that something is *not* a construction. We do not want to admit drawing conclusions from the negation of the statement that something has *not* been constructed. Whether that might ever lead to trouble is doubtful, but it is just not the kind of thing we want to have expressed.

The matter with strong equality is somewhat parallel to this. If we have some kind of definitional equality in the frame, we are unable to express its negation in the books. So if we push that piece of definitional equality into the books, in the form of strong equality, we should not be able to handle its negation either. So it is reasonable to handle strong equality in terms of positive logic.

With the notation explained above this will be expressed by

$$ISSt(X,Y) : \textbf{pprooftype}, \quad ISSo(X,Y,u,x,y) : \textbf{pprooftype}.$$

We leave it at these rather schematic remarks.

7   The project $\Lambda\Sigma$

Introduction

It was expressed already in section 2 that at present $\Lambda\Sigma$ is to be considered as the name of a project rather than as a well-defined language with a satisfactory theory. The project is to define the upper right corner in the following diagram:

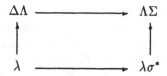

In the lower left corner we have λ, which is ordinary untyped lambda calculus. The one above it is the typed lambda calculus system $\Delta\Lambda$. In the lower right corner we have a modification $\lambda\sigma^*$ of the segment calculus $\lambda\sigma$ (see section 7). The problem is to find a definition and theory of a language $\Lambda\Sigma$ that has both $\Delta\Lambda$ and $\lambda\sigma^*$ as sublanguages.

The calculus $\lambda\sigma$ was introduced in [12] as an attempt to embed abbreviations for strings and telescopes into a system that takes them seriously. Usually one considers such things as a kind of sugaring, and treats them *ad hoc*, but this kind of abbreviations is bound to accumulate: abbreviations inside abbreviations, and then it is hard to build a dependable checker.

The matter is far from easy. One of the troubles with telescopes is that they contain variables to which there are references from other places, so we can get references to variables inside a telescope (or, more generally, a segment) that is only visible in the form of an abbreviation. Moreover, in different references to one and the same telescope we may have to have different sets for the names of the variables, in order to avoid name clashes. It is obviously a situation that asks for namefree calculus.

Some language theory, like the Church-Rosser property, was developed by H. Balsters in [1]. There has not been much activity in the subject since then.

The calculus $\lambda\sigma$

We shall not *define* $\lambda\sigma$ here, but just try to give an impression of what it is about.

We use the word *segment* for any string of applicators and abstractors in (untyped) lambda calculus. Avoiding namefree notation in this and the following examples, we mention the segment

$$(1)\qquad\qquad \langle\langle x\rangle[u]\langle x\rangle u\rangle\ [z]\ \langle\langle z\rangle[t]\langle\langle t\rangle x\rangle\rangle\ [v]$$

(note that the abstractors are untyped, so we have $[x]$ instead of $[x:X]$).

We want to make a calculus that treats segments in a way similar to terms, so we also want to have *segment variables*, and we want to interpret the elimination of segment abbreviations as a kind of β-reduction. As an example we take the abbreviation of the segment $\langle\langle x\rangle[u]\langle x\rangle u\rangle\ [z]$ by the single identifier η. In section 5 we showed how to do this for terms: If the abbreviation is $f := [u]\langle v\rangle u$ then elimination of that definition in a later occurreence of f is effectuated by a local β-reduction, carried out with the applicator-abstractor pair $\langle[u]\langle v\rangle u\rangle\ [f]$. So similarly we want to use for the case of the segment

$$\langle\langle\langle x\rangle[u]\langle x\rangle u\rangle\ [z]\rangle\ [\eta],$$

and there $[\eta]$ is an abstactor that introduces the segment variable η.

But lambda calculus is more than administration of abbreviations: it also concerns variables which are *not* going to be defined like the f above. Accordingly, we will also have undefined segment variables. And since segments may always contain variables that can be referred to, it becomes necessary to have some indication about the number of such referrable variables. To make it worse, some of the variables in the abstractors of a segment can again be segment variables, and the segments to be substituted for them can contain ordinary variables to which it is possible to refer even before these segment variables are replaced by the segments that can be substituted for them.

In order to make that reference system more transparent, the suggestion was made in [12] to attach a kind of norm to the segment variables that shows the structure of the variables contained in them. That norm was called *frame*, but now that the word "frame" has got a completely different meaning it may be better to call that norm the *skeleton*.

The expressions that can be built by means of this segment calculus can sometimes be reduced (by β-reduction) to terms of the lambda calculus, but not always. The segments can begin to lead a life of their own, just like the variables in ordinary lambda calculus achieve more than abbreviations.

We know that segments, in particular telescopes, can be used to describe complex abstract mathematical notions, like the notion "group". A group is usually considered as a mathematical object, but the notion "group" is not. A particular group is represented as a string, and the statement that it represents a group is expressed (with the terminology of [17]) that this string *fits* into the telescope "group". Extensive use of telescope abbreviations for treating modern mathematics was made by Zucker (see [21]).

This segment calculus is something like category theory. The notion "group" may refer to a particular category, represented by a telescope, but if we want to say "let C be any category", then we have to express that by "let η be any telescope", and there we need the telescope variable.

So we see that the title of [12] was not very fortunate: the scope of the paper is wider than the title suggests.

Extending to a typed calculus

What we have in mind with $\Lambda\Sigma$ is primarily a language in which the terms can be reduced to terms of a typed lambda calculus like $\Delta\Lambda$. That means that all segment variables can be eliminated by β-reductions.

If we omit all type information in such a calculus, we get the fragment $\lambda\sigma^*$ of $\lambda\sigma$, containing all $\lambda\sigma$-terms which are reducible to λ-terms. With this limited concept of $\lambda\sigma^*$ one might now say that the diagram given in the beginning of this section describes what we want. This vision on $\Lambda\Sigma$ will hopefully produce a system in which we can efficiently handle accumulated segment abbreviations, both for writing and for checking.

The matter may become harder if we want more than this, like handling segment variables as hinted at in the remark on category theory at the end of the previous subsection.

Bibliography

[1] Balsters, H. (1986). Lambda calculus extended with segments. Ph.D. thesis, Eindhoven University of Technology.

[2] Barendregt, H.P. (1989). Introduction to generalised type systems. *Proceedings 3rd Italian Conference on Theoretical Computer Science*, Eds. A. Bertoni a.o.(World Scientific, Singapore).

[3] Bruijn, N.G. de (1970). The mathematical language Automath, its usage, and some of its extensions. Symposium on Automatic Demonstration (Versailles, December 1968), *Lecture Notes in Mathematics* vol. 125, pp. 29-61 (Springer Verlag).

[4] —— (1971). AUT-SL, a single line version of Automath. Report, Department of Mathematics, Eindhoven University of Technology.

[5] —— (1972). Some abbreviations in the input language for Automath. Report, Department of Mathematics, Eindhoven University of Technology.

[6] —— (1973). Automath, a language for mathematics. *Séminaire Math. Sup.* 1971, 58 p. (Les Presses de l'Université de Montréal).

[7] —— (1974). A framework for the description of a number of members of the Automath family, Memorandum 1974-08, Department of Mathematics, Eindhoven University of Technology.

[8] —— (1974). Some extensions of Automath: the AUT-4 family. Report, Department of Mathematics, Eindhoven University of Technology.

[9] —— (1976). Modifications of the 1968 version of Automath. Memorandum 1976-14, Department of Mathematics, Eindhoven University of Technology.

[10] —— (1977). Some auxiliary operators in AUT-II. Memorandum 1977-10, Department of Mathematics, Eindhoven University of Technology.

[11] —— (1978). AUT-QE without type inclusion. Memorandum 1978-04, Department of Mathematics, Eindhoven University of Technology.

[12] —— (1978). A namefree lambda calculus with facilities for internal definitions of expressions and segments. T.H. Report 78-WSK-03, Department of Mathematics, Eindhoven University of Technology.

[13] —— (1980). A survey of the project Automath. In: *To H.B. Curry: Essays in combinatory logic, lambda calculus and formalism* (ed. J.P. Seldin and J.R. Hindley), pp. 579-606 (Academic Press).

[14] —— (1984). Formalization of constructivity in Automath. In: *Papers dedicated to J.J. Seidel* (ed. P.J. de Doelder, J. de Graaf and J.H. van Lint) EUT-Report 84-WSK-03, ISSN 0167-9708, pp. 76-101. Department of Mathematics and Computing Science, Eindhoven University of Technology.

[15] —— (1987). Generalizing Automath by means of a lambda-typed lambda calculus. In: *Mathematical Logic and Theoretical Computer Science*, Lecture Notes in pure and applied mathematics, 106, (ed. D. W. Kueker, E.G.K. Lopez-Escobar, C.H. Smith) pp. 71-92 (Marcel Dekker, New York).

[16] —— (1990). The use of justification systems for integrated semantics. In: *Colog-88*,(ed. P. Martin-Löf and G. Mints). Lecture Notes in Computer Science vol 417, pp. 9-24 (Springer Verlag).

[17] ——. Telescopic mappings in typed lambda calculus. To be published in *Information and Computation*.

[18] Daalen, D.T. van (1980). *The language theory of Automath*. Ph.D. Thesis, Eindhoven University of Technology.

[19] Jutting, L.S. van Benthem (1979). *Checking Landau's "Grundlagen" in the Automath system*. Ph.D. Thesis, Eindhoven University of Technology, 1977. Mathematical Centre Tracts Nr. 83 (Mathematical Centre, Amsterdam).

[20] Nederpelt, R.P. (1973). Strong normalization in a typed lambda calculus with lambda structured types. Ph.D.thesis, Eindhoven University of Technology.

[21] Zucker, J. (1975) Formalisation of classical mathematics in Automath. In: *Colloques Internationaux du Centre National de la Recherche Scientifique* nr. 249, pp. 135-145.

Nederpelt's calculus extended with a notion of context as a logical framework

Philippe de Groote

Université Catholique de Louvain, Unité d'informatique,
B-1348 Louvain-la-Neuve, Belgique

Abstract

We define an extended version of Nederpelt's calculus which can be used as a logical framework. The extensions have been introduced in order to support the notions of mathematical definition of constants and to internalize the notion of theory. The resulting calculus remains concise and simple, a basic requirement for logical frameworks. The calculus manipulates two kinds of objects: texts which correspond to λ-expressions, and contexts which are mainly sequences of variable declarations, constant definitions, or context abbreviations. Basic operations on texts and contexts are provided. It is argued that these operations allow one to structure large theories. An example is provided.

1 Introduction

This paper introduces the static kernel of a language called DEVA [13]. This language, which has been developed in the framework of the ToolUse Esprit project, is intended to express software development mathematically. The general paradigm which was followed considered *development methods as theories* and *developments as proofs*. Therefore, the kernel of the language should provide a general treatment of formal theories and proofs.

The problem of defining a generic formal system is comparable to the one of defining a general computing language. While, according to Church's thesis, any algorithm can be expressed as a recursive function, one uses higher level languages for the actual programming of computers. Similarly, one could argue that any formal system can be expressed as Post productions, but to use such a formalism as a logical framework is, in practice, inadequate.

The criteria according to which the expressive power of a logical framework should be evaluated are mostly practical and subjective. One speaks of *natural representations* [9] of logics, or expressions close to *ordinary mathematical presentation* [5].

Such requirements were at the origin of the AUTOMATH project [5]; we chose one of the simplest versions of AUTOMATH, as a starting point for our language: Nederpelt's Λ [10].

Nederpelt's calculus, introduced in the next section, is a λ-typed λ-calculus. Its expressive power, as a logical framework, is similar to Edinburgh LF [9]. The systematic use of typed λ-abstraction provides a smooth treatment of syntax, rules, and proofs.

The representation of a theory, in Nederpelt's Λ, amounts to a sequence of declarations of variables. This sequence is the environment in which proofs can be developed, but is not an object of the calculus. The notion of context we have added to Λ is intended to internalize the notion of environment. The goal is to provide simple means for structuring large collections of theories within the calculus.

This problem of structuring theories is not new in the case of software development. It has already been tackled in various ways by work on program specifications. Our approach is somewhat different, since it is merely syntactic. The meaning of the operations we provide on theories is not based on semantics, but explained in terms of reduction relations.

2   Nederpelt's calculus

Definition

In Nederpelt's Λ, there is no syntactic difference between types and terms, and λ-abstraction is used to represent both functional terms and dependent types. For this reason, one rather speaks globally of the expressions of the calculus. These expressions are built from an infinite alphabet of variables and a single constant τ, according to the following formation rules: τ is an expression; any variable is an expression; if e_1, and e_2 are expressions, so are $[x:e_1]e_2$ (typed abstraction) and $(e_1\ e_2)$ (application). The notions of free and bound variables are generalized by adding the following clause to the usual ones: Any free occurrence of a variable x in e_1 is free in $[x_1:e_1]e_2$ (even if $x \equiv x_1$).

β-redices and β-reduction are as usual*. Nevertheless, because of dependent types, contractions and substitutions may now be performed within type labels.

Among expressions, one distinguishes well-typed expressions, i.e. expressions which obey some applicability conditions. To this end, it is necessary to assign types to expressions. This raises a problem for free variables which are a priori untyped. For this reason, the type of an expression will be defined according to some environment assigning a type to each free variable of the expression. An environment is thus a sequence of variable declarations. Let E denote environments, the expression $E, x : e$ will denote the environment obtained by adding the declaration $x : e$ at the end of E. A partial selecting operation $\mathrm{sel}_x(E)$ is defined on environments as follows:

$$\mathrm{sel}_x(E, x : e) \;\equiv\; e$$

$$\mathrm{sel}_x(E, x_1 : e) \;\equiv\; \mathrm{sel}_x(E) \quad \text{if } x \not\equiv x_1.$$

The type of an expression e according to some environment E – in short: $\mathrm{type}(E \mid e)$ – is defined a priori, independently whether e is well-typed or not. There is no type assigned to τ nor to the expressions whose head is τ, which are so to speak the proper types of the calculus.

$$\mathrm{type}(E \mid x) \;\equiv\; \mathrm{sel}_x(E)$$

$$\mathrm{type}(E \mid [x : e_1] e_2) \;\equiv\; [x : e_1] \, \mathrm{type}(E, x : e_1 \mid e_2)$$

$$\mathrm{type}(E \mid (e_1 \, e_2)) \;\equiv\; (\mathrm{type}(E \mid e_1) \, e_2)$$

The typing operator defined above allows to express applicability conditions and to define the notion of well-typed expression:

$$E \vdash \tau$$

$$E \vdash x \quad \text{if } \mathrm{sel}_x(E) \text{ is defined}$$

$$\frac{E \vdash e_1 \quad E, x : e_1 \vdash e_2}{E \vdash [x : e_1] e_2}$$

$$\frac{E \vdash e_1 \quad E \vdash e_2 \quad \mathrm{type}(E \mid e_1) =_\beta [x : \mathrm{type}(E \mid e_2)] e_3}{E \vdash (e_1 \, e_2)}$$

---

*Actually, the calculus which is presented here is a variant of Nederpelt's Λ. The difference is that we do not take η-reduction into account. As is well known [14], the language theory of the calculus with η-reduction is much more complicated, but the main results are preserved.

$$\frac{E \vdash e_1 \quad E \vdash e_2 \quad e_1 =_\beta [\,x\,{:}\,\mathrm{type}\,(E\,|\,e_2)\,]\,e_3}{E \vdash (\,e_1\,e_2\,)}$$

It could seem strange, in the definition above, that there are no correctness conditions on environments. This is justified by the fact that we are interested in closed expressions only. In other words, the correct expressions of the calculus are the ones which are well-typed according to the empty environment.

The main properties of Λ, proof of which may be found in [7, 10, 14], are the following:

Church-Rosser : if $e_1 =_\beta e_2$, then e_1 and e_2 have a common β-reduct[†];

Closure : if e_1 is a correct expression and if $e_1 \to_\beta e_2$, then e_2 is correct;

Strong-normalization : if e is correct, then there is no infinite sequence of β-contractions starting with e.

From these properties, one may infer that the property of being well-typed is decidable.

Λ may be used for representing logics in a way similar to the Edinburgh Logical Framework [9]. The examples developed for LF [1] are quite easily adaptable to Λ. For instance, the following declarations of Λ correspond to the LF-signature Σ_{PA} given in [9]:

ι	$:\tau$	o	$:\tau$
0	$:\iota$	succ	$:[\,x\,{:}\,\iota\,]\,\iota$
$+$	$:[\,x\,{:}\,\iota\,][\,x\,{:}\,\iota\,]\,\iota$	$\times$	$:[\,x\,{:}\,\iota\,][\,x\,{:}\,\iota\,]\,\iota$
$=$	$:[\,x\,{:}\,\iota\,][\,x\,{:}\,\iota\,]\,o$	$<$	$:[\,x\,{:}\,\iota\,][\,x\,{:}\,\iota\,]\,o$
$\neg$	$:[\,x\,{:}\,o\,]\,o$	$\wedge$	$:[\,x\,{:}\,o\,][\,x\,{:}\,o\,]\,o$
$\vee$	$:[\,x\,{:}\,o\,][\,x\,{:}\,o\,]\,o$	$\supset$	$:[\,x\,{:}\,o\,][\,x\,{:}\,o\,]\,o$
$\forall$	$:[\,x\,{:}[\,x\,{:}\,\iota\,]\,o\,]\,o$	$\exists$	$:[\,x\,{:}[\,x\,{:}\,\iota\,]\,o\,]\,o$

Similarly, universal introduction and natural induction, for instance, are given as follows:

AI $: [\,p\,{:}[\,x\,{:}\,\iota\,]\,o\,][\,x\,{:}[\,x\,{:}\,\iota\,]\,(\,p\,x\,)\,]\,(\,\forall\,p\,)$

IND $: [\,p\,{:}[\,x\,{:}\,\iota\,]\,o\,][\,t\,{:}\,\iota\,][\,x\,{:}(\,p\,0\,)\,][\,x\,{:}[\,x\,{:}\,\iota\,][\,y\,{:}(\,p\,x\,)\,]\,(\,p\,(\,\mathrm{succ}\,x\,)\,)\,]\,(\,p\,t\,)$

[†]With the only notion of β-reduction, the Church-Rosser property holds for any pair of well-formed expressions; with the notion of $\beta\eta$-reduction, it holds for correct expressions only.

There is no degree restriction in Λ. This means that any well-typed expression may be used as a type. For this reason, operators turning a term into a type, such as:

$$\text{true} \quad : \quad [x:o]\,\tau$$

are not needed.

Some limitations

Λ was not designed for practical use. In [3], de Bruijn described how to consider a complete AUTOMATH book as a λ-term of a language called AUT-SL (AUTOMATH single line). This idea gave rise to Λ which was essentially used for language-theoretic studies [10, 14].

In [11], Nederpelt presents some translations of mathematical texts into Λ, and discusses translation difficulties.

Some of these difficulties are due to the type structure of Λ. For instance, Λ has uniqueness of types. Therefore, if types are used to represent sets, a natural number x will not be automatically a real number since N and R cannot be convertible expressions. Another example appears if one tries to use the dependent type $[x:a]\,b$ to represent the implication $a \supset b$. A formation rule such as the following is not admissible in Λ:

$$\frac{a \,:\, o \qquad b \,:\, o}{[x:a]\,b \,:\, o}$$

Such translation dificulties arise if one wants as much logical knowledge as possible to be reflected by the internal logic of Λ. But they can be avoided by using Λ as a logical framework in which the logical knowledge is stated by means of axiom and rule declarations. In short, we would say that these difficulties arise when Λ is used with application of the *propositions as types* principle, but that they disappear when Λ is used with application of the *judgements as types* principle.

Another difficulty is related to the handling of definitions. The only way of representing mathematical definitions in Λ is by means of β-redices ($[x : e_1]\,e_2\,e_3$), where the operand e_3 represents the *definiens*, and the variable x the *definiendum*. Such redices, to be well-typed, must obey the following rule:

$$\frac{E \vdash e_1 \quad E \vdash e_3 \quad E, x:e_1 \vdash e_2 \quad \text{type}(E\,|\,e_3) =_\beta e_1}{E \vdash (\,[x:e_1]\,e_2\,e_3\,)}$$

This rule is too strong. It requires that a mathematical text (e_2), in which some defined constant (x) occurs, must make sense (be well-typed) independently of the value (e_3) assigned to the constant. For this reason, when translating an AUTOMATH book into Λ, it is necessary to eliminate all the definitions, by β-reduction. This partial normalization is, in practice, prohibitive. To solve this problem, de Bruijn designed the language $\Lambda\Delta$ [6]. The notion of correctness, in $\Lambda\Delta$, is defined by means of an algorithm. And, while this algorithm does not enforce β-normalisation, it amounts to typing rules which are such that a redex, to be well-typed, must obey the following rule:

$$\frac{E \vdash e_1 \quad E \vdash e_3 \quad E \vdash [e_3/x]\,e_2 \quad \text{type}\,(E\,|\,e_3) =_\beta e_1}{E \vdash (\,[\,x\!:\!e_1\,]\,e_2\,e_3\,)}$$

In the extended system which is introduced in this paper we combine both Λ and $\Lambda\Delta$: Nederpelt's conditions are kept for functional application, but β-redices are not used any more to represent definitions. Instead, we use an explicit mechanism:

$$[\,d := e_1\,]\,e_2$$

whose typing conditions are those of $\Lambda\Delta$.

A last practical drawback when using an expression of Λ to represent a mathematical text is that it gives rise to numerous repetitions inside the expression. The parts of the expression which are often repeated are not mere subexpressions, they are abstractors, pairs made of abstractors and operands, or sequences of these. Therefore, such repetitions cannot be avoided by using β-redices, they require some other abbreviation mechanism. Such a mechanism is proposed by Balsters who extends λ-calculus by introducing the notion of segment [2]. The tailor made notion of context we introduce in the next section is a particular case of segment. While this notion is mainly introduced to internalize the notion of theory within the calculus, it may also serve to avoid the repetitions mentioned above.

3   Contexts

Let us consider some correct expression of Λ representing some proof performed, for instance, in Peano arithmetic. Such an expression starts with a sequence of abstractions corresponding to the signature and the rules of the Peano system:

$$[\,\iota\!:\!\tau\,][\,o\!:\!\tau\,][\,0\!:\!\iota\,]\,[\,\text{succ}\!:\![\,x\!:\!\iota\,]\,\iota\,][\,+\!:\![\,x\!:\!\iota\,]\,[\,x\!:\!\iota\,]\,\iota\,]\,\cdots$$

Hence, at first sight, the representation of a given theory within the calculus corresponds to a sequence of abstractors. Since contexts are intended to represent theories, a context is, in first approximation, such a sequence, and we allow abstraction of such contexts:

$$[\,\iota\!:\!\tau\,;\,o\!:\!\tau\,;\,0\!:\!\iota\,;\,\text{succ}\!:\![\,x\!:\!\iota\,]\,\iota\,;\,+\!:\![\,x\!:\!\iota\,]\,[\,x\!:\!\iota\,]\,\iota\,;\,\cdots\,]\,\cdots$$

To turn contexts into objects of the calculus remains useless as long as we do not provide operations to manipulate them. To this end, we introduce context variables, and the possibility of abbreviating contexts:

$$s := [\,\iota\!:\!\tau\,;\,o\!:\!\tau\,;\,0\!:\!\iota\,;\,\text{succ}\!:\![\,x\!:\!\iota\,]\,\iota\,;\,+\!:\![\,x\!:\!\iota\,]\,[\,x\!:\!\iota\,]\,\iota\,;\,\cdots\,]$$

Such abbreviations must have a scope, hence they are themselves abstractors. At this point, we may refine our notion of context: a context is either a context variable bound to an abbreviation, or a sequence of abstractors. Abstractors, which are atomic contexts, are of three kinds: declarations, definitions, and context abbreviations.

Besides contexts, mere λ-expressions remain: we call them texts. A text is either the constant τ, a variable, a defined constant (i.e. a variable bound to a definition), the application of text to a text, or the abstraction of a context on a text.

Roughly speaking, abstracting a context on a text consists of stating the theory in which the text makes sense. Such an operation would be useful on contexts: it would amount to state the theory in which some subtheory or some enrichment would be developed. Therefore, we add to the calculus the possibility of abstracting a context on another context. Similarly, we allow the application of context on text. This operation serves to instantiate parametric contexts.

Figure 1 gives an example illustrating how contexts and operations on them are useful to structure the presentation of theories. The reader who can not guess the rules according to which this example is a well-typed text is invited to consult the next section.

This example must be understood as follows.

It begins by a large context which may be seen as a library of theories. This context contains, on the one hand, some fundamental declarations common to all the theories of the library, and on the other hand, subcontexts which correspond to different theories (theories of equality, of natural numbers, of lists, ...).

The theory of equality specifies an equivalence relation between the elements of a sort α. This sort α is a parameter of the theory. To specify the theories of natural numbers or of lists, equality between naturals or between lists is needed. Therefore, both theories import the theory of equality, with the proper instantiation of the parameter α. This instantiation is achieved by application of context.

The theory of lists is also parametric. The parameter is the sort α to which the elements of the lists belong. To give the proper equality rules for lists, the equality between elements of sort α is needed. This relation $(=_\alpha)$ is the second parameter of the theory.

```
[   prop : τ;
    sort : τ;
    ⋮
    equ-thy := [  α  : sort;
                  = : [x:α][x:α]prop;
                  REFL : [x:α] x = x;
                  ⋮
               ]  ;
    nat-thy := [  nat : sort
                  succ : [x:nat]nat;
                  + : [x:nat][x:nat]nat;
                  equ-thy(nat);
                  CSUCC :   [n₁:nat][n₂:nat]
                            [x:n₁ = n₂]
                            (succ n₁) = (succ n₂)
                  ⋮
               ]  ;
    list-thy := [  α : sort;
                   =_α : [x:α][x:α]prop;
                   list : [x:sort]sort;
                   nil : (list α);
                   cons : [a:α][l:(list α)](list α);
                   equ-thy(list α);
                   CCONS :   [a₁:α][a₂:α][l₁:(list α)][l₂:(list α)]
                             [x:a₁ =_α a₂][x:l₁ = l₂]
                             ((cons a₁) l₁) = ((cons a₂) l₂);
                   ⋮
                ]  ;
    ⋮
][   nat-thy;
     list-thy(nat)( = )]  ⋯
```

Figure 1.1: example

After the library, one finds a second context. This context is the working context in which proofs (symbolized by the last three dots) are performed. This working context is built by importing some parts of the library. In the example, it specifies the theory of lists of natural numbers. Therefore, the theory of natural numbers is first imported, and then, in the scope of this importation, the theory of lists is imported with the appropriate instantiation[‡].

4 Definition of the extended calculus

Formation rules

The expressions of the extended calculus are built from an infinite alphabet of ξ-variables (variables bound to declarations), an infinite alphabet of δ-variables (variables bound to definitions), an infinite alphabet of σ-variables (variables bound to context abbreviations), and the single constant τ. Let x, d, and s range over ξ-, δ-, and σ-variables respectively. Let c and t range over contexts and texts. The formation rules are the following:

$$
\begin{array}{llll}
c & ::= & x\!:\!t \mid d := t \mid s := [\,c\,] & (\textit{atomic contexts})\\
  & \mid & s & (\textit{context variable})\\
  & \mid & c\,;\,c & (\textit{abstraction on context})\\
  & \mid & (\,c\,)(\,t\,) & (\textit{application of context})
\end{array}
$$

$$
\begin{array}{llll}
t & ::= & \tau & (\textit{constant})\\
  & \mid & x \mid d & (\textit{variables})\\
  & \mid & [\,c\,]\,t & (\textit{abstraction on text})\\
  & \mid & (\,t\,t\,) & (\textit{application of text})\\
  & \mid & (\,t\!:\!t\,) & (\textit{judgement})
\end{array}
$$

Judgement is a simple construction we have not yet described. It allows to explicitly give the type of a text. This is useful, for instance, for giving a typed definition, or intermediate results within a proof.

As it is, the above grammar is ambiguous: a context made of successive abstractions gives rise to different parse trees. This ambiguity is circumvented by considering these different parse trees to be equivalent. In other words, the syntactic equivalence between contexts, at the level of abstract syntax, is modulo associativity of context abstraction.

[‡]An attentive reader could object that this last importation results in hiding some rules of the theory of natural numbers. This problem is related to the concrete syntax we have used, not to the structure of the calculus. At the abstract level, the use of a nameless notation for bound variables makes the problem vanish.

The use of context variables may give rise to problems when defining the notions of bound and free occurrences of a variable. On the one hand, there are the usual problems related to α-conversion; on the other hand, problems related to the possible use of free σ-variables. Consider, for instance, the following text:

$$[s := [x:\tau; y:x]][s]y$$

The last occurrence of y is bound to the declaration $y : x$ which occurs inside the context abbreviated by s. Consider the same example where the abbreviation has been removed:

$$[s]y$$

One needs further information about the σ-variable s in order to know whether the occurrence of y is bound or not.

These problems can be solved by using a name free notation for context variables [2] in the spirit of [4]. We consider that such a notation is used at the level of abstract syntax. Nevertheless, for the sake of readability, we use the concrete syntax above, which is sufficient for our purpose since we are interested in closed expressions only, and clashes between variables can be avoided by requiring that all the variables occurring in an environment have to be distinct.

Environments and typing

The notion of environment has to be adapted to the extended calculus: an environment is a sequence of atomic contexts, i.e. a sequence of declarations, definitions, and abbreviations. Similarly, the operation of selection is extended:

$$\mathrm{sel}_X(E, x:t) \;\equiv\; t \quad \text{if } X \equiv x.$$

$$\mathrm{sel}_X(E, x:t) \;\equiv\; \mathrm{sel}_X(E) \quad \text{if } X \not\equiv x.$$

$$\mathrm{sel}_X(E, d:=t) \;\equiv\; t \quad \text{if } X \equiv d.$$

$$\mathrm{sel}_X(E, d:=t) \;\equiv\; \mathrm{sel}_X(E) \quad \text{if } X \not\equiv d.$$

$$\mathrm{sel}_X(E, s:=[c]) \;\equiv\; c \quad \text{if } X \equiv s.$$

$$\mathrm{sel}_X(E, s:=[c]) \;\equiv\; \mathrm{sel}_X(E) \quad \text{if } X \not\equiv s.$$

where X ranges over ξ-, δ-, and σ-variables.

To define the type of a text, we need a way of turning a context into an environment. To this end, we define the partial normalization of a context, with respect to an environment, as follows:

$$\text{pnc}(E \mid x{:}t) \;\equiv\; x{:}t$$

$$\text{pnc}(E \mid d := t) \;\equiv\; d := t$$

$$\text{pnc}(E \mid s := [c]) \;\equiv\; s := [c]$$

$$\text{pnc}(E \mid s) \;\equiv\; \text{pnc}(E \mid \text{sel}_s(E))$$

$$\text{pnc}(E \mid c_1 \,;\, c_2) \;\equiv\; \text{pnc}(E \mid c_1)\,;\, c_2$$

$$\text{pnc}(E \mid (c)(t)) \;\equiv\;
\begin{array}{ll}
\text{if} & \text{pnc}(E \mid c) \equiv x{:}t_1 \,;\, c_1 \\
\text{then} & \text{pnc}(E \mid [t/x]\,c_1) \\
\text{else} & \text{undefined}
\end{array}$$

Thanks to this last definition, we may define the operation of pushing a context onto an environment:

$$E \oplus x{:}t \;\equiv\; E,\, x{:}t$$

$$E \oplus d := t \;\equiv\; E,\, d := t$$

$$E \oplus s := [c] \;\equiv\; E,\, s := [c]$$

$$E \oplus s \;\equiv\; E \oplus \text{sel}_s(E)$$

$$E \oplus c_1 \,;\, c_2 \;\equiv\; (E \oplus c_1) \oplus c_2$$

$$E \oplus (c)(t) \;\equiv\; E \oplus \text{pnc}(E \mid (c)(t))$$

The typing relation is then a mere extension of the one introduced by Nederpelt:

$$\text{type}(E \mid x) \;\equiv\; \text{sel}_x(E)$$

$$\text{type}(E \mid d) \;\equiv\; \text{type}(E \mid \text{sel}_d(E))$$

$$\text{type}(E \mid [c]\,t) \;\equiv\; [c]\,\text{type}(E \oplus c \mid t)$$

$$\text{type}(E \mid (t_1\, t_2)) \;\equiv\; (\,\text{type}(E \mid t_1)\, t_2\,)$$

$$\text{type}(E \mid (t_1{:}t_2)) \;\equiv\; \text{type}(E \mid t_1)$$

Conversion rules

The various constructions we have added to Nederpelt's calculus extend its practical expressive power. Nevertheless, they remain unessential in the sense that they do not extend the class of normal forms. To obtan this property we introduce reduction relations allowing to remove the different extensions. Because of the presence of definitions and abbreviations, these notions of reduction have to be defined with respect to environments.

In addition to β- (and possibly η-) redices, we introduce the following reducible expressions:

Reducible contexts:

$$E \vdash s \rightarrow \text{sel}_s(E)$$

$$E \vdash (x : t_1 ; c)(t_2) \rightarrow [t_2/x] c$$

Reducible texts:

$$E \vdash d \rightarrow \text{sel}_d(E)$$

$$E \vdash [d := t_1] t_2 \rightarrow t_2 \quad \text{if } d \text{ does not occur free in } t_2$$

$$E \vdash [s := [c]] t \rightarrow t \quad \text{if } s \text{ does not occur free in } t$$

$$E \vdash [c_1 ; c_2] t \rightarrow [c_1][c_2] t \quad ; \text{ if } c_1 \text{ is anatomic context}$$

$$E \vdash (t_1 : t_2) \rightarrow t_1$$

Reduction is then defined as the least reflexive, transitive relation including the notions of reduction above, and obeying the following congruence rules:

$$\frac{E \vdash t_1 \rightarrow t_2}{E \vdash x : t_1 \rightarrow x : t_2} \qquad \frac{E \vdash t_1 \rightarrow t_2}{E \vdash d := t_1 \rightarrow d := t_2}$$

$$\frac{E \vdash c_1 \rightarrow c_2}{E \vdash s := [c_1] \rightarrow s := [c_2]}$$

$$\frac{E \vdash c_1 \rightarrow c_2 \quad E \oplus c_1 \vdash c_3 \rightarrow c_4}{E \vdash c_1 ; c_3 \rightarrow c_2 ; c_4} \qquad \frac{E \vdash c_1 \rightarrow c_2 \quad E \vdash t_1 \rightarrow t_2}{E \vdash (c_1)(t_1) \rightarrow (c_2)(t_2)}$$

$$\frac{E \vdash c_1 \rightarrow c_2 \quad E \oplus c_1 \vdash t_1 \rightarrow t_2}{E \vdash [c_1] t_1 \rightarrow [c_2] t_2} \qquad \frac{E \vdash t_1 \rightarrow t_2 \quad E \vdash t_3 \rightarrow t_4}{E \vdash (t_1 t_3) \rightarrow (t_2 t_4)}$$

$$\frac{E \vdash t_1 \rightarrow t_2 \quad E \vdash t_3 \rightarrow t_4}{E \vdash (t_1 : t_3) \rightarrow (t_2 : t_4)}$$

As usual, conversion ($=$) is the transitive, symmetric closure of reduction.

Well-typedness

The well-typedness conditions for the extended calculus are a straightforward generalization of these introduced by Nederpelt. They are expressed by the following rules:

$$\frac{E \vdash t}{E \vdash x:t} \qquad \frac{E \vdash t}{E \vdash d := t} \qquad \frac{E \vdash c}{E \vdash s := [\,c\,]}$$

$$E \vdash s \quad \text{if } \operatorname{sel}_s(E) \text{ is defined}$$

$$\frac{E \vdash c_1 \quad E \oplus c_1 \vdash c_2}{E \vdash c_1\,;\,c_2} \qquad \frac{E \vdash c \quad E \vdash t \quad c = x:\operatorname{type}(E\,|\,t)\,;\,c_1}{E \vdash (c)(t)}$$

$$E \vdash \tau \qquad E \vdash x \quad \text{if } \operatorname{sel}_x(E) \text{ is defined}$$

$$E \vdash d \quad \text{if } \operatorname{sel}_d(E) \text{ is defined} \qquad \frac{E \vdash c \quad E \oplus c \vdash t}{E \vdash [\,c\,]\,t}$$

$$\frac{E \vdash t_1 \quad E \vdash t_2 \quad E \vdash \operatorname{type}(E\,|\,t_1) = [\,x:\operatorname{type}(E\,|\,t_2)\,]\,t_3}{E \vdash (t_1\,t_2)}$$

$$\frac{E \vdash t_1 \quad E \vdash t_2 \quad E \vdash t_1 = [\,x:\operatorname{type}(E\,|\,t_2)\,]\,t_3}{E \vdash (t_1\,t_2)}$$

$$\frac{E \vdash t_1 \quad E \vdash t_2 \quad E \vdash \operatorname{type}(E\,|\,t_1) = t_2}{E \vdash (t_1:t_2)}$$

This system, which is a conservative extension of Nederpelt's Λ, is such that the properties of Church-Rosser, closure and strong normalization are preserved, and the property of being well-typed is still decidable [7].

5   Evaluation

We argued, in the introduction, that the criteria according to which the expressive power of a logical framework must be evaluated are mainly practical and subjective. In our case, what are these criteria? What are the expected benefits? To our mind, the main features of the calculus we have introduced in this paper are the following:

- it is an extension of Nederpelt's Λ;

- contrarily to de Bruijn's $\Lambda\Delta$, δ-redices (definitions of constants) and β-redices are kept disjoint;

- the approach to contexts is purely syntactic;

- the operations on contexts, i.e. abbreviation, abstraction, and application, remain basic.

These design choices have to be discussed according to practical considerations.

Extension of Nederpelt's Λ

As most of AUTOMATH languages, Λ is a λ-typed λ-calculus: functional terms and dependent types are identified. This characteristic goes so far in the case of Λ that there is no syntactic difference at all between terms and types: any well-typed term may act as a type, without any degree restriction.

This uniformity could sometimes be seen as a drawback. It could be argued that the identification of types and terms is purely syntactic, and that it obscures the structure of the calculus. One might agree with this criticism, when considering logical frameworks as formalisms intended for human communication.

Our standpoint is somewhat different: we consider our calculus as a "machine level language", i.e. a language into which higher level formalisms should be translated. From this point of view, the uniformity of Λ appears to be an advantage. Λ provides a unique set of data structures to handle formal languages as well as rules and proofs. For instance, the same type checking algorithm allows to decide whether a term is well-formed according to some signature, or whether a proof is correct according to some theory.

Distinction between β- and δ-redices

Since we consider our calculus as a kind of machine code, we must justify the distinction made between β- and δ-redices at this level.

Instantiation and definition are surely distinct concepts, but this does not imply that they must be represented by distinct means. They may both be represented as β-redices. Moreover, in the case of the representation of formal languages and theories, we just argued that it was economic to deal with a uniform construct. We must therefore provide further evidence.

A first argument concerns the structure of β-redices. When a definition is coded as a β-redex, this redex represents both the definition and its scope. The definition itself corresponds only to the pair operand-abstractor. As such, it is hardly accessible as an object of the language. This fact would prevent us to turn definitions into atomic contexts. However, this argument is not definitive. Balsters' segments allow one to manipulate operand-abstractor pairs.

The second argument we give is more sensible. Theoretically, the type checking algorithm requires normalizations in order to decide the equality between operand types and operator domains. Practically, such normalizations are too costly, and it is necessary to provide heuristics trying to built common reducts far away from the normal forms.

Such heuristics take advantage of the distinction between β- and δ-redices. If β-redices are used for instantiation only, β-normalisation is not harmful. Experience shows that the oversized growth of normal forms is mainly due to δ-reduction while, in practice, the number of constants to be unfolded remains reasonable.

Similarly, higher order resolution involved a unification process which works on head normal forms. While theoretically too complex, this process is acceptable in practice if unification is not modulo δ-conversion [12].

Another discussion about the distinction between β- and δ-redices may be found in [6], section 6.7.

Syntactic approach to contexts

The goal we followed by defining contexts was to internalize the notion of theory. To this end we defined contexts as constructs of the language and gave them a meaning in term of reduction relations. Other approaches would have been possible: semantics based approaches or type theoretical approaches.

Semantic and syntactic approaches are not exclusive, they are complementary. Nevertheless, with respect to the goal we followed, syntax comes first: we are interested in derivability, rather than in validity. For instance, if we use, in a given context, some induction principle, it will be because the principle is explicitly available as a rule, and not because our semantics would be based on initial algebras as it is the case for some specification languages.

A type theoretical approach would consist in enriching the type structure of the language, by providing existential types, for instance, in order to get types corresponding to theories. Such an enrichment would have destroyed Nederpelt's Λ uniformity. Terms belonging to existential types can hardly be considered as types.

Our goal was to provide a machine level framework, and, in this respect, we will say that we followed a data structure oriented approach. Nevertheless, further work should clarify the relation between the different approaches and provide possible models to contexts.

Basic operations on contexts

Finally, the operations we provide on contexts remain basic, especially when one compares them with operations available in higher level formalisms such as parametrization, instantiation, union, merging, importation, renaming...

Once more, this choice is justified by the fact we consider our calculus as a machine level language. For instance, the example of section 3 shows how parametrization, instantiation, and importation may be expressed by abstractions and applications. What we hope is to provide basic operations easy to implement and powerful enough to be composed into higher level operations.

Contexts have now to be evaluated with that respect: From the point of view of implementation, do they correspond to realistic data structure? From the point of view of utilization, may high level operations on theories be compiled in terms of basic operations on contexts? This evaluation process is under way. Prototypes supporting DEVA partially implement our notion of context [8]. The ToolUse project has provided non trivial examples of structuration of theories into contexts [15].

Bibliography

[1] Avron, A. Honsel, F. and Mason, I. (1987). Using typed lambda calculus to implement formal systems on a machine, in *Proceedings of the workshop on programming logic*, Report 37 ed. P. Dybjer, B. Nordström, K. Petersson, and J. Smith, (University of Göteborg).

[2] Balsters, H. (1986). Lambda Calculus extended with Segments, Technische hogeschool Eindhoven, PhD thesis.

[3] de Bruijn, N.G. (1971). AUT-SL, a single line version of AUTOMATH, Technische hogeschool Eindhoven, Department of Mathematics and Computing Science, Memorandum 71-17.

[4] de Bruijn, N.G. (1972). Lambda Calculus notations with nameless dummies, a tool for automatic formula manipulation, with an application to the Church-Rosser theorem, *Indagationes Mathematicae*, **34** 381–392.

[5] de Bruijn, N.G. (1980). A survey of the project AUTOMATH, in *to H. B. Curry: Essays on Combinatory Logic, Lambda Calculus and Formalism*, ed. J. P. Seldin and J. R. Hindley (Academic Press)

[6] de Bruijn, N.G. (1987). Generalizing AUTOMATH by means of a lambda-typed lambda-calculus, in *Mathematical Logic and Theoretical Computer Science*, Lecture Notes in pure and applied Mathematics, **106** (Marcel Dekker, New York)

[7] de Groote, Ph. (1991). Définition et Propriétés d'un métacalcul de représentation de théories, Université Catholique de Louvain, thèse de doctorat.

[8] Gabriel, R. (1989). ToolUse Project, Task S final Report, GMD, Karlsruhe.

[9] Harper, R., Honsel, F. and Plotkin, G. (1987). A Framework for Defining Logics, in *Proceedings of 2nd annual symposium on logic in computer science*, (IEEE Computer Society Press)

[10] Nederpelt, R.P. (1973). Strong Normalization in a typed lambda calculus with lambda structured types, Technische hogeschool Eindhoven, PhD thesis.

[11] Nederpelt, R.P. (1980). An Approach to theorem proving on the basis of a typed lambda-calculus, in *Proceedings of the 5th international conference on automated deduction*, Lecture Notes in Computer Science, 87 (Springer Verlag).

[12] Paulson L.C. (1986). Natural Deduction as Higher Order Resolution, *Journal of logic programming*, 3 237–258.

[13] Sintzoff, M., Weber, M., de Groote, Ph. and Cazin J. (1989). Definition 1.1. of the generic Development Language DEVA, Université Catholique de Louvain, Unité d'Informatique, Report RR 89-9.

[14] van Daalen D.T. (1980). The language theory of AUTOMATH, Technische hogeschool Eindhoven, PhD thesis.

[15] Weber, M. (1990). Formalization of the Bird-Meertens algorithmic calculus in the DEVA meta-calculus, in *Programming Concepts and Methods*, ed. M. Broy and C. B. Jones (Elsevier Science Publisher B.V., North-Holland)

IMPLEMENTATIONS

The Boyer-Moore Prover and Nuprl: An Experimental Comparison

David Basin
Department of Artificial Intelligence,
University of Edinburgh, Edinburgh Scotland.
Email: basin@aipna.ed.ac.uk

Matt Kaufmann
Computational Logic, Inc.
Austin, Texas 78703 USA
Email: kaufmann@cli.com*

Abstract

We use an example to compare the Boyer-Moore Theorem Prover and the
Nuprl Proof Development System. The respective machine verifications
of a version of Ramsey's theorem illustrate similarities and differences between the two systems. The proofs are compared using both quantitative
and non-quantitative measures, and we examine difficulties in making such
comparisons.

1 Introduction

Over the last 25 years, a large number of logics and systems have been devised for machine verified mathematical development. These systems vary
significantly in many important ways, including: underlying philosophy,
object-level logic, support for meta-level reasoning, support for automated

---

*Earlier related work was supported by ONR Contract N00014-81-K-0634.

proof construction, and user interface. A summary of some of these systems, along with a number of interesting comments about issues (such as differences in logics, proof power, theory construction, and styles of user interaction), may be found in Lindsay's article [14]. The Kemmerer study [13] compares the use of four software verification systems (all based on classical logic) on particular programs.

In this report we compare two interactive systems for proof development and checking: The Boyer-Moore Theorem Prover and the Nuprl Proof Development System. We have based our comparison on similar proofs of a specific theorem: the finite exponent two version of Ramsey's theorem (explained in Section 2). The Boyer-Moore Theorem Prover is a powerful (by current standards) heuristic theorem prover for a quantifier-free variant of first order Peano arithmetic with additional data types. Nuprl is a tactic-oriented theorem prover based on a sequent calculus formulation of a constructive type theory similar to Martin-Löf's [15]. We do not assume any prior knowledge of either system by the reader.

Throughout this paper, we refer to the Boyer-Moore Theorem Prover by its name, NQTHM. "NQTHM" stands for "New Quantified THeorem Prover", in reference to a quantification feature added in about 1984.

Why undertake such a comparison? We believe there is too little communication between those who use different mechanical proof-checking systems. This lack of communication encourages myths and preconceptions about the usability of various systems. Concrete comparisons bring to light the limitations and advantages of different systems, as well as their commonalities and differences. Moreover, comparisons help determine which directions the field is heading and what progress is being made.

Much of our comparison is based on our two proofs of the aforementioned theorem. We make qualitative comparisons, and we also make quantitative comparisons based on metrics that indicate the degree of effort required to prove the theorem. However, we caution that there is a real danger in quantitative comparisons as metrics can oversimply and mislead. Numbers cannot account for much of what is important about proof development systems and their application; e.g.,

- Expressive power of the underlying logic (e.g., first order vs. higher order, definitional extensibility, set theoretic or arithmetic, typed vs. untyped.)

- Domains particularly well-suited to verification with the given system

- Computational content (explicit or implicit), i.e., existence of executable programs associated with existence proofs (written explicitly or derived implicitly from the proof)

- Use of novel techniques in representation or in automated reasoning

- Naturalness/comprehensibility of definitions and proofs, both to experienced users and to a more general community

- Ease of creating, reviewing, and changing definitions and proofs

- Proof discovery capabilities

- Soundness

Moreover, the choice of metrics is difficult. Different metrics can favor different kinds of systems more than one might expect. For example, the number of tokens typed may not correlate with number of keystrokes if one system uses extensive cutting and pasting with an editor, or uses keyboard macros or structure editor facilities. For another example, it may or may not be the case that prover power correlates with replay time; it's not hard to envision scenarios in which a weak system's proofs replay more quickly because there is a large proof script but little heuristic search. Nonetheless, we make quantitative comparisons using the following metrics.

- Lemma and definition counts

- Symbol counts

- User time required

- Replay time

Our paper is organized as follows. Section 2 provides an informal statement and proof of the version of Ramsey's theorem alluded to above. Section 3 contains a description of the proof completed with the Boyer-Moore Theorem Prover, NQTHM. Section 4 contains the Nuprl proof. The final section draws comparisons and conclusions.

Acknowledgements. We thank Gian-Luigi Bellin, Jussi Ketonen, and David McAllester for many interesting and useful discussions on this topic. We thank Andrew Ireland, Bill Pierce, Matt Wilding, and the referees for their very helpful comments on a draft of this paper. Randy Pollack gave us some useful encouragement on this effort. David Basin also gratefully acknowledges assistance provided by Doug Howe during the Nuprl proof effort.

2   Informal Statement and Proof of Ramsey's Theorem

The version of Ramsey's theorem that we prove is about the existence of "order" in symmetric graphs. A *symmetric graph* is a set V of vertices together with a symmetric edge relation E on that set. (Some formulations also require that E is irreflexive; that bears little on the essential mathematics but can bear on the details.) Let G be a symmetric graph with vertex set V and relation E. A *clique* C of G is a subset of V such that all pairs $<x, y>$ of distinct members of C belong to E; an *independent set* I of G is a subset of V such that no pairs $<x, y>$ of members of I belong to E. A set is *homogeneous* if it is a clique or an independent set. For any positive integer l we say that a subset S of V is an *l-clique* (respectively, an *l-independent set*) if it is a clique (respectively, independent set) of cardinality l. Finally, for any positive integers n, l_1 and l_2 we write

$$n \rightarrow (l_1, l_2)$$

to assert that for every graph G with at least n vertices, there is either an l_1-clique or an l_2-independent set in G.

Note: Henceforth all our graphs will be symmetric, i.e., *graph* means *symmetric graph*.

We may now state the main theorem.

Theorem. For all l_1, l_2, there exists an n such that $n \rightarrow (l_1, l_2)$.

Note: The least such n is sometimes called the *Ramsey number* corresponding to l_1 and l_2.

An informal "text-book proof" (similar to one in [9]) proceeds by double induction on l_1 and l_2. (Alternatively, the proof may proceed by a single induction on their sum — this is the tact taken in the NQTHM proof.) To prove the base case observe that $l_1 \rightarrow (l_1, 2)$ as any graph with l_1 vertices either is a clique, or there are at least two vertices that are not connected by an edge. Similarly $l_2 \rightarrow (2, l_2)$. Now assume as an inductive hypothesis that we have some n and m where $n \rightarrow (l_1, l_2 - 1)$ and $m \rightarrow (l_1 - 1, l_2)$.

Claim. $n + m \rightarrow (l_1, l_2)$.

Proof. Given an arbitrary graph G on at least $n + m$ vertices, choose an element v_0 of its vertex set V. Now partition the remaining elements into two sets r_1 and r_2 where

$$
\begin{aligned}
r_1 &= \{x \in (V - \{v_0\}) : E(v_0, x)\} \\
r_2 &= \{x \in (V - \{v_0\}) : \neg E(v_0, x)\}
\end{aligned}
$$

Then $|r_1| + |r_2| \geq m + n - 1$ so either $|r_1| \geq m$ or $|r_2| \geq n$. If $|r_1| \geq m$, then by the induction hypothesis there is a subset S of r_1 where either S is an l_2-independent set (so we are done) or S is an $(l_1 - 1)$-clique. In the latter case set $S' = S + v_0$. Now, since $S \subseteq r_1$, there is an edge between v_0 and all $x \in S$. Hence S' is the desired l_1-clique. The case $|r_2| \geq n$ is analogous.

3   The Boyer-Moore Theorem Prover NQTHM

We present our discussion of the NQTHM proof in five subsections. We begin by giving enough of an introduction to the logic of NQTHM to be able to transform a straightforward first order formalization of the theorem into a formalization in the NQTHM logic (which we also do in the first subsection). Afterwards, we discuss the proof strategy. In the third subsection, we summarize the actual proof steps. We continue with some statistics and general remarks about the proof and we conclude with a discussion of computing in the NQTHM logic.

Background and Formalization of the Theorem

The Boyer-Moore theorem prover NQTHM is a heuristic prover based on a simple version of a traditional first order logic of total functions, with instantiation and induction rules of inference. The logic is quantifier-free, except for the implicit universal quantification surrounding each definition and theorem. A detailed description of the logic and manual for the prover may be found in [6]. The lack of quantifiers together with the presence of induction encourages a style of specification and proof that is "constructive" in nature. In fact, Bob Boyer has pointed out that since definitions in the NQTHM logic (technically speaking, in "thm mode", i.e., without the V&C\$ interpreter and without induction all the way up to ϵ_0) always produce primitive recursive functions, the law of the excluded middle is constructively valid for this logic when all function symbols are introduced with definitions (DEFN events). "Constructive" here also means that rather than specifying the existence of various objects, one explicitly defines functions that yield those objects. The system is equipped with a mechanism for computing with its defined functions (see subsection below entitled *Computing*).

The syntax of the logic is in the Lisp tradition, where the list (f x_1 ... x_n) denotes the application of the function f to the arguments x_1 through x_n. We also allow the let form from Lisp (as it is included in the "PC-NQTHM" system described below), so for example the expression (let ((x a) (y b)) exp) is equivalent to the result of substituting a for x and b for y in exp. Certain functions are built into the logic, such as the ordered pair constructor cons and the atom nil. The list (x_1 x_2 ... x_n) is represented by the term (cons x_1 (cons x_2 ... (cons x_n nil) ...)). The functions car and cdr select (respectively) the first and second component of a pair. Thus car selects the first member of a list. It is an axiom of the logic that every pair x equals (cons (car x) (cdr x)). Note also that since this is a logic of total functions, it makes sense to form the term (car x) for any term x, whether it is a pair (or list) or not . In practice, this lack of typing is generally not much of a problem for users once they become accustomed to it.

Consider now how we might formalize Ramsey's Theorem in this logic. If we had quantifiers then we might simply write the following. Here pairs is a list of pairs that represents a graph on a set domain of nodes, and S is the desired homogeneous set (i.e., a clique or an independent set) with respect to the graph pairs.

```
     For all 11 and 12 there exists N
     such that for all domain and pairs there exists S
     such that:
     N ≤ cardinality(domain)  →
        [S ⊆ domain ∧
(a)     ((11 ≤ cardinality(S) ∧ clique (pairs, S)) ∨
(b)      (12 ≤ cardinality(S) ∧ independent (pairs, S)))]
```

In order to represent this conjecture in the NQTHM logic, we must first eliminate the quantifiers. To that end, we will define N as a function ramsey of 11 and 12, and we will also define S in terms of a function wit ("witness") of 11, 12, domain, and pairs. Actually, it is convenient to define wit to return an ordered pair of the form $<S, f>$, where S is the desired clique or independent set according to whether the "flag" f is 1 or 2, respectively. We'll say that good-hom-set (pairs, domain, 11, 12, flg) holds iff flg is 1 and disjunct (a) above holds, or else flg is not 1 and disjunct (b) above holds, where S is the first component of wit (pairs, domain, 11, 12). The conjecture above thus transforms into the following statement.

```
For all 11, 12, domain, pairs, if
    S = car (wit (pairs, domain, 11, 12)) and
    flg = cdr (wit (pairs, domain, 11, 12)), then:
        ramsey (11,12) ≤ cardinality(domain)
        →
        [S ⊆ domain ∧ good-hom-set (pairs, domain, 11, 12,
flg)]
```

The NQTHM logic has a built-in theory of lists, but not of sets. Therefore it is convenient to recast this formalization in terms of lists. We can define a predicate **setp** for a list having no duplicates. Slipping into Lisp-style syntax, we finally obtain a formalization of Ramsey's theorem. (Only the last conjunct below is new, and it says that if **domain** represents a set then so does the witness set. This is important so that the **length** of a list equals the cardinality of the set it represents; note that **length** is used in the definition of **good-hom-set**, which in turn may be found in the subsection below entitled *Outline of Main Proof Steps.*)

THEOREM.
```
    (implies (leq (ramsey 11 12)
                  (length domain))
             (let ((pair (wit pairs domain 11 12)))
               (let ((hom-set (car pair))
                     (indep-or-clique (cdr pair)))
                 (and (subsetp hom-set domain)
                      (good-hom-set pairs domain 11 12
indep-or-clique)
                      (implies (setp domain)
                               (setp hom-set)))))))
```

Proof Strategy

In the NQTHM prover, a "proof" is a sequence of steps called *events*, typically of two kinds: definition (DEFN) events and theorem (PROVE-LEMMA) events. A major step is to define the function **wit**, referred to above, that constructs the clique or independent set. Unlike Nuprl, the system does not construct such a function from the proof; rather, the function is introduced by the user and its pattern of recursion is available for generating heuristic induction schemes. In fact, the proof is eventually (after some lemmas are proved) accomplished using an induction heuristically chosen by the NQTHM system (see [6] or [4] for more on this topic) to reflect the recursion in the definition of the function **wit** below, i.e., by an induction on **(plus 11 12)**. This function returns a pair for the form **(cons set** flag) where **flag** is 1 or 2 according to whether **set** is a clique or an independent set. Everything to the right of any semicolon is a comment.

```
DEFINITION.
(wit pairs domain l1 l2) =
(if (listp domain)
    (if (zerop l1) (cons nil 1)
      (if (zerop l2) (cons nil 2)
        (let ((set1 (car (partition (car domain) (cdr domain)
pairs)))
              (set2 (cdr (partition (car domain) (cdr domain)
pairs))))
          ;; the function sub1 below is the decrement function on natural num-
bers
          (if (lessp (length set1) (ramsey (sub1 l1) l2))
            ;; then use set2 to form clique or independent set
            (let ((wit-set2 (wit pairs set2 l1 (sub1 l2))))
              (if (equal (cdr wit-set2) 1) wit-set2
                (cons (cons (car domain) (car wit-set2))
                  2)))
            ;; otherwise use set1 to form clique or independent set
            (let ((wit-set1 (wit pairs set1 (sub1 l1) l2)))
              (if (equal (cdr wit-set1) 2) wit-set1
                (cons (cons (car domain) (car wit-set1))
                  1)))))))
  (cons nil 1))
```

This definition is actually presented with a *hint* (lessp (plus l1 l2)) that instructs the prover to verify that the sum of the final two arguments of **wit** decreases in each recursive call of **wit**, thus guaranteeing termination. This informal description of what the prover does with that hint reflects a formal definitional principle in the NQTHM logic, but we omit further discussion of this point.

In this example we use two main techniques to "discover" the proofs. One approach (the traditional one for NQTHM users) is to start by presenting a lemma to NQTHM. If the proof fails or if the output (a mixture of English and formulas) suggests that the proof probably won't complete successfully, then inspection of the output often suggests (to an experienced eye) useful rewrite (simplification) rules that one might wish to prove. The other main technique is to use an interactive enhancement [12] to the NQTHM system as an aid to discovering the structure of the proof. This "PC-NQTHM" enhancement ("PC" for "proof-checker") allows one to create PROVE-LEMMA events by first submitting the proposed theorem and then interactively giving various proof commands in a backward goal-directed, "refinement" style. These commands range from "low-level" commands which invoke a particular definition or rewrite rule, to "medium-level" commands invoking simplification or (heuristic) induction, to "high-level" commands which call the NQTHM prover. There is also a facility for user-defined *macro commands* in the tradition of the "tactics" and "tacticals" of LCF [8] and Nuprl (see Section 4). This "proof-checker" enhancement is helpful, but not crucial, for completion of the proof. The plan was in fact to develop nice rewrite rules rather than to rely on the manual commands provided by the interactive enhancement, and this plan succeeded: the final proof contained only 10 definitions and 26 lemmas (including the final theorem) after loading the standard "ground-zero" base theory, and did not contain any proof-checker commands. The events run successfully in the unenhanced NQTHM system. Other than a few hints – 7 of the lemmas took standard NQTHM "hints" that specify use of one or two previously proved lemmas – the proofs are fully automatic.

Outline of Main Proof Steps

We divide this subsection into four parts: one for the requisite definitions and then one for each of the three conjuncts of the conclusion of the main theorem (see subsection above entitled *Background and Formalization of the Theorem*).

Definitions

Several definitions are necessary for the proof. One of these is the definition of the function wit, provided in the preceding subsection, which picks out a desired clique or independent set. Another important definition is of a function ramsey that provides an upper bound on the Ramsey number. Here is that definition, expressed in the official syntax with formal parameters 11 and 12.

```
(defn ramsey (11 12)
  (if (zerop 11) 1
      (if (zerop 12) 1
          (plus (ramsey (sub1 11) 12)
                (ramsey 11 (sub1 12))))))
  ((lessp (plus 11 12))))
```

The last line of ramsey is a hint to the prover for its proof of termination and suggests that the sum of the two arguments decreases on each recursive call.

The definition of **wit** depends not only on the function **ramsey**, but also on three other functions, which we describe here informally; see [11] for details. For any list **pairs**, (related i j pairs) is *true* (t) if and only if the pair <i,j> or the pair <j,i> belongs to **pairs**; in this way we represent the notion of symmetric binary relation. (partition n rest pairs) returns a pair <x,y> where x consists of all elements of the list **rest** that are related (in the sense above) to n, and y consists of the remaining elements of **rest**. Finally, (length lst) is the length of the list **lst**.

The function **setp** recognizes whether or not a list represents a set by returning t if and only if the list contains no duplicates. Notice the use of primitive recursion to express bounded quantification. This is a common technique for defining universally-quantified concepts in the NQTHM logic.

```
(defn setp (x)
  (if (listp x)
      (and (not (member (car x) (cdr x))) (setp (cdr x)))
    t))
```

The function **homogeneous** defined below recognizes whether a given set **domain** is homogeneous (i.e., a clique or independent set) for the relation (graph) represented by the list **pairs**: it tests whether **domain** is a clique if the formal parameter **flg** is 1, and otherwise it tests whether **domain** is an independent set. Notice that **homogeneous** is defined by recursion on its first argument, using an auxiliary function **homogeneous1** that checks that its first parameter n is related or not related (according to whether or not the parameter **flg** is 1) to every element of **domain**.

```
(defn homogeneous1 (n domain pairs flg)
  (if (listp domain)
      (and (if (equal flg 1)
               (related n (car domain) pairs)
               (not (related n (car domain) pairs)))
           (homogeneous1 n (cdr domain) pairs flg))
    t))
```

```
(defn homogeneous (domain pairs flg)
  (if (listp domain)
      (and (homogeneous1 (car domain) (cdr domain) pairs flg)
           (homogeneous (cdr domain) pairs flg))
    t))
```

Our formalization of Ramsey's theorem also requires the notion of a "sufficiently large" homogeneous set, i.e., one that has at least 11 or 12 elements depending on whether the set is a clique or an independent set.

```
(defn good-hom-set (pairs domain l1 l2 flg)
  (and (homogeneous (car (wit pairs domain l1 l2))
                    pairs
                    flg)
       (not (lessp (length (car (wit pairs domain l1 l2)))
                   (if (equal flg 1) l1 l2)))))
```

Finally, we need the notion of subset. We omit here its straightforward recursive definition as well as several standard related lemmas such as transitivity.

The constructed set is contained in the given set

We wish to prove the following lemma. Notice the syntax for lemmas:

```
(prove-lemma lemma-name lemma-types statement),
```

where *lemma-types* is often **(rewrite)** to indicate that the lemma is to be used in subsequent proofs as a rewrite rule. (See [6] for details.)

```
(prove-lemma subsetp-hom-set-domain (rewrite)
  (subsetp (car (wit pairs domain l1 l2))
           domain))
```

The theorem prover proceeds by an induction suggested by the recursion in the definition of the function **wit**. The proof actually fails at first, but the prover's output suggests some lemmas. Here is one of those, which says that the second component returned by **partition** is a subset of the given set.

```
(prove-lemma subsetp-cdr-partition (rewrite)
  (subsetp (cdr (partition x z pairs))
           z))
```

A similar lemma is required for the first component, and these are used to prove two rather technical lemmas suggested by the attempted proof of the lemma **subsetp-hom-set-domain**. After these four lemmas, the inductive proof of **subsetp-hom-set-domain** succeeds without further interaction.

The constructed set is homogeneous and large enough

The following lemma is at the heart of the theorem.

```
(prove-lemma wit-yields-good-hom-set (rewrite)
  (implies (not (lessp (length domain) (ramsey 11 12)))
    (good-hom-set pairs domain 11 12
                  (cdr (wit pairs domain 11 12)))))
```

Unfortunately, the proof attempt does not succeed at first, so we must prove supporting lemmas. This time we use the proof-checker enhancement PC-NQTHM (see subsection above entitled *proof-strategy*) of NQTHM to explore the situation. Specifically, an INDUCT command is used to invoke a heuristic choice of induction scheme, a PROVE command is used in order to call the NQTHM prover to dispose of the three "base cases", the function **good-hom-set** is expanded in one of the remaining four (inductive) cases, a casesplit is performed to create 8 subgoals, and finally inspection of one of those subgoals suggests the following lemma.

```
(prove-lemma homogeneous1-subset (rewrite)
  (implies (and (subsetp x domain)
                (homogeneous1 elt domain pairs flg))
    (homogeneous1 elt x pairs flg)))
```

The NQTHM prover proves this lemma automatically. Manual application of this rule (in the proof-checker), to the subgoal referred to above, suggests another lemma, which is also proved automatically.

```
(prove-lemma homogeneous1-cdr-partition (rewrite)
  (homogeneous1 elt (cdr (partition elt dom pairs)) pairs 2))
```

Further attempts to prove subgoals inside the proof-checker, as well as attempts to prove the main goal **wit-yields-good-hom-set** in the context of the two lemmas displayed above (and others discovered subsequently), lead to some additional lemmas. One is completely analogous to **homogeneous1-cdr-partition** (displayed just above), but for the **car** of the partition in place of the **cdr**. Another (also proved automatically) asserts that the cardinality of a set equals the sum of the cardinalities of the two sets returned by **partition**. Still another asserts that **ramsey** always returns a positive integer. Four other technical lemmas seem necessary for the prover's rewriter to behave properly; they are omitted here. Finally, the proof of our goal **wit-yields-good-hom-set** (see above) succeeds.

The constructed set is indeed a set

The final goal is to prove that the homogeneous set is really a set.

```
(prove-lemma setp-hom-set (rewrite)
  (implies (setp domain)
           (setp (car (wit pairs domain 11 12))))))
```

The NQTHM prover does not succeed in proving this automatically, but
the output suggests the following useful (though obvious) lemma whose
proof does succeed automatically. It states that the lists returned by
partition are sets if the given list is a set.

```
(prove-lemma setp-partition (rewrite)
  (implies (setp x)
           (and (setp (car (partition a x pairs)))
                (setp (cdr (partition a x pairs)))))))
```

Two technical lemmas discovered using the proof-checker suffice for con-
cluding the proof of setp-hom-set.

More Statistics and General Remarks

The first time we formalized and proved this theorem was in January, 1987.
The resulting proof was very ugly, as the use of the (then new) proof-
checker enhancement was quite undisciplined. It seems best to find a good
combination of elegant rewrite rules even when one has the capabilities
offered by the proof-checker. Perhaps surprisingly, the "manual" proof
takes longer to replay than the "heuristic" one reported here: total time
was 219.7 seconds as opposed to 394.7 seconds for the older proof, both on
a Sun 3/60 with 16 megabytes of main memory.

It took about 7 hours of human time to complete the current proof effort, which resulted in a list of events that is accepted by NQTHM (without
the interactive enhancement). That number may be somewhat misleading
since the new proof effort took advantage of the definitions and a few of
the lemmas created in the earlier version. However, the more disciplined
approach used in the final effort suggested changes that were made in the
definitions, so it seems reasonable to guess that an effort from scratch would
have taken not much longer than 7 hours anyhow. A more detailed anno-
tated chronicle of this proof effort may be found in [11].

Computing

The NQTHM system provides a mechanism for computing values of variable-
free terms in the logic. This mechanism of providing *executable counterparts*
to defined functions is important as part of the theorem proving process.
For one thing, it allows the fast replacement of variable-free terms by constants. This was an important consideration in, for example, the operating

system kernel proof described in [3], where there were many large variable-free terms in the proof; compiling the executable counterparts sped up the proof process significantly.[†] Fast execution is also valuable when executing *metafunctions* [5], which are functions that are written in the logic for the purpose of simplifying terms and can be used as code once they are proved correct.

In this subsection we address the use of the NQTHM logic as a general purpose programming language. For example, if we want a homogeneous set of cardinality 3, execution of the function **ramsey** tells us that such a set exists within any graph with at least 20 vertices:

```
>(r-loop)   ;; We type this in order to enter the NQTHM reduction loop.
Trace Mode: Off    Abbreviated Output Mode:  On
Type ? for help.
*(ramsey 3 3)   ;; We ask the system to compute the value of ramsey on
inputs 3 and 3.....
 20
```

This is however an unsatisfactory answer, given that the Nuprl proof (see next section) provides a value of 6 rather than 20 in this case. Therefore, we have in fact re-done the proof using slightly different definitions of the functions **ramsey** and **wit** that more closely reflect the induction that takes place in the Nuprl proof, which is grounded at 2 rather than at 0. We then obtain 6 rather than 20 for the value of (**ramsey** 3 3). It took roughly 5 hours to redo the proof for these new versions of **ramsey** and **wit**.

Convention. In the remainder of this subsection we refer to the alternate versions of **ramsey** and **wit** mentioned above.

The (new version of the) function **wit** can also be executed, on a particular set and binary relation, with particular values for its parameters 11 and 12. Consider for example the hexagon, represented as a binary relation connecting i to $i + 1$ for i from 1 to 6 (except that 6 is connected to 1).

```
*(wit '((1 . 2) (2 . 3) (3 . 4) (4 . 5) (5 . 6) (6 . 1))
      '(1 2 3 4 5 6)
      3 3)
 (CONS '(1 3 5) F)
```

Thus, the set $\{1, 3, 5\}$ is an independent set, as indicated by the second component F of the value returned above (which corresponds to 2 in the

---

[†]personal communication from Bill Bevier

version discussed in the rest of this paper). We found on a Sun 3/60 that it took an average of about 0.15 seconds to evaluate this **wit** form. However, after compiling an appropriate file, the time was reduced to 0.011 seconds per form.

4 Nuprl

Our presentation of the Nuprl proof is divided into four subsections. The first provides a brief overview of Nuprl. The reader is encouraged to consult [7] for further details. The second summarizes definitions, theorems, and tactics used in our proof. The third presents main proof steps. And the final subsection documents the computational content of our proof.

Background

The basic objects of reasoning in Nuprl are types and members of types. The rules of Nuprl deal with *sequents*, objects of the form

$$x_1 : H_1, \ x_2 : H_2, \ ..., \ x_n : H_n \ >> A.$$

Informally, a sequent is true if, when given members x_i of type H_i (the *hypotheses*), one can construct a member (*inhabitant*) of A (the *goal* or *conclusion*). Nuprl's inference rules are applied in a top down fashion. That is, they allow us to refine a sequent obtaining subgoal sequents such that a goal inhabitant can be computed from subgoal inhabitants. Proofs in Nuprl are trees where each node has associated with it a sequent and a refinement rule. Children correspond to subgoals that result from refinement rule application.

These refinement rules may be either primitive inference rules or ML programs called tactics. Nuprl tactics are similar to those in LCF [8]: given a sequent as input, they apply primitive inference rules and other tactics to the proof tree. The unproved leaves of the resulting tree become the subgoals resulting from the tactic's application. Higher-order combinators called *tacticals* (e.g., *THEN* which sequences two tactics) are used to build complex tactics from simpler tactics. The correctness of the tactic mechanism is justified by the way the type structure of ML is used.

Nuprl's type theory is expressive; its intent is to facilitate the formalization of constructive mathematics. Higher order logic is represented via the propositions-as-types correspondence. Under this correspondence an intuitionistic proposition is identified with the type of its evidence or proof objects. For example, an intuitionistic proof of $A \Rightarrow B$ is a function mapping proofs of A to proofs of B, i.e., a member of the function space $A \rightarrow B$.

Similarly, a proof of $A\&B$ inhabits the cartesian product type $A\#B$. A proposition is true when the corresponding type is inhabited. For example, $\lambda x.x$ is a member of the true proposition $A \Rightarrow A$. Types are stratified in an unbounded hierarchy of universes beginning with U_1. One may quantify over types belonging to a given universe, but the resulting type (predicatively) belongs to a higher universe.

To prove a proposition P of constructive mathematics in Nuprl, one proves ">> P" by applying refinement rules until no unproven subgoals exist. If P is true, a proof will produce a member (the proof object) that embodies the proof's computational content. Nuprl provides facilities to extract and execute this content. Thus, Nuprl may be viewed as a system for program synthesis: Theorem statements are program specifications, and the system extracts proven correct programs.

Theorem proving takes place within the context of a Nuprl *library*, an ordered collection of tactics, theorems, and definitions. Objects are created and modified using window-oriented, structure editors. Nuprl contains a definition facility for developing new notations in the form of templates (display forms) which can be invoked when entering text. Notations are defined using other definitions and ultimately terms within the type theory. Required properties (or axioms) about defined objects may not be assumed; they must be proved within the theory.

Theory Development

Our proof of Ramsey's theorem required approximately two weeks of work. Most of this time was spent building a library of foundations for reasoning about finite sets and graphs. Our self-contained library contains 24 definitions and 25 lemmas (counting the final theorem and excluding "ground zero" definitions such as the direct encodings of the logical connectives of predicate calculus). Nineteen definitions and all of the lemmas are related to finite sets, four definitions are related to graphs, and one definition is relevant to the statement of Ramsey's theorem. A complete list of definitions and lemmas may be found in [1].

Our library is built in a rather general way and has been used by researchers at Cornell (in addition to the first author) to prove theorems in graph theory. Rather than assuming that finite sets are built from some specific type (such as integers) most of our definitions and theorems are parameterized by a type whose members are types with decidable member equalities. This type of types (which we refer to as the type of "discrete type pairs" and display as D) is defined as

$$T:U_1 \# \forall x,y:T.\ x = y \ in \ T \lor \neg(x = y \ in \ T).$$

For example, the type of integers (*int*) paired with a decision procedure for member equality belongs to this type D. If A is a member of D, we denote the first projection (i.e., the type or carrier) of A by $|A|$. Most definitions (e.g., finite set membership $\epsilon\{A\}$ or finite set subset $\subset\{A\}$) and theorems carry along a reference to this type parameter in their statement. Such generality is not required for Ramsey's theorem as we could have fixed a specific discrete type, such as the integers, throughout the proof; hence, in the presentation that follows, we often leave this parameter (A) implicit. A full discussion of the benefits of such parameterization may be found in [1].

Finite sets (displayed as $FS(A)$) are defined as lists without duplication, containing members from the carrier of some discrete type pair A. Specifically, finite sets are defined as the parameterized type[‡]

$$\lambda A.\{l:|A| \; list \mid [nil \to True; h.t,v \to \neg(h\,\epsilon\{|A|\}\,t)\,\&\,v; \,@l]\}.$$

whose members are empty lists (the base case, when l is the empty list, evaluates to $True$), and all non-empty $|A|$ lists whose heads are not members of their tails and the same is recursively required of their tails. Given this definition, finite set membership (displayed as $\epsilon\{A\}$) is defined in the obvious way as list membership, subset (displayed as $\subset\{A\}$) in terms of finite set membership, cardinality as list length, etc.

Many of the theorems we prove about finite sets read like set theory axioms, and their proofs implicitly construct useful functions on finite sets. For example, the following lemma states that the union of two finite sets is a finite set: "for all A of the type D of discrete type pairs, and for all r_1 and r_2 that are finite sets (over A), there exists a finite set r such that for all x in $|A|$, x belongs to r if and only if x belongs to either r_1 or r_2."

$$\forall A:D.\forall r_1,r_2:FS(A).\exists r:FS(A).\forall x:|A|.\,x\,\epsilon\{A\}\,r \Leftrightarrow x\,\epsilon\{A\}\,r_1 \vee x\,\epsilon\{A\}\,r_2$$

As usual, a constructive proof of $\exists x.P$ is a pair $<a,p>$ where p proves $P[a/x]$. Thus, as the proof of the above lemma must be constructive, it provides an actual procedure that given a discrete type pair A, and two finite sets r_1 and r_2, returns a pair, where the first component is the union of r_1 and r_2 and the second is constructive evidence of this fact. This procedure is supplied automatically from the completed proof by Nuprl's

---

[‡]The term $[nil \to b; h.t,v \to w; @l]$ is defined as (a hopefully more readable version of) Nuprl's list recursion combinator $list\_ind(l; b; h,t,v.w)$. When l is nil this term reduces to b and when l is $h'.t'$ it reduces to the term w' where w' is w with h' substituted for (free occurrences of) h, t' substituted for t, and $list\_ind(t'; b; h,t,v.w)$ substituted for v.

```
Graph:
A:D # V:FS(A) # E: (elts{A}(V)->elts{A}(V)->U1) #
  ∀x,y:elts{A}(V). E(x,y) ∨ ¬E(x,y) &
  ∀x,y:elts{A}(V). E(x,y) <=> E(y,x) &
  ∀x:elts{A}(V). ¬E(x,x)

n→ (11,12):
λ n 11 12. ∀G:Graph. n ≤ |V(G)| =>
  ∃s:FS(|G|). s ⊂ {|G|} V(G) &
    |s| = 11 & ∀x,y ∈{|G|} s. ¬(x ={||G||} y) => E(G)(x,y) ∨
    |s| = 12 & ∀x,y ∈{|G|} s. ¬E(G)(x,y)

ramsey:
>> ∀11,12:{2..}. ∃n:N+. n→ (11,12)
```

Figure 1.1: Graph and Ramsey Theory

extractor. An additional library object is created that associates a definition for finite set union (displayed as $∪\{A\}$) with this extraction. Another typical example is the lemma *pick* which states that an element can be picked from any non-empty finite set.

$$∀A:D.∀s:FS(A).0 < |s| ⇒ ∃x:|A|.x ∈ \{A\} s$$

Several additional definitions leading up to the statement of Ramsey's theorem are provided in Figure 1.1. The first defines the type of graphs (displayed as *Graph*). A graph is parameterized by a discrete type pair A, and contains a vertex set V, and an edge relation E that is decidable, symmetric, and irreflexive. Not shown are defined projection functions that access the graph's carrier, vertex set, and edge relation components. Their display forms are $|G|$, $V(G)$, and $E(G)$ respectively.[§] The second definition defines a "ramsey function" (displayed as $n → (l_1, l_2)$), which states that any graph with at least n vertices contains an l_1-clique or an l_2-independent set. The third object is the statement of Ramsey's theorem itself. $\{2..\}$ and $N+$ represent the set of integers at least two and the positive integers, respectively. In our presentation here, we have used indentation to aid the reader in parsing Nuprl terms. In the actual system, a structure editor

---

[§] Note that we have overloaded display forms (i.e., we have distinct definitions that display the same way) such as vertical bars which project carriers from both graphs and discrete type pairs. Hence, in the second definition in Figure 1.1, the term $||G||$ is the type given by projecting out the discrete type pair from a graph tuple G and then projecting out the type from the resulting pair.

is used that has facilities for disambiguating parsing when creating and viewing expressions.

Our development of finite set and graph theory also includes building specialized tactics. Nuprl's standard tactic collection [10] contains a number of modules for automating common forms of logical reasoning. On top of these are special purpose tactics for set theoretic reasoning. The most powerful of these, *FSTactic*, uses a combination of term rewriting, backchaining, propositional reasoning, and congruence reasoning to solve set membership problems. For example, the lemma defining finite set union is automatically used to rewrite membership in a union of sets to a disjunction of membership terms. Our collection consists of about 150 lines of ML code and was written in a day.

Outline of Main Proof Steps

The actual Nuprl proof of Ramsey's theorem closely follows the informal outline in Section 2, albeit with more detail. The following snapshots represent the main steps and are derived from the actual Nuprl session. These steps convey much of the flavor of proof development in Nuprl and indicate how carefully developed definitions, lemmas, and tactics, facilitate high-level, comprehensible proof development.

(Note that some space saving simplifications have been made. Some hypotheses and uninteresting parts (e.g., applications of *FSTactic*) of refinement steps are omitted. Hypothesis numbers are omitted unless referenced in subsequent snapshots. As the proof references only one discrete type pair, such references are dropped whenever possible. For example, expressions like $s_1 \cup \{A\} s_2$ and $x \in \{A\} s$ are replaced with the simpler $s_1 \cup s_2$ and $x \in s$. The complete unaltered proof is found in [1].)

The first snapshot is of the initial proof step. At the top is the goal, our statement of Ramsey's theorem. It is followed by a refinement rule, a combination of tactics that specifies induction on l_1 using j_1 as the induction variable. The next two lines contain the hypothesis and subgoal for the base case, and the last three lines contain the inductive case. This simple looking refinement step hides 64 primitive refinement rules. (That is, the tactics in this refinement step internally generate a 64 node proof tree containing only primitive refinement rules. The size of this underlying proof tree, to a first approximation, roughly indicates the degree of automated proof construction.)

```
>> ∀l1,12:{2..}. ∃n:N+. n→ (11,12)
BY OnVar '11' (NonNegInd 'j1')
j1 = 2
   >> ∀12:{2..}. ∃n:N+. n→ (j1,12)
2 < j1
∀12:{2..}. ∃n:N+. n→ (j1-1,12)
   >> ∀12:{2..}. ∃n:N+. n→ (j1,12)
```

We continue by refining the base case using the tactic *ITerm* ("Instantiate Term"), which provides the witness l_2 for n. Notice some that abbreviations are expanded by this step, such as $n \to (j_1, l_2)$.

```
BY ITerm '12'
G:Graph
12 ≤ |V(G)|
   >> ∃s:FS(|G|). s ⊆ V(G) &
       |s| = j1 & ∀x,y ∈ s. ¬(x=y in ||G ||) => E(G)(x,y) ∨
       |s| = 12 & ∀x,y ∈ s. ¬E(G)(x,y)
```

The result is that, given an arbitrary graph G with at least l_2 vertices, we must find a subset s of its vertex set such that G restricted to s is a 2-clique or an l_2-independent set. To construct such an s, we use a lemma that states that for any decidable predicate P on pairs of elements from some finite set, either P holds for all pairs, or there is a pair for which P fails. This lemma, whose formal statement is

```
>> ∀s:FS(A). ∀P:elts(s)->elts(s)->U1.∀x,y ∈ s.
     P(x)(y) ∨ ¬P(x)(y)
          => ∀x,y ∈ s. P(x)(y) ∨ ∃x,y ∈ s.  ¬P(x)(y),
```

is proved by providing (implicitly via an inductive proof) a search procedure that applies P to all x and y in a given s and returns a proof that either P holds for all x and y or returns a pair for which P fails and a proof of $\neg P(x)(y)$. Instantiating P with the appropriate edge relation justifies the following.

```
BY Cases ['∀x,y ∈ V. (λ z w.  z = w in |A| ∨ ¬E(z,w))(x)(y)';
          '∃x,y ∈ V. ¬((λ z w.   z = w in |A| ∨ ¬E(z,w))(x)(y))']
```

When the first case holds, we are provided with a proof of $\neg E(x, y)$, for all x and y in V such that $x \neq y$. As $|V| \geq l_2$, we can pick a subset of V that is an l_2-independent set. In the second case, we are given an x and a y that have an edge between them. Hence, this subset of V is a 2-clique under the edge relation E. It takes 11 refinement steps to complete this analysis.

To prove the inductive case of the first induction, we perform a second induction whose base cases are proved analogously to the first. Afterwards, we have two induction hypotheses, which after several elimination steps are as follows.

```
(6) n→ (j1,j2-1)
(8) m→ (j1-1,j2)
```

These furnish the required Ramsey number for the second induction step.

```
>> ∃n:N+. n→ (j1,j2)
BY ITerm 'n + m'
G:Graph
n+m ≤ |V(G)|
    >> ∃s:FS(|G|). s ⊂ V(G) &
        |s| = j1 & ∀x,y ∈ s. ¬(x=y in ||G||) => E(G)(x,y) ∨
        |s| = j2 & ∀x,y ∈ s. ¬E(G)(x,y)
```

After expanding G into its constituent components (a discrete type pair A, a vertex set V, an edge relation E, and edge properties p_1, p_2, and p_3 — i.e., the six parts of the graph tuple defined in Figure 1.1), we instantiate the outermost quantifiers of the *pick* lemma to select an element v_0 from V. Then, using finite set comprehension, provided by a lemma *fs_comp* which states that any set (here $V - v_0$) may be partitioned by a decidable property (here $\lambda x. E(v_0)(x)$), we divide V into r_1 and r_2: those elements of V connected to v_0 and those not.

```
BY InstLemma 'pick' ['A';'V'] THEN InstLemma 'fs_comp' ['A';'V - v0';'E(v0)']
```

This leaves our conclusion unchanged and provides the following new hypotheses.

```
v0 ∈ V
(19) ∀x:elts(V - v0). x ∈ r1 <=> x ∈ V - v0 & E(v0,x) &
                         x ∈ r2 <=> x ∈ V - v0 & ¬E(v0,x)
disj(r1,r2)
r1 ∪ r2 = V - v0
```

Using the last two hypotheses and our cardinality lemmas, we prove that $|r_1| + |r_2| \geq m + n - 1$. This takes two refinement steps. It follows (using a tactic for simple monotonicity reasoning) that $|r_1| \geq m \vee |r_2| \geq n$, and we split on the two cases. In the $|r_1| \geq m$ case, we instantiate hypothesis 8, one of our two induction hypotheses as follows.

```
BY EOnThin '<A,<r1,<E,<p1,<p2,p3>>>>>' 8
```

Recall that a Graph is a tuple. The tactic *EOnThin* ("Eliminate On and then Thin (drop) the indicated (uninstantiated) hypothesis") performs an elimination step that instantiates hypothesis 8 with the graph G restricted to the vertex set $r_1 \subset V$. The other components of G are as before. This yields the following hypothesis.

```
(m ≤ |r1|) => ∃s:FS(A). s ⊂ r1 &
    |s| = j1-1 & ∀x,y ∈ s. ¬(x=y in |A|) => E(x,y) ∨
    |s| = j2 & ∀x,y ∈ s.¬E(x,y)
```

Breaking down this hypothesis yields another case split. In the first case, we are given the new hypotheses:

```
(22) s ⊂ r1
|s| = j1-1
(26) ∀x,y ∈ s.¬(x=y in |A|) => E(x,y)
```

Our conclusion remains unchanged. We must still produce a subset s of V that contains a j_1-clique or a j_2-independent set. In this case we prove the left disjunct by introducing the set $s + v_0$ and demonstrate that it constitutes a clique.

```
>> ∃s:FS(A). s ⊂ V &
    |s| = j1 & ∀x,y ∈ s. ¬(x = y in |A|) => E(x,y) ∨
    |s| = j2 & ∀x,y ∈ s. ¬E(x,y)
BY ITerm 's + v0' THEN ILeft

s + v0 ⊂ V
|s + v0| = j1
x ∈ s + v0
y ∈ s + v0
(33) ¬(x=y in |A|)
    >> E(x,y)
```

This step results in the new goal of proving that G restricted to $s + v_0$ is indeed a clique: that is, given an arbitrary x and y in $s + v_0$, proving $E(x, y)$. The first two hypotheses in the display above in fact correspond to two other subgoals produced by the indicated refinement; however, they are proved automatically by the tactic *FSTactic* mentioned previously.¶ This new goal is proved by examining the four possible cases of $x = v_0$ and $y = v_0$. This type of reasoning is routine and each case takes one

---

¶This does not come for free. *FSTactic* undertakes significant amounts of search and this is slow. Its execution time contributes significantly to our replay time (when the tactic must be rerun to construct the underlying primitive inference tree) and library development time discussed in the next section.

refinement step (invoking the suitable tactic or combination of tactics) to verify. If $x = y = v_0$, then this contradicts hypothesis 33. If neither are, than both vertices are in s and $E(x,y)$ follows from hypothesis 26. In the remaining two cases, one vertex is v_0 and the other is not; $E(x,y)$ follows from hypotheses 19 and 22, together with the definition of r_1 and the symmetry of E.

In the second case, our new hypotheses are

```
s ⊂ r1
|s| = j2
∀x,y ∈ s. ¬E(x,y)
```

Instantiating the goal with s now proves the existence of a j_2-independent set.

```
>> ∃s:FS(A). s ⊂ V &
     |s| = j1 & ∀x,y ∈ s. ¬(x=y in |A|) => E(x,y) V
     |s| = j2 & ∀x,y ∈ s. ¬E(x,y)
BY ITerm 's' THEN IRight
```

FSTactic completes the $|r_1| \geq m$ case. The other case is proved analogously.

Overall, the entire proof consists of 64 refinement steps and took about 20 man-hours to prove, including aborted proof attempts. Tactics played a major role in making this development feasible; the 64 refinement steps hide 17531 primitive steps, an expansion factor of 273 to 1.

Computational Content

Although our constructive proof may be more complicated than a corresponding classical proof, our proof constructs three interesting functions that can be automatically synthesized by Nuprl's extractor. They are displayed below. Let us note that *term_of*(*thm*) is a term that evaluates to the extraction from a theorem *thm*, i.e., evaluates to a proof object of *thm*. ".1" and ".2" are defined as first and second projection functions on pairs.

ram_n The outermost type constructors of Ramsey's theorem define an AE ($\forall/\exists$) formula. Hence, its extraction, $\lambda l_1 \, l_2 . term\_of(ramsey)(l_1)(l_2).1$, constitutes a function from integers l_1 and l_2 that evaluates to the first projection of a pair $<n, P_1>$. This function returns n, an upper bound on the Ramsey number for l_1 and l_2.

ram_clique P_1, the second component of the above pair, is the computational part of our proof that $n \to (l_1, l_2)$. This too is an AE statement (see Figure 1.1) and defines a function whose application to a G in

Graph and a trivial proof (*axiom*) that G is sufficiently large evaluates to
$<s, P_2>$. The function $\lambda\, l_1\, l_2\, g.term\_of(ramsey)(l_1)(l_2).2(g)(axiom).1$,
returns the set s, where G restricted to s is an l_1-clique or an l_2-
independent set.

ram_decide P_2 is the computational content of our proof of a disjunction. It provides the basis for a procedure that prints "Clique" or
"Independent Set" depending on which disjunct holds.

Nuprl contains facilities to execute these functions. For example, let
G be a tuple of type *Graph* that encodes the six vertex "hexagon graph"
given in Subsection "Computing" of Section 3. Execution of $ram\_n(3)(3)$
returns 6, so G must contain three vertices that form a clique or an independent set. Execution of $ram\_clique(3)(3)(G)$ returns the set 6.(2.(4.nil)) and
$ram\_decide(3)(3)(G)$ prints *Independent Set*. Their execution takes about
seven seconds on a Symbolics 3670 Lisp Machine.

5   Comparison

At the heart of the differences between NQTHM and Nuprl are the philoso-
phies underlying the two systems. NQTHM is poised on a delicate balance
point between logical strength and theorem proving power. The logic is
just strong enough to express many interesting problems, but not so strong
that proof automation becomes unmanageable. In the case of Ramsey's
theorem, the NQTHM proof was essentially constructive by necessity: as
the logic lacks quantifiers, "existence" cannot be expressed other than by
providing witnessing objects in the theorem statement. Of course, the upside is that around such a restricted logic, Boyer and Moore have been
remarkably successful at designing heuristics for automating theorem proving; this is perhaps reflected in the quantitative comparison in Figure 1.2,‖
and it is certainly reflected in some large proof efforts that have been carried
out using that system and PC-NQTHM (see for example [2] and the other
articles on system verification in that issue of the Journal of Automated

---

‖In Figure 1.2, "# Tokens" refers to (essentially) the total number of identifiers and
numerals in the input submitted to the systems. It does not count Nuprl tactics
or Nuprl definitions or theorem statements leading up to the final proof. Replay
times refer to runs on a Sun 3/60 using akcl for the NQTHM run and a Symbolics
3670 Lisp Machine for the Nuprl run. The Nuprl replay time measures the time
required to expand (i.e., produce a tree of primitive refinement rules) only the
proof of Ramsey's theorem. Nuprl version 3.0 was used for these measurements; a
new version is soon to be released that is substantially (up to a factor of 2) more
efficient.

	NQTHM	Nuprl
# Tokens	933	972
# Definitions	10	24
# Lemmas	26	25
Replay Time	3.7 minutes	57 minutes

Figure 1.2: Comparison Statistics

Reasoning). It is also reflected in the total times for the proof efforts. The Nuprl effort took about 60 hours for library development and about 20 additional hours to complete the proof. (However, much of this time was spenting waiting for Nuprl and could be saved by a more efficient version of the system.) The NQTHM effort took about 7 hours altogether, though (as explained in the subsection above entitled *More Statistics and General Remarks*) a few hours may have been saved because of the existence of a previous proof. Finally, the simplicity and classical nature of the NQTHM logic makes it quite accessible to those with little background in logic.

The philosophy behind Nuprl is to provide a foundation for the implementation of constructive mathematics and verified functional programs. Within this framework, the responsibility for automating reasoning falls almost entirely upon the user, though Nuprl does contain a built-in decision procedure for a fragment of arithmetic and Nuprl's standard tactic collection provides significant theorem proving support. Moreover, the logical complexity of Nuprl's type theory is reflected in the complexity of the tactics. For example, term well-formedness is not merely a syntactic property of terms; it is a proof obligation that is undecidable in general, as it is equivalent to showing that a program meets its specification. Nuprl's standard tactic collection contains procedures that in practice solve well-formedness problems (i.e., that a term belongs to some universe), but nonetheless well-formedness is an additional burden on the user and tactic writer and is reflected in development and replay time. However, the richness of the logic contributes to the ease with which problems may be formulated. And its constructivity enables the system to construct interesting programs as results of the theorem-proving process.

It is difficult to compare the naturalness or the ease with which one finds proofs in different systems — especially when the theorem proving paradigms are as different as NQTHM and Nuprl's. In NQTHM, the user incrementally provides definition and lemma statements that lead up to the desired theorem statement. Each lemma is proved automatically, as is the final theorem. Interaction with the system consists of the user analyzing failed proof attempts and determining what intermediate lemmas, and perhaps hints, are needed to help the prover find a proof. Refinement style proof is possible using the PC-NQTHM interactive enhancement. On the other hand, Nuprl proofs are constructed entirely interactively by refinement.

Interestingly, approximately the same number of lemmas were used for both proofs. However, the lemma statements tend to be rather different. Almost all of the Nuprl lemmas are general purpose propositions about finite sets and are not suggested by failed automated proof attempts. As a result, their statements are often more intuitive than the more technical of the lemmas used in the NQTHM proof. Moreover, the Nuprl proofs seem syntactically close to the style in which mathematics is traditionally presented and provide a formal document of why a theorem is true. Let us return to the question of what is learned from counting the number of lemmas. The sequence of Nuprl refinement steps is probably a more natural analogue of the sequence of NQTHM lemmas than is the sequence of Nuprl lemmas. Both NQTHM lemmas and Nuprl refinement steps are atomic steps carried out automatically without user interaction, and they both take advantage of reasoning capabilities provided by the system (including the tactic libraries, in the case of Nuprl).

Another interesting point, related to proof style, is that, to a certain degree, Nuprl proofs should *not* in general be completely automated. Although any proof is sufficient to demonstrate that a theorem is true, different proofs have different computational content. When algorithmic efficiency is a consideration, the user requires control over the proof steps that affect program complexity. This is not an issue with NQTHM proofs because programs are explicitly given in definitions.

Both Nuprl and NQTHM have strong connections with programming, although the approaches are different. In Nuprl, one may directly verify that an explicitly given program (a term in Nuprl's type theory) meets a specification. However, programs are usually extracted as the implicit "computational content" of proofs. The subsection above entitled *Computational Content* provides examples of t he latter approach. In the NQTHM system one must explicitly provide the programs (though they are usually called definitions or "DEFN events") in a language closely related to pure Lisp. However, those programs are translated quite directly by the system into Common Lisp code, which can then be compiled. Therefore these programs can be considerably more efficient than the unoptimized, interpreted programs extracted by Nuprl. (Recall the numbers in the subsections above entitled *Computing* and *Computational Content*: 0.15 seconds to evaluate an NQTHM form (0.011 if the functions are compiled) corresponds to about

7 seconds for evaluation of an analogous Nuprl form, albeit on different machines.) But we can envision improvements in both systems. The Nuprl term language defines a pure functional programming language that is currently interpreted in a straightforward way. It seems reasonable to assume that (with enough effort) execution could be made as efficient as current ML or Lisp implementations. Furthermore, extracted code is currently unoptimized. Work by Sasaki [17] on an optimizer for an earlier version of Nuprl indicates that type information in proofs can be utilized to extract significantly more efficient code. Improvements are also planned for program development in the NQTHM system. Boyer and Moore are developing a successor to NQTHM called ACL2 that will be based on an applicative subset of Common Lisp. Common Lisp is actually used for serious applications and we expect ACL2 to be more useful for programmers than the current language.

We have spent little time addressing soundness issues. Both systems are based on well-defined formal logics, so at the very least it is possible to ask whether the systems do indeed implement their respective logics. Both systems have been crafted sufficiently carefully and used sufficiently extensively to give us some confidence that when a statement is certified by the system as being a theorem, then it is indeed a theorem. Another soundness issue is the extent to which a system helps users to develop specifications that reflect their informal intentions. The expressiveness of Nuprl's type theory and the ability to create new notions allow users to express specifications in a reasonably naturally and hierarchical way that follows their logical intuitions. Soundness is not compromised by definitions as the definition facility is essentially a macro facility. Furthermore the "strong typing" in Nuprl prevents certain kinds of specification errors that are analogous to errors prevented by strong typing in programming languages (e.g., array subscripts out of range). The NQTHM logic (hence the prover as well) does allow bona fide definitions, even recursive ones, but guarantees conservativity and hence consistency of the resulting theories. The text printed out by the NQTHM prover is also occasionally useful for discovering errors in specifications. For example, experienced users sometimes detect output indicating obviously false subgoals. Similarly, their suspicions may be raised by proofs that succeed "too quickly".

We have also said little in our comparison about user interface issues. However, in practice, actual usability depends greatly on something less glamorous than the logic or the automated reasoning heuristics, namely the editor. Serious users of NQTHM tend to rely heavily on the capabilities offered by an Emacs editor. Nuprl provides special purpose editors for creating and manipulating definitions, tactics, and proofs.

We should re-emphasize that the numbers presented above, as with many metrics, are potentially misleading. Consider, for example, the problem of comparing sizes of related proofs. We measure this by counting user-entered tokens. But even this simple metric is problematic. Our count measures the number of tokens to be input for the completed proof, and hence ignores the issue of how many tokens were entered on misguided parts of the attempt that never found their way into the final proof. (An attempt to measure this total number of tokens might be informative but might well measure a user's style more than it would measure something about a particular system.) Moreover, even the final token count may be quite dependent on the way one goes about doing the proof, and this can vary wildly among users of a given system. For example, in the Nuprl system, any sequence of proof steps can be encoded as a tactic. In the Nuprl effort, we did not count the tactic code in Figure 1.2 since the tactics' development was for the most part fairly general. Similarly, arbitrarily large chunks of the proof can be proved separately as lemmas that can be incorporated into the final proof. Nuprl's definition mechanism also allows text to be bound to a single tokens. Comparable difficulties exist in collecting statistics about the NQTHM prover. Many of the tokens come from technical lemmas whose statements were constructed by using the editor to cut and paste; hence the token count is not necessarily reflective of the amount of user interaction. And as with Nuprl, it is easy to shorten the proof with tricks, especially if we use the `let` construct, which is included with the PC-NQTHM interactive enhancement of NQTHM, to share subexpressions. Of the lemmas proved, six (with 65 tokens altogether) were purely about sets, and two were technical lemmas that were created easily using the Emacs editor (without typing many characters, to our recollection) but which accounted for 116 tokens; and all of these were included in the statistics.

In a similar vein, let us point out that a higher definition count might reflect a lack of expressiveness of the logic, or it might instead reflect an elegance of style (modularity). Similarly, the number of lemmas in an interactive system can reflect the user's desire for modularity or it can reflect the weakness of the prover. Replay time can measure the power of the prover, but instead it may measure the extent to which the system "saves" the decisions that were made during the interactive proof of the theorem.

Of course, in our proofs we tried not to exploit such possibilities. Furthermore, to a certain extent, "cheating" in one area is reflected in another. For example a proof may be shortened by increasing definitions and lemmas, and replay time may be decreased by increasing the size (explicitness) of the proof. Hence, quantitative measurements should all be taken together along with the non-quantitative proof aspects in order to aid understanding of the systems in question.

Perhaps the most important point we can make in closing this comparison is that both of us felt comfortable in using the system that we chose, and we each find the other system to be reasonably natural but difficult to imagine using ourselves. It seems to be the case that it takes most people at least a few weeks to get comfortable enough with a proof-checking environment in order to reasonably assess its strengths and weaknesses. We'd like to hope that the descriptions of the proof efforts presented in this paper, together with our comments about the systems, suggest that both systems are quite manageable once one invests some time to become familiar with them. We'd also like to hope that the various warnings presented in this paper encourage people to be cautious about making too-easy judgments regarding the relative merits of systems.

We would be interested in seeing more comparisons of proof development systems. Perhaps though it would be responsible of us to point out that it took much more effort to write this paper than to carry out the proofs.

Bibliography

[1] David A. Basin. *Building Theories in Nuprl.* Technical Report 88-932, Cornell University, 1988.

[2] William R. Bevier, Warren A. Hunt, Jr., J Strother Moore, and William D. Young. "An Approach to Systems Verification." Journal of Automated Reasoning, November, 1989.

[3] William R. Bevier. "Kit: A Study in Operating System Verification." IEEE Transactions on Software Engineering, November, 1989, pp. 1368-81.

[4] Robert S. Boyer and J Strother Moore. *A Computational Logic.* Academic Press, New York, 1979.

[5] Robert S. Boyer and J Strother Moore. "Metafunctions: Proving Them Correct and Using Them Efficiently as New Proof Procedures." In *The Correctness Problem in Computer Science,* ed. Robert S. Boyer and J Strother Moore, Academic Press, London, 1981 .

[6] Robert S. Boyer and J Strother Moore. *A Computational Logic Handbook.* Academic Press, Boston, 1988.

[7] R.L. Constable et al. *Implementing Mathematics with the Nuprl Proof Development System.* Prentice Hall, 1986.

[8] Michael J. Gordon, Robin Milner, and Christopher P. Wadsworth. *Edinburgh LCF: A Mechanized Logic of Computation.* Volume 78 of *Lecture Notes in Computer Science,* Springer-Verlag, 1979.

[9] Ronald L. Graham, Bruce L. Rothschild, and Joel H. Spencer. *Ramsey Theory.* John Wiley and Sons, 1980.

[10] Douglas J. Howe. *Automating Reasoning in an Implementation of Constructive Type Theory.* PhD thesis, Cornell University, 1988.

[11] Matt Kaufmann. *An Example in NQTHM: Ramsey's Theorem.* Internal Note 100, Computational Logic, Inc., November 1988.

[12] Matt Kaufmann. *A User's Manual for an Interactive Enhancement to the Boyer-Moore Theorem Prover.* Technical Report CLI-19, Computational Logic, Inc., May 1988.

[13] Richard A. Kemmerer. *Verification Assessment Study Final Report.* National Computer Security Center, Fort Meade, Maryland, 1986.

[14] Peter A. Lindsay. "A Survey of Mechanical Support for Formal Reasoning." Software Engineering Journal, January, 1988.

[15] Per Martin-Löf. "Constructive mathematics and computer programming." In *Sixth International Congress for Logic, Methodology, and Philosophy of Science,* pages 153–175, North Holland, Amsterdam, 1982.

[16] J. McCarthy et al. *LISP 1.5 Programmer's Manual.* The MIT Press, Cambridge, Massachusetts, 1965.

[17] James T. Sasaki. *The Extraction and Optimization of Programs from Constructive Proofs.* PhD thesis, Cornell University, 1985.

Goal directed proof construction in type theory

LEEN HELMINK and RENÉ AHN *

Philips Research Laboratories,
P.O. Box 80.000, 5600 JA Eindhoven, the Netherlands

1 Introduction

In this paper, a method is presented for proof construction in Generalised Type Systems. An interactive system that implements the method has been developed. Generalised type systems (GTSs) [4] provide a uniform way to describe and classify type theoretical systems, e.g. systems in the families of AUTOMATH [9, 14], the Calculus of Constructions [13], LF [21]. A method is presented to perform unification based top down proof construction for generalised type systems, thus offering a well-founded, elegant and powerful underlying formalism for a proof development system. It combines clause resolution with higher-order natural deduction style theorem proving. No theoretical contribution to generalised type systems is claimed.

A type theory presents a set of rules to derive types of objects in a given context with assumptions about the type of primitive objects. The objects and types are expressions in typed λ-calculus. The *propositions as types* paradigm provides a direct mapping between (higher-order) logic and type theory. In this interpretation, contexts correspond to theories, types correspond to propositions, and objects correspond to proofs of propositions. Type theory has successfully demonstrated its capabilities to formalise many parts of mathematics in a uniform and natural way. For many generalised type systems, like the systems in the so-called λ-cube, the typing relation is decidable. This permits automatic proof checking, and such proof checkers have been developed for specific type systems [29, 11].

A preliminary version of this article appeared as [24].
*Second author's current address: *Institute for Language Technology and Artificial Intelligence, Tilburg University, P.O.Box 90153, 5000 LE Tilburg, the Netherlands.*

The problem addressed in this paper is to construct an object in a given context, given its type. This amounts to higher-order theorem proving. This paper demonstrates that this construction problem can be handled by a form of clause inference, provided that the collection of available clauses is continuously adapted to the context in which the proof is conducted. This rests on a mechanism that provides a simple clausal interpretation for the assumptions in a context. The method presented is not complete, due to the expressive power of GTS. To illustrate the method, a full derivation example is included. A proof environment based on the method, named *Constructor*, has been developed within Esprit project 1222: 'Genesis' [23, 24]. Experiments with this system demonstrate the power and efficiency of the method.

The paper is organised in 8 sections. Section 2 summarizes generalised type systems. The inference method is presented in Section 3. In Section 4, incompleteness of the proposed method is discussed. Section 5 illustrates the method by means of a derivation example. The *Constructor* proof development environment is described in Section 6. Section 7 discusses related work, and Section 8 concludes with a discussion. Finally, the appendix demonstrates soundness of the inference method.

2   Generalised type systems (GTS)

Barendregt has introduced the notion of generalised type systems, including the λ-cube. This classification describes many constructive type systems, by controlling which abstractions are permitted. This section summarizes the type rules for GTS. For details, see [4, 5, 7].

Terms

We assume a predefined set of constants C. The syntactic formation rules for GTS terms are defined as:

- constants, viz. $c \in C$.

- variables, denoted by an identifier.

- $\lambda x{:}A.B$, typed abstraction, where A and B are terms, and x an identifier denoting a variable.

- $\Pi x{:}A.B$, generalised cartesian product of types B indexed over x of type A, where A and B are terms, and x an identifier denoting a variable. We will write $A \rightarrow B$ if x does not occur free in B.

- $(A \; B)$, application, where A and B are terms (function and argument). Application associates to the left, so we will write (a b c) for ((a b) c).

Correctness rules

The terms in the system are typed, and types are terms themselves. This imposes a hierarchy of types. A *typing* is a construction of the form $[t{:}T]$, denoting that T is the type of t. Correctness of typings containing free variables is always relative to a certain *context*. A context is a list of assumptions and definitions:

$$\text{assdef}_1 \; , \dots , \text{assdef}_n \quad (n \geq 0)$$

An *assumption* is of the form $[x_i{:}A_i]$ and introduces x_i as a variable of type A_i. A *definition* is of the form $[x_i \equiv a_i{:}A_i]$ and introduces x_i as an abbreviation of the term a_i of type A_i. We will use Γ and Δ as metavariables over contexts. A *sequent* is an expression of the form $\Gamma \vdash [a{:}A]$, denoting that $[a{:}A]$ is a correct typing in the well-formed context Γ. Well-formedness of a context Γ will be denoted as *well-formed*(Γ). We will write $\Gamma, [x{:}A]$ to denote the context Γ extended with the assumption $[x{:}A]$, and Γ_1, Γ_2 for the concatenation of contexts Γ_1 and Γ_2. We will write $B[a/x]$ to denote substitution of the term a for the free occurrences of the variable x in the expression B. We will write '$=_{\beta\delta}$' to denote the transitive reflexive closure of β- and δ-reduction. β-reduction corresponds to the usual notion in typed lambda-calculus, and δ-reduction denotes local expansion of definitions (unfolding). Note that both β- and δ-reduction are context-dependent.

We ignore here all problems concerning renaming of bound variables (in case of clash of variable names): all variable names are considered unique here, and all equality is modulo α-conversion. This can be achieved by using De Bruijn indices [8] or Barendregt's variable convention [3].

A specification of a GTS consists of a triple (S,A,R) such that

- $S \subseteq C$, called *sorts*.

- A is a set of axioms of the form $[c{:}s]$, where $c \in C$ and $s \in S$.

- R is a set of rules of the form (s_1, s_2, s_3), with $s_1, s_2, s_3 \in S$. A pair (s_1, s_2) abbreviates the rule (s_1, s_2, s_2).

Given a specification (S,A,R), the correctness rules for the associated GTS are defined as:

(empty)	*well-formed*()
(axiom)	if *well-formed*(Γ), then $\Gamma \vdash [c{:}s]$ ($[c{:}s] \in A$)
(introduction)	if $\Gamma \vdash [A{:}s]$, then *well-formed*($\Gamma, [x{:}A]$) ($s \in S$)
(introduction)	if $\Gamma \vdash [a{:}A]$, then *well-formed*($\Gamma, [c \equiv a{:}A]$)
(selection)	if *well-formed*(Γ) and $[x{:}A] \in \Gamma$, then $\Gamma \vdash [x{:}A]$
(selection)	if *well-formed*(Γ) and $[c \equiv a{:}A] \in \Gamma$, then $\Gamma \vdash [c{:}A]$
(λ-abstraction)	if $\Gamma \vdash [A{:}s_1]$ and $\Gamma, [x{:}A] \vdash [B{:}s_2]$ and $\Gamma, [x{:}A] \vdash [b{:}B]$,
	then $\Gamma \vdash [\lambda x{:}A.b : \Pi x{:}A.B]$ $((s_1, s_2, s_3) \in R)$
(Π-abstraction)	if $\Gamma \vdash [A{:}s_1]$ and $\Gamma, [x{:}A] \vdash [B{:}s_2]$,
	then $\Gamma \vdash [\Pi x{:}A.B{:}s_3]$ $((s_1, s_2, s_3) \in R)$
(application)	if $\Gamma \vdash [a{:}A]$ and $\Gamma \vdash [b : \Pi x{:}A.B]$,
	then $\Gamma \vdash [(b\ a){:}B[a/x]]$
(type conversion)	if $\Gamma \vdash [a{:}A]$ and $\Gamma \vdash [B{:}s]$ and $A =_{\beta\delta} B$,
	then $\Gamma \vdash [a{:}B]$ ($s \in S$)

Note that the introduction rule and the selection rule are given here for assumptions as well as for definitions.

3   Proof construction method

In the method, GTS sequents will be derived using a form of clause resolution. The problem of interest is to find an object of a given type. More precisely: given a context Γ and a type A, the objective is to construct an object p such that $\Gamma \vdash [p{:}A]$.

To this end, we will first need a notion of logical variables. Logical variables play the role of meta variables ranging over GTS terms given in section 2. During proof construction, they serve as placeholders for finding GTS terms. To avoid confusion with GTS variables, we will denote logical variables by identifiers prefixed will a '$\sharp$' symbol. If σ is a substitution of terms for logical variables, then $[t]_\sigma$ is the term obtained from t by simultaneously replacing the logical variables in t by the associated terms given in σ. $[t]_\sigma$ is called an instantiation of t. A term is grounded if it does not contain logical variables. A context will be called grounded if it contains grounded terms only.

Derivations

Central in the proof development process is the notion of a derivation. A derivation will be of the following form:

$$\Gamma \vdash [p{:}A] \Leftarrow \Gamma, \Gamma_1 \vdash [p_1{:}A_1]$$
$$\dots$$
$$\Gamma, \Gamma_n \vdash [p_n{:}A_n].$$

where $n \geq 0$. The sequent to the left of the $\Leftarrow$ symbol will be referred to as the conclusion or the head of the derivation, and the sequents to the right of the $\Leftarrow$ symbol are referred to as the antecedents or goals of the derivation. The objects $p, p_1, ..., p_n$ and the types $A, A_1, ...A_n$ may contain logical variables that are considered to be universally quantified over the derivation. However, we will impose the restriction that the contexts $\Gamma, \Gamma_1, ..., \Gamma_n$ in a derivation are always grounded.

Definition: *Validity of a derivation.*

$$valid(\Gamma \vdash [p{:}A] \Leftarrow \Gamma, \Gamma_1 \vdash [p_1{:}A_1] \dots \Gamma, \Gamma_n \vdash [p_n{:}A_n].) \quad \text{if}$$
$$\Gamma, \Gamma_1 \vdash [p_1{:}A_1] \land \dots \land \Gamma, \Gamma_n \vdash [p_n{:}A_n] \Rightarrow \Gamma \vdash [p{:}A].$$

Thus, a derivation is considered *valid* if for any substitution of GTS terms for the logical variables in the derivation such that the derivation is grounded, if the substitution applied to the formulas of the antecedents are correct GTS sequents, then the substitution applied to the conclusion is a correct GTS sequent. From the definition it follows immediately that validity of a derivation is monotonic under substitutions, i.e. any (partial) substitution applied to a derivation results in a new valid derivation. During the proof construction process, the following invariant properties will hold for all derivations:

1. all contexts Γ and $\Gamma_1 \dots \Gamma_n$ will be grounded and well-formed.

2. all derivations will be valid.

3. for any logical variable $\sharp P$ occurring in the type field A_i of a goal $\Gamma_i \vdash [p_i{:}A_i]$, $\sharp P \in \{p_1 \dots p_{i-1}\}$. If an object field p_i of a goal $\Gamma_i \vdash [p_i{:}A_i]$ is not a logical variable, then for any logical variable $\sharp P$ occurring in p_i, $\sharp P \in \{p_1 \dots p_{i-1}\}$.

4. for any logical variable $\sharp P$ occurring in the object field p of the conclusion $\Gamma \vdash [p{:}A]$, $\sharp P \in \{p_1 \dots p_n\}$.

The first property is essential to the method and reflects the fact that construction always takes place within a known context. The second property ensures that the method is sound. The third and fourth property will ensure that logical variables are 'introduced before use'. It will turn out that only the first property affects completeness of the method. The rest of the properties impose no restrictions to our objectives.

In goal-directed proving, the main idea is to start off with the goal to be proven, and to replace this goal with appropriate goals by application of inference rules or clauses. Clauses will be described in detail in the next section. For now, it is sufficient to know that valid clauses can transform valid derivations into new valid derivations by replacement of goals by appropriate new goals. During such an inference step, logical variables in the derivation may become instantiated. The resulting derivations will have the described properties. For GTS, the aim is to find, in a given context Γ, an inhabitant $\sharp A$ of a given type B. To achieve this, the proof inference process starts with the following trivial derivation:

$$\Gamma \vdash [\sharp A{:}B] \Leftarrow \Gamma \vdash [\sharp A{:}B].$$

which is obviously valid and obeys the other derivation properties. An inference step by application of a valid clause on the goal of this derivation will replace the goal by new goals and results in a new valid derivation:

$$\Gamma \vdash [A{:}B] \Leftarrow \ \Gamma, \Gamma_1 \vdash [A_1{:}B_1]$$
$$\dots$$
$$\Gamma, \Gamma_n \vdash [A_n{:}B_n].$$

A is a partial instantiation of $\sharp A$. New logical variables may appear in the derivation. The objective is to repeat this process of transforming the derivation until all goals have disappeared and a derivation of the form:

$$\Gamma \vdash [A'{:}B] \Leftarrow .$$

has been reached. The fourth property for derivations guarantees that the conclusion of this derivation will be grounded (the type field B of a derivation conclusion is grounded from the start). A' is a grounded instantiation of $\sharp A$. Because this derivation will still be valid, this means that $\Gamma \vdash [A'{:}B]$ is a correct GTS sequent, i.e. a correct object A' of the requested type B has been constructed.

Clauses

The clauses that provide valid transformations on derivations will be of the following form:

$$[A{:}B] \;\Leftarrow\; [A_1{:}B_1]_{\Delta_1}$$
$$\ldots$$
$$[A_k{:}B_k]_{\Delta_k}.$$

where $k \geq 0$. Clauses may contain logical variables that are considered to be universally quantified over the clause. Validity of clauses is always with respect to a certain context Γ:

Definition: *Validity of a clause with respect to a context.*

$$valid([A{:}B] \Leftarrow [A_1{:}B_1]_{\Delta_1} \ldots [A_k{:}B_k]_{\Delta_k}., \Gamma) \text{ if}$$
$$\Gamma, \Delta_1 \vdash [A_1{:}B_1] \wedge \ldots \wedge \Gamma, \Delta_k \vdash [A_k{:}B_k] \Rightarrow \Gamma \vdash [A{:}B].$$

Thus, a clause of the given form is called valid in a context Γ if for any substitution of GTS terms for the logical variables in the clause such that the clause is grounded, if the substitution applied to $\Gamma, \Delta_1 \vdash [A_1{:}B_1]$ ... $\Gamma, \Delta_k \vdash [A_k{:}B_k]$ are correct GTS sequents, then the substitution applied to $\Gamma \vdash [A{:}B]$ is a correct GTS sequent.

Let $\mathcal{D}$ be the valid derivation:

$$\Gamma \vdash [P{:}Q] \;\Leftarrow\; \Gamma, \Gamma_1 \vdash [P_1{:}Q_1]$$
$$\ldots$$
$$\Gamma, \Gamma_i \vdash [P_i{:}Q_i]$$
$$\ldots$$
$$\Gamma, \Gamma_n \vdash [P_n{:}Q_n].$$

Let $\mathcal{C}$ be the clause:

$$[A{:}B] \;\Leftarrow\; [A_1{:}B_1]_{\Delta_1}$$
$$\ldots$$
$$[A_k{:}B_k]_{\Delta_k}.$$

and assume that $\mathcal{C}$ is valid in context Γ, Γ_i. Let θ be a unifying substitution for A and P_i and for B and Q_i, i.e. $[A]_\theta = [P_i]_\theta$ and $[B]_\theta = [Q_i]_\theta$. Derivation $\mathcal{D}$ and clause $\mathcal{C}$ remain valid under any substitution, a forteriori under θ, so $[\mathcal{D}]_\theta$ and $[\mathcal{C}]_\theta$ are valid. From the definitions of validity of derivations and clauses it follows immediately that the derivation

$$[\Gamma \vdash [P{:}Q] \Leftarrow \Gamma, \Gamma_1 \vdash [P_1{:}Q_1]$$

$$\ldots$$
$$\Gamma, \Gamma_{i-1}, \vdash [P_{i-1}{:}Q_{i-1}]$$
$$\Gamma, \Gamma_i, \Delta_1 \vdash [A_1{:}B_1]$$
$$\ldots$$
$$\Gamma, \Gamma_i, \Delta_k \vdash [A_k{:}B_k]$$
$$\Gamma, \Gamma_{i+1}, \vdash [P_{i+1}{:}Q_{i+1}]$$
$$\ldots$$
$$\Gamma, \Gamma_n \vdash [P_n{:}Q_n]]_\theta.$$

is also a valid derivation. This is similar to resolution. Note that contexts can only be extended during backward proof construction, like in natural deduction style theorem proving. This avoids the need of unification over contexts, and allows efficient implementations.

In the subsequent sections, valid clauses for proof construction in a given GTS will be derived. The reader is invited to verify that these clauses will not violate the given invariant properties for derivations. Some of the clauses correspond directly to correctness rules for the generalised type theory and are valid in any well-formed context. These clauses will be called system clauses, and they are of interest to all goals in a derivation.. The problem with backward proof construction in GTS is that no suitable clause can be given for the application rule, on account of the substitution. A solution for this problem is presented, that provides a clausal interpretation for the assumptions in a context. The requirement that contexts in derivations are grounded is essential for this translation. The derived clauses thus obtained cover derivation steps that can construct the necessary application terms. For any given goal $\Gamma_i \vdash [p_i{:}A_i]$, this mechanism, when applied to the context Γ_i, allows derivation of a set of clauses that are valid in Γ_i and that are available candidates for resolution on this particular goal. A first proposal for this mechanism can be found in [1].

System clauses

The clauses presented in this section follow directly from the specific GTS in question. They are valid in any well-formed context and will be available for all goals in a derivation.

Axiom clauses

The axioms A from a GTS specification are directly available as inference rules. The valid axiom clauses are:

$$[c : s] \Leftarrow .$$

One for each associated axiom $[c{:}s]{\in}A$. For any goal $\Gamma_i \vdash [p_i{:}A_i]$, such a rule applies if the typing $[p_i{:}A_i]$ unifies with $[c{:}s]$. Note that the context Γ is not affected. Because contexts in our derivations are always grounded and well-formed, the well-formedness check on Γ_i (required in the axiom rules) is needless.

Lambda abstraction clauses

The λ-abstraction rules correspond to a set of valid clauses, one for each (s_1, s_2) pair for which there exists an s_3 such that $(s_1, s_2, s_3) \in$ R. The λ-abstraction clauses are:

$$[\lambda x{:}\natural A.\natural B : \Pi x{:}\natural A.\natural T] \Leftarrow [\natural A{:}s_1]$$
$$[\natural T{:}s_2]_{[x:\natural A]}$$
$$[\natural B{:}\natural T]_{[x:\natural A]}.$$

where $\natural A, \natural B, \natural T$ are logical variables. The typing of a goal of the form $\Gamma_i \vdash [P : \Pi x{:}A.T]$ may be unified with the typing in the conclusion of this rule, unifying P with $\lambda x{:}\natural A.\natural B$ and resulting in the new stripped goal $[\natural B{:}\natural T]$, to be solved in the context Γ_i extended with the typing $[x{:}\natural A]$. The first two goals that arise will ensure that the new context is well-formed and that the abstractions are permitted. Thus, application of this rule introduces context extensions for goals, similar to natural deduction style theorem proving. To ensure that this new context is grounded, the restriction is imposed that A must be grounded after unification, thus preventing logical variables from occurring in the context. The restriction implies that this rule for example can not be used to find a proof for an implication $\natural A \Rightarrow B$, because this would introduce an unknown assumption $[p{:}\natural A]$ in the context.

Pi abstraction clauses

The Π-abstraction rules correspond to a set of valid Π-abstraction clauses, one for each triple $(s_1, s_2, s_3) \in$ R:

$$[\Pi x{:}\natural A.\natural B : s_3] \Leftarrow [\natural A{:}s_1]$$
$$[\natural B{:}s_2]_{[x:\natural A]}.$$

where $\sharp A, \sharp B$ are logical variables. Application of this rule results, after unification of typings, in a stripped goal $[B{:}s_2]$, to be solved in the context Γ_i extended with the typing $[x{:}A]$. Note that the first goal that arises verifies that the abstraction is permitted and that the new context is well-formed, Again the restriction is imposed that A must be grounded. The restriction prevents e.g. using this rule on a goal of the form $\Gamma \vdash [\sharp P{:}s_i]$.

Derived clauses

The application rule cannot be translated directly into a clause, on account of the substitution. A solution is offered, the soundness of which is justified by the following theorem:

Theorem: *Soundness of the method.*

Correctness of a sequent of the form

$$\Gamma \vdash [C : \Pi x_1{:}A_1. \, ... \, \Pi x_n{:}A_n.B]$$

implies that the following clause is valid in context Γ:

$$[(C \; \sharp x_1 \; ... \; \sharp x_n) : B[\sharp x_1/x_1, ..., \sharp x_n/x_n]] \Leftarrow$$
$$[\sharp x_1{:}A_1]$$
$$[\sharp x_2{:}A_2[\sharp x_1/x_1]]$$
$$...$$
$$[\sharp x_n{:}A_n[\sharp x_1/x_1, ..., \sharp x_{n-1}/x_{n-1}]].$$

where $\sharp x_1 \; ... \; \sharp x_n$ are the logical variables of the clause. Note that all possible occurrences of the GTS variables x_i have been replaced by logical variables $\sharp x_i$. For $n = 0$, the set of premises is empty and the application in the consequent simplifies to the object C. Intuitively, the theorem is a version of the heuristic application principle. A proof of the theorem is given in the appendix.

The selection rule justifies that the theorem is in particular applicable to all introductions and definitions occurring in any well-formed context Γ, i.e.

For all GTS variables c, if

$$[c : \Pi x_1{:}A_1. \, ... \, \Pi x_n{:}A_n.B] \in \Gamma \text{ or } [c \equiv C : \Pi x_1{:}A_1. \, ... \, \Pi x_n{:}A_n.B] \in \Gamma$$

this theorem ensures that the following is a valid clause in context Γ:

$$[(c \; \sharp x_1 \; ... \; \sharp x_n) : B[\sharp x_1/x_1, ..., \sharp x_n/x_n]] \Leftarrow$$
$$[\sharp x_1 : A_1]$$
$$[\sharp x_2 : A_2[\sharp x_1/x_1]]$$
$$...$$
$$[\sharp x_n : A_n[\sharp x_1/x_1, ..., \sharp x_{n-1}/x_{n-1}]].$$

This result is now used to interpret the introductions and definitions in a context in clausal form, thus providing the possible application candidates. The intuition behind this is to translate the top-level Π-abstractions for context elements to clauses. For any goal $\Gamma \vdash [A : B]$, all clauses thus obtained from the context Γ are available as valid clauses for resolution on this goal. Note that the context is not affected by these clauses, i.e. the context of the new goals is identical to the context of the original goal.

Because contexts can be extended by the λ- and the Π-abstraction clauses, the set of clauses depends on the particular goal in question and changes dynamically as the proof search proceeds: there is an interleaving between resolution steps and clause translations. The translation mechanism covers both the application rule and the selection rule. The context introduction rule is handled by the λ- and the Π-abstraction clauses, and they enable us to create natural deduction style proofs.

Although for a given context element of type $\Pi x_1 : A_1. \; ... \; \Pi x_n : A_n . B$ (where B is not itself a Π-abstraction) this mechanism gives $n + 1$ different valid clauses, it is sufficient to provide a completely unfolded clause with n antecedents. If the clause has been unfolded too far to unify directly with a sequent, this can be compensated by first resolving the sequent with the λ-abstraction rule. η-conversion is essential here.

Unification and type conversion

Unification is not the subject of this paper, but a few remarks should be made here. It is important to observe that inference steps in the method are correct for any substitution that makes the head of a clause equal to the typing in a goal of interest. Thus the method is sound for any sound procedure that yields unifying substitutions. In implementations, unification algorithms determine whether a clause is applicable to a given goal. Unification will also handle the type conversion rule, dealing with equality of types. It is sufficient to provide unification over typings, not over contexts (although context information is of course relevant for correctness of β- and δ-reductions during unification). Unifying typings $[P{:}A]$ and $[P'{:}A']$ will be achieved by unifying the objects P and P' and subsequently unifying the types A and A'. For types, the unification is with respect to β- and δ-equality. Although β-equality for objects is not explicit in the correctness rules, it is also desirable to identify β- (and δ-) equivalent terms. This is justified by the closure under reduction property and corresponds to proof normalisation [14, 21]. If derived clauses are unfolded completely, it is desirable to augment object unification with outermost η-equality, to ensure reachability of objects in η-normal form.

Unification for expressions in typed λ-calculus with respect to α, β and possibly η-conversion requires complete higher-order unification. This problem depends on the particular GTS of interest. For GTS in general, the problem is not decidable (this is easy to see: even for grounded terms equality is not necessarily decidable because strong normalisation of terms is not guaranteed for all generalised type systems). See also [26, 20]. For simply typed λ-calculus, this problem has a possibly infinite set of solutions. There is no complete and always terminating search algorithm. [27] gives a complete semi-algorithm for this problem in simply typed λ-calculus. In the case of generalised type systems, it is more complicated. Elliott [17] and Pym [36] have independently extended Huets algorithm to dependent types for the logical framework LF (see also [35]). Dowek [15, 16] is working towards extending the algorithm to the Barendregt λ-cube [4], an important class of GTS systems. For implementations of the method, sound approximations for higher-order unification can always be used. Approximations can be very usable in practice (section 6 gives an example) although they affects completeness, of course.

4   Incompleteness

An interesting question is whether the method is complete in the sense that a top down derivation can be constructed for all correct inhabitants (modulo object conversion) of a given type. Completeness is determined by two issues:

- completeness of the higher-order unification procedure.

- the synthesis method itself

Unification is outside the scope of this paper. Let us assume that, for a given GTS, a complete unification procedure is used, then what exactly are the consequences of the restriction imposed on the context, viz. that it is always grounded?

We already saw that our queries of interest are not affected by the restriction. Consider the effect of the restriction during the inferencing process. It should be clear that only the λ-clauses and the Π-clauses are affected by the restriction, as they are the only rules that can extend a context during resolution. For all issues related to completeness (at least in a non-deterministic sense), the following observation is important: due to the third invariant property on derivations, we only need to consider goals where the type field of the conclusion is grounded, because any logical variable $\sharp P$ occurring there can be instantiated by first solving the associated goal where $\sharp P$ is introduced. This implies that the partiality of the λ-abstraction rule poses no fundamental restrictions, because it can be circumvented by postponing resolution on the goal in question. The restriction on the applicability of the Π-abstraction clause does however pose real limitations: it explicitly restricts construction of inhabitants of sorts, e.g. it refuses to enumerate all Π-abstracted propositions or types. For instance, in λC, suppose an object $\sharp P$ is sought, such that $\vdash [\sharp P{:}*]$. Then the correct inhabitant $\Pi a{:}*.a$ cannot be synthesized, because this would require that during construction an unknown type were introduced in the context. The expressive power of type theory is such, that it does allow the construction of proofs that involve e.g. induction loading, where a stronger proposition needs to be constructed in order to infer a proof for a weaker one. Top down construction of such proofs is unattainable in general. The limitations imposed on the Π-abstraction clause are related to this fundamental problem. Note that for checking the restriction does not apply, because the abstraction is known then.

Thus, the method as presented is not complete. Despite extensive experiences with the *Constructor* implementation the authors have never encountered a correct proof that could not be constructed, albeit with the use of auxiliary definitions. It seems that the use of lemmas to build up the proof can circumvent incompleteness issues.

Upon completion of this article, the authors get notice from Gilles Dowek [16] that he has developed a complete proof synthesis method for type systems of the λ-cube. His method seems a generalisation of the method presented here.

5 Derivation example

To illustrate the method, a top down derivation will be presented for a simple theorem in number theory. The particular type theoretical system we use is λC, one of the versions of the theory of constructions introduced by Coquand and Huet [11, 13]. λC is formalised by the following GTS specification:

$$
\begin{array}{ll}
\mathbf{S} & *, \square \\
\mathbf{A} & * : \square \\
\mathbf{R} & (*,*), (\square,*), (*,\square), (\square,\square)
\end{array}
$$

Consider the following correct context Γ_0:

$[nat : *]$,
$[0 : nat]$,
$[s : nat \rightarrow nat]$,
$[< : nat \rightarrow nat \rightarrow *]$,
$[axiom1 : \Pi x{:}nat.\,(<\ x\ (s\ x))]$,
$[trans : \Pi x,y,z{:}nat.\,(<\ x\ y) \rightarrow (<\ y\ z) \rightarrow (<\ x\ z)]$,
$[ind :\ \Pi\,p : nat \rightarrow *.$
  $\Pi\,g : (p\ 0).$
  $\Pi\,h : \Pi n{:}nat.\,(p\ n) \rightarrow (p\ (s\ n)).$
  $\Pi\,z : nat.\,(p\ z)]$,
$[pred1 \equiv \lambda x{:}nat.\,(<\ 0\ (s\ x)) : nat \rightarrow *]$

Possible interpretation:

nat is a type.
0 is a nat.
s is a function from nat to nat (the successor function).
$<$ is a binary predicate over nats.
$axiom1$ states that $\forall x : nat.\,(<\ x\ (s\ x))$.
$trans$ states that $<$ is transitive.
ind axiomatises induction for natural numbers.
$pred1$ abbreviates the predicate $\lambda x{:}nat.\,(<\ 0\ (s\ x))$

A top down proof will now be synthesized for the theorem $\forall y{:}nat.\,(pred1\ y)$, i.e. $\forall y{:}nat\ (<\ 0\ (s\ y))$. This means that a proof object $\sharp P$ is sought, such that $\Gamma_0 \vdash [\sharp P : \Pi y{:}nat.\,(pred1\ y)]$. The derivation process starts of with the associated trivial derivation:

$$\Gamma_0 \vdash [\sharp P : \Pi y{:}nat.\,(pred1\ y)] \Leftarrow \Gamma_0 \vdash [\sharp P : \Pi y{:}nat.\,(pred1\ y)].$$

The available valid system clauses are:

$[* : \Box] \Leftarrow .$

$[\lambda x{:}\natural A.\natural B : \Pi x{:}\natural A.\natural T] \Leftarrow \quad [\natural A{:}s_1]$
$[\natural T{:}s_2]_{[x:\natural A]}$
$[\natural B{:}\natural T]_{[x:\natural A]}.$

$[\Pi x{:}\natural A.\natural B : s_2] \Leftarrow \quad [\natural A{:}s_1]$
$[\natural B{:}s_2]_{[x:\natural A]}.$

viz. an axiom clause and λ- and Π-abstraction clauses for all pairs $s_1, s_2 \in \{*, \Box\}$. These clauses will be available for all goals. For a given goal, they are extended with clauses that can be obtained from the unfolded context elements of the goal by translation. For the antecedent in the given trivial derivation this results in the clauses:

$[nat : *] \Leftarrow .$
$[0 : nat] \Leftarrow .$
$[(s \,\natural X) : nat] \Leftarrow [\natural X : nat].$
$[(< \,\natural X \,\natural Y) : *] \Leftarrow [\natural X : nat]\,[\natural Y : nat].$
$[(axiom1 \,\natural X) : (< \,\natural X \,(s \,\natural X))] \Leftarrow [\natural X : nat].$
$[(trans \,\natural X \,\natural Y \,\natural Z \,\natural P \,\natural Q) : (< \,\natural X \,\natural Z)] \Leftarrow$
$[\natural X{:}nat]\,[\natural Y{:}nat]\,[\natural Z{:}nat]$
$[\natural P{:}(< \,\natural X \,\natural Y)]\,[\natural Q{:}(< \,\natural Y \,\natural Z)].$
$[(ind \,\natural P \,\natural G \,\natural H \,\natural Z) : (\natural P \,\natural Z)] \Leftarrow$
$[\natural P : nat \rightarrow *]\,[\natural G : (\natural P \,0)]$
$[\natural H : \Pi n{:}nat.\,(\natural P \,n) \rightarrow (\natural P \,(s \,n))]\,[\natural Z : nat].$
$[(pred1 \,\natural X) : *] \Leftarrow [\natural X : nat].$

Similar clauses will be constructed for extensions of Γ_0. The only clause applicable to our derivation is a λ-abstraction clause. Resolution gives:

$\Gamma_0 \vdash [\natural P : \Pi y{:}nat.\,(pred1 \,y)] \Leftarrow \quad \Gamma_0 \vdash [nat : *]$
$\Gamma_0, [y{:}nat] \vdash [(pred1 \,y) : *]$
$\Gamma_0, [y{:}nat] \vdash [\natural P' : (pred1 \,y)].$

instantiating $\natural P$ to $\lambda y{:}nat.\natural P'$. Note the different context extensions for the different goals. In the extended context of the second and third goal, a derived clause for y (viz. $[y{:}nat] \Leftarrow .$) is now available. The first two goals are grounded and can be checked immediately. Resolving the remaining third goal with the induction clause (*ind*) gives:

$$\Gamma_0 \vdash [\sharp P : \Pi y{:}nat. (pred1\ y)] \Leftarrow$$
$$\Gamma_0, [y{:}nat] \vdash [pred1 : nat \rightarrow *]$$
$$\Gamma_0, [y{:}nat] \vdash [\sharp G : (pred1\ 0)]$$
$$\Gamma_0, [y{:}nat] \vdash [\sharp H : \Pi n{:}nat. (pred1\ n) \rightarrow (pred1\ (s\ n))]$$
$$\Gamma_0, [y{:}nat] \vdash [y : nat].$$

instantiating $\sharp P'$ to $(ind\ \sharp P''\ \sharp G\ \sharp H\ \sharp Z)$, $\sharp P''$ to *pred1*, and $\sharp Z$ to *y*. Note that this requires higher-order unification. Other possible unifiers are ignored here. The first goal is grounded and can be checked, but this goal can also be solved after resolution with a λ-abstraction clause, provided that the unification knows that *pred1* is equivalent to [*x:nat*](*pred1 x*) (outermost η-equivalence). The last goal is solved directly with the clause for *y* from the context. The derivation thus becomes:

$$\Gamma_0 \vdash [\sharp P : \Pi y{:}nat. (pred1\ y)] \Leftarrow$$
$$\Gamma_0, [y{:}nat] \vdash [\sharp G : (pred1\ 0)]$$
$$\Gamma_0, [y{:}nat] \vdash [\sharp H : \Pi n{:}nat. (pred1\ n) \rightarrow (pred1\ (s\ n))].$$

The first goal resolves with the clause for *axiom1* from the context. Note that this requires δ- and β-reduction of (*pred1 0*). $\sharp G$ is instantiated to (*axiom1 0*) and [*0:nat*] is left as trivial goal that can be resolved immediately. The remaining goal is stripped twice with the appropriate λ-abstraction clause. The derivation is now:

$$\Gamma_0 \vdash [\sharp P : \Pi y{:}nat. (pred1\ y)] \Leftarrow \Gamma_1 \vdash [\sharp H' : (pred1\ (s\ n))].$$

instantiating $\sharp H$ to $\lambda n{:}nat.\lambda hyp{:}(pred1\ n). \sharp H'$. Γ_1 stands for Γ_0, [*y:nat*], [*n:nat*], [*hyp:*(*pred1 n*)]. The remaining proof obligation is now resolved with the context clause for transitivity (*trans*):

$$\Gamma_0 \vdash [\sharp P : \Pi y{:}nat. (pred1\ y)] \Leftarrow \quad \Gamma_1 \vdash [0 : nat]$$
$$\Gamma_1 \vdash [\sharp Y : nat]$$
$$\Gamma_1 \vdash [(s\ (s\ n)) : nat]$$
$$\Gamma_1 \vdash [\sharp P1 : (<\ 0\ \sharp Y)]$$
$$\Gamma_1 \vdash [\sharp Q : (<\ \sharp Y\ (s\ (s\ n)))].$$

instantiating $\sharp H'$ to $(trans\ 0\ \sharp Y\ (s\ (s\ n))\ \sharp P1\ \sharp Q)$. The first and third goal are eliminated with context clauses from Γ_1 for *0*, *s* and *n*. Because these goals are grounded, this amounts to checking. Resolving the last goal with *axiom1* instantiates $\sharp Q$ to (*axiom1 (s n)*) and $\sharp Y$ to (*s n*). The derivation has become:

$$\Gamma_0 \vdash [\sharp P : \Pi y{:}nat.\,(pred1\ y)] \Leftarrow \Gamma_1 \vdash [(s\ n) : nat]$$
$$\Gamma_1 \vdash [\sharp P1 : (<\ 0\ (s\ n))]$$
$$\Gamma_1 \vdash [(s\ n) : nat].$$

The proof is completed with the context clauses for s, n and hyp. The complete proof $\sharp P$ is now:

$$\lambda y{:}nat.\,(ind\ \ pred1$$
$$(axiom1\ \ 0)$$
$$\lambda n{:}nat.\ \lambda hyp{:}(pred1\ n).\,(trans\ \ \ 0$$
$$(s\ n)$$
$$(s\ (s\ n))$$
$$hyp$$
$$(axiom1\ (s\ n)))$$
$$y)$$

Note that this proof is an η-redex. This is due to the fact that derived clauses are unfolded as far as possible here, thus constructing applications that are provided with the full number of arguments. If outermost η-conversion of objects is provided, the η-normal proof can also be derived.

6   The *Constructor* proof environment

This section gives a short description of an interactive proof environment, named *Constructor*, that implements an inference machine based on the described method. The machine enforces correctness of proof construction in generalised type systems. The mouse-based interface has been built using the *Genesis* system, a tool generator that resulted from Esprit project 1222. Details of the *Constructor* system can be found in [22, 23, 24]. Here, we will explain its most important features.

When using *Constructor*, there is always a global context present, which is the theory that formalises a domain of interest. A global context is prefixed with a GTS specification for the desired type system. The system clauses are generated from this specification. The translation mechanism to obtain derived clauses is identical for all GTS variants. A proof editor is provided in which conjunctions of queries can be posed and which allows application of correct proof steps only. Queries are interpreted in the global context. Queries are typings of the form $[A{:}B]$. Goals consist of a typing and a local context extension. The typing needs to be constructed in the global context, extended with the local context extension. Figures 1 and 2 present some screen images of the system (the syntax used in the figures will be explained below).

Both interactive user-guided inference and automatic search are possible and may intermingle. In interactive mode the user may, for a selected goal, choose a clause from a menu with resolution candidates. Optionally, the system checks instantiated goals that may arise after resolution steps. Currently, only one default search strategy or *tactic* (*tactical* in LCF terminology) is present for automatic search. It uses a consecutively bounded depth-first search strategy. This behaves much like breadth-first search, and can be regarded as a brute-force approach. The maximum search depth is specified interactively. Alternative solutions are generated upon request. Facilities to 'undo' user or tactic choices are provided. The resolution method itself is used for correctness checking of contexts and local context introductions. Completed derivations may be added to the global context as lemmas. To this end, they must be given a name and will be available for use in subsequent queries. It is possible to 'freeze' definitions, i.e. to hide their contents and treat them as axioms. In case of clash of variable names (α-clash), unique variable names are generated by numbering. Textual editing of theories and queries is provided in the *Constructor* environment itself.

The special handling of contexts can be implemented efficiently. For example, translation of context elements to clauses only needs to be done once, because clauses remain valid in extended contexts (due to the fact that generalised type systems are monotonic). Verifying well-formedness of contexts can be done incrementally. Contexts with associated clauses can be shared amongst goals.

Technical details

In *Constructor*, typed abstraction is denoted $[x{:}A]B$, whereas typed product is denoted as $\{x{:}A\}B$. Multiple variable introductions are permitted, e.g. $[x\ y{:}A]B$ denotes $[x{:}A][y{:}A]B$. Variables and definitions that are introduced can be declared as operators with a fixity, much like in a Prolog fashion. For example, '$[=> ==[a\ b{:}*]\{p{:}a\}b : \{a\ b{:}*\}*]\ xfy\ 100$' declares '$=>$' (implication) as a right associative infix operator with priority level *100*. Application is treated as a left-associative infix operator. Bracketing is used in the usual way to over-rule priorities. Logical variables are prefixed with a '$\sharp$' symbol.

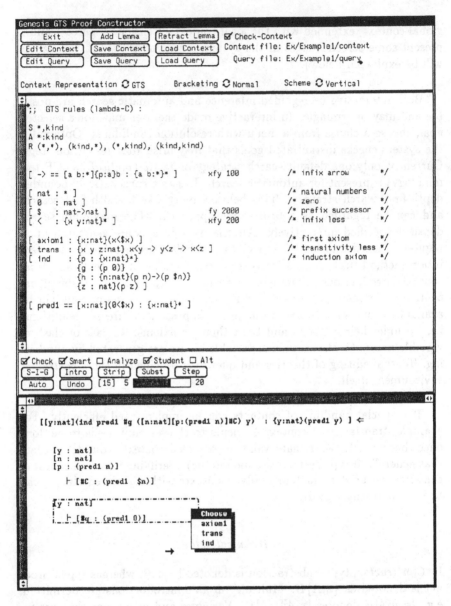

Figure 1.1: Here, we are in the middle of an interactive session, solving the example from section 5. The second window contains the global context. It starts with a GTS specification of λC. For each goal, candidate clauses for resolution can be selected from a menu. The proof under construction is collected in the head of the derivation. Note the different local context extensions for the different subgoals.

The built-in unification procedure implements a simple approximation of higher-order unification with the following characteristics:

- *Higher Order Structural Matching*
  First order unification where logical variables for functors match structurally, e.g. '($\sharp$F 0)' unifies with '(suc 0)' yielding unifier $\sharp$F=suc.

- *Alpha conversion*
  The unification is modulo the name of bound variables, e.g. '[x:nat]x' equals '[y:nat]y'.

- *Beta conversion*
  The built in unification procedure will reduce β-redexes if necessary. To ensure that the reduction is always sound, a goal is added to ensure that the argument will have the required domain type, in the context in question.

- *Delta conversion*
  The built in unification procedure will do δ-reduction on definitions if necessary, i.e. it may expand abbreviating names.

In addition, the provided unification also recognizes outermost η-equality for objects, so that it can use the λ-abstraction clause to verify given application objects where the functor has not been provided with the full number of arguments. This can be regarded as the inverse operation of 'unfolding' Π-abstractions to clauses. The simple unification procedure always yields at most one unifier. If complicated higher-order unification is required, two options are available: (1) provide appropriate auxiliary definitions to obtain the desired result (cf. *pred1* in the derivation example) (2) Interactively substitute a template of the desired proof object by hand. Checking objects (also those that can not be constructed by the unification) is possible for most type systems, because all relevant terms are then known.

The *Constructor* system automatically proves the example from the previous section without delay. As another example, the system constructs the proof for Tarski's Lemma as formalised by Huet [28], a famous example from constructive mathematics, either by first proving the lemmas as proposed in [28], or by direct automatic construction of the complete proof. The example runs within seconds. The search strategy confirms that Huet's proofs are indeed the shortest possible proofs. See figure 2. As an example of a large proof (2000 lines), the system has been used to interactively construct a proof of Girard's paradox, formalising a proof in [6]. This proof was conducted in a GTS known as λU. The system's contribution to

Figure 1.2: Proving Tarski's Lemma [28]. The proof is conducted in a version of the Calculus of Constructions. After automatically constructing a proof of the fixed point property for the given witness, the proof has been added to the context as a lemma (definition) named *'Theorem'*. The associated completed derivation in the bottom window is only partly visible here.

this effort was essential. All lemmas were constructed top-down, in close cooperation between user and machine. In a scenario like this, the system does the clerical work of automatically solving the 'easy' lemmas and proof obligations, while the user selects the crucial proof steps (cf. [12, 25]).

The performance of the system is good: on an average, the system performs 4000 unifications every second (including possible β and δ-reductions). Currently, no clause compilation takes place. Automatic construction of the proofs shown in the figures runs in seconds.

7 Related systems

The Nuprl system by Constable *et al.* ([10]) offers an interesting and impressive interactive proof development environment that is based on Martin-Löf's Type Theory [31]. It is a significant improvement on the LCF proof system ([19]) that strongly influenced it. The Nuprl system has a shortcoming that may have been overcome by the proposed method. The Nuprl inference rules are the correctness rules for the underlying type theory, and implications in a context cannot be used directly as derived rules to resolve goals. Defining a new rule requires a detailed knowledge of the system and the programming language ML. As unification is not directly available, derivation of new hypotheses by instantiating others is often demanded, i.e. variables need to be given that could have been calculated. Automated theorem proving has not yet been accomplished with the system ([10, p.13]).

One of the most powerful existing proof systems is *Isabelle* [33, 34]. Comparison with this system is difficult, because Isabelle is a generic theorem prover, whereas the proof method proposed here is dedicated to only one single proof formalism, viz. type theory. The same remark can be made for a comparison with the work of Felty and Miller on theorem provers [18].

To the knowledge of the authors, three systems are currently under development that have similar objectives to the method proposed here, viz. assistance for proof construction in type theory. One of them is the interesting LEGO system of Pollack [30] in Edinburgh. First prototype implementations of this system are operational. Another promising effort is the ALF system that is implemented by Nordström and Coquand [2]. Finally, Dowek [15, 16] is working on a mathematical vernacular for the Calculus of Constructions. As these systems are still under development, it is too early for a comparison.

8 Discussion

The method presented combines the power of type theory with the advantages of resolution inference and natural deduction style theorem proving.

The method described is non-deterministic in the choice of the inference clause. For GTS in general, the method is also non-deterministic in the choice of the unifier. Therefore, strategic information has to be provided by users, either in the form of interactive choices, or in the form of algorithms (tactics). Although the provided inference steps suggest certain tactics and user interaction modes, these issues are outside the scope of this paper.

The method presented may have some potential to be used as a logic programming language, that includes all the essential features of e.g. Prolog, but that also provides typing, higher-order facilities (this implies correct handling of expressions containing binders) and the use of local assumptions, thereby creating the possibility to handle queries containing universal quantification or implication (similar to λProlog [32] and Elf [35]).

As a meta language, the GTS formalism is suitable to specify logical systems. The method presented makes the inference rules of a logic directly available for resolution instead of just the underlying correctness rules of generalised type systems, thus offering the appropriate inference level. The abbreviation mechanism provides the possibility of hiding and the use of derived lemmas.

The requirement that contexts are always grounded in derivations is essential to the method, because it allows the creation of derived clauses while preventing the undesired generation of new axioms. Also, it avoids the need for unification over contexts: they can be treated in a special way. The restriction seems related to fundamental problems in higher-order theorem proving.

Note that derivations are in a natural deduction style. Proofs constructed by the method are in β-normal form, aside from definitions. In other words, the proofs constructed are cut-free. The proofs are not guaranteed in η-normal form, unless outermost η-reduction on objects is provided in the unification or as an explicit derivation step (as demonstrated in the derivation example of section 5).

Actual implementations of proof systems can efficiently handle many issues. An interactive version of such a proof system, *Constructor*, equipped only with a 'brute force' tactic and using a simple approximation to higher-order unification, gives good results and automatically constructs many non-trivial proofs, including the example proof. Of course, fully automated theorem proving cannot be the objective of proof systems. Proof construction is an interactive process between user and proof system, where the system plays the role of an interactive assistant. The user does the essential proof steps. This includes proposing useful lemmas and selecting crucial inference steps during the proof process. The machine task consists of the verification of details and solving the 'easy' lemmas and goals during the assembly of the main proof. Machines cannot do everything.

1 Proof of the soundness theorem

The following theorem is necessary to ensure soundness of the method:

Theorem: *Soundness of the method.*

Let S be a sequent of the form:

$$\Gamma \vdash [C : \Pi x_1{:}A_1. \ldots \Pi x_n{:}A_n.B]$$

Let C be the clause:

$$[(C \, \natural x_1 \ldots \natural x_n) : B[\natural x_1/x_1, \ldots, \natural x_n/x_n]] \Leftarrow$$
$$[\natural x_1{:}A_1]$$
$$[\natural x_2{:}A_2[\natural x_1/x_1]]$$
$$\ldots$$
$$[\natural x_n{:}A_n[\natural x_1/x_1, \ldots, \natural x_{n-1}/x_{n-1}]].$$

Then:

$$S \Rightarrow valid(C, \Gamma).$$

Proof:

Lemma 1:
$$\Gamma \vdash [C : \Pi x{:}A.B] \Rightarrow \Gamma, [x'{:}A] \vdash [(C \, x') : B[x'/x]]$$

Proof:

Assume $\Gamma \vdash [C : \Pi x{:}A.B]$

Monotonicity guarantees that:

$$\Gamma, [x'{:}A] \vdash [C : \Pi x{:}A.B] \tag{1}$$

The selection rule proves:

$$\Gamma, [x'{:}A] \vdash [x'{:}A] \tag{2}$$

From the application rule applied to (1) and (2) we can infer:

$$\Gamma, [x'{:}A] \vdash [(C\ x') : B[x'/x]]$$

A uniform substitution of a fresh variable x' for x is performed to avoid name clashes thus ensuring a well-formed context $\Gamma, [x'{:}A]$. Discharging the assumption:

$$\Gamma \vdash [C : \Pi x{:}A.B] \Rightarrow \Gamma, [x'{:}A] \vdash [(C\ x') : B[x'/x]]$$

This completes the proof of Lemma 1.   ∎

By induction, it follows that:

$\Gamma \vdash [C : \Pi x_1{:}A_1. \ ... \ \Pi x_n{:}A_n.B]$
$\Rightarrow$
$\Gamma, [x_1'{:}A_1], \ ... \ , [x_2'{:}A_2[x_1'/x_1]], \ ... \ , [x_n'{:}A_n[x_i'/x_i]] \vdash [(C\ x_1' \ ... \ x_n') : B[x_i'/x_i]]$

To complete the proof, the right hand side of this expression must imply that the clause $\mathcal{C}$ is valid in context Γ.

Lemma 2:
$\Gamma, [x'{:}A] \vdash [(C\ x') : B[x'/x]]$
$\Rightarrow$
$valid([(C\ \sharp x') : B[\sharp x'/x]] \Leftarrow [\sharp x'{:}A], \Gamma)$

Proof:

Directly from the definition of clause validity and the substitutivity property of generalised type systems:

If $\Gamma_1, [x{:}A], \Gamma_2 \vdash E$ and $\Gamma_1 \vdash [a{:}A]$
then $\Gamma_1, \Gamma_2[a/x] \vdash E[a/x]$. ∎

Induction completes the proof of the soundness theorem. ∎

Although it is irrelevant for the soundness of the method, it can be demonstrated that a stronger theorem holds [22]. Let S and C be the sequent and clause given in the soundness theorem. Then:

$$S \Leftrightarrow \forall \Gamma'. valid(C, (\Gamma, \Gamma')).$$

The extension Γ' arises automatically as a result of the monotonocity of generalised type systems. The forward implication shows that clauses that have been derived in a context Γ remain valid in arbitrary extensions of Γ. This allows efficient implementations. The reverse implication is related to completeness, although it does not guarantee it.

Acknowledgements

The authors grateful to Jan Bergstra, Loe Feijs, Ton Kalker, Frank van der Linden, Rob Wieringa and the referees for numerous suggestions and corrections. Special thanks are due to Bert van Benthem Jutting, who provided the soundness proofs, to Marcel van Tien, who implemented most of *Constructor*, to Paul Gorissen, who provided the dynamic parsing facilities for the system, and finally to Henk Barendregt, for many stimulating and clarifying discussions, and for assisting with the construction of his version of Girard's paradox.

Bibliography

[1] Ahn, R.M.C. *Some extensions to Prolog based on* AUTOMATH. Internal Philips technical note no. 173/85, 1985.

[2] Augustsson, L., Coquand, T, & Nordström, B. *A short description of Another Logical Framework.* Preliminary roceedings of the First Annual Workshop on Logical Frameworks, Antibes, May 1990.

[3] Barendregt, H. *The Lambda-Calculus: Its Syntax and Semantics.* North-Holland, 1981.

[4] Barendregt, H. *Introduction to Generalised Type Systems.* Proceedings of the third Italian conference on theoretical computer science, Mantova 1989. World Scientific Publ. Also to appear in: J. Functional Programming.

[5] Barendregt, H. & Hemerik. *Types in Lambda Calculi and Programming Languages.* Proceedings of European Symposium on Programming, Copenhagen, 1990.

[6] Barendregt, H. *Lambda Calculi with Types.* To appear in: *Handbook of Logic in Computer Science, Oxford University Press.* (Ed. Abramsky, S., Gabbay, D. & Maibaum, T.).

[7] Barendregt, H. & Dekkers, W. *Typed Lambda-Calculi, Syntax and Semantics.* To appear.

[8] De Bruijn, N.G. *Lambda-Calculus Notation with Nameless Dummies, a Tool for Automatic Formula Manipulation, with Application to the Church-Rosser Theorem.* Indag. Math. 34, 5, pp 381-392, 1972.

[9] De Bruijn, N.G. *A survey of the project Automath.* In: *To H.B. Curry: Essays on Combinatory Logic, Lambda Calculus and Formalisms.* (Seldin & Hindley, Eds.), Academic Press, 1980.

[10] Constable, R.L. et al. *Implementing Mathematics with the Nuprl Proof Development System.* Prentice Hall, 1986.

[11] Coquand, T. & Huet, G.P. *Constructions: A Higher Order Proof System for Mechanizing Mathematics.* EUROCAL85, Linz, Springer-Verlag LNCS 203, 1985.

[12] Coquand, T. *An Analysis of Girard's Paradox.* Symposium on Logic in Computer Science, IEEE, pp 227-236, 1986, pp. 27-57, 1975.

[13] Coquand, T. & Huet, G.P. *The Calculus of Constructions.* Information and Computation 76, pp 95-120, 1985.

[14] van Daalen, D.T. *The Language Theory of Automath.* Ph. D. Dissertation, Eindhoven University of Technology, Dept of Mathematics, 1980.

[15] Dowek, G. *A Proof Synthesis Algorithm for a Mathematical Vernacular.* Preliminary roceedings of the First Annual Workshop on Logical Frameworks, Antibes, May 1990.

[16] Dowek, G. *A Complete Proof Synthesis Method for Type Systems of the Cube.* Draft paper version January 11, 1991. Personal communication.

[17] Elliott, C.M. *Higher-order Unification with Dependent Function Types.* RTA-89, Chapel Hill, Springer-Verlag LNCS 355, 1989.

[18] Felty, A. & Miller, D.A. *Specifying Theorem Provers in a Higher-Order Logic Programming Language.* CADE-9, Argonne, pp 61-80, Springer-Verlag LNCS 310, 1988.

[19] Gordon, M.J., Milner, R. & Wadsworth, C.P. *Edingburgh LCF.* Springer-Verlag LNCS 78, 1979.

[20] Goldfarb, W.D. *The Undecidability of the Second-Order Unification Problem.* Theoretical Computer Science 13, pp. 225-230, 1981.

[21] Harper, R., Honsell, F. & Plotkin, G. *A Framework for defining logics.* Second Annual Symposium on Logic in Computer Science, Ithaca, IEEE, pp. 194-204, 1987.

[22] Helmink, L. & Ahn, R.M.C. *Goal Directed Proof Construction in Type Theory.* Internal Philips technical note nr. 229/88, 1988. Also available as document 28.3 of Esprit project 1222: 'Genesis'.

[23] Helmink, L. & Tien, M. van. *Genesis Constructive Logic Machine: User's Guide.* Available as document 28.5 of Esprit project 1222: 'Genesis', August 1989.

[24] Helmink, L. *Resolution and Type Theory.* Proceedings of European Symposium on Programming, Copenhagen, May 1990. Springer-Verlag LNCS 432, 1990.

[25] Howe, D.J. *The Computational Behaviour of Girard's Paradox.* Symposium on Logic in Computer Science, IEEE, pp 205-214, 1987, pp. 27-57, 1975.

[26] Huet, G.P. *The Undecidability of Unification in Third Order Logic.* Information and Control 22, pp. 257-267, 1973.

[27] Huet, G.P. *A Unification Algorithm for Typed λ-calculus.* Theoret. Comput. Sci. Vol.1, pp. 27-57, 1975.

[28] Huet, G.P. *Induction Principles Formalized in the Calculus of Constructions.* Tapsoft '87, Pisa, Springer-Verlag LNCS 250, Vol. 1, 1987.

[29] Jutting, L.S. *A Translation of Landau's "Grundlagen" in AUTOMATH.* Ph.D. Dissertation, Eindhoven University of Technology, Dept of Mathematics, 1976.

[30] Luo, Z., Pollack, R. & Taylor. *How to Use LEGO.* Preliminary User's Manual, Dept. of Computer Science, University of Edinburgh, 1989.

[31] Martin-Löf, P. *Intuitionistic Type Theory.* Bibliopolis, Napoli, 1984.

[32] Nadathur G. & Miller, D.A. *An overview of λProlog.* In: *Logic Programming: Proceedings of the Fifth International Conference and Symposium.* (Kowalski & Bowen, Eds.), MIT Press, Cambridge, Massachusetts, Vol. 1, pp 820-827, August 1988.

[33] Paulson, L.C. *Natural Deduction as Higher-Order Resolution.* J. Logic Programming 3, pp 237-258, 1986.

[34] Paulson, L.C. *The Foundation of a Generic Theorem Prover.* J. Automated Reasoning 5, pp 363-379, 1989.

[35] Pfenning, F. *Elf: a language for logic definition and verified metaprogramming.* This Volume.

[36] Pym, D. *A unification algorithm for the logical framework.* LFCS report, Laboratory for Foundations of Computer Science, University of Edinburgh, November 1988.

Logic programming in
the LF logical framework

Frank Pfenning
Carnegie Mellon University

In [12], Harper, Honsell, and Plotkin present LF (the Logical Framework) as a general framework for the definition of logics. LF provides a uniform way of encoding a logical language, its inference rules and its proofs. In [2], Avron, Honsell, and Mason give a variety of examples for encoding logics in LF. In this paper we describe Elf, a meta-language intended for environments dealing with deductive systems represented in LF.

While this paper is intended to include a full description of the Elf core language, we only state, but do not prove here the most important theorems regarding the basic building blocks of Elf. These proofs are left to a future paper. A preliminary account of Elf can be found in [25]. The range of applications of Elf includes theorem proving and proof transformation in various logics, definition and execution of structured operational and natural semantics for programming languages, type checking and type inference, *etc.* The basic idea behind Elf is to unify logic definition (in the style of LF) with logic programming (in the style of λProlog, see [22, 23]). It achieves this unification by giving *types* an operational interpretation, much the same way that Prolog gives certain formulas (Horn-clauses) an operational interpretation. An alternative approach to logic programming in LF has been developed independently by Pym [27].

Here are some of the salient characteristics of our unified approach to logic definition and meta-programming. First of all, the Elf search process automatically constructs terms that can represent object-logic proofs, and thus a program need not construct them explicitly. This is in contrast to logic programming languages where executing a logic program corresponds to theorem proving in a meta-logic, but a meta-proof is never constructed or used and it is solely the programmer's responsibility to construct object-logic proofs where they are needed. Secondly, the partial correctness of many meta-programs with respect to a given logic can be expressed and proved by Elf itself (see the example in Section 4). This creates the possibility of deriving verified meta-programs through theorem proving in Elf (see Knoblock & Constable [18] or Allen *et al.* [14] for other approaches).

Elf is quite different in look and feel to the standard meta-programming methodology of writing tactics and tacticals in ML [11]. On the positive side, Elf programs tend to be more declarative and easier to understand. Often one can take what authors bill as an "algorithmic" version of an inference system and implement it in Elf with very little additional work. Moreover, it is possible to implement tactics and tacticals in Elf along the lines proposed by Felty [8]. Such tactics are also often easier to write and understand than tactics written in a functional style, since they inherit a notion of meta-variable (the *logic variable*, in logic programming terminology), a notion of unification, and nondeterminism and backtracking in a uniform way from the underlying logic programming language. The Isabelle system [24] also provides support for meta-variables and higher-order unification in tactics, but they are generally not as accessible as in Elf. On the negative side we encounter problems with efficiency when manipulating larger objects, something which we hope to address in future work with compilation techniques from logic programming adapted to this setting. Also, on occasion, it is difficult to express the operations we would like to perform as a pure logic program. For example, neither the cut operator ! familiar from logic programming nor a notion of negation-by-failure are available in Elf. For some initial ideas to address these deficiencies see Section 5.

We conclude this introduction with an overview of the remainder of this paper. After a brief review of the LF Logical Framework, we begin with an exposition of unification as used in Elf. The general unification problem for the LF type theory is undecidable and non-deterministic, which immediately calls into question the whole enterprise of designing a logic programming language based on LF, given that unification is such a central operation. However, inspired by Miller's work on L_λ [21], we design an algorithm which solves the "easy" unification problems (without branching, for example) and postpones all other equalities which may arise as *constraints*. Since dependent types and explicit Π-quantification further complicate unification, we found it necessary to develop a new view of unification as theorem proving in a very simple logic (the *unification logic*). A unification algorithm is then described as a set of transformations on formulas in that logic, reminiscent of the description of first-order unification by transformations on a set of equations. In Section 2 we develop this view by first presenting the main ideas for an untyped, first-order language and then generalizing it to the LF type theory.

Besides unification, execution of a logic program also requires back-chaining search. In Elf, this search takes the form of finding a term of a given type (possibly containing logic variables) over a given signature. This necessitates a form of resolution, which we express through an extension of the unification logic by a notion of *immediate implication*. When restricted to ordinary first-order logic programming, we would say that a clause $H \leftarrow B_1, \ldots, B_n$ immediately implies an atomic goal G, if G unifies with H under substitution θ and the remaining subgoals (θB_i) are all provable. A formalization of this concept in this more general setting can be found in Section 3.

Back-chaining search and unification describe a non-deterministic interpreter. In order to make this useful as a programming language, search control must be added. This takes two forms. First we distinguish those types which are subject to search (and thus play the role of goals) from those types whose elements are subject only to unification (and thus play the role of ordinary logic variables). We call these *closed* and *open* type families, respectively. Second we make a commitment to depth-first search. These conclude the (partly informal) definition of the operational semantics of Elf in Section 3.

In Section 4 we then introduce the concrete syntax for Elf and present examples which illustrate some of its unique features and common patterns of usage. The main example is an implementation of a decision procedure for term equality in the simply-typed λ-calculus. We also describe some aspects of the implementation Elf in this Section. In particular, we sketch our method of type reconstruction, since, we believe, it has independent interest.

We conclude the paper with speculation about future work.

1 The LF logical framework

We review here only the basic definitions and properties of the LF Logical Framework. For more details, the reader is referred to [12]. A number of examples of representations of logical systems in LF can be found in [2].

The LF calculus is a three-level calculus for *objects*, *families*, and *kinds*. Families are classified by kinds, and objects are classified by *types*, that is, families of kind Type.

$$
\begin{array}{llll}
\textit{Kinds} & K & ::= & \text{Type} \mid \Pi x{:}A.K \\
\textit{Families} & A & ::= & a \mid \Pi x{:}A.B \mid \lambda x{:}A.B \mid A\,M \\
\textit{Objects} & M & ::= & c \mid x \mid \lambda x{:}A.M \mid M\,N
\end{array}
$$

We use K to range over kinds, A, B to range over families, M, N to range over objects. a stands for constants at the level of families, and c for constants at the level of objects. In order to describe the basic judgments we consider contexts (assigning types to variables) and signatures (assigning kinds and types to constants at the level of families and objects, respectively).

$$\text{Signatures} \quad \Sigma \quad ::= \quad \langle\rangle \mid \Sigma, a{:}K \mid \Sigma, c{:}A$$
$$\text{Contexts} \quad \Gamma \quad ::= \quad \langle\rangle \mid \Gamma, x{:}A$$

Since families (and thus types) may be indexed by objects, it is important that signatures and contexts be ordered lists, rather than sets. We stipulate that constants can appear only once in signatures and variables only once in contexts. This can always be achieved through renaming. $[M/x]N$ is our notation for the result of substituting M for x in N, renaming variables as necessary to avoid name clashes. We also use the customary abbreviation $A \to B$ and sometimes $B \leftarrow A$ for $\Pi x{:}A.B$ when x does not appear free in B.

The notion of definitional equality we consider here is $\beta\eta$-conversion. Harper *et al.* [12] formulate definitional equality only with β-conversion and conjecture that the system resulting from adding the η-rule would have the properties we list below. This has recently been proved by Coquand [3] and independently by Salvesen [29]. For practical purposes the formulation including the η-rule is superior, since every term has an equivalent canonical form. Thus, for us, $\equiv$ is the least congruence generated by $\beta\eta$-conversions in the usual manner. The basic judgments are $\Gamma \vdash_\Sigma M : A$ and $M \equiv N$ and analogous judgments at the levels of families and kinds. We assume that a well-formed signature Σ is given, but omit the signature subscript of the various judgments in our presentation. As examples, we show the rules for abstraction, application, and type conversion at the level of objects.

$$\frac{\Gamma, x{:}A \vdash M : B}{\Gamma \vdash \lambda x{:}A.M : \Pi x{:}A.B} \qquad \frac{\Gamma \vdash M : \Pi x{:}A.B \qquad \Gamma \vdash N : A}{\Gamma \vdash M\,N : [N/x]B}$$

$$\frac{\Gamma \vdash M : A \qquad A \equiv A' \qquad \Gamma \vdash A' : \text{Type}}{\Gamma \vdash M : A'}$$

We state a selection of the crucial properties of the LF type theory as given and proven in [12] and [3].

1. (Unicity of Types) If $\Gamma \vdash M : A$ and $\Gamma \vdash M : A'$ then $A \equiv A'$.

2. (Strong Normalization) If $\Gamma \vdash M : A$ then M is strongly normalizing.

3. (Canonical Forms for Types) If $\Gamma \vdash A$: Type then for some family a and objects $M_1, \ldots, M_n$, $A \equiv \Pi u_1{:}A_1 \ldots \Pi u_n{:}A_n.a\,M_1 \ldots M_n$.

4. (Decidability) All judgments of the LF type system are decidable.

The existence of canonical forms for types will be used tacitly in the remainder of this paper. For example, the phrase "*in the case that M has the form $\lambda x : \Pi x{:}A.B$. M'*" is to be interpreted as "*in the case that M has the form $\lambda x : A'$. M' where $A' \equiv \Pi x{:}A.B$*".

2 A meta-logic for unification

The foundation of the logic programming paradigm is goal-directed search and unification. Due to the nature of LF, both of these differ significantly from first-order logic programming languages. In particular, proof search and unification become intertwined and unification is no longer a simple subroutine. This phenomenon is already familiar from constraint logic programming [17, 23], but Elf has at least one additional complication: goals are identified with logic variables (see Section 3).

This set of circumstances calls for a new approach to describe the operational semantics of Elf. The key idea is to develop an explicit meta-logic for LF, not to prove properties about LF, but to describe the operational behavior of Elf. This meta-logic was called *state logic* in [25], since it is used to describe the states of an abstract interpreter for Elf. An alternative approach was taken by Pym & Wallen [28] who give a sequent presentation for LF which allows free meta-variables to appear in the sequents.

We begin with the discussion of unification which will be extended to a logic strong enough to describe the complete state of the interpreter in Section 3. One important property of the unification logic is that it is separated from the formalism of LF and has its own, independent judgments. It is possible to construct such a meta-logic for unification over a number of different term languages and type theories, but a further exploration of this possibility is beyond the scope of this paper.

Miller's *mixed prefixes* [20] and the *existential variables* considered by Dowek [4] perform a function similar to our unification logic. Though Dowek deals with a more expressive logical framework (the Calculus of Constructions) we believe that our meta-logic is more expressive, since we can represent not only a formula in a context with some existential variables, but also several formulas simultaneously which share some context. This allows the natural specification and manipulation of unsolved equations as constraints.

A first-order unification logic with quantifier dependencies

The unification logic arises most naturally from a generalization of the usual view of unification as transformations of a set of equations [19, 30]. There we are given set of equations with some free variables. This set is *unifiable* if there is a substitution for the free variables such that all the equations become true. A unification algorithm is described as a set of transformations which can be used to transform the original set of equations into a *solved form* from which a satisfying substitution can be extracted easily.

We transform this view, first by replacing the notion *set of equations* by the notion *conjunction of equations*. The second step is to existentially quantify explicitly over the free variables. Thus the logical content of a unification problem becomes apparent.

Now the problem of determining unifiability becomes one of establishing the truth of a certain closed formula. When function symbols are uninterpreted, this view gives rise to a deductive system in which provable formulas correspond to unifiable equations. We further generalize the usual unification by allowing explicit universal quantification. In first-order unification, this generalization is not necessary, since one can use Skolemization, though even there it may have some interest for efficient implementation. In the higher-order case Skolemization is more problematic and thus explicit variable dependency is desirable not only from the point of view of implementation, but also in order to simplify the theory.

In summary, the unification logic is built upon the following fragment of first-order logic, defined inductively by a BNF grammar.

$$\textit{Formulas} \quad F ::= u \doteq v \mid \top \mid F \wedge G \mid \exists x.F \mid \forall y.F$$

We use x and y to stand for variables, u and v to stand for terms, and F and G to stand for formulas. The basic judgment is $\Vdash F$ (F is provable) is defined by the following inference rules:

$$\frac{}{\Vdash u \doteq u} \qquad\qquad \frac{}{\Vdash \top} \qquad\qquad \frac{\Vdash F \quad\quad \Vdash G}{\Vdash F \wedge G}$$

$$\frac{\Vdash [u/x]F}{\Vdash \exists x.F} \qquad\qquad \frac{\Vdash F}{\Vdash \forall y.F}$$

Here $[u/x]F$ is the result of substituting u for x in F, renaming bound variables if necessary to avoid capturing free variables in u.

Transformations for first-order unification

In the representation of unification problems as sets, one might have the following set of transformations

$$\{u = u\} \cup S \implies S$$
$$\{u = v\} \cup S \implies \{v = u\} \cup S$$
$$\{f(u_1, \ldots, u_n) = f(v_1, \ldots, v_n)\} \cup S \implies \{u_1 = v_1, \ldots, u_n = v_n\} \cup S$$
$$\{x = v\} \cup S \implies \{x = v\} \cup [v/x]S$$

where x is not free in v in the last rule (called *variable elimination*). A pair $x = u$ in S is in *solved form* if x does not occur in u or elsewhere in S, and S is in solved form if every member of S is in solved form. A set of equations S is said to unify iff there is a sequence of transformations $S \implies \cdots \implies S'$ such that S' is in solved form.

Here, we take an analogous approach. Instead of writing "$\ldots \cup S$" we stipulate that our transformations can be applied to an arbitrary subformula occurrence matching the left-hand side.

$$u \doteq u \longrightarrow \top$$
$$u \doteq v \longrightarrow v \doteq u$$
$$f(u_1, \ldots, u_n) \doteq f(v_1, \ldots, v_n) \longrightarrow u_1 \doteq v_1 \wedge \ldots \wedge u_n \doteq v_n$$
$$\exists x. F[x \doteq t] \longrightarrow \exists x. x \doteq t \wedge [t/x](F[x \doteq t])$$

where x is not bound in F, no free variable in t is bound in F, and x does not occur in t. We refer to the last rule also as *variable elimination*. Here $F[G]$ is our notation for a formula F with a subformula occurrence G. However, these rules are not sufficient to perform unification: we also need some structural rules which allow us to exchange quantifiers (with the obvious provisos regarding variable occurences in the rules dealing with conjunction):

$$\exists y. \exists x. F \longrightarrow \exists x. \exists y. F$$
$$F \wedge (\exists x. G) \longrightarrow \exists x. F \wedge G$$
$$(\exists x. F) \wedge G \longrightarrow \exists x. F \wedge G$$
$$\forall y. \exists x. F \longrightarrow \exists x. \forall y. F$$

A formula is in *solved form* if it has the form S defined inductively by

$$S ::= \top \mid S \wedge S' \mid \exists x. x \doteq u \wedge S \mid \exists x. S \mid \forall y. S$$

where x is not free in u.

It is important that the opposite of the last transformation, namely $\exists x. \forall y. F \longrightarrow \forall y. \exists x. F$ is *not* valid. The reason why the quantifier exchange rules are required is somewhat subtle. Consider an example of the form

$$\exists x. \forall y. \exists z. \ x \doteq f(z) \wedge F.$$

z appears in the "substitution term" $f(z)$ for x, and it would thus be illegal to instantiate z to a term containing y, since this would violate the condition on variable elimination for x ("no free variable in t may be bound in F"). Thus, in order to put the example formula into solved form, we will have to move the quantifier on z outward past the quantifiers on y and x, yielding

$$\exists z.\exists x.\forall y.\ x \doteq f(z) \wedge F.$$

Now variable elimination can be applied, yielding

$$\exists z.\exists x.\ x \doteq f(z) \wedge \forall y.\ f(z) \doteq f(z) \wedge [f(z)/x]F.$$

It is now obvious that z can no longer depend on y.

These rules are sound and complete for unification as specified by the inference rules for the $\Vdash$ judgment, and, with some additional control structure, can be guaranteed to terminate. We will not formulate these theorems here, as our real interest is in the generalization of this idea to the LF type theory.

A unification logic for LF

LF poses two new problems over the first-order setting discussed above: the presence of types and a non-trivial notion of equality between terms. In the specification of the unification logic, this is a rather simple change: in order to prove an equality, we have to show that the terms are $\beta\eta$-convertible, and the rule for the existential quantifier must check that the substituted term is of the correct type. The generalized class of formulas is defined inductively by

$$F \ ::= \ M \doteq N \mid \top \mid F \wedge G \mid \exists x{:}A.F \mid \forall y{:}A.F$$

We will use M, N, A, B, as in LF, and F and G will again range over formulas. The generalization of the basic provability judgment $\Vdash$ now requires a context Γ assigning types to variables. As we will see later, the unification transformations do not need to deal with this context — it maintains its own notion of context and quantifier dependencies through universal and existential quantification. Throughout we make the simplifying assumption that all variable names bound by $\exists$, $\forall$, or λ in a formula are distinct. We can then say that y is *quantified outside* of x if the (unique) quantifier on x is in the scope of the quantifier on y. The defining inference rules for this unification logic exhibit the connection between the equality formula $M \doteq N$ and $\beta\eta$-convertibility ($M \equiv N$).

$$\frac{\Gamma \vdash M : A \qquad M \equiv N \qquad \Gamma \vdash N : A}{\Gamma \Vdash M \doteq N} \qquad \frac{\Gamma \vdash F \qquad \Gamma \vdash G}{\Gamma \Vdash F \wedge G}$$

$$\frac{\Gamma \Vdash [M/x]F \qquad \Gamma \vdash M : A}{\Gamma \Vdash \exists x{:}A.F} \qquad \frac{\Gamma, x{:}A \vdash F}{\Gamma \vdash \forall x{:}A.F} \qquad \frac{}{\Gamma \Vdash \top}$$

Substitution at the level of formulas must, of course, substitute into the types attached to the meta-quantifiers and, as before, rename variables when necessary.

A generalization of L_λ unification to LF

The general problem of higher-order unification is undecidable even for the second-order simply-typed λ-calculus with only one binary function constant [10]. This result notwithstanding, a complete pre-unification algorithm for the simply-typed λ-calculus with generally good operational behavior has been devised by Huet [15]. Extensions to LF have been developed independently by Elliott [5, 7] and Pym [27]. "Pre-unification" here refers to the fact that the algorithm will not enumerate unifiers, but simply reduce the original problem to a satisfiable set of constraints (so-called *flex-flex* pairs) whose unifiers are difficult to enumerate.

While this unification algorithm has proven quite useful in the context of automated theorem proving [1, 13], as the basis for a a logic programming language it has some drawbacks. In particular, the potentially high branching factor and the possibility of non-termination make it difficult to exploit the full power of Huet's algorithm in a safe and predictable way.

Observing the actual practice of programming, both in λProlog and Elf, it is noticable that almost all defensible uses of unification are deterministic. Based on this observation, Miller designed a syntactically restricted logic programming language L_λ [21] in which it is guaranteed that only deterministic unification problems arise during program execution. However, the restricted subset disallows important LF representation techniques. For example, the natural rule for universal elimination in an encoding of first-order logic (see [12])

$$\forall E : \Pi F{:}i \to o \, . \, \Pi x{:}i \, . \, true(\forall F) \to true(F\,x)$$

would not satisfy Miller's restriction (once generalized to LF), since the variable x (which is subject to instantiation during Elf search) appears in an argument to F, which is also subject to instantiation.

Thus, unlike Miller, we make no static restriction of the language. Unification problems which arise during Elf program execution and are not in the decidable subset are simply postponed as constraints. The disadvantage of this approach is that, unlike in Huet's algorithm, constraints cannot be guaranteed to have solutions. For example, given two distinct constants $c : i$ and $c' : i$, the formula $\exists x{:}i \rightarrow i \,.\, \exists z{:}i \,.\, x\,z \doteq c \land x\,z \doteq c'$ has no proof and none of the transformations we list are applicable, since the left-hand side of both equations, $x\,z$, is not in the form of a generalized variable (see below). On the other hand the formula $\exists x{:}i \rightarrow i \,.\, \exists z{:}i \,.\, x\,z \doteq c$ has many proofs, but no transitions are applicable either. We say that a formula from which no transformations apply is in *reduced form*.

In Elf the fact that reduced forms do not always have solutions has not shown itself to be a practical problem. On the contrary: some programs (such as a program for type reconstruction for the polymorphic λ-calculus) now show markedly improved performance and behavior.

We briefly review the ideas behind the unification in L_λ through some special cases. The central concept is that of a *generalized variable* which in turn depends on the notion of a *partial permutation*.

Given n and p, a *partial permutation* ϕ from n into p is an injective mapping from $\{1,\ldots,n\}$ into $\{1,\ldots,p\}$, that is, $\phi(i) = \phi(i')$ implies $i = i'$.

Assume we are considering a formula of the form

$$\exists x_1 \ldots \exists x_q \,.\, \forall y_1 \ldots \forall y_p \,.\, N \doteq M$$

(omitting types for the moment). In this special case, N will be a *generalized variable* or *Gvar* if it has the form $x_j\, y_{\phi(1)} \ldots y_{\phi(n)}$ for some partial permutation ϕ from n into p and $1 \le j \le q$. The following examples should provide some intuition about the way generalized variables are unified with terms. Restore the types of all universal variables as some base type, say i, and the remaining types so as to lead to well-typed equations at type i. Without formally defining substitutions, the annotations shown below should give an indication of the substitution term used for the existential variable in the proof of $\vdash F$, where F is the formula on the left.

(i) $\exists x.\forall y_1.\forall y_2 \,.\, x\, y_1\, y_2 \doteq y_1$ $[(\lambda u_1.\lambda u_2.u_1)\,/\,x]$

(ii) $\exists x.\forall y_1.\forall y_2 \,.\, x\, y_1\, y_2 \doteq g\, y_2$ $[(\lambda u_1.\lambda u_2.g\, u_2)\,/\,x]$

(iii) $\exists x.\forall y_1.\forall y_2.\forall y_3 \,.\, x\, y_2\, y_3\, y_1 \doteq x\, y_1\, y_3\, y_2$ $[(\lambda u_1.\lambda u_2.\lambda u_3.x'\, u_2)\,/\,x]$
where x' is a new existential variable.

(iv) $\exists x_1.\exists x_2.\forall y_1.\forall y_2.\forall y_3 \,.\, x_2\, y_3\, y_1 \doteq x_1\, y_2\, y_3$ $[(\lambda v_1.\lambda v_2.x_3\, v_2)\,/\,x_1]$
                                                              $[(\lambda u_1.\lambda u_2.x_3\, u_1)\,/\,x_2]$
where x_3 is a new existential variable.

The remaining are counterexamples to illustrate branching when restrictions on generalized variables are violated. Each of these have two most general solutions.

$$\forall y_1.\exists x \,.\, x \, y_1 \doteq y_1 \qquad [(\lambda u_1.u_1) \,/\, x]$$
$$\text{or} \quad [(\lambda u_1.y_1) \,/\, x]$$
$$\exists x.\forall y_1 \,.\, x \, y_1 \, y_1 \doteq y_1 \qquad [(\lambda u_1.\lambda u_2.u_1) \,/\, x]$$
$$\text{or} \quad [(\lambda u_1.\lambda u_2.u_2) \,/\, x]$$
$$\forall y.\exists x_1.\exists x_2 \,.\, x_1 \, x_2 \doteq y \qquad [(\lambda u_1.u_1) \,/\, x_1] \, [y \,/\, x_2]$$
$$\text{or} \quad [(\lambda u_1.y) \,/\, x_1]$$

Now we state the transformations, beginning with those common to L_λ and Elliott's algorithm and then introduce the notion of a generalized variable. We omit some types in the presentation below—they can be inferred easily from the context. As before, transformations may be applied at any subformula occurrence which matches the left-hand side.

$$\lambda x{:}A.M \doteq \lambda x{:}A.N \quad \longrightarrow \quad \forall x{:}A \,.\, M \doteq N \qquad \text{Lam-Lam}$$
$$\lambda x{:}A.M \doteq N \quad \longrightarrow \quad \forall x{:}A \,.\, M \doteq N \, x \qquad \text{Lam-Any}$$
$$M \doteq \lambda x{:}A.N \quad \longrightarrow \quad \forall x{:}A \,.\, M \, x \doteq N \qquad \text{Any-Lam}$$

$$(\lambda x{:}A.M_0) \, M_1 \, M_2 \ldots M_n \doteq N \quad \longrightarrow \quad ([M_1/x]M_0) \, M_2 \ldots M_n \doteq N$$
$$\text{Beta-Any}$$
$$M \doteq (\lambda x{:}A.N_0) \, N_1 \, N_2 \ldots N_n \quad \longrightarrow \quad M \doteq ([N_1/x]N_0) \, N_2 \ldots N_n$$
$$\text{Any-Beta}$$

$$c \, M_1 \ldots M_n \doteq c \, N_1 \ldots N_n \quad \longrightarrow \quad M_1 \doteq N_1 \wedge \ldots \wedge M_n \doteq N_n$$
$$\text{Const-Const}$$
$$\forall y.F[y \, M_1 \ldots M_n \doteq y \, N_1 \ldots N_n] \quad \longrightarrow \quad \forall y.F[M_1 \doteq N_1 \wedge \ldots \wedge M_n \doteq N_n]$$
$$\text{Uvar-Uvar}$$

$$\forall y.\exists x.F \quad \longrightarrow \quad \exists x.\forall y.F \qquad \text{Forall-Exists}$$
$$\exists y.\exists x.F \quad \longrightarrow \quad \exists x.\exists y.F \qquad \text{Exists-Exists}$$
$$F \wedge (\exists x.G) \quad \longrightarrow \quad \exists x.F \wedge G \qquad \text{And-Exists}$$
$$(\exists x.F) \wedge G \quad \longrightarrow \quad \exists x.F \wedge G \qquad \text{Exists-And}$$

Our assumption that no variable name is bound twice entails, for example, that x cannot be free in F in the And-Exists transformation. The term *Uvar* in the names of the rules stands for *universal variable*.

In first-order unification, unifying a variable x with itself or another variable is of course trivial—here possible arguments add complications. Huet [15] has shown for the simply-typed λ-calculus that such equations (Huet calls them *flex-flex*) can always be unified, but that enumeration of all unifiers of such problems is very undirected. This analysis has been extended to LF by Elliott [7]. Here some flexible-flexible pairs can be solved completely, but other unification problems for which Elliott's algorithm would have enumerated solutions or failed, will be postponed. Thus Huet's algorithm and extended L_λ unification as presented here are in some sense incomparable: each will postpone some equations as constraints which could have been solved by the other algorithm. In the eLP implementation of λProlog [6] a combination of the two algorithms is used.

The remaining transitions we consider have a left-hand side of the form

$$\exists x : \Pi u_1{:}A_1 \ldots \Pi u_n{:}A_n.A \ .$$
$$F[\forall y_1{:}A_1' \ . \ G_1[\ldots \forall y_p{:}A_p' \ . \ G_p[x \, y_{\phi(1)} \ldots y_{\phi(n)} \doteq M]\ldots]]$$

for some partial permutation ϕ from n into p. We refer to $x\,y_{\phi(1)} \ldots y_{\phi(n)}$ in the context above as a *generalized variable*. Depending on the form of M, we consider various subcases. For some of the transitions there is a symmetric one (M is on the left-hand side) which we will not state explicitly.

The formulation below does not carry along the substitutions made for existential variables, that is, instead of $\exists x.F \longrightarrow \exists x.x \doteq L \wedge [L/x]F$ the transitions have the form $\exists x.F \longrightarrow [L/x]F$. This simplifies the presentation and no essential properties are lost. The substitutions for the original variables can be recovered from the sequence of transformations.

Gvar-Const M has the form $c\,M_1 \ldots M_m$ for a constant c. In this case we perform an *imitation* [15]. Let

$$L = \lambda u_1{:}A_1 \ldots \lambda u_n{:}A_n \ . \ c\,(x_1 u_1 \ldots u_n)\ldots(x_m u_1 \ldots u_n)$$

and make the transition to

$$\exists x_1 : \Pi u_1{:}A_1 \ldots \Pi u_n{:}A_n.B_1' \ldots$$
$$\exists x_m : \Pi u_1{:}A_1 \ldots \Pi u_n{:}A_n.B_m' \ . \ [L/x]F$$

where $c : \Pi v_1{:}B_1 \ldots \Pi v_m{:}B_m.B$ and

$$B_j' = [x_{j-1}\,u_1 \ldots u_n/v_{j-1}]\ldots[x_1\,u_1 \ldots u_n/v_1]B_j.$$

Solution of example (ii) above would begin with this step.

Gvar-Uvar-Outside M has the form $y\,M_1 \ldots M_m$ for a y universally quantified outside of x. Here an analogous transition applies (replace c by y in Gvar-Const).

Gvar-Uvar-Inside M has the form $y_{\phi(i)}\,M_1 \ldots M_m$ for $1 \leq i \leq n$. In this case we perform a *projection* [15]. Let $L = \lambda u_1{:}A_1 \ldots \lambda u_n{:}A_n \ .$

$u_i (x_1 u_1 \ldots u_n) \ldots (x_m u_1 \ldots u_n)$ and then perform the same transition as in Gvar-Const where $B_1, \ldots, B_m$ and B are determined (up to conversion) by $A_i \equiv \Pi v_1 {:} B_1 \ldots \Pi v_m {:} B_m . B$.

The solution of example (i) above would be generated by this transformation.

Gvar-Identity M is identical to $x \, y_{\phi(1)} \ldots y_{\phi(n)}$. In this case we simply replace the equation by $\top$.

Gvar-Gvar-Same M has the form $x \, y_{\psi(1)} \ldots y_{\psi(n)}$. In this case, pick a partial permutation ρ satisfying $\phi(i) = \psi(i)$ iff there is a k such that $\rho(k) = \phi(i)$. Such a partial permutation ρ always exists and is unique up to a permutation: it simply collects those indices for which the corresponding argument positions in $x \, y_{\phi(1)} \ldots y_{\phi(n)}$ and $x \, y_{\psi(1)} \ldots y_{\psi(n)}$ are identical. Let $L = \lambda u_1 {:} A_1 \ldots \lambda u_n {:} A_n \, . \, x' \, u_{\rho(1)} \ldots u_{\rho(l)}$ and make the transition to

$$\exists x' : \Pi u_1 {:} A_{\rho(1)} \ldots \Pi u_l {:} A_{\rho(l)} \, . \, [L/x] F$$

Example (iii) above illustrates this case.

Gvar-Gvar-Diff M has the form $z \, y_{\psi(1)} \ldots y_{\psi(m)}$ for some existentially quantified variable z distinct from x and partial permutation ψ. In this case we only apply a transition if we have the following situation:

$$\exists z : \Pi v_1 {:} B_1 \ldots \Pi v_m {:} B_m . B \, . \, \exists x : \Pi u_1 {:} A_1 \ldots \Pi u_n {:} A_n . A \, .$$
$$F[\forall y_1 {:} A'_1 \, . \, G_1[\ldots \forall y_p {:} A'_p \, . \, G_p[x \, y_{\phi(1)} \ldots y_{\phi(n)} \doteq z \, y_{\psi(1)} \ldots y_{\psi(m)}]]]$$

for partial permutations ϕ and ψ, that is, the quantifiers and z and x are consecutive, with z outside of x.

In this case, pick two new partial permutations ϕ' and ψ' such that $\phi(i) = \psi(j)$ iff there is a k such that $\phi'(k) = i$ and $\psi'(k) = j$. ϕ' and ψ' always exist and are unique up to a permutation. Given such partial permutations, we define

$$L = \lambda u_1 {:} A_1 \ldots \lambda u_n {:} A_n . x' \, u_{\phi'(1)} \ldots u_{\phi'(l)}$$
$$L' = \lambda v_1 {:} B_1 \ldots \lambda v_m {:} B_m . x' \, v_{\psi'(1)} \ldots v_{\psi'(l)}$$

and transform the initial formula to

$$\exists x' : \Pi u_1 {:} A_{\phi'(1)} \ldots \Pi u_l {:} A_{\phi'(l)} \, . \, [L'/z][L/x] F$$

An example of this transformation is given by (iv) above.

The last case might seem overly restrictive, but one can use the quantifier exchange rules to transform an equation of two generalized variables into one where Gvar-Gvar-Diff applies. For example

$$\exists z.\forall y_1.\exists x.\forall y_2 \, . \, z\,y_1\,y_2 \doteq x\,y_2$$
$$\longrightarrow \quad \exists z.\exists x.\forall y_1.\forall y_2 \, . \, z\,y_1\,y_2 \doteq x\,y_2 \qquad \text{by Forall-Exists}$$
$$\longrightarrow \quad \exists x'.\forall y_1.\forall y_2 \, . \, (\lambda u_1.\lambda u_2 \, . \, x'\,u_2)\,y_1\,y_2 \doteq (\lambda v_1.x'\,v_1)\,y_2$$
$$\qquad\qquad\qquad\qquad\qquad\qquad\qquad \text{by Gvar-Gvar-Diff}$$
$$\longrightarrow^* \quad \exists x'.\forall y_1.\forall y_2 \, . \, x'\,y_2 \doteq x'\,y_2 \qquad \text{by Beta-Anys and Any-Beta}$$
$$\longrightarrow \quad \exists x'.\forall y_1.\forall y_2 \, . \, \top \qquad\qquad\quad \text{by Gvar-Identity}$$

If we make no restrictions, the transformations stated are not sound. Consider, for example, $\forall y{:}a.\exists x{:}b \, . \, x \doteq y$. This is clearly not provable, since y and x have different types. On the other hand, using Gvar-Uvar-Outside, we can make a transition to $\forall y{:}a.y \doteq y$ which is provable. In the case of the simply-typed λ-calculus, it is enough to require that any equation $M \doteq N$ in a formula is well-typed (both M and N have the same type in the appropriate context). Here, it is not possible to maintain such a strong invariant due to the dependent types. Instead, we maintain the rather technical invariant that F is *acceptable*. The Definitions 4.37 and 4.38 in [7] can be transcribed into this setting. Following the ideas of Elliott it is then possible to show that if $F \longrightarrow F'$ and F is acceptable, then F' is acceptable. Initially, acceptability is established by type-checking. Definition of these concepts and the proof of the soundness theorem below are beyond the scope of this paper.

Theorem (Soundness of Unification) *If F is acceptable, $F \longrightarrow F'$, and $\Gamma \vdash F'$ then $\Gamma \vdash F$.*

Precompleteness of the transformations for unification

The set of transformations given above is weak in the sense that many unification problems cannot be transformed, regardless of whether they have a solution or not (see the earlier examples).

On the other hand, there are some desirable properties of this restricted form of unification which can be stated once we have fixed an algorithm by imposing a control structure on the rules which explicitly allows for the possibility of failure (indicated by an additional atomic formula $\perp$ which has no proof). The resulting algorithm is deterministic (up to some equivalence, as in the case of first-order unification) and preserves provability, that is if $\Gamma \Vdash F$ and $F \Longrightarrow F'$ then $\Gamma \vdash F'$. Thus there is no branching in the unification algorithm, and logic program execution can never fail due to incompleteness in unification.

The basis for the more committed formulation of the transformation rules (written as $F \implies F'$) is formed by the transformations defining the $\longrightarrow$ relation. We restrict the quantifier exchange rules (they can lead to incompleteness and non-termination) as described below. We also add explicit rules for failure as shown below (assuming $c \neq c'$).

$$c\, M_1 \ldots M_n \doteq c'\, N_1 \ldots N_m \implies \bot \qquad \text{Const-Clash}$$
$$\forall y.F[\forall y'.F'[y\, M_1 \ldots M_n \doteq y'\, N_1 \ldots N_n] \implies \bot \qquad \text{Uvar-Clash}$$

There are also two circumstances under which unification of a generalized variable with a term must fail. Consider as examples:

$$\exists x.\forall y_1.\forall y_2 \,.\, x\, y_1 \doteq y_2$$
$$\exists x \,.\, x \doteq g\, x$$

Then, when unifying a generalized variable with a term (where the equation in question has the form $x\, y_{\phi(1)} \ldots y_{\phi(n)} \doteq M$) we may apply:

Gvar-Uvar-Depend M has the form $y_i\, M_1 \ldots M_m$ such that i is not in the range of ϕ. In this case we make a transition to $\bot$.

A variable x is said to *occur rigidly in* M iff *(i)* M is $x\, M_1 \ldots M_n$, or *(ii)* M is $c\, M_1 \ldots M_m$ or $y\, M_1 \ldots M_m$ for a universally quantified y, and x occurs rigidly in at least one M_j, or *(iii)* M is $\lambda u{:}A.M'$ and x occurs rigidly in A or M' (the definition of rigid occurrence in a type A is analogous). The next rule takes precedence over the Gvar-Const and Gvar-Uvar rules.

Occurs-Check The Gvar-Gvar-Same rule does not apply and x occurs rigidly in M. In this case we make the transition to $\bot$.

The final case to consider is the case where we unify two distinct generalized variables, but the condition on the transition Gvar-Gvar-Diff is not satisfied. In this case we pick the inner variable, say z and move its quantifier outwards using the quantifier exchange rules until the condition holds.

Theorem (Precompleteness of Unification) *If $\Gamma \Vdash F$ and $F \implies F'$ then $\Gamma \vdash F'$.*

A brief aside: in the implementation, the rules dealing with generalized variables are combined into a form of *generalized occurs-check* which performs three functions: the usual occurs-check along rigid paths [15], the dependency check, which also might lead to failure, and finally it generates constraints (equations which cannot be reduced further) from flexible subformulas which are not generalized variables.

If we also maintain an approximate well-typedness condition [5] we can show termination of unification. Approximate well-typedness is necessary in order to guarantee termination of successive applications of the β-reduction transformations. This is beyond the scope of this paper, but both approximate well-typing and occurs-check are realized in the implementation.

3 Adding proof search

Besides the basic notion of unification, the interpreter must be able to perform back-chaining search. This search is modelled after the behavior of ordinary logic programming interpreters, though there are a number of complicating factors. For example, due to the presence of constraints, back-chaining search through a program and unification cannot be completely decoupled. The other complication is that the logic program (represented as a signature) does not remain static, but changes during execution. In order to describe the form of search necessary here, we extend the unification logic introduced in the previous section to a logic expressive enough to describe the full state of the interpreter. The interpreter is then described in two steps analogous to our presentation of unification: first non-deterministic transformations are presented, and then a control structure is imposed.

A state logic for the interpreter

We add two new atomic formulas to the unification logic: $M \in A$ which represents the goal of finding an M of type A, and *immediate implication* $M \in A \gg N \in C$, where C must be atomic, that is, of the form $a\, M_1 \ldots M_n$ for a family a. The former is used to represent *goals*, the latter to describe *back-chaining*. Formulas now follow the grammar

$$F \quad ::= \quad M \doteq N \mid M \in A \mid N \in A \gg M \in C \mid \mathsf{T}$$
$$\mid F \wedge G \mid \exists x{:}A.F \mid \forall y{:}A.F$$

It may be possible to formulate this logic without the formulas of the form $M \in A$, since the existential quantifier is typed and thus also imposes a typing constraint (albeit only on existential variables, not arbitrary terms). Economizing the system along these lines would significantly complicate the description of the operational semantics of Elf, since typing information available to unification and typing information necessary for search are not separated.

The meaning of the two new kinds of formulas is defined by the following inference rules.

$$\frac{M \equiv M' \qquad C \equiv C'}{\Gamma \Vdash M \in C \gg M' \in C'} \qquad\qquad \frac{\Gamma \vdash M : A}{\Gamma \Vdash M \in A}$$

$$\frac{\Gamma \Vdash N\,N' \in [N'/x]B \gg M \in C \qquad \Gamma \Vdash N' \in A}{\Gamma \Vdash N \in \Pi x{:}A.B \gg M \in C}$$

The following lemma illustrates the significance of immediate implication and formulas of the form $M \in C$:

Lemma (Immediate Implication)

 1. *If* $\Gamma \vdash M \in A$ *then* $\Gamma \vdash M : A$.

 2. *If* $\Gamma \vdash M \in A$ *and* $\Gamma \Vdash M \in A \gg N \in C$ *then* $\Gamma \vdash N \in C$.

From the inference rule one can see that $(N \in \Pi x_1{:}A_1 \ldots x_n{:}A_n.C) \gg M \in C'$ iff there are appropriately typed terms $N_1, \ldots, N_n$ such that $[N_1/x_1] \ldots [N_n/x_n]C \equiv C'$ and $N\,N_1 \ldots N_n \equiv M$. If there are no dependencies and N is a constant c, we can think of C as "the head of the clause named c". Then we have that $c \in (A_1 \to \ldots \to A_n \to C) \gg M \in D$ iff $C \equiv D$ and, for proofs $N_i : A_i$, $M \equiv c\,N_1 \ldots N_n$. Now the relation to the back-chaining step in Prolog should become clear: the difference here is that we also have to maintain proof objects. Moreover, the implicit universal quantifier is replaced by Π, and conjunction in the body of a clause is replaced by nested implication. Thus, for example, the Prolog clause

    p(X) :- q(X,Y), r(X).

would be expressed as the constant declaration

$$c : \Pi x{:}i \,.\, \Pi y{:}i \,.\, r\,x \to q\,x\,y \to p\,x$$

where c can be thought of as the name of the clause, and i : Type is the type of first-order terms. In order to improve readibility of the clauses, we introduce the notation $B \leftarrow A$ to stand for $A \to B$. The $\leftarrow$ operator is right associative. Moreover, type reconstruction will add implicit quantifiers and their types, so in Elf's concrete syntax the clause above would actually be written as

    c : p X <- q X Y <- r X.

In this manner pure Prolog programs can be transcribed into Elf programs.

Transformations for proof search

The operational meaning of $M \in A$ and immediate implication is given by the following transformations (recall that C stands for an atomic type of the form $a N_1 \ldots N_n$ for some family a).

$$
\begin{aligned}
G_\Pi : &\quad M \in \Pi x{:}A.B &\longrightarrow&\quad \forall x{:}A . \exists y{:}B . y \doteq M x \wedge y \in B \\
G_{\text{Atom}}^1 : &\quad \forall x{:}A . F[M \in C] &\longrightarrow&\quad \forall x{:}A . F[x \in A \gg M \in C] \\
G_{\text{Atom}}^2 : &\quad M \in C &\longrightarrow&\quad c_0 \in A \gg M \in C \quad \text{for } c_0{:}A \text{ in } \Sigma.
\end{aligned}
$$

$$
\begin{aligned}
D_\Pi : &\quad N \in \Pi x{:}A.B \gg M \in C \\
&\quad\longrightarrow \exists x{:}A.(N\,x \in B \gg M \in C) \wedge x \in A \\
D_{\text{Atom}} : &\quad N \in a N_1 \ldots N_n \gg M \in a M_1\, ldots M_n \\
&\quad\longrightarrow N_1 \doteq M_1 \wedge \ldots \wedge N_n \doteq M_n \wedge N \doteq M
\end{aligned}
$$

The soundness theorem below is the crucial theorem in the context of logic programming. It has been argued elsewhere [22] that non-deterministic completeness is also an important criterion to consider. Here, completeness fails (even non-deterministically), due to the incompleteness of unification. On the other hand, there is an analogue to the precompleteness theorem for unification which is beyond the scope of this paper. But the practical importance of such (pre)completeness theorems is not clear: an early version of Elf as described in [25] based on Elliott's unification algorithm was non-deterministically complete, but in practice less useful than the version we describe here.

Theorem (Soundness of Search) *If F is acceptable, $F \longrightarrow F'$, and $\Gamma \Vdash F'$, then $\Gamma \vdash F$.*

Search control

What we have described so far could be considered a non-deterministic proof search procedure for LF. However, as the basis of a proof procedure it has some serious drawbacks, such as incompleteness of unification and a very high branching factor in search.

The transitions for unification and search we gave are more amenable to an interpretation as a method for *goal reduction*: rather than completely solve an original goal (given as a formula), we reduce it to another goal (also represented as a formula). In practice, the final reduced goal will often be in a solved form with obvious solutions.

To turn this view of the transformations as goal reductions into a useful programming language, we need mechanisms to control applications of the transformations. The basic ideas for the control mechanisms come from logic programming. This is in contrast to the approach taken in many current proof development systems where *tactics* and *tacticals* are used to describe when inference rules should be applied. Elf gives meta-programs a much more declarative flavor, and programs tend to be easier to read and have more predictable behavior than tactics. Moreover, tactics can easily be defined within Elf (similarly to Felty's formulation [8]). Finally, by programming directly in a language with dependent types, static typechecking can make stronger correctness guarantees than functional metalanguages without dependent types (such as ML, for example).

The way dependent types can be used to impose constraints on logic variables is one of the attractive features of Elf. This feature is missing if one follows the proposal by Felty & Miller [9] to interpret LF signatures in Hereditary Harrop logic. While their encoding is adequate on the declarative level, it is inadequate on the operational level, since typing constraints are expressed as predicates which are checked after the execution of a goal, thus potentially leading to much backtracking and generally undesirable operational behavior.

Open and closed type families

Since we now would like to think operationally, we speak of a formula in the state logic as a *goal*. The first control mechanism we introduce is to distinguish goals we would like to be fully solved from those we would like to postpone if possible. This is done by declaring families to be either *open* or *closed*. If a family a has been declared open, then any atomic type of the form $a M_1 \ldots M_n$ is defined to be open, if a family a has been declared closed, then any atomic type of the form above is also defined to be closed. Every family-level constant must be declared as open or closed, but the syntactic form of this declaration depends on Elf's module system whose design is still in progress, and thus we do not address such syntactic issues here.

Intuitively, if A is open, then a goal $\exists x{:}A.F[x \in A]$ should be postponed. Otherwise, the current context of x will be searched for entries which could construct a term of type A. The type of x then acts purely as a restriction on the instantiations for x which might be made by unification. Thus *open* and *closed* declarations function purely as search control declarations—they do not affect the soundness of the interpreter.

In most examples, types which classify syntactic entities will be declared as open. To illustrate this, consider the following simple signature.

$$nat \quad : \quad \mathsf{Type}$$
$$zero \quad : \quad nat$$
$$succ \quad : \quad nat \to nat$$

$$eqnat \quad : \quad nat \to nat \to \mathsf{Type}$$
$$refl \quad : \quad \Pi n{:}nat \,.\, eqnat\, n\, n$$

There are four possibilities of open/closed declarations. We consider each of them in turn. For the sake of brevity, we omit the types of the quantified variables.

1. If *nat* is open and *eqnat* closed, then the formula

$$\exists N.\exists M.\exists Q \,.\, N \in nat \wedge M \in nat \wedge Q \in eqnat\,(succ\,N)\,(\sqsubset tsucc\,M)$$

   will be reduced to $\exists N.N \in nat$ (with some added $\top$ conjuncts). During this transformation, the substitution for Q will be *refl N*. In the actual top-level interaction with Elf, the answer substitutions would be M = N and Q = refl N. This is the typical case and the desired behavior.

2. If *nat* and *eqnat* are both closed the goal above will be fully solved (transformed to a conjunction of $\top$'s). Both N and M are instantiated to *zero* for the first solution. Upon backtracking, N and M will be instantiated to *succ zero*, *etc.* The problem with this scheme of "eager" solution is that solving any free variable of type *nat* may be an overcommittment, leading to a potentially large amount of backtracking. In most applications it is better to leave types such as *nat* open—variables of such type will then only be instantiated by unification.

3. If *nat* and *eqnat* are both open, then the original goal is already in reduced form and no reductions will be applied. This may lead to very undesirable behavior. For example, the formula $\exists Q.Q \in eqnat\,zero\,(succ\,zero)$ is also in reduced form! What the interpreter establishes in such a case is that

   $$\lambda Q.Q \,:\, eqnat\,zero\,(succ\,zero) \to eqnat\,zero\,(succ\,zero)$$

   which is a valid LF typing judgment, given the signature above, but not very useful.

4. If *nat* is closed and *eqnat* is open, then the formula

$$\exists N.\exists M.\exists Q \; . \; Q \in eqnat \, N \, (succ \, M) \wedge N \in nat \wedge M \in nat$$

would be reduced with the substitution of *zero* for M and *zero* for N (Q remains uninstantiated). Upon backtracking, M will be increased to *succ zero*, etc. Clearly, this is very undesirable behavior, as there are no solutions to Q in most of these cases.

Depth-first search

In the spirit of logic programming, search is committed to be depth-first. The enables an efficient implementation without overly constraining the programmer. Of course, this means that search will be incomplete, and the programmer will have to take account of this when formulating programs. Let us make the point again: Elf is a *programming language* and not a theorem prover. Given a signature defining a logic, in Elf one will generally have to *program* a theorem prover—the signature alone will usually not be sufficient.

The operational semantics of Elf is given by imposing a control structure on the application of the transformation rules in the previous sections, that is, the transitions for unification and the transitions for search. The state of the interpreter is completely described by a formula G without free variables. The interpreter traverses this formula G from left to right until it encounters an atomic formula F. Depending on the structure of F, it takes one of the following actions.

1. If F has the form $M \in \Pi x{:}A.B$ the transformation G_Π is applied.

2. If F is of the form $M \in C$ for atomic and closed C, it applies G^1_{Atom} to the innermost quantifier $\forall x{:}A$ such that A is closed and $M \in C$ is in its scope. On backtracking, further universal quantifiers are considered (from the inside out). Finally the signature Σ is scanned from left to right, applying G^2_{Atom} to declarations $c_0 \in A$ for closed A. We backtrack when the entire signature has been scanned.

3. If F is an immediate implication, we apply rule D_Π if it matches. Finally we apply D_{Atom} if both atomic types begin with the same family-level constant. Otherwise we backtrack over previous choices.

4. If F is an equality not in reduced form, we repeatedly apply unification transformations to all of G until all equalities are in reduced form or unification fails. In the latter case we backtrack.

5. If F is $\top$, an equality in reduced form (no transformation applies), or $M \in C$ for open C, we pass over it, looking for the next atomic formula in G (still searching from left to right). Thus, equalities in reduced form are postponed as constraints which are reexamined whenever unification transitions are applied. If we have scanned all of G and none of cases 1 through 4 apply, the formula is in reduced form and we "succeed". In this case the problem of proving the initial formula has been reduced to proving the current formula (in the extended unification logic).

4 An extended example

We now illustrate Elf and its operation through an extended example. In order to closely match the implementation and describe some of its features, we use concrete syntax in these examples.

Elf concrete syntax

In the syntax, the level of kinds, families, and objects are not distinguished, but they can be determined by type reconstruction. We use *expression* to refer to an entity which may be from any of the three levels. In the last column we list the corresponding cases in the definition of LF in Section 1.

Expressions	e	::=	$\mid c \mid x$	a or c or x
			$\mid \{x{:}e\}e$	$\Pi x{:}A.B$ or $\Pi x{:}A.K$
			$\mid [x{:}e]e$	$\lambda x{:}A.M$ or $\lambda x{:}A.B$
			$\mid e\,e$	$A\,M$ or $M\,N$
			$\mid$ **type**	Type
			$\mid e \rightarrow e \mid e \leftarrow e$	
			$\mid \{x\}e \mid [x]e \mid \_ \mid e{:}e$	
			$\mid (e)$	
Signatures	*sig*	::=	*empty* $\mid c : e.$ *sig*	

Here c stands for a constant at the level of families or objects. **A** -> **B** and **B** <- **A** both stand for $A \rightarrow B$. The later is reminiscent of Prolog's "backwards" implication and improves the readability of some Elf programs. Type reconstruction fills in the omitted types in quantifications $\{x\}$ and abstractions $[x]$. Omitted expressions (indicated by an underscore $\_$) will also be filled in by type or term reconstruction, though in case of ambiguity a warning or error message results. Bound variables and constants in Elf can be either uppercase or lowercase, but free variables in a clause or query must be in uppercase (an undeclared, unbound lowercase identifier is flagged as an undeclared constant).

Because of the different roles of signature entries we sometimes refer to the declaration of a constant of closed type as a *clause*, and a constant of open type as a *constructor*.

Equality in the simply-typed λ-calculus

We begin with a representation of the simply typed λ-calculus ($\lambda^{\rightarrow}$) in LF. In this formulation, the types are "intrinsic" to the representation: we can only represent well-typed terms. tp is the syntactic category of types of $\lambda^{\rightarrow}$. We include a single base type tp and the **arrow** type constructor to form function types. Both families are *open*: they will only be instantiated via unification, not through a search of the signature.

```
tp    : type.
arrow : tp -> tp -> tp.
nat   : tp.
```

The representation of a *term* of $\lambda^{\rightarrow}$ is indexed by its type. The constructors of terms represent 0, successor, λ-abstraction, and application. In order to obtain the maximal benefits of the expressiveness of the metalanguage (LF), the variables of the object language $\lambda^{\rightarrow}$ are represented as variables in the metalanguage.

```
term : tp -> type.
z    : term nat.
s    : term (arrow nat nat).
lam  : (term A -> term B) -> term (arrow A B).
app  : term (arrow A B) -> term A -> term B.
```

Note the free variables A and B in the declaration for lam. In a pure LF signature, one would have to specify

$$lam : \Pi A{:}tp.\Pi B{:}tp \, . \, (term(A) \rightarrow term(B)) \rightarrow term(arrow\, A\, B).$$

In Elf, the quantifiers on A and B are inferred, including the type of the variables. The omitted quantifier also has another role: wherever lam is encountered subsequently it is replaced by lam _ _, where _ stands for an (LF) object or type to be reconstructed.

In this representation, the simply-typed term $(\lambda x{:}nat \rightarrow nat.x)\, z$ is encoded as the following term:

```
app nat nat (lam nat nat [x:term nat] x) z.
```

In concrete syntax this will be accepted and printed as

```
app (lam [x] x) z.
```

The next part of the signature defines $\beta\eta$-equality between terms in $\lambda^{\rightarrow}$. Before showing it, we give the usual two-dimensional representation of three of the inference rules which are discussed below.

$$\frac{}{(\lambda x{:}A.M)\,N \approx [N/x]M}\,\beta \qquad \frac{}{(\lambda x{:}A.M\,x) \approx M}\,\eta$$

$$\frac{M \approx M'}{\lambda x{:}A.M \approx \lambda x{:}A.M'}\,\lambda$$

with the proviso that x is not free in M in the η-rule. The equiv judgment is declared as *closed*, since we hardly would want to accept free variables ranging over equivalence proofs in an answer to a query. On the other hand the signature below should never be used for search, as it very quickly gets into infinite loops. In the implementation this is handled by allowing the programmer to specify which signatures will be used in search. The concrete syntax for these language features are likely to change in the near future as the design of the module system for Elf matures, and thus not described here.

```
equiv : term A -> term A -> type.

e_beta : equiv (app (lam M) N)     (M N).
e_eta  : equiv (lam [x] (app M x)) M.

e_app : equiv (app M N) (app M' N')
           <- equiv M M' <- equiv N N'.
e_lam : equiv (lam M)     (lam M')
           <- {x} equiv (M x) (M' x).

e_refl  : equiv M M.
e_sym   : equiv M N <- equiv N M.
e_trans : equiv M N <- equiv M R <- equiv R N.
```

A number of common techniques are illustrated in this signature. The formulation of the β-rule takes advantage of LF-level application in order to represent substitution. The usual side-condition on η-conversion is also implicit: the quantifier on M (which we omitted) is on the outside. If we tried to instantiate this quantifier with a term containing x free, substitution would actually rename the bound variable x in order to avoid a name clash. The rule e_lam illustrates the way we descend into abstractions by using the LF-level context.

This signature is never used for search, only for type-checking purposes. One can easily see why: depth-first search using this signature, or any other naive control structure will almost inevitably lead to non-termination. Instead we take the approach of explicitly giving an *algorithmic* formulation of equivalence in terms of a signature which *can* be used for search. The soundness of the algorithmic formulation with respect to the definition can then also be expressed in Elf (see later in this section).

An algorithmic formulation

The algorithmic version of equality requires three separate judgments: M and N are equal at type A (the main judgment), M weakly head reduces to N, and M and N have the same head and equal arguments. All three judgments are declared to be *closed*.

We begin with weak head reduction, whr. As an inference system, the above might have been written as

$$\frac{}{(\lambda x{:}A.M)\,N \longrightarrow_{\text{whr}} [N/x]M}\ \text{redex} \qquad \frac{M \longrightarrow_{\text{whr}} M'}{M\,N \longrightarrow_{\text{whr}} M'\,N}\ \text{left}$$

The Elf formulation is not much more verbose than the formulation through inference rules. Moreover, it expresses and verifies directly that weak head reduction relates terms of the same type! The possibility of statically verifying this property during type reconstruction stems from the use of dependent types in the declaration of whr: we explicitly state that both arguments to whr have the same type A (in $\lambda^{\rightarrow}$).

```
whr : term A -> term A -> type.

whr_redex : whr (app (lam M) N) (M N).
whr_left  : whr (app M N)       (app M' N) <- whr M M'.
```

Next we introduce the main judgments, eq and eq', which are mutually recursive. eq reduces equality at function types to equality at base type by using extensionality, and eq' checks whether two terms have the same head and correspondingly eq arguments. The type argument to eq is made explicit, since the program unifies against this type. This is only a stylistic decision: if the explicit quantifier over A were omitted, we could, for example, formulate the rule eq_base as eq (M:nat) N <- eq' M N.

```
eq   : {A:tp} term A -> term A -> type.
eq'  : term A -> term A -> type.


eq_arrow : eq (arrow A B) M N
                <- ({x:term A} eq' x x
                                -> eq B (app M x) (app N x)).

eq_base : eq nat M N <- eq' M N.

eq_whrl : eq nat M N <- whr M M' <- eq nat M' N.
eq_whrr : eq nat M N <- whr N N' <- eq nat M N'.

eq'_z   : eq' z z.
eq'_s   : eq' s s.
eq'_app : eq' (app M N) (app M' N')
                <- eq' M M' <- eq _ N N'.
```

From the formulation of the inference rules for `eq'` it may seem that there is no case for variables. However, when a variable is added to the context (in the right-hand side of the `eq_arrow` rule), we also add to the context a proof that this variable is equal (`eq'`) to itself—another common programming technique in Elf.

The use of _ in the last clause indicates that the omitted type should be inferrable from the context. We have no explicit name for the type here, since it appears only in the synthesized and thus suppressed arguments to `eq'` and app. We could have easily created such a name through an explicit type annotation, as in

```
eq'_app : eq' (app M (N:term A)) (app M' N')
                <- eq' M M' <- eq A N N'.
```

To see the practical utility of implicit syntax and implicit quantification as realized in Elf, consider the explicit version of the `eq'_app` rule:

```
eq'_app : {A:tp} {N:term A} {N':term A} {A':tp}
             {M:term (arrow A A')} {M':term (arrow A A')}
                eq A N N' -> eq' (arrow A A') M M'
                    -> eq' A' (app A A' M N) (app A A' M' N').
```

In particular deductions where the 6 implicit arguments are shown are completely unreadable.

Here is a sample query as given to the interactive top-level loop of Elf which is modeled after Prolog.

```
?- eq A (app (lam [x] x) s) M.

M <- s ,
A <- arrow nat nat .

Query <- eq_arrow ([x:term nat] [p:eq' x x] eq_whrl
              (eq_base (eq'_app (eq_base p) eq'_s))
              (whr_left whr_redex)) .
```

Here the substitution for A is determined during type reconstruction, the substitutions for M and Query are constructed by search and unification.

Soundness of the algorithmic formulation

We would now like to show that the program for eq given above is sound with respect to the definition of equiv—so far we have made no formal connection. The most immediate one is to interpret whr, eq, and eq' all as establishing equivalence between two terms, and then show that the rules for those judgments are derived rules. In an extension of Elf currently under development this interpretation will be in the form of a functor (in the terminology of the Standard ML module system). Here we simply show the definitions as they might appear in the body of such a functor.

```
def whr = equiv.

def whr_redex = e_beta.
def whr_left P = e_app e_refl P.

def eq A = equiv.
def eq'  = equiv.

def eq_arrow P = e_trans (e_trans e_eta (e_lam P))
                          (e_sym e_eta).
def eq_base P  = P.

def eq_whrl Q P = e_trans P Q.
def eq_whrr Q P = e_trans (e_sym Q) P.

def eq'_z        = e_refl.
def eq'_s        = e_refl.
def eq'_app Q P = e_app P Q.
```

The fact that these definitions are type-correct is enough to guarantee the soundness of our algorithm for deciding equality for $\lambda^{\rightarrow}$, since it allows

us to interpret the "trace" (algorithmic deduction) of eq A M N as a proof
of equiv M N. Of course, such a direct interpretation will not always be
possible. This is because the LF type theory has no recursion operator, as
the addition of operators for recursion would render many encodings as not
adequate. In such cases the soundness of an operational formulation can
only be expressed as a relation. In our example, the following signature
relates algorithmic deductions to proofs of equivalence.

```
treq  : eq A M N -> equiv M N -> type.
treq' : eq' M N -> equiv M N -> type.
trwhr : whr M N -> equiv M N -> type.


tr_redex  : trwhr whr_redex      e_beta.
tr_redexl : trwhr (whr_left Tr) (e_app e_refl P)
                   <- trwhr Tr P.


tr_z   : treq' eq'_z e_refl.
tr_s   : treq' eq'_s e_refl.
tr_app : treq' (eq'_app Tr Tr') (e_app P P')
               <- treq Tr P <- treq' Tr' P'.


tr_base  : treq (eq_base Tr') P <- treq' Tr' P.
tr_arrow : treq (eq_arrow F)
                (e_trans (e_trans e_eta (e_lam P))
                         (e_sym e_eta))
                <- {x} {tr'} treq' tr' e_refl
                                -> treq (F x tr') (P x).


tr_whrl : treq (eq_whrl Tr TrW) (e_trans P Q)
               <- treq Tr P <- trwhr TrW Q.
tr_whrr : treq (eq_whrr Tr TrW) (e_trans (e_sym Q) P)
               <- treq Tr P <- trwhr TrW Q.
```

Thus while the method of direct interpretation allows a form of compile-
time soundness proof through the type checker, the second method requires that we explicitly transform a proof Tr of eq M N into a proof P of
equiv M N by calling treq Tr P. We are guaranteed that P is an equivalence proof for M and N only when this translation succeeds.

Type reconstruction for Elf

The method of type reconstruction for Elf is different from what is used
in LEGO [26] or the implementation of the Calculus of Constructions at

INRIA [16] in that (1) argument synthesis and type and term reconstruction are completely decoupled, and (2) there is no restriction on which types and terms can be omitted in the input. We only sketch the algorithm here.

If a constant declaration has implicit quantifiers, these arguments are assumed to be implicit and are inserted as underscores during parsing (see the earlier example). In the second phase, the type reconstruction algorithm performs unification as described in Section 2 augmented with straightforward transitions to deal with variables at the level of types. Underscores are converted into logic variables during this phase, and their value may depend on all bound variables it is in the scope of. At present, we do not attempt to infer types for undeclared constants, though underscores may be inserted in any place where a term or type would be legal.

Thus we presuppose no particular flow of information, except that the analysis is done one constant declaration at a time. This avoids some unnatural problems which sometimes arise in other systems. For example, in many synthesis algorithms polymorphic constants with no arguments (such as nil) or constructors with only implicit arguments (such as the inference rule e_beta in the example above) must be supplied with arguments, even though the context often determines unambiguously what these arguments should be.

This algorithm has surprisingly good operational behavior: it is very efficient, gives good error messages most of the time, and one rarely has to disambiguate by giving additional information. If a type has been reconstructed without any remaining constraints it is a principal type, since unification as described by the transitions in Section 2 does not branch. Moreover, type reconstruction will not fail if there is a valid typing, due to the precompleteness of unification. However, in some, in practice rare cases, constraints remain after type reconstruction. These may or may not be satisfiable and the programmer will be advised to further annotate his program.

Elf has no explicit way to specify that an argument should be synthesized, or to explicitly override synthesis. In the case where the latter would be necessary, one can use the general : operator to annotate arbitrary subexpressions and achieve the same effect as the | annotation provides in LEGO, though somewhat more verbosely.

5   Conclusion and future work

To summarize, we have presented the design and preliminary implementation of the logic programming language Elf based on the LF logical framework. As in classical first-order logic programming, Elf proof search is sound, but not complete with respect to a given LF signature. Unlike Prolog, the interpreter constructs proof terms during the solution of a query, and such proof terms can be used later. In this framework logic variables and goals are identified, a distinction which is replaced by a similar distinction between open and closed families—a distinction made purely for reasons of search control.

Dependent types and can be used as expressive constraints on logic variables. Moreover, dependent types can internally (through Elf type checking) give correctness guarantees which are not possible in a system with only simple types. Elf has been used to specify and write meta-programs in the domains of theorem proving, type checking and inference, natural semantics, program extraction and proof transformation. Some of these are partially verified internally.

The primary deficiencies of Elf as it currently stands are the lack of a module system (under development), the absence of notational definition and polymorphism (both of which are actually provided in the implementation, but for which the theoretical consequences have not been fully investigated), and the inefficiency of the implementation on large problems. We hope to address the latter through a number of improvements, such as dependency analysis to avoid redundant unification, elimination of the construction of proofs whenever it can be shown statically that they will be discarded, and the compilation of signatures to take advantage of indexing techniques and to optimize unification. In particular, the costly (generalized) occurs-check can be avoided in many cases without loss of soundness.

Finally, Elf lacks some control constructs such as cut (!), assert, var, etc. that are familiar from logic programming, and occasionally this presents some difficulties. Our basic design principle in extending the language has to be to preserve the declarative reading of a signature at all costs, that is, the operational behavior of a language extension will have to be sound with respect to its declarative interpretation (though usually incomplete). This is more or less forced, as Elf, unlike Prolog, will deliver *proofs*, not just substitutions. On the other hand, we try to be circumspect and only incorporate extensions which in some sense appear necessary. The addition of Σ-types (strong sums) as first envisioned in [25] has not been necessary as anticipated and has, for the moment at least, been abandoned.

It is possible, however, to include some search control operators in Elf programs without destroying the basic promise to deliver proofs for the original query. An example of such an operator is *once*, where we define that $\Gamma \vdash M : once A$ iff $\Gamma \vdash M : A$, though search for proofs of *once A* will behave differently from search for proofs of A (operationally, by delivering only the first proof M but deliver no more on backtracking). The theoretical and practical properties of such extensions have not yet been fully investigated.

Bibliography

[1] Andrews, P. B. (1989). On connections and higher-order logic. *Journal of Automated Reasoning*, 5:257–291.

[2] Avron, A., Honsell, F. A., and Mason, I. A. (1987). Using typed lambda calculus to implement formal systems on a machine. Technical Report ECS-LFCS-87-31, University of Edinburgh.

[3] Coquand, T. (1991). An algorithm for testing conversion in type theory. This volume.

[4] Dowek, G. (1991). A proof synthesis algorithm for a mathematical vernacular in a restriction of the Calculus of Constructions. Unpublished manuscript.

[5] Elliott, C. (1989). Higher-order unification with dependent types. In *Rewriting Techniques and Applications*, pages 121–136. Springer-Verlag LNCS 355.

[6] Elliott, C. and Pfenning, F. (1989). eLP: A Common Lisp implementation of λProlog in the Ergo Support System. Available via ftp over the Internet. Send mail to elp-request@cs.cmu.edu on the Internet for further information.

[7] Elliott, C. M. (1990). *Extensions and Applications of Higher-Order Unification*. PhD thesis, School of Computer Science, Carnegie Mellon University. Available as Technical Report CMU-CS-90-134.

[8] Felty, A. (1989). *Specifying and Implementing Theorem Provers in a Higher-Order Logic Programming Language*. PhD thesis, Department of Computer and Information Science, University of Pennsylvania.

[9] Felty, A. and Miller, D. (1990). Encoding a dependent-type λ-calculus in a logic programming language. In Stickel, M., editor, *10th International Conference on Automated Deduction, Kaiserslautern, Germany*, pages 221–235. Springer-Verlag LNCS 449.

[10] Goldfarb, W. D. (1981). The undecidability of the second-order unification problem. *Theoretical Computer Science*, 13:225–230.

[11] Gordon, M. J., Milner, R., and Wadsworth, C. P. (1979). *Edinburgh LCF*. Springer-Verlag LNCS 78.

[12] Harper, R., Honsell, F., and Plotkin, G. (1987). A framework for defining logics. In *Symposium on Logic in Computer Science*, pages 194–204. An extended and revised version is available as Technical Report CMU-CS-89-173, School of Computer Science, Carnegie Mellon University.

[13] Helmink, L. and Ahn, R. (1991). Goal directed proof construction in type theory. This volume.

[14] Howe, D. J. (1988). Computational metatheory in Nuprl. In Lusk, E. and Overbeek, R., editors, *9th International Conference on Automated Deduction, Argonne, Illinois*, pages 238–257. Springer-Verlag LNCS 310.

[15] Huet, G. (1975). A unification algorithm for typed λ-calculus. *Theoretical Computer Science*, 1:27–57.

[16] Huet, G. (1989). The calculus of constructions, documentation and user's guide. Rapport technique 110, INRIA, Rocquencourt, France.

[17] Jaffar, J. and Lassez, J.-L. (1987). Constraint logic programming. In *Proceedings of the Fourteenth Annual ACM Symposium on Principles of Programming Languages*, pages 111–119.

[18] Knoblock, T. B. and Constable, R. L. (1986). Formalized metareasoning in type theory. In *First Annual Symposium on Logic in Computer Science*, pages 237–248.

[19] Martelli, A. and Montanari, U. (1982). An efficient unification algorithm. *ACM Transactions on Programming Languages and Systems*, 4(2):258–282.

[20] Miller, D. (1990). Unification under a mixed prefix. *Journal of Symbolic Computation*. To appear.

[21] Miller, D. (1991). A logic programming language with lambda-abstraction, function variables, and simple unification. In Schroeder-Heister, P., editor, *Extensions of Logic Programming*, pages 253–281. Springer-Verlag LNCS 475.

[22] Miller, D., Nadathur, G., Pfenning, F., and Scedrov, A. (1988). Uniform proofs as a foundation for logic programming. *Journal of Pure and Applied Logic*. To appear.

[23] Nadathur, G. and Miller, D. (1988). An overview of λProlog. In Kowalski, R. A. and Bowen, K. A., editors, *Logic Programming: Proceedings of the Fifth International Conference and Symposium, Volume 1*, pages 810–827, Cambridge, Massachusetts. MIT Press.

[24] Paulson, L. C. and Nipkow, T. (1990). Isabelle tutorial and user's manual. Technical Report 189, Computer Laboratory, University of Cambridge.

[25] Pfenning, F. (1989). Elf: A language for logic definition and verified meta-programming. In *Fourth Annual Symposium on Logic in Computer Science*, pages 313–322.

[26] Pollack, R. (1990). Implicit syntax. Unpublished notes to a talk given at the First Workshop on Logical Frameworks in Antibes, May 1990.

[27] Pym, D. (1990). *Proofs, Search and Computation in General Logic*. PhD thesis, University of Edinburgh. Available as CST-69-90, also published as ECS-LFCS-90-125.

[28] Pym, D. and Wallen, L. (1990). Investigations into proof-search in a system of first-order dependent function types. In Stickel, M., editor, *10th International Conference on Automated Deduction, Kaiserslautern, Germany*, pages 236–250. Springer-Verlag LNCS 449.

[29] Salvesen, A. (1990). The Church-Rosser theorem for LF with $\beta\eta$-reduction. Unpublished notes to a talk given at the First Workshop on Logical Frameworks in Antibes, May 1990.

[30] Snyder, W. and Gallier, J. H. (1989). Higher-order unification revisited: Complete sets of transformations. *Journal of Symbolic Computation*, 8:101–140.

REPRESENTING FORMAL SYSTEMS

Operational semantics in a natural deduction setting[*]

Rod Burstall[†] Furio Honsell[‡]
University of Edinburgh University of Udine

June 15, 1990

Abstract

We show how Natural Deduction extended with two replacement operators can provide a framework for defining programming languages, a framework which is more expressive than the usual Operational Semantics presentation in that it permits hypothetical premises. This allows us to do without an explicit environment and store. Instead we use the hypothetical premises to make assumptions about the values of variables. We define the extended Natural Deduction logic using the Edinburgh Logical Framework.

1 Introduction

The Edinburgh Logical Framework (ELF) provides a formalism for defining Natural Deduction style logics [5]. Natural Deduction is rather more powerful than the notation which is commonly used to define programming

---

[*]Work partially supported by the UK SERC, by the Italian MPI 40% and 60% grants, by the Project Stimulation Lambda Calcul Type' and by the Basic Research Action project: Logical Frameworks.

[†]Dept of Computer Science, Edinburgh University, JCMB, King's Bdgs., Mayfield Rd., Edinburgh EH9 3JZ, U.K.

[‡]Dipartimento di Informatica, Universita di Udine, via Zanon 6, 33100- Udine, Italy

languages in "inference-style" Operational Semantics, following Plotkin [12] and others, for example Kahn [6] [§]. So one may ask

"Can a Natural Deduction style be used with advantage to define programming languages?".

We show here that, with a slight extension, it can, and hence that the ELF can be used as a formal meta-language for defining programming languages. However ELF employs the "judgements as types" paradigm and takes the form of a typed lambda calculus with dependent types. We do not need all this power here, and in this paper we present a slight extension of Natural Deduction as a semantic notation for programming language definition. This extension can itself be defined in ELF.

The inspiration for using a meta-logic for Natural Deduction proofs comes from Martin-Löf. Our work benefited from that of Mason [8] who did a proof system for Hoare logic in the ELF, encountering problems about the treatment of program variables. In particular he adopted the non-interference relation originally used by Reynolds [3]. The main feature of Natural Deduction proofs, used in our semantics but not used in the usual style of Operational Semantics, is that the premises of a rule may be hypothetical: they may themselves be of the form "Q is derivable from P_1 and ... and P_n". We write a premise of this form thus

$$
\begin{array}{c}
(P_1, \ldots, P_n) \\
\vdots \\
Q \\
\hline
R
\end{array}
$$

Using these techniques we are able to give an operational semantics which dispenses with the traditional notions of environment and store. This makes our semantic definitions and our proofs of evaluations appreciably simpler than the traditional ones. Our proofs are the same shape as the traditional ones, but each formula is simpler; the environment and store do not appear repeatedly in formulas as they do in the traditional system. We exploit in fact the structural rules inherent in Natural Deduction. Instead of environment and store we use the notions of expression with an attached substitution and evaluation of an expression after a command (compare Dynamic Logic). Instead of evaluating an expression M with respect to an environment we consider its value given some assumptions about the values

---

[§]Kahn uses the term "Natural Semantics", but this is different from "Natural Deduction style semantics" in our sense.

of the variables which occur in it. We discuss also an alternative approach in which commands evaluate to "partial stores".

The main technical difficulty is to define the necessary substitution operations; these play a crucial roles in our semantics. For instance we need to define substitutions of values for identifiers in expressions, declarations and commands. This is not a textual substitution; it depends on the binding operators in the language being defined. For example the meaning of $[m/x]M$ (substitute value m for identifier x in expression M of the programming language) is that when we come to evaluate M we assume the value of x to be m and ignore any previous assumptions about the value of x. To express this we use the hypothetical premises of Natural Deduction, with side conditions to ensure that we have a fresh variable. However we are not able to express substitution purely in a Natural Deduction logic. The difficulty can be reduced to substituting a (new) identifier for an (old) one. Thus we have to add a primitive operator for identifier replacement, just textual replacement, which we call α. (It is named from α conversion in lambda calculus.) We define this with a special rule schema. We also need an "dual" to a which we call $\underline{\alpha}$.

In using an editor or a programming language you probably learn from a "Users' Manual" and then, having got some experience, look up the fine points in a "Reference Manual". For our style of doing operational semantics the "Reference Manual" is a formal description in ELF. We try to provide also a less formal "Users' Manual" which describes the form of the semantic rules and the criteria for proofs utilizing a particular notation called alpha notation. Alpha notation will be described with about the degree of precision with which the rules of predicate logic might be defined in a text book. As usual we will give the Users' Manual first, asking the reader to suspend critical judgement while getting an intuitive feel for the style of semantics we propose.

We proceed in four steps.

- We define alpha notation: Natural Deduction extended with operators α and $\underline{\alpha}$ to replace variables.

- We use this notation to define the notion of an Evaluation System, by introducing evaluation predicates, $\Rightarrow$, and substitution operators, $[\ /\ ]$, obeying suitable rules.

- We use an evaluation system to define the semantic rules for a sample programming language which features lambda expressions, commands, exceptions, declarations, procedures and expressions with side effects.

- We give a formal definition of an Evaluation System in the Edinburgh Logical Framework.

In this last step we show the connection of our approach with the ELF treatment of logical languages. First we give a literal encoding of evaluation systems in ELF. We thus show how to put alpha notation on a firm foundation by explaining it in terms of higher order constructions. Finally we give an alternative encoding which does not mention alpha notation at all.

Comparison with the Edinburgh Logical Framework

Our original aim was to use the ELF as a definition medium for Programming Languages. We achieve this in the last step above. Our semantic rules can be written in ELF notation by mere transliteration. However the rules do not use all the power of the ELF except in defining the substitution operations. It seemed to us better to present Evaluation systems as a simpler framework for semantics. These do not need a higher order description of syntax and do not introduce involved judgements which use the dependent types structure of ELF. Instead they makes use of the primitive operators α and $\underline{\alpha}$. The semantic rules do not even mention α or $\underline{\alpha}$, once we have defined the appropriate substitution rules. In short:

ELF approach: If you understand lambda calculus with dependent types you can define many logics formally.

Evaluation systems approach: If you understand Natural Deduction with variable replacement you can define many programming languages formally.

In using evaluation systems we lose the ELF advantage of a built-in type checker for dependent types, so that we have to write a separate static semantics (not treated in this paper). Even in ELF we may have to write a static semantics, for example to handle phenomena such as the polymorphism in ML.

How this paper evolved

This work started while Furio Honsell was at Edinburgh University. An early version of this paper appeared as an invited paper in Proc. 8th Conf. on Foundations of Software Technology held in Pune (India) 1988 [1] and as an LFCS Report [2]. This is a revised and expanded version with some corrections. The main changes with respect to the earlier versions are (i) the rules for applying a closure or a primitive; (ii) the example proofs; (iii) removal of explicit equality in alpha notation; (iv) the rule of substitution uses $\underline{\alpha}$; (v) recursive function definition; (vi) rules for complex declarations; (vii) alternative rules for commands; (viii) expressions with side-effects; (ix) a concise ELF encoding which does not use α s nor $\underline{\alpha}$ s.

Since this first version of this paper appeared a lot of work has been carried out in the direction of representing operational semantics in a Logical Framework. In particular Hannan and Miller [9] discussed operational semantics for a purely functional language in λ-Prolog utilizing full-blown higher order syntax. C.-E. Ore [11] discussed a more efficient but perhaps less uniform encoding of our notion of Evaluation System in ELF and argued against the possibility of using Natural Deduction in reasoning about heaps.

Acknowledgements

We thank our colleagues at the Laboratory for Foundations of Computer Science for stimulating interaction. We would like to thank Randy Pollack who coded our semantics in his LEGO ELF [13] system and thereby brought to light two errors in our earlier version of the paper. Rod Burstall also thanks Butler Lampson of DEC SRC for experience gained in their joint work on the semantics of the Pebble language. Thanks to Claire Jones for kindly Texing this paper.

2   Definition of a framework for operational semantics

Alpha notation is about syntactic entities, namely identifiers and expressions. As we pointed out in the introduction, the main reason for introducing it is that of simplifying our framework. In particular using alpha notation we succeed in doing without a higher order representation of syntax and complex judgement constructions.

Alpha notation

Let Σ be a first order signature with two sorts, *Id* (identifiers) and *Expr* (expressions), some predicates P and some function symbols F, which include two distinguished function symbols α, $\underline{\alpha}$: *Id* $\times$ *Id* $\times$ *Expr* $\rightarrow$ *Expr* ; α denotes replacement of all occurrences of an identifier in a term by another identifier, whilst $\underline{\alpha}$ is "dual" to it.

We define Terms and (atomic) Formulas over the signature and variables as usual. Rules are defined as in Natural Deduction.

Alpha notation over a signature Σ with sorts Id and $Expr$ uses the distinguished function symbols α and $\underline{\alpha}$. These are subject to a set of rules $\mathbf{R} \cup \underline{\mathbf{R}}$ which we now define.

An element of $\mathbf{R}$ is a well formed instance of the following schema:

$$\frac{C[J]}{C[\alpha_{j/i} I]}$$

where $C[\ ]$ is any context (formula with a hole) and where J is the term obtained from the term I by replacing all occurrences of identifier i with j.

Thus to prove $\alpha_{j/i}(i+k) < 3$ we have to prove $j + k < 3$.

An element of $\underline{\mathbf{R}}$ is a well formed instance of the following schema:

$$\frac{C[J]}{C[\underline{\alpha}_{j/i} I]}$$

where $C[\ ]$ is any context (formula with a hole) and where I is the term obtained from the term J by replacing all occurrences of identifier j with i.

Thus if we have proved $i + j < 3$ we may conclude $\underline{\alpha}_{j/i}(i+i) < 3$. (We may reach the same conclusion from $i + i < 3$ or $j + i < 3$ or $j + j < 3$.) The reader may like to think of $\underline{\alpha}_{j/i}$ as dual to $\alpha_{i/j}$.

A proof in alpha notation is a natural deduction proof [14]. In explaining the set of rules $\mathbf{R} \cup \underline{\mathbf{R}}$ we appealed to the intuitive understanding of the phrase "replacing all occurrences of identifier j with i". In the appendix we will give a formal account of the notion of a proof in alpha notation in the Edinburgh Logical Framework. The main step will be to reflect in the system the notion of syntactic identity so as to make it possible to reason formally about what we use informally at this stage.

More generally a "many sorted alpha notation" has sorts $Id_{s_1}, \ldots, Id_{s_n}$ and $Expr_{t_1}, \ldots, Expr_{t_n}$, function symbols, $\alpha_{st}, \underline{\alpha}_{st} : Id_s \times Id_s \times Expr_t \to Expr_t$ and corresponding sets of rules.

Evaluation systems—1

We now use alpha notation to define evaluation systems. We consider first the case with two sorts Id (identifiers) and Expr (expressions). An evaluation system in alpha notation is a formal system which contains, in addition to the function symbols and the rules of alpha notation, at least two distinguished predicates, a distinguished function and certain rules which these obey. An evaluation system will contain also functions, predicates and rules specific to the object language it defines.

The distinguished predicates correspond to the notions of evaluation and value denoted $\Rightarrow$ over $Expr \times Expr$ (written infix) and $Value$ over $Expr$ respectively.

The distinguished functions are $expr$ (to convert Id to $Expr$) and substitution; denoted $expr : Id \rightarrow Expr$ and $[\quad / \quad] : Expr \times Id \times Expr \rightarrow Expr$ respectively.

For ease of reading we will usually omit the conversion function $expr$ hereafter, treating Id as a subsort of $Expr$.

We use the following symbols (possibly primed): x, y, z for identifiers; M, N, m, n, p for expressions.

There are two rules. The first rule is

$$(x' \Rightarrow n)$$
$$\vdots$$
$$\frac{value\ n \quad \alpha_{x'/x}M \Rightarrow \alpha_{x'/x}m}{[n/x]M \Rightarrow m} \quad x' \text{ is a new variable}$$

By "x' is a new variable" we mean that it does not occur in n, x, M and m nor does it occur in any assumption except those of the form $x' \Rightarrow n$; such assumptions are discharged by an application of this rule.

This rule is really no more complex than the usual rule for, say, existential elimination. The reason for this simplicity is our appeal to the intuitive understanding of the alpha operators. The ELF encoding of this rule, that we will give in the appendix, will be much more convoluted. In establishing the minor premise, three more assumptions will be allowed, all of which will be discharged by an application of the rule itself. The reason for this is due to the fact that, x' is a new variable, has to be reflected in the system itself in order to apply the formal versions of the rules governing the alpha operators. We will give also an encoding of evaluation systems with no formal counterpart for the alpha operators. The encoding of the substitution rule will then be even more complex. Hence there is a case for alpha operators even in the ELF encoding. They factorize a complex rule into more elementary ones.

The second rule is :-

$$\frac{value\ n}{n \Rightarrow n}.$$

The rule for substitution is the key definition. It encapsulates the way we handle object language variables. One of the virtues of the Natural Deduction framework used in evaluation systems is that it provides uniformity in handling scopes of variables, avoiding side conditions on rules. This is important in practice because handling variables is a traditional pitfall in defining logics or programming languages. Our approach is to define substitution in terms of evaluation. A naïve version of the substitution rule might have been:-

$$(x \Rightarrow n)$$

$$\vdots$$

$$\frac{value \; n \quad M \Rightarrow m}{[n/x]M \Rightarrow m}$$

but the evaluation of M in the hypothetical premise could make use not only of $x \Rightarrow n$, but also of any other statement about the value of x in the context in which the rule is used; we might be evaluating $[n/x]M$ in a context in which $x \Rightarrow n'$ and this should not affect the value. Thus we need to introduce a new variable x' local to the hypothetical premise. We have to replace x by x' in M in the right subproof. Just in case the resulting value m in the subproof contains an x' we have to replace the x' by an x (This will occur in our example language only for closures).

We will mostly use infix syntax for expressions, e.g. "let $x = M$ in N" for "let(x, M, N)". When we introduce a syntax for a particular object language in what follows this is to be understood as syntactic sugar.

Example proof

We now give a proof using alpha notation with the substitution rule above, constants 1,2,3, an operation + and three extra rules

$$\frac{M \Rightarrow 1 \quad N \Rightarrow 2}{M + N \Rightarrow 3} \qquad \frac{}{value \; 1} \qquad \frac{}{value \; 2}$$

We will show that $[1/x][2/y]x + y \Rightarrow 3$.

$$\frac{value \; 1 \quad \dfrac{value \; 2 \quad \dfrac{\dfrac{[x' \Rightarrow 1]_{(1)} \quad [y' \Rightarrow 2]_{(2)}}{x' + y' \Rightarrow 3}}{[2/y]x' + y \Rightarrow 3}(2) \; y'}{[1/x][2/y]x + y \Rightarrow 3}}{} (1) \; x'$$

The square brackets enclose hypotheses which are discharged at the level indicated by the subscript. The scope of a variable is shown by writing it at the end of the line below the scope.

We could write this proof more briefly omitting the applications of the α and $\underline{\alpha}$ rules. We may think of the α expression brought in by the substitution rule being immediately reduced. A proof editor could do this step automatically. We recommend this style of proof display. Introducing α and $\underline{\alpha}$ is a technical device for making the machinery of substitution explicit. They do not appear in the semantic rules once we have defined substitution, and they can well be omitted from the proofs.

$$
value\ 1 \cfrac{value\ 2 \cfrac{[x' \Rightarrow 1]_{(1)} \quad [y' \Rightarrow 2]_{(2)}}{x' + y' \Rightarrow 3}}{\cfrac{[2/y]x' + y \Rightarrow 3}{[1/x][2/y]x + y \Rightarrow 3}} \begin{array}{l} (2)\ y' \\[2mm] (1)\ x' \end{array}
$$

Evaluation systems — 2, The multisorted case

So far we have treated the case with one sort Id and one sort $Expr$, in a many sorted case these would be indexed families Id_s and $Expr_t$. We may define an evaluation system over a multi-sorted alpha notation with sorts Id_s and $Expr_t$ and possibly with more than one evaluation predicate, value predicate and substitution function. Thus we have

$$\alpha_{ij}, \underline{\alpha}_{ij} : Id_i \times Id_i \times Expr_j \rightarrow Expr_j$$

$$expr_{ik} : Id_i \rightarrow Expr_k$$

predicates $\Rightarrow_k$ over $Expr_k \times Expr_k$, $value_k$ over $Expr_k$ and

$$[\ \ /\ \ ]_{ikm} : Expr_k \times Id_i \times Expr_m \rightarrow Expr_m.$$

Corresponding to each substitution function an appropriate substitution rule schema is added, or even several rule schemas corresponding to different evaluation predicates. These schemas will always be of a similar pattern, often just polymorphic variants of the single-sorted case. We will not give a precise definition of these schemata here. Examples of multi sorted evaluation systems with more than one substitution operation and evaluation predicate will be found in the semantics for local variables in commands and for complex declarations.

Conventions for syntax

Here are some conventions which will be used in the rest of the paper.

We will mostly use infix syntax for expressions, e.g. "let $x = M$ in N" for "let(x, M, N)". When we introduce a syntax for a particular object language in what follows this is to be understood as syntactic sugar.

To extend the evaluation system signature $(Id, Expr, \Rightarrow, value, [\ \ /\ \ ])$ we will use the usual conventions of syntax. These allow us to introduce function symbols together with the infix notation for them. We will use the names allocated to schematic variables for the syntax classes. For example using x, y, z for identifiers; M, N, m, n, p for expressions. The syntax definition

$$M ::= K \mid \textbf{let } x = M \textbf{ in } N \mid \textbf{lambda } x.M$$

introduces the new function symbols K: *Expr*, let: *Id* × *Expr* × *Expr* → *Expr* and **lambda**: *Id* × *Expr* → *Expr*.

3 Example semantics

A basic functional language

In this section we will give the semantics for a simple functional language as a signature and a set of rules of an evaluation system.

Signature   We use the signature with sorts *Id* and *Expr*. We use the following symbols (possibly primed): x, y, z for identifiers; M, N, m, n, p, f, k for expressions and

$$M ::= 0 \mid succ \mid plus \mid Y \mid \ldots \mid MN \mid \textbf{let } x = M \textbf{ in } N \mid$$

$$\textbf{lambda } x.M \mid m.n$$

To be explicit, MN means $apply(M, N)$. We explain $m.n$ below.

We need a new unary predicate over expressions *closed M* — (informally) M has no free variables. When *closed M* appears in a correct proof there might occur free variables in the ordinary sense in M. But then, hypotheses of the form *closed x* for any such variable x must also appear in the proof. The evaluation of a let and the application of a lambda expression (assuming call by value) are formulated in terms of our substitution operation.

Since our language allows a lambda expression to appear as the result of evaluating an expression, we must ensure that it carries with it enough information about the values of its free variables to enable it to be applied in any context, so we use Landin's notion of "closure" (Landin [7]). Our Natural Deduction technique really corresponds to stack discipline and we cannot expect it to handle function values without some further device. We do not have an explicit environment, instead we give rules which successively bind the variables appearing in the body until the body is "closed". We have to define closed, essentially by induction on the syntax. This means that for each syntactic constructor (let , **lambda** and so on) we need not only a rule for ⇒ but also a rule for closed. The predicate closed conveys the binding nature of the operators; it really belongs to the static semantics.

We have to give rules for the application of closures and primitive functions to argument values. For this we introduce a new syntactic construct "*m.n*" for such applications with appropriate rules. These rules allow us to take a closure to pieces and apply its body in the correct context .

An illustrative proof follows the rules.

Evaluation rules

$$\frac{N \Rightarrow n \quad [n/x]M \Rightarrow m}{\text{let } x = N \text{ in } M \Rightarrow m}$$

$$\frac{M \Rightarrow m \quad N \Rightarrow n \quad m.n \Rightarrow p}{MN \Rightarrow p}$$

$$\frac{value \; n \quad [p/y](f.n) \Rightarrow m}{([p/y]f).n \Rightarrow m}$$

$$\frac{value \; n \quad [n/x]M \Rightarrow m}{(\textbf{lambda } x.M).n \Rightarrow m}$$

Example of "delta rules" for primitive functions :-

$$\frac{}{value \; 0}$$

$$\frac{}{value \; n} \qquad\qquad \frac{value \; m}{succ.n \Rightarrow succ.n}$$

$$\frac{}{value \; plus} \qquad\qquad \frac{value \; m}{plus.m \Rightarrow plus.m}$$

$$\frac{value \; n}{(plus.0).n \Rightarrow n} \qquad\qquad \frac{(plus.m).n \Rightarrow p}{(plus.(succ.m)).n \Rightarrow succ.p}$$

$$\frac{}{value \; Y}$$

$$\frac{value \; f}{Y.f \Rightarrow Y.f} \qquad\qquad \frac{(f.(Y.f)).m \Rightarrow n}{(Y.f).m \Rightarrow n}$$

Rules for evaluating lambda expressions to closures :-

$$(closed\ x)$$

$$\vdots$$

$$\frac{closed\ M}{\textbf{lambda } x.M \Rightarrow (\textbf{lambda } x.M)}$$

$$(closed\ y)$$

$$\vdots$$

$$\frac{y \Rightarrow p \quad \textbf{lambda } x.M \Rightarrow m}{\textbf{lambda } x.M \Rightarrow [p/y]m}$$

The reader might like to compare these with the usual treatment using an explicit environment, ρ. For example :

$$\frac{\rho \vdash N \Rightarrow n \quad \rho[n/x] \vdash M \Rightarrow m}{\rho \vdash \textbf{let } x = N \textbf{ in } M \Rightarrow m}$$

$$\frac{\rho \vdash M \Rightarrow m \quad \rho \vdash N \Rightarrow n \quad m.n \Rightarrow p}{\rho \vdash MN \Rightarrow p}$$

In the latter rule the environment is not used; it is simply passed down. This is implicit in our Natural Deduction formulation. We only mention the environment when it is used and therefore succeed in eliminating various redundancies.

Rules for closed

$$(closed\ x)$$

$$\vdots$$

$$\frac{closed\ n \quad closed\ M}{closed([n/x]M)}$$

$$\frac{}{closed\ 0}$$

and similarly for the other constants.

$$\frac{closed\ M \quad closed\ N}{closed(MN)}$$

$$\frac{closed\ m \quad closed\ n}{closed(m.n)}$$

$$\frac{(closed\ x)}{\vdots}$$

$$\frac{closed\ N \quad closed\ M}{closed(\text{let } x = N \text{ in } M)}$$

$$\frac{(closed\ x)}{\vdots}$$

$$\frac{closed\ M}{closed(\text{lambda } x.M)}$$

Rule for value

$$\frac{M \Rightarrow m}{value\ m}$$

Example of evaluation As an example of proofs using these rules we evaluate (**let** $y = 2$ **in lambda** $x.x + y$)1. We use two Lemmas, A and B, to simplify the layout. They are proved below. We will omit the proofs of such exciting facts as "*value 1*" and "$1 + 2 \Rightarrow 3$", and we use λ for **lambda** to save space.

$$\frac{2 \Rightarrow 2 \quad \dfrac{value\ 2 \quad \dfrac{\dfrac{[y' \Rightarrow 2]_{(1)}}{A}}{\lambda x.x + y' \Rightarrow [2/y'](\lambda x.x + y')}}{[2/y](\lambda x.x + y) \Rightarrow [2/y](\lambda x.x + y)}\ (1)}{\dfrac{\text{let } y = 2 \text{ in } \lambda x.x + y \Rightarrow [2/y](\lambda x.x + y) \quad 1 \Rightarrow 1 \quad \dfrac{B}{([2/y]\lambda x.x + y).1 \Rightarrow 3}}{(\text{let } y = 2 \text{ in } \lambda x.x + y)1 \Rightarrow 3}}$$

Lemma A Show that if $y' \Rightarrow 2$ then $(\lambda x.x + y') \Rightarrow [2/y'](\lambda x.x + y')$.

$$\frac{y' \Rightarrow 2 \quad \dfrac{\dfrac{[closed\ (y')]_{(4)} \quad [closed(x)]_{(5)}}{closed\ (x + y')}\ (5)}{\lambda x.x + y' \Rightarrow \lambda x.x + y'}}{\lambda x.x + y' \Rightarrow [2/y'](\lambda x.x + y')}\ (4)$$

Lemma B   Show $([2/y]\lambda x.x + y).1 \Rightarrow 3$.

$$\cfrac{value\ 1 \quad \cfrac{value\ 2 \quad \cfrac{value\ 1 \quad \cfrac{\cfrac{[x' \Rightarrow 1]_{(1)} \quad [y' \Rightarrow 2]_{(1)}}{x' + y'}}{(\lambda x.x + y').1 \Rightarrow 3}}{[2/y]((\lambda x.x + y).1) \Rightarrow 3}}{([2/y]\lambda x.x + y).1 \Rightarrow 3}}$$

Complex Declarations

This is the first example which necessitates multisorted alpha notation and multisorted evaluation systems. We now consider allowing **let** to be followed by a complex declaration, formed with "**and**" (parallel declarations) and "**;**" (sequential declarations). Such declarations will form a new syntax class and will need to have as values just the environments which we have otherwise succeeded in eliminating. This seems unavoidable for languages, such as Standard ML, which permit such a declaration feature. However these "environments" only appear as values (declaration values) and then consist only of the sublist of variables which are mentioned in the declaration.

Signature   We extend the previous signature as follows. We introduce a new *Expr*-like sort *Declaration* with a new evaluation predicate $\Rightarrow_d$, a new closure predicate $closed_d$ and a new substitution function

$$[\ /\ ]_d : Expr \times Id \times Declarations \rightarrow Declarations.$$

Since we use multisorted alpha notation we also have the functions

$$\alpha_d, \underline{\alpha}_d : Id \times Id \times Declarations \rightarrow Declarations.$$

We use the following symbols: R, S, r, s, t for declarations;

$$R ::= x = M \mid R \textbf{ and } S \mid R; S \mid \{r\}S \mid r@s$$

We generalise the syntax class *Expr*, introducing a new **let** and $\{\ \}$:

$$M ::= \textbf{let } R \textbf{ in } N \mid \{r\}M$$

The intended meaning of $\{r\}S$ is the declaration obtained from S by replacing the variables occurring in r with their corresponding values in r. Thus $\{r\}S$ is a generalisation of $[n/x]S$ to multiple substitution. Similarly for $\{r\}M$.

Finally we introduce the new rules for $\Rightarrow, \Rightarrow_d, closed$ and $closed_d$. It is worth while remarking that by having introduced declarations as an

Expr-like sort we do not have to explain how to evaluate expressions of the form $[n/x]S \Rightarrow_d s$, since the rule for this new sort of substitution follows from our earlier conventions. We will give it anyway, although it is just a polymorphic variant of the one we discussed for expressions, for the benefit of the reader.

We want a rule for substituting expressions for identifiers in declarations. The rule is

$$(x' \Rightarrow n)$$
$$\vdots$$
$$\frac{value\ n \quad \alpha_{x'/x}S \Rightarrow_d \underline{\alpha}_{x'/x}s}{[n/x]_d S \Rightarrow_d s} \quad x' \text{ is a new variable}$$

provided that x' is a new variable, that is it does not occur in any assumption except the ones on the top line nor in s, x, S, N and n. We will omit subscripts to predicates in the two following lists of rules.

Evaluation rules

$$\frac{M \Rightarrow m}{x = M \Rightarrow m/x}$$

$$\frac{R \Rightarrow r \quad S \Rightarrow s}{R \text{ and } S \Rightarrow r@s}$$

$$\frac{R \Rightarrow r \quad \{r\}S \Rightarrow s}{R\,;S \Rightarrow r@s}$$

$$\frac{[n/x]S \Rightarrow s}{\{n/x\}S \Rightarrow s}$$

$$\frac{\{r\}(\{t\}S) \Rightarrow s}{\{r@t\}S \Rightarrow s}$$

$$\frac{[n/x]M \Rightarrow m}{\{n/x\}M \Rightarrow m}$$

$$\frac{R \Rightarrow r \quad \{r\}M \Rightarrow m}{\text{let } R \text{ in } M \Rightarrow m}$$

$$\frac{\{r\}(\{s\}M) \Rightarrow m}{\{r@s\}M \Rightarrow m}$$

Rules for closed   (This is just a selection)

$$\frac{closed([n/x]M)}{closed(\{n/x\}M)}$$

$$\frac{R \Rightarrow r \quad closed(\{r\}M)}{closed(\text{let } R \text{ in } M)}$$

$$\frac{closed(\{r\}(\{s\}M))}{closed(\{r \text{ and } s\}M)}$$

An assignment language

We will now discuss the operational semantics of a language with imperative features. We will give two alternative signatures, both extending the one defined in the previous section, with a new kind of expressions $[C]M$, the intended meaning of this being "evaluate M after doing the command C". In the first signature we will introduce a new *Expr*-like sort *Command*. These commands do not have a value of their own and their effect appears only in relation to an expression. The second signature is more denotational in nature. It is suggested by the natural remark that there is no conceptual difference between a command and a complex declaration, both denote transformations of an environment. In this case we merely extend the class of declarations. This allows commands to have an explicit value. We will only sketch this signature.

Future concrete experiments may suggest comparative advantages and disadvantages of these two signatures.

A first signature   We extend the previous signature as follows. We introduce a new *Expr*-like sort *Command*. We do not need to introduce a new substitution function right now. We use the following symbols: C, D for commands;

$$C ::= x := M \mid C; D \mid \text{if } M \text{ do } C \mid \text{while } M \text{ do } C$$

We extend the syntax class M to be $M ::= [C]M$. As remarked earlier, the intended meaning of this new kind of expression is "evaluate M after doing the command C". For example if $x \neq y$ then $[x := 1; y := 2]x + y$ evaluates to 3. These expressions have no side effect. The use of $[\ ]$ for commands should not be confused with the notation for substitution. However there is a suggestive analogy. We introduce a new predicate over *Command*, *closed comm*(C), which we will write simply as $closed(C)$. Finally we introduce the new rules for $\Rightarrow$ and *closed*. As usual we omit subscripts.

Evaluation rules

$$\frac{M \Rightarrow m \quad [m/x]N \Rightarrow n}{[x := M]N \Rightarrow n}$$

$$\frac{[C]([D]M) \Rightarrow m}{[C; D]M \Rightarrow m}$$

$$\frac{N \Rightarrow true \quad [C]M \Rightarrow m}{[\mathbf{if}\ N\ \mathbf{do}\ C]M \Rightarrow m}$$

$$\frac{N \Rightarrow false \quad M \Rightarrow m}{[\mathbf{if}\ N\ \mathbf{do}\ C]M \Rightarrow m}$$

$$\frac{[\mathbf{if}\ N\ \mathbf{do}\ (C; \mathbf{while}\ N\ \mathbf{do}\ C)]M \Rightarrow m}{[\mathbf{while}\ N\ \mathbf{do}\ C]M \Rightarrow m}$$

Rules for closed

$$\frac{closed\ C \quad closed\ M}{closed\ [C]M}$$

$$\frac{closed\ M}{closed(x := M)}$$

$$\frac{closed\ C \quad closed\ D}{closed(C; D)}$$

$$\frac{closed\ N \quad closed\ C}{closed(\mathbf{if}\ N\ \mathbf{do}\ C)}$$

$$\frac{closed\ N \quad closed\ C}{closed(\mathbf{while}\ N\ \mathbf{do}\ C)}$$

An alternative signature   We do not extend the signature with a new *Expr*-like sort *Command* as we did before. We extend instead the *Expr*-like sort *Declarations*. We use the following symbols: S, R, C, D for complex declarations; and

$$S ::= x := M \mid C; D \mid \mathbf{if}\ M\ \mathbf{do}\ C \mid \mathbf{while}\ M\ \mathbf{do}\ C \mid [\ ]$$

The intended meaning of [ ] is the empty declaration. We extend the syntax class M to $M ::= [C]M$.

Evaluation rules

$$\frac{C \Rightarrow s \quad \{s\}M \Rightarrow m}{[C]M \Rightarrow m}$$

$$\frac{M \Rightarrow m}{[\ ]M \Rightarrow m}$$

$$\frac{M \Rightarrow true \quad C \Rightarrow s}{\textbf{if } M \textbf{ do } C \Rightarrow s}$$

$$\frac{M \Rightarrow false}{\textbf{if } M \textbf{ do } C \Rightarrow [\ ]}$$

$$\frac{\textbf{if } N \textbf{ do } (C; \textbf{while } N \textbf{ do } C) \Rightarrow s}{\textbf{while } N \textbf{ do } C \Rightarrow s}$$

Expressions with side effects

How can we extend the system to deal with expressions which may have side effects? Here are some tentative thoughts. In the above C had a side effect but with the given semantics for the functional language $[C]M$ had no side effects. Now let us change the semantics of the functional language to allow expressions, M, to have side effects. To accomplish this we adopt the following device: write $[M]N$ to mean the value of N after evaluating the expression M. Now for example $[M+N]P$ has the same value as $[M]([N]P)$ and $M + N \Rightarrow p$ if $M \Rightarrow m$ and $[M]N \Rightarrow n$ and $m + n \Rightarrow p$.

The revised semantic rules might be as follows. We do not give them all, just enough to illustrate the idea.

$$\frac{N \Rightarrow n}{[x]N \Rightarrow n}$$

$$\frac{N \Rightarrow n}{[0]N \Rightarrow n}$$

and similarly for the other constants.

$$\frac{N \Rightarrow n}{[\textbf{lambda } x.M]N \Rightarrow n}$$

The rule for evaluating an application becomes

$$\frac{M \Rightarrow m \quad [M]N \Rightarrow n \quad m.n \Rightarrow p}{MN \Rightarrow p}$$

$$\frac{P \Rightarrow p}{[m.n]P \Rightarrow p} \quad (m.n \text{ has no side effect})$$

$$\frac{[C]([M]N) \Rightarrow n}{[[C]M]N \Rightarrow n}$$

Exceptions

To handle exceptions we introduce a new basic syntax class *e*— exception names and a new ternary judgement, "$\_ \Rightarrow \_!\_$". $M \Rightarrow e!m$ — evaluating M produces an exception e with value m. The exception is raised by "raise" and the value m is caught by a "handle" clause (we follow the notation of Standard ML). The extension to the syntax is

$M ::=$ **raise** $e\ M \mid M$ **handle** $e\ x$ **in** N

The handle expression is the same as M if M evaluates normally or evaluates to an exception other than e; but if M evaluates to exception e with value m then the result is found by evaluating N with x bound to m.

Example:[¶]

    raise *help* $999 \Rightarrow$ it help !999

    1 **handle** *help* x **in** $x\ times10 \Rightarrow 1$

    $(1 + (\textbf{raise}\ \ help\ 999))$ h andle *help* x **in** $x \times 10 \Rightarrow 9990$

We need rules for **raise** and **handle**. We must also add rules to cope with the exception cases of application, let and other constructions above; we just give the rules for application as the others follow a similar pattern. We get a lot more rules, but the normal (non-exception) rules are unchanged. This makes it easier to understand the semantics; you can study the normal rules first. We do not discuss exception declarations but only global exceptions: **handle** does not bind exception names. Subscripts are omitted.

[¶] The italian reader can get an example with the same connotation by replacing the string 999 with 113 throughout the example

$$\frac{M \Rightarrow m}{\mathbf{raise}\ e\ M \Rightarrow e!m}$$

$$\frac{M \Rightarrow e!m}{MN \Rightarrow e!m}$$

$$\frac{M \Rightarrow m \quad N \Rightarrow n \quad m.n \Rightarrow e!p}{MN \Rightarrow e!p}$$

$$\frac{M \Rightarrow m \quad N \Rightarrow e!n}{MN \Rightarrow e!n}$$

$$\frac{M \Rightarrow m}{M\ \mathbf{handle}\ ex\ \mathbf{in}\ N \Rightarrow m}$$

$$\frac{M \Rightarrow e!m \quad [m/x]N \Rightarrow n}{M\ \mathbf{handle}\ ex\ \mathbf{in}\ N \Rightarrow n}$$

$$\frac{M \Rightarrow e!m \quad [m/x]N \Rightarrow e'!n}{M\ \mathbf{handle}\ ex\ \mathbf{in}\ N \Rightarrow e'!n}$$

$$\frac{M \Rightarrow e!m}{M\ \mathbf{handle}\ e'x\ \mathbf{in}\ N \Rightarrow e!m}$$

Since we have two different judgements for normal and exceptional evaluation, we have to duplicate some of the rules, even if these are conceptually very close. We have to keep in our signature e.g. both the second rule for application above and the corresponding normal evaluation rule, and both the first and last rule for **handle** above. The use of subsorts in the meta language would enable a more economical treatment here; we would then have subsorts of normal and exceptional values instead of two judgements, compare [4]. We lose the advantage that normal values can be treated without mentioning exceptions. The Standard ML semantics [10] is slightly informally presented but seems to implicitly use subsorts.

Recursive function definitions

Amongst the primitive operations defined above was Y, the fixed point operator. This gives us the ability to define recursive functions by applying Y to a functional. However we can define recursive definitions more directly by a "letrec" construction. This has an unwinding rule rather like the one for **while** , but a little more subtle. The new syntax, using f for function identifiers, is:

$$M ::= \text{letrec } f(x) = M \text{ in } N$$

The rules are

$$\frac{\text{let } f = (\text{lambda } x. \text{ } \text{letrec } f(x) = N \text{ in } M) \text{ in } M \Rightarrow p}{\text{letrec } f(x) = N \text{ in } M \Rightarrow p}$$

$$\frac{(\textit{closed } f \quad \textit{closed } x) \quad (\textit{closed } f) \\ \vdots \qquad\qquad \vdots \\ \textit{closed } N \qquad \textit{closed } M}{\textit{closed}(\text{letrec } f(x) = N \text{ in } M)}$$

Mysterious? Let us try an example. We will do it upside down.

letrec $f(x) = (\text{if } x = 0 \text{ then } 0 \text{ else } f(x-1)+1) \text{ in } f(1) \Rightarrow$?

let $f = \text{lambda } x.(\text{letrec } f(x) = (\text{if } x = 0 \text{ then } 0 \text{ else } f(x-1)+1) \text{ in } (\text{if } x = 0 \text{ then } 0 \text{ else } f(x-1)+1) \text{ in } f(1) \Rightarrow$?

$[1/x]$letrec $f(x) = (\text{if } x = 0 \text{ then } 0 \text{ else } f(x-1)+1) \text{ in } (\text{if } x = 0 \text{ then } 0 \text{ else } f(x-1)+1)(x) \Rightarrow$?

letrec $f(x) = (\text{if } x = 0 \text{ then } 0 \text{ else } f(x-1)+1) \text{ in } (\text{if } x = 0 \text{ then } 0 \text{ else } f(x-1)+1)(1) \Rightarrow$?

Local declarations and procedures with parameters

In this example we illustrate the semantics of a language with local variables in commands and with procedure declaration facilities. More precisely we discuss procedures with one parameter, passed by value, and possibly with local variables. We do not consider kinds of parameters other than value ones nor procedures as parameters. We do not address the issue of recursive procedures here. Also this example uses multisorted alpha notation. It is perhaps the most involved example so far. We need to introduce the new substitution function corresponding to the syntax class *Command* and hence the appropriate rule to manipulate it.

Signature We extend the signature of the assignment language as follows. We introduce a new substitution function, which enables us to take care of local variables, $[\quad / \quad]_{Comm}: Expr \times Id \times Command \rightarrow Expr$. Correspondingly we add the appropriate substitution rule (dropping subscripts).

$$(x' \Rightarrow m)$$
$$\vdots$$
$$\frac{\textit{value } n \quad [\alpha_{x'/x}C]N \Rightarrow \underline{\alpha}_{x'/x}n}{[[m/x]C]N \Rightarrow n} \qquad x' \text{ is a new variable}$$

provided that x' is a new variable, that is it does not occur in any assumption except the ones on the top line nor in m, x, C, N and n. We have in the background the function α_d: $Id \times Id \times Command \rightarrow Command$.

We introduce a new *Expr*-like sort *Procedures* and an *Id*-like sort *Procedure_names*, with a corresponding evaluation predicate $\Rightarrow_{proc}$. We use the following symbols: Q, h for *Procedures*; P for *Procedure_names*.

$$P ::= P_0 \mid \ldots \mid P_k$$

$$Q ::= \text{lambda } x.C$$

We generalise the syntax class *Command* to

$$C ::= \text{begin new } x = M \text{ in } D \text{ end } \mid \text{proc } P(x) = C \text{ in } D \mid P(M)$$

In giving the rules we will omit subscripts.

The mechanism for procedure call is given by $[P/h]_{Proc}C$, where we use a new substitution function $[\ /\ ]_{Proc}$: $Proc \times Id \times Command \rightarrow Expr$ for substituting procedures for procedure identifiers in commands. We omit the rule to which it obeys since it is similar to the one for $[m/x]C$. Finally we introduce the new rules for $\Rightarrow$ and *closed* . As usual we drop subscripts.

We do not introduce procedure closures which package up the values of the free variables in the procedure body. In fact, procedure values are never passed outside the context in which they are created, as happens for lambda expression values. However if a procedure application $P(e)$, occurs inside a lambda expression, when the corresponding closure is passed around $P(e)$ might be evaluated in an environment which has a different definition of P. So we ban such occurrences; to permit them we could presumably allow bindings for procedure variables in the closures of lambda expressions (an exercise for the reader).

Evaluation rules

$$\frac{M \Rightarrow m \quad [[m/x]C]N \Rightarrow n}{[\text{begin new } x = M; C \text{ end }]N \Rightarrow n}$$

$$\frac{[[\text{lambda } x.C/P]D]N \Rightarrow n}{[\text{proc } P(x) = C \text{ in } D]N \Rightarrow n}$$

$$\frac{P \Rightarrow \text{lambda } x.C \quad M \Rightarrow m \quad [[m/x]C]N \Rightarrow n}{[P(M)]N \Rightarrow n}$$

Rules for closed

$$(closed\,x)$$
$$\vdots$$

$$\frac{closed\ n \quad closed\ C}{closed([n/x]C)}$$

$$(closed\,x)$$
$$\vdots$$

$$\frac{closed\ M \quad closed\ C}{closed(\text{begin new } x = M; C \text{ end })}$$

$$\frac{closed\ [[\text{lambda } x.C/P]D]}{closed\ [\text{proc } P(x) = C \text{ in } D]}$$

$$\frac{closed\ M \quad closed\ N}{closed\ [P(M)]N}$$

$$(closed\,x)$$
$$\vdots$$

$$\frac{closed(C) \quad closed([D]N)}{closed([[\text{lambda } x.C/P]D]N)}$$

An alternative Signature Again we can explain local variables in commands and hence procedures by reducing them to complex declarations. First we introduce procedures and procedure names as before. Then we extend the syntax class of complex declarations as follows:

$$S ::= \textbf{begin new } x = M \textbf{ in } R \textbf{ end } \mid \textbf{proc } P(x) = R \textbf{ in } S$$

and add the rules

$$\frac{M \Rightarrow m \quad m/xS \Rightarrow s}{\textbf{begin new } x = M; S \textbf{ end } \Rightarrow s}$$

$$\frac{[\text{lambda } x.S/P]D \Rightarrow n}{\textbf{proc } P(x) = S \textbf{ in } D \Rightarrow n}$$

$$\frac{P \Longrightarrow \text{lambda } x.S \quad M \Rightarrow m \quad m/xS \Rightarrow s}{P(M) \Rightarrow s}$$

In this case we have just to introduce the substitution rule for procedures. Again it is a polymorphic variant of the one for declarations

4   Defining evaluation systems in the Edinburgh Logical Framework

In this section we outline two alternative definitions of an Evaluation System with a minimal signature in the Edinburgh Logical Framework. This is a signature which has two sorts *Id* and *Expr*, three function symbols α, $\underline{\alpha}$: *Id* → *Id* → *Expr* → *Expr*, and [/   ]: *Expr* → *Id* → *Expr* → *Expr* and two predicates *value* over *Expr* and ⇒ over *Expr* × *Expr*. The first encoding introduces explicit formal counterparts for the operators α, $\underline{\alpha}$ of alpha notation and therefore counts also as a rigorous explanation of such a notation. The second encoding does not have formal counterparts for α, $\underline{\alpha}$. Hence it illustrates how evaluation systems can be used without the need of alpha notation if one is willing to work with the full higher order power of ELF.

The first ELF signature for the minimal Evaluation System   In order to encode in ELF such an Evaluation System we proceed as follows. First of all we introduce an ELF type corresponding to the collection of sorts and a type constructor, *Term*, defined on sorts.

Sorts : *Type*

Term : *Sorts* → *Type*

Then we introduce constants corresponding to *Id* and *Expr* and two new constants. The first ⊃, is intended to denote the higher order sort constructor (written as an infix and bracketed to the right), while the second is intended to denote syntactic application.

Id : *Sorts*

Exp r: *Sorts*

⊃: *Sorts* → *Sorts* → *Sorts*

app: $\Pi_{s,t}$: *Sorts*.*Term* $(s \supset t)$ → *Term* (s) → *Term* (t)

Corresponding to a function in the signature we declare a constant of type *Term(s)* for the appropriate *s*, that is

$\alpha, \underline{\alpha}$: *Term* $(Id \supset$ it $Id \supset Expr \supset Expr)$

expr : *Term* $(Id \supset Expr)$

$$[\ / \ ]: Term \ (Expr \supset Id \supset Expr \supset Expr)$$

Corresponding to the class of formulae in the system we introduce an ELF type *Form* : *Type* . Corresponding to a predicate in the signature we introduce a functional constant with domain *Term(s)* for appropriate sorts s, that is

$$value : Term \ (Expr) \rightarrow Form$$

and

$$\Rightarrow: Term \ (Expr) \rightarrow Term \ (Expr) \rightarrow Form.$$

Finally we introduce a judgement forming operator, asserting the truth of formulae in the evaluation system

$$True : Form \ \rightarrow \ Type \ .$$

We now encode the rules for the replacement operators α and $\underline{\alpha}$. This is the most elaborate part. We have to introduce in the ELF signature a number of new predicates, new constants, new formula forming operators, and new rules governing the provability of these new formulae. More precisely we define

$$\in: \Pi_s: Sorts. Term(Id) \rightarrow Term(s) \rightarrow \ Type$$

$$\notin: \Pi_s: Sorts. Term(Id) \ \rightarrow \ Term(s) \rightarrow \ Type.$$

The judgement $x \in M$ says that the identifier x occurs in M, while $x \notin M$ says that it does not occur. To translate the rules of Alpha notation we introduce constants of the types which follow. (For ease of reading we will write rules using a somewhat more suggestive notation than the ELF Π and $\rightarrow$. We will use the notation τs instead of *Term(s)* and subscript arguments which are sorts to other functions).

$$\frac{x \in_s M}{x \in_t app_{st} N M} \quad s, t: Sorts \quad x: \tau Id \ \ M: \tau s \ \ N: \tau s \supset t$$

$$\frac{x \in_s \supset t N}{x \in_t app_{st} N M} \quad s, t: Sorts \quad x: \tau Id \ \ M: \tau s \ \ N: \tau s \supset t$$

$$\frac{x \notin_s M \quad x \notin_{s \supset t} N}{x \notin_t app_{st} N M} \quad s, t: Sorts \quad x: \tau Id \ \ M: \tau s \ \ N: \tau s \supset t$$

$$\frac{}{x \in_{Id} x} \quad x: \tau Id$$

$$\frac{y \notin_{Id} x}{x \notin_{Id} y} \quad x,y{:}\tau Id$$

$$\frac{}{x \notin_{Id \supset Expr \supset Expr \supset Expr} [\ /\ ]} \quad x{:}\tau Id$$

$$\frac{}{x \notin_{Id \supset Expr} expr} \quad x{:}\tau Id$$

$$\frac{}{x \notin_{Id \supset Id \supset Expr \supset Expr} \alpha} \quad x{:}\tau Id \text{ (and similarly for } \underline{\alpha})$$

When we come to add identifier constants to the signature, for each pair of distinct constants, i,j in *Term(Id)*, we will need a rule,

$$\frac{}{\notin_{Id} j}.$$

We are now ready to illustrate how to encode the set of rules about the α and $\underline{\alpha}$ operators in ELF. We introduce constants of the following ELF types.

$$\frac{x \notin_{Expr} F(y) \quad True(G(F(y)))}{True(G(\alpha_{y/x} F(x)))}$$

$$\frac{y \notin_{Expr} F(x) \quad True(G(F(y)))}{True(G(\underline{\alpha}_{y/x} F(x)))}$$

In both rules $F{:}\tau Id \rightarrow \tau Expr$, $G{:}\tau Expr \rightarrow Form$, and x, $y{:}\tau Id$. In the last rule we have omitted *app* before α and $\underline{\alpha}$ for ease of reading.

The translations of the first rule specific to evaluation systems in ELF is straightforward:

$$\frac{True(value\ (n))}{True(n \Rightarrow n)} \quad n{:}\tau Expr$$

The encoding of the substitution rule is instead quite a delicate matter. One has to reflect in the system the fact that the variable local to the minor premise is indeed different from any other variable in the system. This can be achieved using the higher order nature of ELF by allowing to establish the minor premise assuming appropriate rules which are then discharged by an application of the substitution rule itself. This is an interesting example of a second order rule, i.e. a rule with hypothetical rule assumptions. We omit the *Id* and *Expr* subscripts on $\in$; they are *Id* except before M or m.

$$\cfrac{True(value(n)) \quad \cfrac{True(x'\!\Rightarrow\! n) \quad \cfrac{w \in x}{w \notin x'}\; w{:}\tau Id \quad \cfrac{w \in M}{w \notin x'}\; w{:}\tau Id \quad \cfrac{w \in m}{w \notin x'}\; w{:}\tau Id}{True(\alpha_{x'/x}M \Rightarrow \underline{\alpha}_{x'/x}m)}\; \begin{array}{l} x'{:}\tau Id \\[2pt] x, M{:}\tau Id \\[2pt] m, n{:}\tau Id \end{array}}{True([x/n]M \Rightarrow m)}$$

In the last rule for ease of reading we have omitted *expr*, also *app* before α, $\underline{\alpha}$ and [/]. As one can see now, the main benefit of using directly alpha notation is that in the informal substitution rule the higher order syntactic notions $M, m{:}\tau Id \to Expr$ and the hypothetical rules premises do not appear.

This ELF signature can be easily extended to the case of multi-sorted Evaluation systems. Care has to be taken only in encoding hypothetical premises in the informal rules (e.g. substitution rules or rules for closed). One has to introduce hypothetical rule premises analogous to the ones in the rule above.

Another ELF signature for the minimal Evaluation System This signature is much the same as the one we defined above. We have all the constants we had in the previous signature but the ones which involve α $\underline{\alpha}$. In particular we have:

Sorts	:	*Type*
Term	:	*Sorts* → *Type*
Form	:	*Type*
True	:	*Form* → *Type*
Id	:	*Sorts*
Expr	:	*Sorts*
⊃	:	*Sorts* → *Sorts* → *Sorts*
app	:	$\Pi_{s,t}{:}\,Sorts.Term(s \supset t) \to Term(s) \to Term(t)$
expr	:	$Term(Id \supset Expr)$
[/]	:	$Term(Expr \supset Id \supset Expr \supset Expr)$
value	:	$Term(Expr) \to Form$
⇒	:	$Term(Expr) \to Term(Expr) \to Form$
∈	:	$\Pi_s{:}\,Sorts.Term\,(Id) \to Term\,(s) \to Type$
∉	:	$\Pi_s{:}\,Sorts.Term\,(Id) \to Term\,(s) \to Type$

$$\cfrac{x \in_s M}{x \in_t app_{st} N M}\quad s,t{:}Sorts,\, x{:}\tau Id,\, M{:}\tau s,\, N{:}\tau s \supset t$$

$$\frac{x \in_{s \supset t} N}{x \in_t app_{st} N M} \quad s,t: Sorts, x: \tau Id, M: \tau s, N: \tau s \supset t$$

$$\frac{x \notin_s M \quad x \notin_{s \supset t} N}{x \notin_t app_{st} N M} \quad s,t: Sorts, x: \tau Id, M: \tau s, N: \tau s \supset t$$

$$\frac{}{x \in_{Id} x} \quad x: \tau Id$$

$$\frac{y \notin_{Id} x}{x \notin_{Id} y} \quad x,y: \tau Id$$

$$\frac{}{x \notin_{Id \supset Expr \supset Expr \supset Expr} [\quad / \quad]} \quad x: \tau Id$$

$$\frac{}{x \notin_{Id \supset Expr} expr} \quad x: \tau Id$$

$$\frac{True(value(n))}{True(n \Rightarrow n)} \quad n: \tau Expr$$

The encoding of the substitution rule is much more involved. In order to get the same conclusion as before we need to have more premises. We omit the *Id* and *Expr* subscripts on $\in$; they are *Id* except before *M* or *m*.

$$\frac{True(value(n)) \quad x \notin M \quad x \notin m \quad \dfrac{\dfrac{w \in x}{w \notin x'} \; w:\tau Id \quad \dfrac{w \in M}{w \notin x'} \; w:\tau Id \quad \dfrac{w \in m}{w \notin x'} \; w:\tau Id \quad x':\tau Id \quad True(M(x') \Rightarrow m(x'))}{True([x/n]M(x) \Rightarrow m(x))}}{\begin{array}{l} x:\tau Id \\ n:\tau Expr \\ M,m:\tau Id \to Expr \end{array}}$$

As one can see now the main benefit of alpha operators in the ELF encoding is to reduce the number of premises in this rule.

5 Concluding remarks

We have shown how to define semantics of a simple but non-trivial language in our Natural Deduction style. We have not treated reference variables and data types, nor have we defined the type discipline by a static semantics. These remain to be investigated. Another area for exploration would be the application of the technique to defining logics. We would also like to consider program verification and transformation in this formalism. Although our system relies on the Edinburgh Logical Framework for a formal definition, it can be applied without explicit reference to ELF, basing it on Alpha notation.

Bibliography

[1] Rod Burstall and Furio Honsell. A natural deduction treatment of operational semantics. In *Proc. 8th Conf. on Foundations of Software Technology, Pune (India)*. Springer LNCS, 1988.

[2] Rod Burstall and Furio Honsell. A natural deduction treatment of operational semantics. LFCS, Comp. Sci. Dept., Edinburgh University, UK, 1989.

[3] Reynolds J. C. Syntactic control of interference. In *Proc. 5th Annual Symp. on Principles of Prog. Langs., Tucson,*. ACM, 1978.

[4] J.A. Goguen. Order Sorted Algebra. Technical Report 14, Computer Science Dept., University of Calif. at Los Angeles, US, 1978.

[5] Robert Harper, Furio Honsell, and Gordon Plotkin. A framework for defining logics. In *Proceedings of the Second Annual Conference on Logic in Computer Science, Cornell, USA*, 1987.

[6] Gilles Kahn. Natural semantics. Rapport de Recherche 601, INRIA, France, 1987.

[7] P.J. Landin. The mechanical evaluation of expressions. *Computer Journal*, 6, 1964.

[8] Ian Mason. Hoare's logic in the LF. Technical Report LFCS-87-32, Comp. Science Dept. Edinburgh University, UK, 1987.

[9] Hannan J and Miller D., Enriching a Meta-Language with Higher Order Features In Proceedings of the 1988 Workshop on Meta-Programming in Logic Programming, Bristol, UK.

[10] R. Milner. Notes on relational semantics, 1987.

[11] C.-E. Ore. On Natural Deduction Style Semantics, Environments and Stores Technical report, LFCS 89-88, Comp. Science Dept. Edinburgh University, UK, 1989.

[12] Gordon Plotkin. A structural approach to operational semantics. Technical Report DAIMI FN-19, Computer Science Department, Aarhus University, Denmark, 1981.

[13] Luo Z., Pollack R. A. and Taylor P. (1989), LEGO User Manual, LFCS, Dept. of Computer Science, Edinburgh University, UK.

[14] D. Prawitz. *Natural Deduction: A Proof-Theoretic study.* Almqvist & Wiksel, Stockholm, 1965.

Encoding Dependent Types in an Intuitionistic Logic

Amy Felty

INRIA Rocquencourt

Domaine de Voluceau

78153 Le Chesnay Cedex, France

Abstract

Various languages have been proposed as specification languages for representing a wide variety of logics. The development of typed λ-calculi has been one approach toward this goal. The *logical framework* (LF), a λ-calculus with dependent types is one example of such a language. A small subset of intuitionistic logic with quantification over the simply typed λ-calculus has also been proposed as a framework for specifying general logics. The logic of *hereditary Harrop* formulas with quantification at all non-predicate types, denoted here as hh^ω, is such a meta-logic. In this paper, we show how to translate specifications in LF into hh^ω specifications in a direct and natural way, so that correct typing in LF corresponds to intuitionistic provability in hh^ω. In addition, we demonstrate a direct correspondence between proofs in these two systems. The logic of hh^ω can be implemented using such logic programming techniques as providing operational interpretations to the connectives and implementing unification on λ-terms. As a result, relating these two languages makes it possible to provide direct implementations of proof checkers and theorem provers for logics specified in LF.

1   Introduction

The design of languages that can express a wide variety of logics has been the focus of much recent work. Such languages attempt to provide a general theory of inference systems that captures uniformities across different logics, so that they can be exploited in implementing theorem provers and proof systems. One approach to the design of such languages is the development of various typed λ-calculi. Examples that have been proposed include the AUTOMATH languages [4], type theories developed by Martin-Löf [16], the Logical Framework (LF) [10], and the Calculus of Constructions [3]. A second approach is the use of a simple intuitionistic logic as a meta-language for expressing a wide variety of logics. The Isabelle theorem prover [20] and the λProlog logic programming language [18] provide implementations of a common subset of intuitionistic logic, called hh^ω here, that can be used for this purpose.

In this paper, we will illustrate a strong correspondence between one language in the first category and a language in the second. In particular, we shall show how the Logical Framework (LF), a typed λ-calculus with dependent types, has essentially the same expressive power as hh^ω. We do so by showing how to translate LF typing judgments into hh^ω formulas such that correct typing in LF corresponds to intuitionistic provability in hh^ω.

Both Isabelle and λProlog can turn specifications of logics into proof checkers and theorem provers by making use of the unification of simply typed λ-terms and goal-directed, tactic-style search. Thus, besides answering the theoretical question about the precise relationship between these two meta-languages, this translation also describes how LF specifications of object logics can be implemented within such systems.

The translation we present here extends a translation given in [9]. As in that paper, we consider a form of LF such that all terms in derivable assertions are in *canonical* form, a notion which corresponds to $\beta\eta$-long normal form in the simply typed λ-calculus. In the translation given there, the form of proofs was also greatly limited. As we will illustrate, although we also restrict the form of terms here, we retain essentially the same power of provability as in LF as presented in [10]. As a result, theorem provers implemented from the hh^ω specifications obtained from this translation have a greater degree of flexibility.

In the next section, we provide some further motivation for establishing a formal relation between these two meta-languages. Then, in Section 3 we present LF, and in Section 4 we present the meta-logic hh^ω. Section 5 presents a translation of LF into hh^ω and Section 6 contains a proof of its correctness. Section 7 provides examples of this translation using an LF specification of natural deduction for first-order logic. Finally, Section 8 concludes.

2 Motivation

Our objectives in defining an encoding from LF into hh^ω are both theoretical and practical. On the theoretical side, we hope that by providing an alternate presentation of LF (via its encoding into a different formalism), we can provide some insight into the information contained in dependent types. In addition, we wish to formally establish the correspondence between two different approaches to specifying general logics. On the practical side, as already mentioned, we wish to provide an approach to implementing proof checkers and theorem provers for logics specified in these meta-languages. We address both of these concerns below.

Dependent Types as Formulas

A dependent type in LF has the structure $\Pi x : A.B$ where A and B are types and x is a variable of type A bound in this expression. The type B may contain occurrences of x. This structure represents a "functional type." If f is a function of this type, and N is a term of type A, then fN (f applied to N) has the type B where all occurrences of x are replaced by N, often written $[N/x]B$. Thus the argument type is A and the result type *depends* on the value input to the function. Another way to read such a type is as follows: "for any element x, if x has type A then fx has type B." This reading suggests a logical interpretation of such a type: "for any" suggests universal quantification while "if then" suggests implication. It is exactly this kind of "propositional content" of dependent types that will be made explicit by our encoding. When x does not occur in B, such a dependent type corresponds to the simple functional type $A \to B$. Note that the logical reading remains the same in this simpler case. For the case when x occurs in B, we can think of B as a predicate over x.

In the LF encoding of natural deduction for first-order logic, for example, first-order formulas are represented as LF terms of type *form* and a function *true* of type *form* $\to$ Type is defined which takes formulas into LF types. The constant *true* is used to encode the provability judgment of first-order logic: the type (*true* A) represents the statement "formula A is provable," and LF terms of this type are identified with natural deduction proofs for this formula. (This is an example of the LF "judgments as types" principle, similar to the "formulas as types" principle as in [14].) Via the encoding in hh^ω, we will view *true* as a predicate over first-order formulas. Proofs of the predicate (*true A*) in hh^ω can be identified with natural deduction proofs of *A*. Our results establish a very close connection between hh^ω proofs of such predicates and LF proofs of their corresponding typing judgments.

Implementing Goal Directed Search in Dependent-Type Calculi

In general, the search for terms inhabiting types in LF corresponds to object-level theorem proving. For example, searching for a term of type (*true C* ∧ *D*) corresponds to searching for a natural deduction proof of the conjunction *C* ∧ *D*. To find a term of this type we may use, for example, the following item which encodes the ∧-introduction rule for natural deduction.

$$\wedge\text{-I} : \Pi A : form.\Pi B : form.(true\ A) \to (true\ B) \to (true\ A \wedge B)$$

(We will say a type is "atomic" if it has no leading Π. We call the rightmost atomic type, (*true A* ∧ *B*) in this case, the "target" type. The types *form*, (*true A*), and (*true B*) are said to be "argument" types.) This type can be read: for any formulas *A* and *B*, if *A* is provable and *B* is provable, then the conjunction *A* ∧ *B* is provable. Thus, if *C* and *D* indeed have type *form*, and there exist terms *P* and *Q* inhabiting types (*true C*) and (*true D*), then (∧-I *C D P Q*) is a term of the desired type.

Consider the following general goal directed approach to the search for an inhabiting term of a given type. If the type is atomic, attempt to match it with the target type of an existing axiom or hypothesis. If there is a match, attempt to find inhabitants of each of the argument types. If the type is of the form Π*x* : *A.B*, add *x* : *A* as a new hypothesis, and attempt to find an inhabitant of *B*. It is exactly this kind of approach to search that we obtain via the translation. More specifically, our encoding will map each LF axiom such as the one above specifying the ∧-introduction rule to an hh^ω formula. With respect to a logic programming interpreter implementing hh^ω that will be described in Section 4, search using such translated LF axioms will correspond exactly to the above description of goal directed search in LF.

We will see that a set of hh^ω formulas obtained by translating an LF representation of an object logic can serve directly as a proof checker for that logic. In other words, a given hh^ω formula will be provable with respect to the depth-first interpreter implementing hh^ω described in Section 4 if and only if the corresponding LF typing judgment is provable in the LF type system. For theorem proving, or searching for a term inhabiting a type, more sophisticated control is necessary. In [7], it is shown that a theorem proving environment with tactic style search can be implemented in λProlog. The clauses obtained by the translation can serve as the basic operations to such a theorem prover. In fact, tactic theorem provers for many of the example LF specifications given in [1] have been implemented and tested in λProlog. Within such a tactic environment, more complex search strategies can be written from the basic operations. For example, for a theorem prover obtained by translating an LF specification of natural deduction, a simple tactic can be written that automates the application of introduction rules, performing all possible applications of such rules to a given input formula.

The hh^ω specification of natural deduction described in Section 7 obtained via translation is in fact quite similar to the direct specification given in [7]. Thus, the tactic theorem prover described in that paper is very similar in behavior to the one obtained via translation. One difference is that an alternate specification of the elimination rules is given in [7] such that goal-directed search in hh^ω corresponds to forward reasoning in natural deduction. Using this approach, it is possible to apply rules to existing hypotheses in a forward direction, a capability which is quite useful for theorem proving in natural deduction style systems. (See also [6] for more on this kind of reasoning in natural deduction and its correspondence to backward reasoning on the left in sequent style inference systems.) It is in fact straightforward to define an LF specification of natural deduction in first-order logic whose translation has the property that rules can be applied to hypotheses in a forward direction. Thus a goal directed strategy at the meta-level (LF or hh^ω) does not necessarily impose a goal directed strategy at the object-level.

3 The Logical Framework

There are three levels of terms in the LF type theory: objects (often called just terms), types and families of types, and kinds. We assume two given denumerable sets of variables, one for object-level variables and the other for type family-level variables. The syntax of LF is given by the following classes of objects.

$$K \;:=\; \mathsf{Type} \mid \Pi x\!:\!A.K$$
$$A \;:=\; x \mid \Pi x\!:\!A.B \mid \lambda x\!:\!A.B \mid AM$$
$$M \;:=\; x \mid \lambda x\!:\!A.M \mid MN$$
$$\Gamma \;:=\; \langle\rangle \mid \Gamma, x\!:\!K \mid \Gamma, x\!:\!A \mid \Gamma, A\!:\!K \mid \Gamma, M\!:\!A$$

Here M and N range over expressions for objects, A and B over types and families of types, K over kinds, x over variables, and Γ over contexts. The empty context is denoted by $\langle\rangle$. We will use P and Q to range over arbitrary objects, types, type families, or kinds. We write $A \to P$ for $\Pi x : A.P$ when x does not occur in type or kind P. We will say that a type or type family of the form $x N_1 \ldots N_n$ where $n \geq 0$ and x is a type family-level variable is a *flat type*.

Terms that differ only in the names of variables bound by λ or Π are identified. If x is an object-level variable and N is an object then $[N/x]$ denotes the operation of substituting N for all free occurrences of x, systematically changing bound variables in order to avoid variable capture. The expression $[N_1/x_1, \ldots, N_n/x_n]$ will denote the simultaneous substitution of the terms $N_1, \ldots, N_n$ for distinct variables $x_1, \ldots, x_n$, respectively.

The notion of β-conversion at the level of objects, types, type families, and kinds can be defined in the obvious way using the usual rule for β-reduction at the level of both objects and type families: $(\lambda x : A.P)N \to_\beta [N/x]P$ where P is either an object or type/type family. The relation of convertibility up to β is written as $=_\beta$. All well-typed LF terms are strongly normalizing [10]. We write P^β to denote the normal form of term P.

Let Q be a type or kind whose normal form is $\Pi x_1 : A_1 \ldots \Pi x_n : A_n.P$ where P is Type, a variable, or an application. We define the *order* of Q to be 0 if n is 0, and 1 greater than the maximum order of $A_1, \ldots, A_n$ otherwise.

We present a version of the LF proof system that constructs only terms in canonical form. Several definitions from [11] are required to establish this notion. We define the *arity* of a type or kind to be the number of Πs in the prefix of its normal form. The arity of a variable with respect to a context is the arity of its type in that context. The arity of a bound variable occurrence in a term is the arity of the type label attached to its binding occurrence. An occurrence of a variable x in a term is *fully applied* with respect to a context if it occurs in a subterm of the form $x M_1 \ldots M_n$, where n is the arity of x. A term P is *canonical* with respect to a context Γ if P is in β-normal form and every variable occurrence in P is fully applied with respect to Γ. A term P is *pre-canonical* if its β-normal form is canonical. Flat types $x N_1 \ldots N_n$ such that x is fully applied will be called *base types*.

The following four kinds of *assertions* are derivable in the LF type theory.

$$\vdash \Gamma \text{ context} \qquad (\Gamma \text{ is valid context})$$
$$\Gamma \vdash K \text{ kind} \qquad (K \text{ is a kind in } \Gamma)$$
$$\Gamma \vdash A : K \qquad (A \text{ has kind } K \text{ in } \Gamma)$$
$$\Gamma \vdash M : A \qquad (M \text{ has type } A \text{ in } \Gamma)$$

For the special form $\Gamma \vdash A :$ Type of the third type of assertion, we also say A is a type in Γ. For the latter three assertions, we say that K, A, or

$$\vdash \langle \rangle \text{ context} \quad \text{(EMPTY-CTX)}$$

$$\frac{\vdash \Gamma \text{ context} \qquad \Gamma \vdash K \text{ kind}}{\vdash \Gamma, x : K \text{ context}} \text{(FAM-INTRO)}$$

$$\frac{\vdash \Gamma \text{ context} \qquad \Gamma \vdash A : \text{Type}}{\vdash \Gamma, x : A \text{ context}} \text{(OBJ-INTRO)}$$

$$\frac{\vdash \Gamma \text{ context} \qquad \Gamma \vdash A : K}{\vdash \Gamma, A : K \text{ context}} \text{(FAM-LEMMA)}$$

$$\frac{\vdash \Gamma \text{ context} \qquad \Gamma \vdash M : A}{\vdash \Gamma, M : A \text{ context}} \text{(OBJ-LEMMA)}$$

$$\Gamma \vdash \text{Type kind} \quad \text{(TYPE-KIND)}$$

$$\frac{\Gamma \vdash A : \text{Type} \qquad \Gamma, x : A \vdash K \text{ kind}}{\Gamma \vdash \Pi x : A.K \text{ kind}} \text{(PI-KIND)}$$

$$\frac{\Gamma \vdash A : \text{Type} \qquad \Gamma, x : A \vdash B : \text{Type}}{\Gamma \vdash \Pi x : A.B : \text{Type}} \text{(PI-FAM)}$$

$$\frac{\Gamma \vdash A : \text{Type} \qquad \Gamma, x : A \vdash B : K}{\Gamma \vdash \lambda x : A.B : \Pi x : A.K} \text{(ABS-FAM)}$$

$$\frac{\Gamma \vdash A : \text{Type} \qquad \Gamma, x : A \vdash M : B}{\Gamma \vdash \lambda x : A.M : \Pi x : A.B} \text{(ABS-OBJ)}$$

Figure 1.1: LF contexts and abstraction rules

M, respectively, is a *well-typed term* in Γ. We write $\Gamma \vdash \alpha$ for an arbitrary assertion of one of these three forms, where α is called an LF *judgment*. In deriving an assertion of this form, we always assume that we start with a valid context Γ.

We extend the notation for substitution and β-normalization to contexts and judgments. We write $[N/x]\Gamma$ and $[N/x]\alpha$ to denote the substitution of N for x in all terms in context Γ and judgment α, respectively. Similarly, we write Γ^β and α^β to denote the context and judgment obtained by replacing every term in Γ and α, respectively, by their normal forms.

The inference rules of LF are given in Figures 1.1 and 1.2. The set of variables on the left of the colon in a context Γ is denoted as

$$B : \Pi x_1 : A_1 \ldots \Pi x_n : A_n.\mathsf{Type} \in \Gamma$$
$$\Gamma \vdash N_1 : A_1$$
$$\Gamma \vdash N_2 : ([N_1/x_1]A_2)^\beta$$
$$\vdots$$

$$\frac{\Gamma \vdash N_n : ([N_1/x_1, \ldots, N_{n-1}/x_{n-1}]A_n)^\beta}{\Gamma \vdash (BN_1 \ldots N_n)^\beta : \mathsf{Type}} \quad \text{(APP-FAM)}$$

$$M : \Pi x_1 : A_1 \ldots \Pi x_n : A_n.B \in \Gamma$$
$$\Gamma \vdash N_1 : A_1$$
$$\Gamma \vdash N_2 : ([N_1/x_1]A_2)^\beta$$
$$\vdots$$

$$\frac{\Gamma \vdash N_n : ([N_1/x_1, \ldots, N_{n-1}/x_{n-1}]A_n)^\beta}{\Gamma \vdash (MN_1 \ldots N_n)^\beta : ([N_1/x_1, \ldots, N_n/x_n]B)^\beta} \quad \text{(APP-OBJ)}$$

Figure 1.2: LF application rules

$\mathrm{dom}(\Gamma)$. In (FAM-INTRO), (OBJ-INTRO), (PI-KIND), (PI-FAM), (ABS-FAM), and (ABS-OBJ) in Figure 1.1, we assume that the variable x does not occur in Γ, and in (APP-FAM) and (APP-OBJ) in Figure 1.2, we assume that the variables $x_1, \ldots, x_n$ do not occur free in $N_1, \ldots, N_n$. Note that bound variables can always be renamed to meet these restrictions. In addition, in (APP-OBJ) B must be a base type. Note that when B is a base type, so is $([N_1/x_1, \ldots, N_n/x_n]B)^\beta$.

Items introduced into contexts by (FAM-LEMMA) or (OBJ-LEMMA) will be called *context lemmas*. The main differences between this presentation and the usual presentation of the LF type system are the appearance of such lemmas in contexts and the form of the (APP-FAM) and (APP-OBJ) rules. Here, in any derivation, all terms that are used on the left of an application must occur explicitly in the context.

We say that a context Γ is canonical (pre-canonical) if for every item $x : P$ in Γ where x is a variable, P is canonical (pre-canonical), and for every context lemma $P : Q$ in Γ, both P and Q are canonical (pre-canonical) with respect to Γ. We say that an assertion is canonical (pre-canonical) if the context is canonical (pre-canonical) and all terms in the judgment on the left of the turnstile are canonical (pre-canonical). In this presentation, all derivable assertions are canonical. To see why, first note that no new β-redexes are introduced in the conclusion of any rule. Second, consider the application rules. In the (APP-OBJ) or (APP-FAM) rule, if the term on the left of the application is a variable x, then it has arity

n and is applied in the conclusion to n terms and thus this occurrence of x is fully applied. Hence, as long as $N_1, \ldots, N_n$ are canonical, so is $xN_1 \ldots N_n$. If the term on the left of the application is a canonical term, then it has the form $\lambda x_1 : A_1 \ldots \lambda x_n : A_n.P$. The term in the conclusion has the form $((\lambda x_1 : A_1 \ldots \lambda x_n : A_n.P)N_1 \ldots N_n)^\beta$ which is equivalent to $([N_1/x_1, \ldots, N_n/x_n]P)^\beta$. The fact that this latter term is canonical follows from the fact that for any object, type, type family, or kind Q and any object N, if Q and N are canonical, then so is $([N/x]Q)^\beta$. For the same reason, the type $([N_1/x_1, \ldots, N_n/x_n]B)^\beta$ in the (APP-OBJ) rule is canonical.

In Appendix A, we show formally the correspondence between LF as presented in [10], which we call *full LF*, and LF as presented here, which we will call *canonical LF*. In full LF, terms in derivable judgments are not necessarily canonical or β-normal. For a provable assertion $\Gamma \vdash \alpha$ in full LF, we say that $\Gamma^\beta \vdash \alpha^\beta$ is its *normal form*. In Appendix A, we demonstrate that any derivation of a pre-canonical assertion in full LF can be mapped directly to a derivation in canonical LF of its normal form. Conversely, any derivation of $\Gamma \vdash \alpha$ in canonical LF has a corresponding derivation of a pre-canonical assertion in full LF whose normal form is $\Gamma \vdash \alpha$. It is important to emphasize that these results demonstrate not only a correspondence between what is provable in each system, but also a direct correspondence between derivations in each system. In other words, full LF restricted to pre-canonical terms is essentially the same system as canonical LF presented here.

It can now be seen how the goal directed strategy discussed in Section 2 can be applied to construct a proof of an LF assertion in this system. For example to find an object inhabiting an LF type, the (ABS-OBJ) rule is applied if the type has a leading Π, and the (APP-OBJ) rule is attempted if the type is atomic. In this case, goal directed proof corresponds to searching for a term in the context whose target type matches with the atomic type.

4 The Intuitionistic Logic hh^ω

The terms of the logic hh^ω are the simply typed λ-terms. Let S be a fixed, finite set of *primitive types*. We assume that the symbol o is always a member of S. Following Church [2], o is the type for propositions. The set of *types* is the smallest set of expressions that contains the primitive types and is closed under the construction of function types, denoted by the binary, infix symbol $\rightarrow$. The Greek letter τ is used as a syntactic variable ranging over types. The type constructor $\rightarrow$ associates to the right. If τ_0 is a primitive type then the type $\tau_1 \rightarrow \cdots \rightarrow \tau_n \rightarrow \tau_0$ has $\tau_1, \ldots, \tau_n$ as *argument types* and τ_0 as *target type*. The *order* of a primitive type is 0 while the order or a non-primitive type is one greater than the maximum order of its argument types.

For each type τ, we assume that there are denumerably many constants and variables of that type. Constants and variables do not overlap and if two constants (variables) have different types, they are different constants (variables). A *signature* is a finite set Σ of constants and variables whose types are such that their argument types do not contain o. A constant with target type o is a *predicate constant*.

Simply typed λ-terms are built in the usual way. An abstraction is written as $\lambda x\ t$, or $\lambda x : \tau.t$ when we wish to be explicit about the type of the bound variable x. The logical constants are given the following types: $\wedge$ (conjunction) and $\supset$ (implication) are both of type $o \to o \to o$; $\top$ (true) is of type o; and $\forall_\tau$ (universal quantification) is of type $(\tau \to o) \to o$, for all types τ not containing o. A formula is a term of type o. The logical constants $\wedge$ and $\supset$ are written in the familiar infix form. The expression $\forall_\tau(\lambda x\ t)$ is written $\forall_\tau x\ t$ or simply as $\forall x\ t$ when types can be inferred from context.

If x and t are terms of the same type then $[t/x]$ denotes the operation of substituting t for all free occurrences of x, systematically changing bound variables in order to avoid variable capture. The expression $[t_1/x_1, \ldots, t_n/x_n]$ will denote the simultaneous substitution of the terms $t_1, \ldots, t_n$ for distinct variables $x_1, \ldots, x_n$, respectively.

We shall assume that the reader is familiar with the usual notions and properties of α, β, and η conversion for the simply typed λ-calculus. The relation of convertibility up to α and β is written as $=_\beta$ (as it is for LF), and if η is added, is written as $=_{\beta\eta}$. A λ-term is in β-normal form if it contains no beta redexes, that is, subformulas of the form $(\lambda x\ t)s$. We say that an occurrence of a variable or constant h in a simply typed λ-term is *fully applied* if it occurs in a subterm of the form $ht_1 \ldots t_n$ having primitive type. The term h is called the *head* of this subterm. A λ-term is in $\beta\eta$-long form if it is in β-normal form and every variable and constant occurrence is fully applied. All λ-terms $\beta\eta$-convert to a term in $\beta\eta$-long form, unique up to α-conversion. See [13] for a fuller discussion of these basic properties of the simply typed λ-calculus.

Let Σ be a signature. A term is a Σ-*term* if all of its free variables and nonlogical constants are members of Σ. Similarly, a formula is a Σ-*formula* if all of its free variables and nonlogical constants are members of Σ. A formula is either *atomic* or *non-atomic*. An atomic Σ-formula is of the form $(Pt_1 \ldots t_n)$, where $n \geq 0$, P is given type $\tau_1 \to \cdots \to \tau_n \to o$ by Σ, and $t_1, \ldots, t_n$ are terms of the types $\tau_1, \ldots, \tau_n$, respectively. The predicate constant P is the *head* of this atomic formula. Non-atomic formulas are of the form $\top$, $B_1 \wedge B_2$, $B_1 \supset B_2$, or $\forall_\tau x\ B$, where B, B_1, and B_2 are formulas.

$$\frac{\Sigma \, ; \, B,C,\mathcal{P} \; \longrightarrow \; C}{\Sigma \, ; \, B \wedge C,\mathcal{P} \; \longrightarrow \; C} \wedge\text{-L} \qquad \frac{\Sigma \, ; \, \mathcal{P} \; \longrightarrow \; B \qquad \Sigma \, ; \, \mathcal{P} \; \longrightarrow \; C}{\Sigma \, ; \, \mathcal{P} \; \longrightarrow \; B \wedge C} \wedge\text{-R}$$

$$\frac{\Sigma \, ; \, \mathcal{P} \; \longrightarrow \; B \qquad \Sigma \, ; \, C,\mathcal{P} \; \longrightarrow \; A}{\Sigma \, ; \, B \supset C,\mathcal{P} \; \longrightarrow \; A} \supset\text{-L} \qquad \frac{\Sigma \, ; \, B,\mathcal{P} \; \longrightarrow \; C}{\Sigma \, ; \, \mathcal{P} \; \longrightarrow \; B \supset C} \supset\text{-R}$$

$$\frac{\Sigma \, ; \, [t/x]B,\mathcal{P} \; \longrightarrow \; C}{\Sigma \, ; \, \forall_\tau x \, B,\mathcal{P} \; \longrightarrow \; C} \forall\text{-L} \qquad \frac{\Sigma \cup \{c\} \, ; \, \mathcal{P} \; \longrightarrow \; [c/x]B}{\Sigma \, ; \, \mathcal{P} \; \longrightarrow \; \forall_\tau x \, B} \forall\text{-R}$$

Figure 1.3: Left and right introduction rules for hh^ω

The logic we have just presented is very closely related to two logic programming extensions that have been studied elsewhere [17]. *First-order hereditary Harrop* formulas (*fohh*) have been studied as an extension to first-order Horn clauses as a basis for logic programming. Similarly *higher-order hereditary Harrop* formulas (*hohh*) are a generalization of *fohh* that permits some forms of predicate quantification. Because our meta-language is neither higher-order, since it lacks predicate quantification, nor first-order, since it contains quantification at all function types, we shall simply call it hh^ω. The set of hh^ω formulas in which quantification only up to order n is used will be labeled as hh^n.

Provability for hh^ω can be given in terms of sequent calculus proofs. A *sequent* is a triple $\Sigma \, ; \, \mathcal{P} \longrightarrow B$, where Σ is a signature, B is a Σ-formula, and $\mathcal{P}$ is a finite (possibly empty) sets of Σ-formulas. The set $\mathcal{P}$ is this sequent's *antecedent* and B is its *succedent*. Later, when discussing an interpreter for this language, we also say that $\mathcal{P}$ is a *program*, that each formula in $\mathcal{P}$ is a *clause*, and that B is a *goal formula*. The expression $B,\mathcal{P}$ denotes the set $\mathcal{P} \cup \{B\}$; this notation is used even if $B \in \mathcal{P}$. The inference rules for sequents are presented in Figure 1.3. The following provisos are also attached to the two inference rules for quantifier introduction: in $\forall$-R c is a constant of type τ not in Σ, and in $\forall$-L t is a Σ-term of type τ.

A *proof* of the sequent $\Sigma \, ; \, \mathcal{P} \longrightarrow B$ is a finite tree constructed using these inference rules such that the root is labeled with $\Sigma \, ; \, \mathcal{P} \longrightarrow B$ and the leaves are labeled with *initial sequents*, that is, sequents $\Sigma' \, ; \, \mathcal{P}' \longrightarrow B'$ such that either B' is $\top$ or $B' \in \mathcal{P}'$. The non-terminals in such a tree are instances of the inference figures in Figure 1.3. Since we do not have an inference figure for $\beta\eta$-conversion, we shall assume that in building a proof, two formulas are equal if they are $\beta\eta$-convertible. If the sequent $\Sigma \; ; \; \mathcal{P} \longrightarrow B$ has a sequent proof then we write $\Sigma; \mathcal{P} \vdash_I B$ and say that B is provable from Σ and $\mathcal{P}$. The following two theorems establish the main proof theoretic results of hh^ω we shall need. These theorems are direct consequences of the proof theory of a more expressive logic studied in [17].

Theorem 0.1 Let Σ be a signature, let $\mathcal{P}$ be a finite set of Σ-formulas, and let B be a Σ-formula. The sequent $\Sigma \; ; \; \mathcal{P} \longrightarrow B$ has a proof if and only if it has a proof in which every sequent containing a non-atomic formula as its succedent is the conclusion of a right introduction rule.

To state our second theorem, we need the following definition.

Definition 0.2 Let Σ be a signature and let $\mathcal{P}$ be a finite set of Σ-formulas. The expression $|\mathcal{P}|_\Sigma$ denotes the smallest set of pairs $\langle \mathcal{G}, D \rangle$ of finite set of Σ-formulas $\mathcal{G}$ and Σ-formula D, such that

- If $D \in \mathcal{P}$ then $\langle \emptyset, D \rangle \in |\mathcal{P}|_\Sigma$.

- If $\langle \mathcal{G}, D_1 \wedge D_2 \rangle \in |\mathcal{P}|_\Sigma$ then $\langle \mathcal{G}, D_1 \rangle \in |\mathcal{P}|_\Sigma$ and $\langle \mathcal{G}, D_2 \rangle \in |\mathcal{P}|_\Sigma$.

- If $\langle \mathcal{G}, \forall_\tau x D \rangle \in |\mathcal{P}|_\Sigma$ then $\langle \mathcal{G}, [t/x]D \rangle \in |\mathcal{P}|_\Sigma$ for all Σ-terms t of type τ.

- If $\langle \mathcal{G}, G \supset D \rangle \in |\mathcal{P}|_\Sigma$ then $\langle \mathcal{G} \cup \{G\}, D \rangle \in |\mathcal{P}|_\Sigma$.

Theorem 0.3 Let Σ be a signature, let $\mathcal{P}$ be a finite set of Σ-formulas, and let A be an atomic Σ-formula. Then A is provable from Σ and $\mathcal{P}$ if and only if there is a pair $\langle \mathcal{G}, A \rangle \in |\mathcal{P}|_\Sigma$ so that for each $G \in \mathcal{G}$, G is provable from Σ and $\mathcal{P}$.

Given these two theorems, it is clear how a non-deterministic search procedure for hh^ω can be organized using the following four search primitives.

AND: $B_1 \wedge B_2$ is provable from Σ and $\mathcal{P}$ if and only if both B_1 and B_2 are provable from Σ and $\mathcal{P}$.

GENERIC: $\forall_\tau x B$ is provable from Σ and $\mathcal{P}$ if and only if $[c/x]B$ is provable from $\Sigma \cup \{c\}$ and $\mathcal{P}$ for any constant c of type τ not in Σ.

AUGMENT: $B_1 \supset B_2$ is provable from Σ and $\mathcal{P}$ if and only if B_2 is provable from Σ and $\mathcal{P} \cup \{B_1\}$.

BACKCHAIN: The atomic formula A is provable from Σ and $\mathcal{P}$ if and only if there is a pair $\langle \mathcal{G}, A \rangle \in |\mathcal{P}|_\Sigma$ so that for every $G \in \mathcal{G}$, G is provable from Σ and $\mathcal{P}$.

To implement an interpreter which implements these search operations, choices must be made which are left unspecified in the high-level description above. Here, we assume choices as in the λProlog language. For example, logic variables are employed in the BACKCHAIN operation to create universal instances of definite clauses. As a result, unification on λ-terms is necessary since logic variables of arbitrary functional type can occur inside λ-terms. Also the equality of terms is not a simple syntactic check but a more complex check of $\beta\eta$-conversion. Unification on λ-terms is not in general decidable. In λProlog, this issue is addressed by implementing a depth-first version of the unification search procedure described in [15]. (See [19, 17].) In this paper, the unification problems that result from programs we present are all decidable and rather simple.

In the AUGMENT search operation, clauses get added to the program dynamically. Note that as a result, clauses may in fact contain logic variables. The GENERIC operation must be implemented so that the new constant c introduced for x, must not appear in the terms eventually instantiated for logic variables free in the goal or in the program when c is introduced.

A deterministic interpreter must also specify the order in which conjuncts are attempted and definite clauses are backchained over. One possibility is to attempt conjuncts and backchain on definite clauses in the order in which they appear in the goal or in $\mathcal{P}$, respectively, using a depth-first search paradigm to handle failures as in Prolog.

5 Translating LF Assertions to hh^ω Formulas

In this section we present the translation of LF assertions to formulas in hh^ω. This translation will require an encoding of LF terms as simply typed λ-terms. We begin by presenting this encoding. We then present the translation, which has three parts. The first translates context items to a set of hh^ω formulas to be used as assumptions, while the second translates LF judgments to a formula to be proven with respect to such a set of assumptions. The third translation is defined using the previous two, and translates an LF assertion $\Gamma \vdash \alpha$ to a single formula whose proof verifies that Γ is a valid context before proving that α holds within the context Γ.

In this section, since we encode LF in hh^ω, we consider hh^ω as the meta-language and LF as the object-language. Since both languages have types and terms, to avoid confusion we will refer to types and terms of hh^ω as *meta-types* and *meta-terms*. In order to define an encoding of LF terms as simply typed λ-terms, we change slightly the notion of LF syntax. We will associate to each object and type variable, a tag which indicates the "syntactic structure" of types and kinds, respectively, which can be associated with it in forming a binder or a context item. These tags will be "simple types" built up from two primitive types ob and ty and the arrow constructor $\rightarrow$, with the additional restriction that ty can only appear as a target type. We assume that there is an infinite number of object-level and type-level variables associated with every simple type whose target type is ob and ty, respectively.

Let x be an object or type variable and $\tau_1 \rightarrow \cdots \rightarrow \tau_n \rightarrow \tau_0$ be the tag associated with x, where $n \geq 0$ and τ_0 is ob or ty. We say that variable x *admits* type or kind $\Pi x_1 : A_1 \ldots x_n : A_n.P$ if the following hold: if τ_0 is ty then P is Type; if τ_0 is ob, then P is a flat type; for $i = 1, \ldots, n$, the tag associated with x_i is τ_i and x_i admits type A_i. We add a restriction when forming the λ or Π binder $x : A$, or the context item $x : A$ or $x : K$, that x admits type A or kind K. Note that this restriction requires that the "simple type" in a variable tag has exactly the same order as the LF type or kind used in forming the binder.

We only define the encoding of LF terms as simply typed λ-terms for LF objects and flat types since this is all that is required by the translation. We introduce two primitive types at the meta-level, *ob* and *ty*, for these two classes of LF terms. The types ob and ty in variable tags correspond to these meta-types in the obvious way. When we wish to be explicit, we write $\mathcal{T}(x)$ to denote the meta-type associated with the tag on LF variable x obtained by replacing each occurrence of ob by *ob* and ty by *ty*. We will assume a fixed mapping ρ which associates each LF variable x to a meta-variable of type $\mathcal{T}(x)$. For readability in our presentation, this mapping will be implicit. A variable x will represent both an LF variable and its corresponding meta-variable. It will always be clear from context which is meant.

We denote the encoding of term or type P as $\langle\!\langle P \rangle\!\rangle$. The full encoding is defined in Figure 1.4. Note that the encoding maps abstraction in LF

$$
\begin{aligned}
\langle\!\langle x \rangle\!\rangle &:= x \\
\langle\!\langle \lambda x : A.M \rangle\!\rangle &:= \lambda x : \mathcal{T}(x).\langle\!\langle M \rangle\!\rangle \\
\langle\!\langle M N \rangle\!\rangle &:= \langle\!\langle M \rangle\!\rangle\, \langle\!\langle N \rangle\!\rangle \\
\langle\!\langle A M \rangle\!\rangle &:= \langle\!\langle A \rangle\!\rangle\, \langle\!\langle M \rangle\!\rangle
\end{aligned}
$$

Figure 1.4: Encoding of LF Terms

objects directly to abstraction at the meta-level, and that both application of objects to objects and application of type families to objects are mapped directly to application at the meta-level. The difference at the meta-level is that the former application will be a meta-term with target type *ob* while the latter application will be a meta-term with target type *ty*.

We can easily define a function Φ which maps an LF type or kind to the simple type corresponding to the tag on a variable that admits this type or kind: $\Phi(\Pi x\!:\!A.P)$ is $\Phi(A) \to \Phi(P)$, $\Phi(\mathsf{Type})$ is *ty*, and $\Phi(xN_1\ldots N_n)$ is *ob*. It is easy to see that for object or type family P having, respectively, type or kind Q, $\langle\!\langle P \rangle\!\rangle$ is a meta-term of meta-type $\Phi(Q)$.

Two predicates will appear in the atomic hh^ω formulas resulting from the translation: *hastype* of type $ob \to ty \to o$ and *istype* of type $ty \to o$. We will name the signature containing these two predicates Σ_{LF}. We denote the translation of the context item $P\!:\!Q$ as $[\![P\!:\!Q]\!]^+$. This translation is defined in Figure 1.5 (a). It is a partial function since it is defined by cases and undefined when no case applies. It will in fact always be defined on valid context items. When applied to a valid context item, P in the first two clauses in Figure 1.5 (a) will always be either an object or type family, and Q a type or kind, respectively. As was noted earlier, valid contexts are always in canonical form. Note that in a canonical context item $x\!:\!P$, the variable x is not necessarily canonical since it may not be fully applied. Such judgments with non-canonical terms on the left are handled by the second clause of the definition. Note the direct mapping of Π-abstraction in LF types and kinds to instances of universal quantification and implication in hh^ω formulas, as discussed earlier. In the first two clauses of the definition, the variable bound by Π is mapped to a variable at the meta-level bound by universal quantification. Then, in the resulting implication, the left hand side asserts the fact that the bound variable has a certain type, while the right hand side contains the translation of the body of the type or kind which may contain occurrences of this bound variable. The base cases occur when there is no leading Π in the type or kind, resulting in atomic formulas for the *hastype* and *istype* predicates.

To illustrate this translation, we consider an example from an LF context specifying natural deduction for first-order logic. The following context item introduces the constant for universal quantification and gives it a type: $\forall^* : (i \to \textit{form}) \to \textit{form}$. (We write $\forall^*$ for universal quantification at the object-level to distinguish it from universal quantification in hh^ω.) To make all bound variables explicit, we expand the above type to its unabbreviated form: $\Pi A\!:\!(\Pi y\!:\!i.\textit{form}).\textit{form}$. Note that the tag associated to $\forall^*$ must be $(ob \to ob) \to ob$. Both the LF type and the corresponding meta-type have order 2. The translation of this context item is as follows.

$$[\![\lambda x\!:\!A.P : \Pi x\!:\!A.Q]\!]^+ \quad := \quad \forall x \left([\![x\!:\!A]\!]^+ \supset [\![P : Q]\!]^+\right)$$

$$[\![P : \Pi x\!:\!A.Q]\!]^+ \quad := \quad \forall x \left([\![x\!:\!A]\!]^+ \supset [\![Px : Q]\!]^+\right)$$

where P is not an abstraction.

$$[\![M : A]\!]^+ \quad := \quad \textit{hastype } \langle\!\langle M \rangle\!\rangle \, \langle\!\langle A \rangle\!\rangle$$

where A is a flat type.

$$[\![A : \mathsf{Type}]\!]^+ \quad := \quad \textit{istype } \langle\!\langle A \rangle\!\rangle \quad \text{where } A \text{ is a flat type.}$$

(a) Translation of context items

$$[\![\lambda x\!:\!A.P : \Pi x\!:\!A.Q]\!]^- \quad := \quad [\![A : \mathsf{Type}]\!]^- \wedge \forall x \left([\![x\!:\!A]\!]^+ \supset [\![P : Q]\!]^-\right)$$

$$[\![M : A]\!]^- \quad := \quad \textit{hastype } \langle\!\langle M \rangle\!\rangle \, \langle\!\langle A \rangle\!\rangle$$

where A is a flat type.

$$[\![A : \mathsf{Type}]\!]^- \quad := \quad \textit{istype } \langle\!\langle A \rangle\!\rangle \quad \text{where } A \text{ is a flat type.}$$

$$[\![\Pi x\!:\!A.B : \mathsf{Type}]\!]^- \quad := \quad [\![A : \mathsf{Type}]\!]^- \wedge \forall x \left([\![x\!:\!A]\!]^+ \supset [\![B : \mathsf{Type}]\!]^-\right)$$

$$[\![\mathsf{Type\ kind}]\!]^- \quad := \quad \top$$

$$[\![\Pi x\!:\!A.K \text{ kind}]\!]^- \quad := \quad [\![A : \mathsf{Type}]\!]^- \wedge \forall x \left([\![x\!:\!A]\!]^+ \supset [\![K \text{ kind}]\!]^-\right)$$

(b) Translation of LF judgments

Figure 1.5: Translating LF contexts and judgments to hh^ω formulas

$$\llbracket x\!:\!A,\Gamma;\alpha\rrbracket \quad := \quad \llbracket A:\mathsf{Type}\rrbracket^- \wedge \forall x \left(\llbracket x\!:\!A\rrbracket^+ \supset \llbracket \Gamma;\alpha\rrbracket \right)$$

$$\llbracket x\!:\!K,\Gamma;\alpha\rrbracket \quad := \quad \llbracket K\ \mathsf{kind}\rrbracket^- \wedge \forall x \left(\llbracket x\!:\!K\rrbracket^+ \supset \llbracket \Gamma;\alpha\rrbracket \right)$$

$$\llbracket P\!:\!Q,\Gamma;\alpha\rrbracket \quad := \quad \llbracket P:Q\rrbracket^- \wedge \left(\llbracket P\!:\!Q\rrbracket^+ \supset \llbracket \Gamma;\alpha\rrbracket \right)$$

$$\llbracket \langle\rangle;\alpha\rrbracket \quad := \quad \llbracket \alpha\rrbracket^-$$

Figure 1.6: Translating LF assertions to hh^ω formulas

$$\llbracket \forall^* : \Pi A\!:\!(\Pi y\!:\!i.form).form\rrbracket^+ \equiv$$

$$\forall A \left(\forall y \left(\llbracket y:i\rrbracket^+ \supset \llbracket Ay:form\rrbracket^+ \right) \supset \llbracket \forall^*A:form\rrbracket^+ \right) \equiv$$

$$\forall A \left(\forall y((hastype\ y\ i) \supset (hastype\ (Ay)\ form)) \supset (hastype\ (\forall^*A)\ form) \right)$$

This formula provides the following description of the information contained in the above dependent type: for any A, if for arbitrary y of type i, Ay is a formula, then $\forall^*A$ is a formula.

Figure 1.5 (b) contains the definition of the translation for LF judgments. The translation of judgment α is denoted $\llbracket \alpha\rrbracket^-$. Several clauses of this definition are similar to the clauses of the previous one. For example, judgments containing a λ and Π-abstraction pair again translate to a universally quantified implication (using the first clause of the definition). In this case, an additional conjunct is also required to verify that the type in the abstraction is valid. Note that in the left-hand side of the implication, the binder $x:A$ is translated as a context item (using $\llbracket\rrbracket^+$), and represents an additional assumption available when proving that P has type or kind Q. Since the term on the left of a colon in a canonical assertion is always canonical, we do not need a clause corresponding to the second clause of $\llbracket\rrbracket^+$. Note that the base cases resulting in atomic formulas for *hastype* and *istype* are identical to those for translating context items. Finally, the last three clauses handle the remaining possible LF judgments. Again Π-abstraction maps to universal quantification and implication, with an additional conjunct to verify that the type in the binder is valid. The judgment Type kind simply maps to $\top$.

Figure 1.6 contains the general translation for LF assertions. Given assertion $\Gamma \vdash \alpha$, the pair $(\Gamma;\alpha)$ is mapped to a single formula containing subformulas whose proofs will insure that each context item is valid and that the judgment holds in this context. The translation of such a pair is denoted $\llbracket \Gamma;\alpha\rrbracket$. The first two clauses of this translation map each context item to a conjunctive formula where the first conjunct verifies that the type or kind is valid (using the translation on LF judgments), and the second conjunct is a universally quantified implication where the left hand side asserts the fact that the context item has the corresponding type (using the translation on contexts), and the right side contains the translation of the pair consisting of the remaining context items and judgment. The third clause handles context lemmas. Again there are two conjuncts. The first translates the lemma as a judgment to verify that it holds, while the second translates it as a context item which will be available as an assumption in proving that the rest of the context is valid and that the judgment holds within the entire context. The last clause in the translation is for the base case. When the context is empty, the judgment is simply translated using $\llbracket\;\rrbracket^-$. In the next section, we will show formally that for LF assertion $\Gamma \vdash \alpha$, Γ is a valid context and $\Gamma \vdash \alpha$ is provable in LF if and only if $\llbracket \Gamma; \alpha \rrbracket$ is a provable hh^ω formula.

6 Correctness of Translation

The following two properties hold for the encoding $\langle\!\langle \rangle\!\rangle$ on terms. They will be important for establishing the correctness of the translation.

Lemma 0.4 Let P be an LF object or base type, and N an LF object. Then $[\langle\!\langle N \rangle\!\rangle / x]\langle\!\langle P \rangle\!\rangle = \langle\!\langle [N/x]P \rangle\!\rangle$.

Lemma 0.5 Let P and Q be two LF objects or base types. If $P =_\beta Q$, then $\langle\!\langle P \rangle\!\rangle =_\beta \langle\!\langle Q \rangle\!\rangle$.

Lemma 0.4 is proved by induction on the structure of LF terms, while Lemma 0.5 is proved by induction on a sequence of β-reductions to convert P to Q.

In proving the correctness of the translation, we consider a slightly modified LF. Our modified system replaces the (ABS-FAM) and (ABS-OBJ) rules with the following two rules.

$$\frac{\Gamma, x : A \vdash B : K}{\Gamma \vdash \lambda x : A.B : \Pi x : A.K} \text{(ABS-FAM$'$)} \qquad \frac{\Gamma, x : A \vdash M : B}{\Gamma \vdash \lambda x : A.M : \Pi x : A.B} \text{(ABS-OBJ$'$)}$$

These rules are the same as presented earlier except that the left premise is omitted. We call this system LF$'$. Proving an assertion of the form $\Gamma \vdash \lambda x : A.P : \Pi x : A.Q$ in valid context Γ in the unmodified version of LF is equivalent to proving $\Gamma, x : A \vdash P : Q$ in valid context $\Gamma, x : A$. In Appendix B, we show that for valid context Γ and judgment α, the assertion

$\Gamma \vdash \alpha$ is provable in LF if and only if it is provable in LF' and all types bound by outermost abstractions in the term on the left in α are valid.

In proving correctness of the translation, we prove a stronger statement from which correctness will follow directly. This stronger statement will talk about the provability of an arbitrary LF' assertion $\Gamma \vdash \alpha$ even in the case when Γ and the types bound by outermost abstractions in α are not valid. We make the following modifications to the definition of $[\![\,]\!]^-$ for translating such judgments: we replace the first clause of Figure 1.5 (b) with the first clause below, and add the second as a new clause.

$$[\![\lambda x{:}A.P : \Pi x{:}A.Q]\!]^- \quad := \quad \forall x \left([\![x{:}A]\!]^+ \supset [\![P:Q]\!]^- \right)$$

$$[\![P : \Pi x{:}A.Q]\!]^- \quad := \quad \forall x \left([\![x{:}A]\!]^+ \supset [\![Px:Q]\!]^- \right)$$

where P is not an abstraction.

In the first clause, the removal of the left conjunct in these formulas corresponds to the removal of the left premise in the (ABS) rules. The second clause will be needed for proving our general form of the correctness theorem. Note that with these two clauses, the positive and negative translation are identical on judgments for which they are both defined.

One further lemma about LF' is needed to prove the correctness of the (modified) translation. Lemma 0.4 shows that substitution commutes with the encoding operation. The lemma below extends this result to the translation operation on judgments which translate to provable hh^ω formulas. Given a context Γ, we write $\rho(\Gamma)$ to denote the set of meta-variables obtained by mapping, for each signature item $x{:}P$ in Γ, the variable x to the corresponding meta-variable of type $\mathcal{T}(x)$. We write $[\![\Gamma]\!]^+$ to denote the set of formulas obtained by translating separately each item in Γ using $[\![\,]\!]^+$.

Lemma 0.6 Let $\Gamma, x_1{:}A_1, \ldots, x_n{:}A_n, x{:}A$ $(n \geq 0)$ be a canonical context. Let $N_1, \ldots, N_n, N$ be canonical objects with respect to Γ. Let Σ be the signature $\Sigma_{LF} \cup \rho(\Gamma)$. Then $\Sigma; [\![\Gamma]\!]^+ \vdash_I [\![N : ([N_1/x_1, \ldots, N_n/x_n]A)^\beta]\!]^-$ iff

$$\Sigma; [\![\Gamma]\!]^+ \vdash_I [\langle\!\langle N_1\rangle\!\rangle/x_1, \ldots, \langle\!\langle N_n\rangle\!\rangle/x_n, \langle\!\langle N\rangle\!\rangle/x][\![x : A]\!]^-.$$

Proof: The forward and backward direction is proved by simultaneous induction on the structure of A with the following statement. Let C be any $\Sigma \cup \{x\}$-formula. Then

$$\Sigma \cup \{x\}; [\![\Gamma]\!]^+, [\![x : ([N_1/x_1, \ldots, N_n/x_n]A)^\beta]\!]^+ \vdash_I C \quad \text{iff}$$

$$\Sigma \cup \{x\}; [\![\Gamma]\!]^+, [\langle\!\langle N_1\rangle\!\rangle/x_1, \ldots, \langle\!\langle N_n\rangle\!\rangle/x_n][\![x : A]\!]^+ \vdash_I C.$$

∎

Theorem 0.7 (Correctness of Translation I) Let Γ be a valid context and α a canonical judgment such that all types bound by outermost abstractions in the term on the left in α are valid. Let Σ be $\Sigma_{LF} \cup \rho(\Gamma)$. Then $\Gamma \vdash \alpha$ is provable in LF' iff $\Sigma; [\![\Gamma]\!]^+ \vdash_I [\![\alpha]\!]^-$ holds.

Proof: We prove a modified form of the above statement from which the theorem will follow directly. We relax the requirement that Γ is valid and that the types bound by outermost abstractions in α are valid. Instead, we simply require that $[\![\Gamma]\!]^+$ and $[\![\alpha]\!]^-$ are well-defined.

The proof of this theorem is constructive, *i.e.*, it provides a method for constructing an hh^ω proof from an LF proof, and vice versa. We begin with the forward direction which is proved by induction on the height of an LF' proof of the assertion $\Gamma \vdash \alpha$. For the one node proof $\Gamma \vdash \mathsf{Type\ kind}$, clearly $[\![\mathsf{Type\ kind}]\!]^- \equiv \top$ is provable from Σ and $[\![\Gamma]\!]^+$. For the case when the last rule is (PI-FAM), we build the following sequent proof fragment, where the root is the translation of the conclusion of the (PI-FAM) rule, and the leaves are the translations of the premises which we know to be provable by the induction hypothesis.

$$
\cfrac{
  \Sigma; [\![\Gamma]\!]^+ \longrightarrow [\![A:\mathsf{Type}]\!]^- \qquad
  \cfrac{
    \cfrac{
      \cfrac{
        \Sigma \cup \{x\}; [\![\Gamma, x:A]\!]^+ \longrightarrow [\![B:\mathsf{Type}]\!]^-
      }{
        \Sigma \cup \{x\}; [\![\Gamma]\!]^+ \longrightarrow [\![x:A]\!]^+ \supset [\![B:\mathsf{Type}]\!]^-
      } \scriptstyle \supset\text{-R}
    }{
      \Sigma; [\![\Gamma]\!]^+ \longrightarrow \forall x\,([\![x:A]\!]^+ \supset [\![B:\mathsf{Type}]\!]^-)
    } \scriptstyle \forall\text{-R}
  }{
    \Sigma; [\![\Gamma]\!]^+ \longrightarrow [\![A:\mathsf{Type}]\!]^- \wedge \forall x\,([\![x:A]\!]^+ \supset [\![B:\mathsf{Type}]\!]^-)
  } \scriptstyle \wedge\text{-R}
}
$$

The case when the last rule is (PI-KIND) is similar. The cases for (ABS-OBJ') and (ABS-FAM') are also similar, except that the translations do not have the left conjunct and the corresponding LF' proofs have only one premise. Next, consider the case when the last rule is (APP-OBJ) with context lemma $M : \Pi x_1 : A_1 \ldots \Pi x_n : A_n.B \in \Gamma$ and objects $N_1, \ldots, N_n$ appearing on the right of the colon in the n premises. We must show that the formula below (the translation of the conclusion) is provable from Σ and $[\![\Gamma]\!]^+$.

$$(hastype\ \langle\!\langle (MN_1 \ldots N_n)^\beta \rangle\!\rangle\ \langle\!\langle ([N_1/x_1, \ldots, N_n/x_n]B)^\beta \rangle\!\rangle) \tag{1.1}$$

(Note that we can assume that $x_1, \ldots, x_n$ do not appear free in M, otherwise we rename them in the above type.) By the induction hypothesis for the n premises and Lemma 0.6, the following are provable from Σ and $[\![\Gamma]\!]^+$.

$$[\langle\!\langle N_1 \rangle\!\rangle/x_1][\![x_1:A_1]\!]^-, \ldots, [\langle\!\langle N_1 \rangle\!\rangle/x_1, \ldots, \langle\!\langle N_n \rangle\!\rangle/x_n][\![x_n:A_n]\!]^- \tag{1.2}$$

M has the form $\lambda x_1 : A_1 \ldots \lambda x_n : A_n.M'$. Since $M : \Pi x_1 : A_1 \ldots \Pi x_n : A_n.B$ is in Γ the formula below (the translation of this context item using $[\![\,]\!]^+$) is in $[\![\Gamma]\!]^+$.

$$\forall x_1 \left([\![x_1\!:\!A_1]\!]^+ \supset \ldots \forall x_n \left([\![x_n\!:\!A_n]\!]^+ \supset (hastype \,\langle\!\langle M'\rangle\!\rangle \,\langle\!\langle B\rangle\!\rangle)\right)\ldots\right)$$

By Definition 0.2 applied to this formula with instances $\langle\!\langle N_1\rangle\!\rangle, \ldots, \langle\!\langle N_n\rangle\!\rangle$ for the variables $x_1, \ldots, x_n$, we know that the following pair is in $\left|[\![\Gamma]\!]^+\right|_{\Sigma}$.

$$\Big\langle \{[\langle\!\langle N_1\rangle\!\rangle/x_1][\![x_1\!:\!A_1]\!]^+, \ldots, [\langle\!\langle N_1\rangle\!\rangle/x_1, \ldots, \langle\!\langle N_n\rangle\!\rangle/x_n][\![x_n\!:\!A_n]\!]^+\},$$
$$(hastype \,[\langle\!\langle N_1\rangle\!\rangle/x_1, \ldots, \langle\!\langle N_n\rangle\!\rangle/x_n]\langle\!\langle M'\rangle\!\rangle \,[\langle\!\langle N_1\rangle\!\rangle/x_1, \ldots, \langle\!\langle N_n\rangle\!\rangle/x_n]\langle\!\langle B\rangle\!\rangle)\Big\rangle$$

Hence, by Theorem 0.3, the fact that the formulas (1.2) are provable from Σ and $[\![\Gamma]\!]^+$, and the fact that the positive and negative translation are identical on these judgments, we can conclude that the formula on the right of this pair is provable from Σ and $[\![\Gamma]\!]^+$. By Lemmas 0.4 and 0.5, the following hold.

$$[\langle\!\langle N_1\rangle\!\rangle/x_1, \ldots, \langle\!\langle N_n\rangle\!\rangle/x_n]\langle\!\langle M'\rangle\!\rangle =_\beta \langle\!\langle (MN_1 \ldots N_n)^\beta\rangle\!\rangle$$

$$[\langle\!\langle N_1\rangle\!\rangle/x_1, \ldots, \langle\!\langle N_n\rangle\!\rangle/x_n]\langle\!\langle B\rangle\!\rangle =_\beta \langle\!\langle ([N_1/x_1, \ldots, N_n/x_n]B)^\beta\rangle\!\rangle$$

Thus the formula on the right of the above pair is equivalent to (1.1) and we have our result. The case when M is a variable, and the case when the last rule in the proof of the LF$'$ assertion is (APP-FAM) are similar to this case.

The proof of the backward direction is by induction on the structure of the term on the left in α, and is similar to the proof of the forward direction. The proof of the case when the term on the left is an abstraction or Π relies on the fact that there is a sequent proof of the corresponding hh^ω formula of the form described by Theorem 0.1. The proof of the case when the term on the left is an application uses Theorem 0.3. ∎

The correctness of the translation $[\![\,]\!]$ is stated as the following corollary of this theorem. We state it with respect to the unmodified canonical LF.

Corollary 0.8 (Correctness of Translation II)
Let Γ be a canonical context and α a canonical judgment. Then Γ is a valid context and $\Gamma \vdash \alpha$ is provable in LF iff $\Sigma_{LF}; \emptyset \vdash_I [\![\Gamma; \alpha]\!]$ holds.

7 Encoding a Specification of First-Order Logic

In this section, we consider some further examples from an LF specification of natural deduction in first-order logic. We begin by illustrating the translation of context items specifying some of the inference rules. We then consider some example LF judgments provable from this context, and discuss both proof checking and theorem proving of the corresponding goals in hh^ω.

Note that in general, formulas obtained by translating context items have the form on the left below, but can be rewritten to have the form on the right:

$$\forall X_1 (G_1 \supset \ldots \forall X_n (G_n \supset D)\ldots) \qquad \forall X_1 \ldots \forall X_n (G_1 \wedge \cdots \wedge G_n \supset D)$$

where $n \geq 0$, $X_1, \ldots, X_n$ are variables, and $G_1, \ldots, G_n, D$ are hh^ω formulas. (Here we assume that for $i = 1, \ldots, n$, $X_{i+1}, \ldots, X_n$ do not appear free in G_i). For readability, we will write hh^ω formulas in the examples in this section simply as $G_1 \wedge \cdots \wedge G_n \supset D$ (or just D when $n = 0$), and assume implicit universal quantification over all free variables written as capital letters.

The fragment of an LF specification for first-order logic that we are concerned with is the following.

$$i : \mathsf{Type}$$
$$form : \mathsf{Type}$$
$$true : form \to \mathsf{Type}$$
$$\wedge^* : form \to form \to form$$
$$\supset^* : form \to form \to form$$
$$\forall^* : (i \to form) \to form$$
$$\wedge^*\text{-}I : \Pi A{:}form.\Pi B{:}form.(true\ A) \to (true\ B) \to (true\ A \wedge^* B)$$
$$\wedge^*\text{-}E_1 : \Pi A{:}form.\Pi B{:}form.(true\ A \wedge^* B) \to (true\ A)$$
$$\wedge^*\text{-}E_2 : \Pi A{:}form.\Pi B{:}form.(true\ A \wedge^* B) \to (true\ B)$$
$$\forall^*\text{-}E : \Pi A{:}i \to form.\Pi t{:}i.(true\ \forall^* A) \to (true\ At)$$
$$\forall^*\text{-}I : \Pi A{:}i \to form.(\Pi y{:}i.(true\ Ay)) \to (true\ \forall^* A)$$
$$\supset^*\text{-}I : \Pi A{:}form.\Pi B{:}form.((true\ A) \to (true\ B)) \to (true\ A \supset^* B)$$
$$\supset^*\text{-}E : \Pi A{:}form.\Pi B{:}form.(true\ A \supset^* B) \to (true\ A) \to (true\ B)$$

For readability, we do not always present context items in canonical form. The corresponding canonical term can always be easily deduced. For example, to apply the translation to the inference rules for universal quantification, the term $(\forall^* A)$ must be replaced by $(\forall^* \lambda x{:}iAx)$.

First, consider the $\forall^*$-elimination rule specified by $\forall^*$-E and its type. Its translation (using $\llbracket \rrbracket^+$) is the following formula.

$$\forall y((hastype\ y\ i) \supset (hastype\ Ay\ form)) \wedge (hastype\ t\ i) \wedge$$
$$(hastype\ P\ (true\ \forall^* A)) \supset (hastype\ (\forall^*\text{-}E\ A\ t\ P)\ (true\ At))$$

This formula reads: if for arbitrary y of type i, Ay is a formula, and if t is a term of type i and P is a proof of $\forall^* A$, then the term $(\forall^*$-E $A\ t\ P)$

is a proof of the formula At. Note that, as in the translation of the $\forall^*$ connective given in Section 5, A is a function at the meta-level having syntactic type $ob \to ob$. It maps first-order terms to formulas just as it does at the object-level. We next consider the translation of the $\forall^*$-I rule as the following formula.

$$\forall y((\text{hastype } y\ i) \supset (\text{hastype } Ay\ \text{form})) \wedge$$
$$\forall y((\text{hastype } y\ i) \supset (\text{hastype } Py\ (\text{true } Ay))) \supset$$
$$(\text{hastype } (\forall^*\text{-I } A\ P)\ (\text{true } \forall^* A))$$

This clause provides the following description of the information contained in the dependent type: if for arbitrary y of type i, Ay is a formula and Py is a proof of Ay, then the term $(\forall^*\text{-I } A\ P)$ is a proof of $\forall^* A$. Here, both A and P are functions at the meta-level having syntactic type $ob \to ob$. Again, A maps first-order terms to formulas, while P maps first-order terms to proofs. As a final inference rule example, consider the declaration for $\supset^*$-I, which translates to the following formula.

$$(\text{hastype } A\ \text{form}) \wedge (\text{hastype } B\ \text{form}) \wedge$$
$$\forall q((\text{hastype } q\ (\text{true } A)) \supset (\text{hastype } Pq\ (\text{true } B))) \supset$$
$$(\text{hastype } (\supset^*\text{-I } A\ B\ P)\ (\text{true } A \supset^* B))$$

This formula reads: if A and B are formulas and P is a function which maps an arbitrary proof q of A to the proof Pq of B, then the term $(\supset^*\text{-I } A\ B\ P)$ is a proof of $A \supset^* B$. Note that P in this formula is a function which maps proofs to proofs.

We consider an example from [21] which is provable in the LF specification for natural deduction. The following LF type represents the fact that in first-order logic, a universal quantifier can be pulled outside a conjunction.

$$\Pi A\!:\!i \to \text{form}.\Pi B\!:\!i \to \text{form}.$$
$$(\text{true } (\forall^* A \wedge^* \forall^* B)) \to (\text{true } \forall^* (\lambda x\!:\!i(Ax \wedge^* Bx)))$$

Let the term T be the following LF term of this type, which represents a natural deduction proof of this fact.

$$\lambda A\!:\!i \to \text{form}.\lambda B\!:\!i \to \text{form}.\lambda p\!:\!(\text{true } (\forall^* A \wedge^* \forall^* B)).$$
$$(\forall^*\text{-I } \lambda x\!:\!i.(Ax \wedge^* Bx)\ \lambda x\!:\!i.(\wedge^*\text{-I } Ax\ Bx$$
$$(\forall^*\text{-E } A\ x\ (\wedge^*\text{-E}_1\ \forall^* A\ \forall^* B\ p))\ (\forall^*\text{-E } B\ x\ (\wedge^*\text{-E}_2\ \forall^* A\ \forall^* B\ p))))$$

Let T' be the following simply typed λ-term of type $(ob \to ob) \to (ob \to ob) \to ob \to ob$.

$$\lambda A\!:\!ob \to ob.\lambda B\!:\!ob \to ob.\lambda p\!:\!ob.$$
$$(\forall^*\text{-I } \lambda x\!:\!ob.(Ax \wedge^* Bx)\ \lambda x\!:\!ob.(\wedge^*\text{-I } Ax\ Bx$$
$$(\forall^*\text{-E } A\ x\ (\wedge^*\text{-E}_1\ \forall^* A\ \forall^* B\ p))\ (\forall^*\text{-E } B\ x\ (\wedge^*\text{-E}_2\ \forall^* A\ \forall^* B\ p))))$$

The encoding of the above judgment using $\llbracket \rrbracket^-$ is an hh^ω formula equivalent to the conjunction of the three formulas below, which are provable from the set of formulas encoding the entire LF context specifying natural deduction in first-order logic.

$(istype\ i) \wedge \forall y((hastype\ y\ i) \supset (istype\ form))$

$\forall y((hastype\ y\ i) \supset (hastype\ Ay\ form)) \wedge$
$\quad \forall y((hastype\ y\ i) \supset (hastype\ By\ form)) \supset (istype\ (true\ (\forall^*A\ \wedge^*\ \forall^*B)))$

$\forall y((hastype\ y\ i) \supset (hastype\ Ay\ form)) \wedge$
$\quad \forall y((hastype\ y\ i) \supset (hastype\ By\ form)) \wedge$
$\quad (hastype\ p\ (true\ (\forall^*A\ \wedge^*\ \forall^*B))) \supset$
$\quad\quad (hastype\ (T'ABp)\ (true\ \forall^*(\lambda x : ob.(Ax \wedge^* Bx))))$

Once a fact is proved it can be considered a part of the context and used to prove new judgments. In this case, the translation of the above judgment as a context item is the latter of the three formulas above. Thus this formula can be added as an assumption and used in proving new hh^ω goals. For example, consider the LF type below.

$$true((\forall^*r\ \wedge^*\ \forall^*s) \supset^* (ra \wedge^* sa))$$

(We assume that a is a constant and r, s are unary predicates in our first-order logic. Thus the context contains $a : i, r : i \to form, s : i \to form$, and the set of hh^ω formulas contains their corresponding translations.) The following two LF terms represent proofs of this fact. The first uses the above LF judgment as a lemma.

$(\supset^*\text{-I}\ (\forall^*r\ \wedge^*\ \forall^*s)\ (ra \wedge^* sa)\ \lambda p : (true\ (\forall^*r\ \wedge^*\ \forall^*s)).$
$\quad (\forall^*\text{-E}\ \lambda x : i.(rx \wedge^* sx)\ a\ (Trsp)^\beta)$

$(\supset^*\text{-I}\ (\forall^*r\ \wedge^*\ \forall^*s)\ (ra \wedge^* sa)\ \lambda p : (true\ (\forall^*r\ \wedge^*\ \forall^*s)).(\wedge^*\text{-I}\ ra\ sa$
$\quad (\forall^*\text{-E}\ r\ a\ (\wedge^*\text{-E}_1\ \forall^*r\ \forall^*s\ p))\ (\forall^*\text{-E}\ s\ a\ (\wedge^*\text{-E}_2\ \forall^*r\ \forall^*s\ p))))$

These judgments translate to the following two provable hh^ω formulas.

$(hastype\ (\supset^*\text{-I}\ (\forall^*r\ \wedge^*\ \forall^*s)\ (ra \wedge^* sa)$
$\quad\quad \lambda p : ob.(\forall^*\text{-E}\ \lambda x : ob.(rx \wedge^* sx)\ a\ (T'rsp))$
$\quad\quad (true\ (\forall^*r\ \wedge^*\ \forall^*s) \supset^* (ra \wedge^* sa))$

$(hastype\ (\supset^*\text{-I}\ (\forall^*r\ \wedge^*\ \forall^*s)\ (ra \wedge^* sa)\ \lambda p : ob.(\wedge^*\text{-I}\ ra\ sa$
$\quad\quad (\forall^*\text{-E}\ r\ a\ (\wedge^*\text{-E}_1\ \forall^*r\ \forall^*s\ p))$
$\quad\quad (\forall^*\text{-E}\ s\ a\ (\wedge^*\text{-E}_2\ \forall^*r\ \forall^*s\ p))))$
$\quad\quad (true\ (\forall^*r\ \wedge^*\ \forall^*s) \supset^* (ra \wedge^* sa))$

With respect to the interpreter described in Section 4, we will say that an hh^ω formula with no logic variables is *closed*. The formulas we obtain by applying the translation, for example, are all closed. Proving one of the above two formulas, for instance, corresponds to verifying that the closed term represents a natural deduction proof of the first-order formula in the closed type, *i.e.*, proving closed formulas corresponds to object-level proof checking. The deterministic interpreter described in Section 4 is in fact sufficient to prove such goals. Each BACKCHAIN step will produce new closed subgoals. Consider the first of the two formulas above. In proving this formula, we obtain a subgoal of the form:

$$(hastype\ (T'rsp)\ (true\ (\forall\lambda x:ob.(rx \wedge^* sx)))).$$

The term at the head of (the normal form of) $(T'rsp)$ is $\forall^*$-I. At this point in the proof there will be two possible definite clauses that can be used in backchaining: the translation of the $\forall^*$-I context item, and the translation of the lemma T, and either will lead to proof of the subgoal. In fact, for proof checking, we can restrict the set of definite clauses used to those obtained by translating context items that introduce new variables, discarding those that translate context lemmas, and still retain a complete program with respect to a deterministic control. In this restricted setting, at each step depending on the constant at the head of the term, there will be exactly one clause that can be used in backchaining.

To use such a set of hh^ω formulas for object-level theorem proving, we simply use a logic variable in the first argument to the *hastype* predicate. For example, to prove the first-order formula $(\forall^*r \wedge^* \forall^*s) \supset^*(ra \wedge^* sa)$, we begin with the goal:

$$(hastype\ \texttt{M}\ (true\ (\forall^*r \wedge^* \forall^*s) \supset^*(ra \wedge^* sa)))$$

where M is a logic variable to be instantiated with a term of the given type. A closed instance of M can easily be mapped back to an LF term having the given type. As discussed in Section 2, depth-first search is not sufficient for such a theorem proving goal since there may often be many definite clauses to choose from to use in backchaining. For example, for a subgoal of the form:

$$(hastype\ \texttt{M'}\ (true\ (\forall\lambda x:ob.(rx \wedge^* sx))))$$

among the options available are backchaining on the clause for the lemma T or backchaining directly on the clause for $\forall^*$-I. As discussed earlier, the tactic environment of [7] provides an environment in which such choices can be made.

8 Conclusion

We have not yet considered the possibility of translating hh^ω formulas into LF. This translation is particularly simple. Let Σ be a signature for hh^ω and let $\mathcal{P}$ be a set of Σ-formulas. For each primitive type τ other than o in S, the corresponding LF judgment is τ : Type. For each non-predicate constant c of type τ in Σ, the corresponding LF judgment is $c : \tau$. For each predicate constant p of type $\tau_1 \to \cdots \to \tau_n \to o \in \Sigma$, the corresponding LF judgment is $p : \tau_1 \to \cdots \to \tau_n \to$ Type. Finally, let $D \in \mathcal{P}$ and let k be a new constant not used in the translation to this point. Then the corresponding LF judgment is $k : D'$ where D' is essentially D with $B_1 \supset B_2$ written as $\Pi x : B_1.B_2$ and $\forall_\tau x\ B$ written as $\Pi x : \tau.B$.

Notice that the translation presented in this paper works via recursion over the structure of types. Thus, λ-calculi that contain quantification over types such as the polymorphic λ-calculus or the Calculus of Constructions cannot be directly translated in this manner. For example, we cannot define the same notion of base type. Translating A : Type when A is a base type, for instance, results in an atomic formula for the *istype* predicate. In systems with quantification over types, whether or not A is a base type may depend on its instances, and cannot be determined at the time of translation.

The translation we have described provides a method of directly translating an LF specification, so that there is one hh^ω formula corresponding to each LF context item. Since each context item represents a concept of the logic being specified, in the resulting proof checkers and theorem provers, each (BACKCHAIN) step is on a clause for a particular constant representing an object-level notion. Another approach to implementing LF specifications is to implement the inference rules of LF directly as hh^ω formulas, coding the provability relation directly into the meta-language. An LF context specifying a particular logic would serve as a parameter to such a specification. Such an approach adds one level of indirection in implementing object logics since now each (BACKCHAIN) step corresponds to the application of an LF rule. This approach to implementing typed λ-calculi is taken in [8], where it is also shown that it can be applied to systems with quantification over types.

Such an approach requires an encoding of terms at all levels of the calculus being specified. In LF, for instance, meta-level constants for the various notions of application and abstraction must be introduced. For example, at the level of types a constant of type $ty \to ob \to ty$ can be introduced to represent application, while constants of type $(ob \to ty) \to ty$ can be introduced for Π and λ-abstraction. A coding of the convertibility relation on terms is also required in this setting. Note that the above simple types have order 1 and 2 respectively. In fact hh^2 is all that is required to encode provability of typed λ-calculi in this manner. In [5], using such an encoding on terms, it was shown that a direct encoding of LF specifications using the approach in this paper can be defined in just hh^2. The proofs of the correctness of that encoding are similar to those presented here.

In [12], a similar approach based on recursion over types is adopted to implement a subset of the Calculus of Constructions. In the meta-language used there, terms are the terms of the Calculus of Constructions, and a simple language of clauses over these terms is defined. During goal-directed proof, when a new assumption is introduced, the clause corresponding to this assumption is added dynamically and is then available for backchaining. In this way, certain forms of quantification over types can be handled. Such an approach can be implemented in λProlog by implementing the translation as a λProlog program and performing the translation dynamically as types become instantiated to obtain new assumptions which can be used in subsequent proof checking and theorem proving subgoals.

In the Elf programming language [21], a logic programming language is described that gives operational interpretations directly to LF types similar to the way in which the interpreter described in Section 4 gives operational interpretations to the connectives of hh^ω. Logic variables are also used in this implementation, and the more complex operation of unification on LF terms is required. The LF specification for first-order logic discussed in Section 7, for example, can serve directly as a program in this language. The operational behavior, of such a program, although similar to the execution of an hh^ω specification, has several differences. For instance, certain operations which are handled directly at the meta-level by unification on types in an Elf implementation are expressed explicitly as type-checking subgoals in the hh^ω formulas, and thus handled by logic programming search. For example, consider a goal of the form $(true\ A \supset^* B)$ in the first-order logic specification. In Elf, before backchaining on the context item specifying the $\supset^*$-introduction rule, the interpreter verifies that $A \supset^* B$ has type *form*. In the corresponding hh^ω program, the term $A \supset^* B$ in the head of the clause translating the $\supset^*$-I context item will unify with any term of type *ob*. It is the subgoals $(hastype\ A\ form)$ and $(hastype\ B\ form)$ which will succeed or fail depending on whether A and B represent first-order formulas. In addition, when such programs are used as theorem provers, LF proofs are built at the meta-level by Elf, whereas they are explicit arguments to the *hastype* predicate in hh^ω specifications and are built by unification on simply typed λ-terms.

Acknowledgements

The author would like to thank Dale Miller, Frank Pfenning, and Randy Pollack for helpful comments and discussions related to the subject of this paper.

References

[1] Arnon Avron, Furio A. Honsell, and Ian A. Mason. Using typed lambda calculus to implement formal systems on a machine. Technical Report ECS-LFCS-87-31, Laboratory for the Foundations of Computer Science, University of Edinburgh, June 1987.

[2] Alonzo Church. A formulation of the simple theory of types. *Journal of Symbolic Logic*, 5:56–68, 1940.

[3] Thierry Coquand and Gérard Huet. The calculus of constructions. *Information and Computation*, 76(2/3):95–120, February/March 1988.

[4] N.G. deBruijn. A survey of the project AUTOMATH. In *To H. B. Curry: Essays in Combinatory Logic, Lambda Calculus, and Formalism*, pages 589–606. Academic Press, New York, 1980.

[5] Amy Felty. *Specifying and Implementing Theorem Provers in a Higher-Order Logic Programming Language*. PhD thesis, University of Pennsylvania, August 1989.

[6] Amy Felty. A logic program for transforming sequent proofs to natural deduction proofs. In Peter Schroeder-Heister, editor, *Proceedings of the 1989 International Workshop on Extensions of Logic Programming*, Tübingen, West Germany. Springer-Verlag LNAI series, 1991.

[7] Amy Felty and Dale Miller. Specifying theorem provers in a higher-order logic programming language. In *Ninth International Conference on Automated Deduction*, Argonne, IL, May 1988.

[8] Amy Felty and Dale Miller. A meta language for type checking and inference: An extended abstract. Presented at the 1989 Workshop on Programming Logic, Bålstad, Sweden, 1989.

[9] Amy Felty and Dale Miller. Encoding a dependent-type λ-calculus in a logic programming language. In *Tenth International Conference on Automated Deduction*, Kaiserslautern, Germany, July 1990.

[10] Robert Harper, Furio Honsell, and Gordon Plotkin. A framework for defining logics. In *Second Annual Symposium on Logic in Computer Science*, Ithaca, NY, June 1987.

[11] Robert Harper, Furio Honsell, and Gordon Plotkin. A framework for defining logics. Technical Report CMU-CS-89-173. To appear, 1989.

[12] Leen Helmink. Resolution and type theory. In *Proceedings of the European Symposium on Programming*, Copenhagen, 1990.

[13] J. Roger Hindley and Jonathan P. Seldin. *Introduction to Combinatory Logic and Lambda Calculus*. Cambridge University Press, 1986.

[14] William A. Howard. The formulae-as-type notion of construction, 1969. In *To H. B. Curry: Essays in Combinatory Logic, Lambda Calculus, and Formalism*. Academic Press, 1980.

[15] Gérard Huet. A unification algorithm for typed λ-calculus. *Theoretical Computer Science*, 1:27–57, 1975.

[16] Per Martin-Löf. *Intuitionistic Type Theory*. Studies in Proof Theory Lecture Notes. BIBLIOPOLIS, Napoli, 1984.

[17] Dale Miller, Gopalan Nadathur, Frank Pfenning, and Andre Scedrov. Uniform proofs as a foundation for logic programming. To appear in the *Annals of Pure and Applied Logic*.

[18] Gopalan Nadathur and Dale Miller. An overview of λProlog. In K. Bowen and R. Kowalski, editors, *Fifth International Conference and Symposium on Logic Programming*. MIT Press, 1988.

[19] Gopalan Nadathur and Dale Miller. Higher-order horn clauses. *Journal of the ACM*, 37(4):777 – 814, October 1990.

[20] Lawrence C. Paulson. The foundation of a generic theorem prover. *Journal of Automated Reasoning*, 5(3):363–397, September 1989.

[21] Frank Pfenning. Elf: A language for logic definition and verified metaprogramming. In *Fourth Annual Symposium on Logic in Computer Science*, Monterey, CA, June 1989.

A   Full and Canonical LF

In this section, we show the correspondence between canonical LF as presented in Section 3, and full LF as presented in [10]. The rules of full LF are the rules of Figure 1.1 in Section 3 except for (FAM-LEMMA) and (OBJ-LEMMA) plus the application and conversion rules given in Figure 1.7 which replace the application rules in Figure 1.2. The following two prop-

$$\frac{x:K \in \Gamma}{\Gamma \vdash x : K} \text{ (VAR-KIND)} \qquad \frac{x:A \in \Gamma}{\Gamma \vdash x : A} \text{ (VAR-FAM)}$$

$$\frac{\Gamma \vdash A : \Pi x:B.K \qquad \Gamma \vdash M : B}{\Gamma \vdash AM : [M/x]K} \text{ (APP-FAM)}$$

$$\frac{\Gamma \vdash M : \Pi x:A.B \qquad \Gamma \vdash N : A}{\Gamma \vdash MN : [N/x]B} \text{ (APP-OBJ)}$$

$$\frac{\Gamma \vdash A : K \qquad \Gamma \vdash K' \text{ kind} \qquad K =_\beta K'}{\Gamma \vdash A : K'} \text{ (β-KIND)}$$

$$\frac{\Gamma \vdash M : A \qquad \Gamma \vdash A' \text{ kind} \qquad A =_\beta A'}{\Gamma \vdash M : A'} \text{ (β-FAM)}$$

Figure 1.7: Full LF application and conversion rules

erties of full LF are shown to hold in [10], and will be used in proving the results below.

Lemma 0.9 (Subderivation)

1. If $\Gamma \vdash A : K$ holds then $\Gamma \vdash K$ kind also holds.

2. If $\Gamma \vdash M : A$ holds then $\Gamma \vdash A :$ Type also holds.

Lemma 0.10 (Subject Reduction)

1. If $\Gamma \vdash K$ kind holds and K β-reduces to K', then $\Gamma \vdash K'$ kind also holds.

2. If $\Gamma \vdash A : K$ holds and A β-reduces to A', then $\Gamma \vdash A' : K$ also holds.

3. If $\Gamma \vdash M : A$ holds and M β-reduces to M', then $\Gamma \vdash M' : A$ also holds.

We establish some further properties about canonical and full LF that will be needed to show the correspondence between these two systems.

Definition 0.11 Let Γ be a valid context (in canonical or full LF), and $x : P$ an item in Γ. We define the function $\mathcal{C}$ which maps variable x and context Γ to a canonical term. P has the form $\Pi x_1 : A_1 \ldots \Pi x_n : A_n.Q$ where $n \geq 0$ and Q is Type or a base type. For $i = 1, \ldots, n$, let Γ_i be the context $\Gamma, x_1 : A_1, \ldots, x_i : A_i$. We define $\mathcal{C}(x, \Gamma)$ to be the term:

$$\lambda x_1 : A_1 \ldots \lambda x_n : A_n.x(\mathcal{C}(x_1, \Gamma_1)) \ldots (\mathcal{C}(x_n, \Gamma_n)).$$

(We will abbreviate $\mathcal{C}(x, \Gamma)$ as $\mathcal{C}(x)$ in the remainder of this section, since Γ can always be determined from context.)

The following lemma holds for both canonical and full LF.

Lemma 0.12 Let Γ be a valid context containing $x : P$ where P is canonical. Then $\Gamma \vdash \mathcal{C}(x) : P$ is provable.

Proof: The proof is by induction on the structure of P and relies on the fact that for any variable z and well-typed canonical term Q, $([\mathcal{C}(z)/z]Q)^\beta = Q$. ∎

Using this lemma, the following result about canonical LF can be proven.

Lemma 0.13 If $\Gamma_1, x : A, P : Q, \Gamma_2$ is a valid context with $P : Q$ a context lemma, and $\Gamma_1, x : A, P : Q, \Gamma_2 \vdash \alpha$ is provable in canonical LF, then $\Gamma_1, \lambda x : A.P : \Pi x : A.Q, x : A, \Gamma_2$ is a valid context and the assertion $\Gamma_1, \lambda x : A.P : \Pi x : A.Q, x : A, \Gamma_2 \vdash \alpha$ is provable

Proof: We let Γ' and Γ'' be the contexts $\Gamma_1, x : A, P : Q, \Gamma_2$ and $\Gamma_1, \lambda x : A.P : \Pi x : A.Q, x : A, \Gamma_2$, respectively. We first prove the lemma with the added assumption that Γ'' is a valid context by induction on the height of a derivation of $\Gamma' \vdash \alpha$. The only non-trivial case occurs when the context item from Γ' used in an application of (APP-OBJ) or (APP-FAM) is $P : Q$. To show $\Gamma'' \vdash \alpha$, we use the corresponding item $\lambda x : A.P : \Pi x : A.Q$ from Γ'', with the additional hypothesis $\Gamma'' \vdash \mathcal{C}(x) : A$, which we know to be provable by Lemma 0.12. Using this result, the proof that Γ'' is valid is by a straightforward induction on the length of Γ_2. ∎

Definition 0.14 A *canonical derivation* in full LF is a derivation such that the following hold.

1. The assertion at the root is pre-canonical (*i.e.*, its normal form is canonical).

2. All assertions in the derivation except for those that occur as the conclusion of (VAR-KIND) or (VAR-OBJ), or as the conclusion *and* left premise of (APP-FAM) or (APP-OBJ) are pre-canonical.

3. In all assertions that occur as the conclusion, but not a left premise of (APP-FAM) or (APP-OBJ), the term on the right of the judgment is Type or a base type.

We will only consider canonical derivations in full LF when demonstrating the relative soundness and completeness of canonical LF. By imposing this restriction we are eliminating exactly those derivations such that a term used on the left of an application is not applied to the maximum number of arguments. A derivation that does not meet this requirement can, in fact, be mapped in a straightforward manner to one that does by introducing context items of the appropriate types and discharging them with an (ABS) rule. For example, a derivation of $\Gamma \vdash P : \Pi x : A.Q$ where P is not an abstraction can be mapped to a derivation of $\Gamma, x : A \vdash P : \Pi x : A.Q$ to which we can apply the corresponding (APP) rule to obtain $\Gamma, x : A \vdash P(\mathcal{C}(x)) : Q$, followed by an (ABS) rule to obtain $\Gamma \vdash \lambda x : A.P(\mathcal{C}(x)) : \Pi x : A.Q$.

We now define by induction an operation $\mathcal{L}$ which maps a derivation in full LF to a sequence of typing judgments. As we will see, the sequence of judgments associated to a canonical derivation is exactly the set of lemmas that will be added to the context to obtain the corresponding derivation in canonical LF.

Definition 0.15 $\mathcal{L}$ maps a derivation in full LF to a sequence of typing judgments Δ defined by induction on the derivation as follows.

- If the last rule in the derivation is (TYPE-KIND), (VAR-KIND), (VAR-FAM), or (EMPTY-CTX), then Δ is the empty sequence.

- If the last rule is a (PI) or (ABS) rule, then let Δ_1 be the sequence associated by $\mathcal{L}$ to the derivation of the left premise $\Gamma \vdash A :$ Type, and Δ_2 be the sequence associated to the derivation of the right premise. Let Δ_2' be the sequence that replaces every judgment $P : Q$ in Δ_2 with $\lambda x : A^\beta.P : \Pi x : A^\beta.Q$. Then Δ is Δ_1, Δ_2'.

- If the last rule is an (APP) rule, then let Δ_1 be the sequence associated by $\mathcal{L}$ to the derivation of the left premise $\Gamma \vdash P : Q$, and Δ_2 be the sequence associated to the derivation of the right premise. If the left premise is pre-canonical, and is not the conclusion of another (APP) rule or of a (VAR) rule, then Δ is $\Delta_1, P^\beta : Q^\beta, \Delta_2$. Otherwise, Δ is Δ_1, Δ_2.

- If the last rule is a β rule, Δ is the sequence associated to the derivation of the leftmost premise.

- If the last rule is (FAM-INTRO) or (OBJ-INTRO), then let Δ_1 and Δ_2 be the sequences associated by $\mathcal{L}$ to the derivation of the left and right premises, respectively. Then Δ is Δ_1, Δ_2.

It can be shown by a straightforward induction on a derivation of $\Gamma \vdash \alpha$ that for each judgment $P : Q$ in the sequence associated to this assertion by $\mathcal{L}$, $\Gamma \vdash P : Q$ holds.

Let $x_1 : P_1, \ldots, x_n : P_n$ be a valid context in full LF. For $i = 1, \ldots, n$, we denote the subcontext whose last element is $x_i : P_i$ as Γ_i. Given a derivation of $\vdash \Gamma_n$ context, for $i = 1, \ldots, n$, let Δ_i be the context associated to the subderivation of $\Gamma_{i-1} \vdash P_i$ kind or $\Gamma_{i-1} \vdash P_i :$ Type. We say that the context $\Delta_1, x_1 : P_1^\beta, \ldots, \Delta_n, x_n : P_n^\beta$ is the *extended normal context* associated to this derivation.

Theorem 0.16 (Completeness of Canonical LF) Let Γ be a context and α a judgment such that $\vdash \Gamma$ context and $\Gamma \vdash \alpha$ have canonical derivations in full LF. Let Γ' be the extended normal context associated to the derivation of $\vdash \Gamma$ context, and let Δ be the set of typing judgments associated to the derivation of $\Gamma \vdash \alpha$ by the function $\mathcal{L}$. Then Γ', Δ is a valid context and $\Gamma', \Delta \vdash \alpha^\beta$ is provable in canonical LF.

Proof: We first prove the above statement under the additional hypotheses that Γ' is a valid context in canonical LF. Using this result, it can be proved by a straightforward induction on the length of Γ that Γ' is valid. The proof is by induction on the height of a canonical derivation in full LF of $\Gamma \vdash \alpha$. For the case when the last rule is an (APP) rule, we must consider the subproof that contains a series of n (APP) rules, where $n \geq 1$ and the leftmost premise $\Gamma \vdash P : Q$ is not the conclusion of an (APP) rule. We consider the case when this premise is not the conclusion of a (VAR) rule. Thus P and Q are pre-canonical. First, we show that Γ', Δ is a valid context. Let Δ_0 be the sequence associated to $\Gamma \vdash P : Q$ by $\mathcal{L}$, and for $i = 1, \ldots, n$, let Δ_i be the sequence associated with the right premise in the ith (APP) rule application. Then Δ is $\Delta_0, P^\beta : Q^\beta, \Delta_1, \ldots, \Delta_n$. By the induction hypothesis applied to $\Gamma \vdash P : Q$, the context Γ', Δ_0 is valid and $\Gamma', \Delta_0 \vdash P^\beta : Q^\beta$ holds. Hence $\Gamma', \Delta_0, P^\beta : Q^\beta$ is a valid context. Also, by the induction hypothesis, for $i = 1, \ldots, n$, Γ', Δ_i is a valid context. Thus, we can conclude that Γ', Δ is valid. We now show $\Gamma', \Delta \vdash \alpha^\beta$ holds. By the induction hypothesis, for $i = 1, \ldots, n$, for each right premise $\Gamma \vdash \alpha_i$ in the series of (APP) rules, $\Gamma', \Delta_i \vdash \alpha_i^\beta$ holds. Clearly $\Gamma', \Delta \vdash \alpha_i^\beta$ also holds. Using the context item $P^\beta : Q^\beta$, we can simply apply the canonical LF rule (APP-FAM) or (APP-OBJ) to these n assertions to obtain that $\Gamma', \Delta \vdash \alpha^\beta$ holds. The case when $\Gamma \vdash P : Q$ is the conclusion of a (VAR) rule is similar.

For the case when the last rule is a (PI) or (ABS) rule, let Δ_1 be the sequence of judgments associated to the left premise $\Gamma \vdash A :$ Type by $\mathcal{L}$. Let Δ_2 be the sequence associated to the right premise $\Gamma, x : A \vdash \alpha_0$, and Δ_2' be the sequence that contains $\lambda x : A^\beta . P : \Pi x : A^\beta . Q$ for every $P : Q$ in Δ_2. Then Δ is Δ_1, Δ_2'. We first show that $\Gamma', \Delta_1, \Delta_2'$ is a valid context. By the induction hypothesis for the left premise, Γ', Δ_1 is a valid context, and $\Gamma', \Delta_1 \vdash A^\beta :$ Type holds. Thus, $\Gamma', \Delta_1, x : A^\beta$, the extended normal context associated to $\Gamma, x : A$ is also valid. We now apply the induction hypothesis to the right premise to obtain that $\Gamma', \Delta_1, x : A^\beta, \Delta_2$ is a valid context. By Lemma 0.13, $\Gamma', \Delta_1, \Delta_2', x : A^\beta$ is also a valid context. Since Γ', Δ is a subcontext of this context, it is valid also. Next, we show that $\Gamma', \Delta_1, \Delta_2' \vdash \alpha^\beta$ holds. By the induction hypothesis for the right premise and Lemma 0.13, $\Gamma', \Delta_1, \Delta_2', x : A^\beta \vdash \alpha_0^\beta$ holds. Since $\Gamma', \Delta_1 \vdash A^\beta :$ Type holds, clearly also $\Gamma', \Delta_1, \Delta_2' \vdash A^\beta :$ Type holds. Thus, by an application of the corresponding canonical LF (PI) or (ABS) rule, $\Gamma', \Delta_1, \Delta_2' \vdash \alpha^\beta$ holds. The remaining cases follow directly from the induction hypothesis and the definition of $\mathcal{L}$.   ∎

Theorem 0.17 (Soundness of Canonical LF) Let $\Gamma \vdash \alpha$ be a provable assertion in canonical LF. Let Γ' be the subcontext of Γ containing only variables associated with their types or kinds. Then $\Gamma' \vdash \alpha$ is provable in full LF.

Proof: We first prove the above statement under the additional hypotheses that Γ' is a valid context in full LF and $\Gamma' \vdash P : Q$ for every item $P : Q$ in Γ. Using this result, it can then be shown by induction on the length of Γ that this hypothesis follows from the fact that Γ is valid in canonical LF. We proceed by induction on the height of a canonical LF derivation of $\Gamma \vdash \alpha$. For the (APP) rules, we replace a single application of the rule by a series of n applications of the corresponding rule in full LF. (If n is 0, we simply apply the corresponding (VAR) rule.) If the rule uses a context lemma, we replace it with a full LF derivation of this lemma, which we know to be provable by assumption. The conclusion of each (APP) rule application is a judgment of the form $\Gamma \vdash P : [N/x]Q$ where P and $[N/x]Q$ are not necessarily in β-normal form. We must show that the corresponding β-normal assertion is also provable. $[N/x]Q$ must be a type or kind by Proposition 0.9. By Proposition 0.10, we obtain that $([N/x]Q)^\beta$ is also a type or kind. Then, by the corresponding β rule, $\Gamma \vdash P : ([N/x]Q)^\beta$ is provable. By Proposition 0.10, we know that $\Gamma \vdash P^\beta : ([N/x]Q)^\beta$ is also provable. The remaining cases follow directly from the induction hypothesis. ∎

B LF with Simplified Abstraction Rules

In this section we show that for LF assertions such that all types bound by outermost abstraction in the term on the left in the judgment are valid, the canonical LF system presented in Section 3 is equivalent to LF′, the system obtained by replacing the (ABS-FAM) and (ABS-OBJ) rules with the (ABS-FAM′) and (ABS-OBJ′) rules of Section 6, which drop the left premise $\Gamma \vdash A : \mathsf{Type}$. In such derivations, this premise is redundant.

To prove this result, we need the following transitivity lemma for LF′.

Lemma 0.18 (Transitivity) If $\Gamma, x:A, \Gamma' \vdash \alpha$ and $\Gamma \vdash N : A$ are provable, then $\Gamma, ([N/x]\Gamma')^\beta \vdash ([N/x]\alpha)^\beta$ is provable.

Proof: The proof is by induction on the structure of proofs. A similar result is stated for the more general presentation of LF in [10]. ∎

The following lemma shows that the left premise is redundant in all derivations of assertions such that the term on the left in the judgment is not an abstraction.

Lemma 0.19 Let Γ be a valid context and $\Gamma \vdash \alpha$ a provable assertion in LF′ that has a proof whose last rule is an application of (APP-FAM) or (APP-OBJ), and that has an application of (ABS-OBJ′) above the root such that there are no other applications of (APP-FAM) or (APP-OBJ) below it. Let Γ' be the context, and $x:A$ be the variable and its type bound by λ in the conclusion of this application of (ABS-OBJ′). Then $\Gamma' \vdash A : \mathsf{Type}$ is provable.

Proof: Let $Q : \Pi x_1:A_1 \ldots \Pi x_n:A_n.P$ be the context item used in the rule application at the root, and $N_1, \ldots, N_n$ the terms on the right of the colon in the remaining premises. Since there is an (ABS-OBJ′) application above the root, then for some i such that $1 \leq i \leq n$, A_i has the form $\Pi z:B.C$, the corresponding premise of the (APP) rule has the form

$$\Gamma \vdash N_i : ([N_1/x_1, \ldots, N_{i-1}/x_{i-1}]\Pi z:B.C)^\beta,$$

where N_i has the form $\lambda z:([N_1/x_1, \ldots, N_{i-1}/x_{i-1}]B)^\beta.M$, and the rule application at the root of this premise is (ABS-OBJ′). We show that $([N_1/x_1, \ldots, N_{i-1}/x_{i-1}]B)^\beta$ is a type. We know that $\Pi x_1:A_1 \ldots \Pi x_n:A_n.P$ is a type or kind, since Γ is a valid context. A proof of this fact contains a subproof of

$$\Gamma, x_1:A_1, \ldots, x_{i-1}:A_{i-1} \vdash \Pi z:B.C : \mathsf{Type}.$$

By Lemma 0.18, using the premises of the (APP) rule, we can conclude that the assertion $\Gamma \vdash ([N_1/x_1, \ldots, N_{i-1}/x_{i-1}]\Pi z:B.C)^\beta$: Type is provable. A proof of this fact contains a proof of the desired result. By similar reasoning, all other $x:A$ bound by λ in an application of (ABS-OBJ') can be shown to be types with respect to the corresponding context. ∎

Theorem 0.20 Let Γ be a context that is valid in LF and LF', and let α be a judgment.

1. If $\Gamma \vdash \alpha$ is provable in LF, then it is also provable in LF'.

2. If $\Gamma \vdash \alpha$ is provable in LF' and all types bound by λ in outermost abstractions in the term on the left in α are valid in LF', then $\Gamma \vdash \alpha$ is provable in LF.

Proof: (1) is proved by a straightforward induction on the height of an LF derivation of $\Gamma \vdash \alpha$. (2) is proved by induction on the structure of the term on the left in α. For the case when the term is an application, the last rule in a derivation must be an (APP) rule. Lemma 0.19 is required to show that all of the types bound by λ in outermost abstractions in the premises are valid in LF', so that the induction hypothesis can be applied to these assertions. All other cases follow directly from the induction hypothesis. ∎

TYPE THEORY

TYPE THEORY

An algorithm for testing conversion in Type Theory

THIERRY COQUAND

INRIA and University of Göteborg/Chalmers

Introduction

The goal of this note is to present a "modular" proof, for various type systems with η-conversion, of the completeness and correctness of an algorithm for testing the conversion of two terms. The proof of completeness is an application of the notion of logical relations (see Statman 1983 [14], that uses also this notion for a proof of Church-Rosser for simply typed λ-calculus).

An application of our result will be the equivalence between two formulations of Type Theory, the one where conversions are judgement, like in the present version of Martin-Löf set theory, and the one where conversion is defined at the level of raw terms, like in the standard version of LF (for a "conversion-as-judgement" presentation of LF, see Harper 1988 [6]). Even if we don't include η-conversion, the equivalence between the "conversion-as-judgement" and "conversion defined on raw terms" formulation appears to be a non-trivial property.

In order to simplify the presentation we will limit ourselves to type theory with only Π, and one universe. This calculus contains LF. After some motivations, we present the algorithm, the proof of its completeness and, as a corollary, its correctness. As a corollary of our argument, we prove normalisation, Church-Rosser, and the equivalence between the two possible formulations of Type Theory.

---

*This research was partly supported by ESPRIT Basic Research Action "Logical Frameworks".

1 Informal motivation

The algorithm

The idea is to compute the weak head-normal form of the two terms (in an untyped way), and, in order to take care of η-conversion, in the case where one weak-head normal form is an abstraction $(\lambda x{:}A)M$ and the other is N a variable or an application, to compare recursively apply(N, ξ) and $M[\xi]$.

This algorithm can be applied also for Authomath like system (and General Type Systems extended with η-conversion). But it is not complete if the type system does not have the normalisation property. It is directly used for type-checking and proof-checking in Type Theory.

Some remarks about the rules of Type Theory

The syntax is the following

$$M := \xi \mid U \mid \mathsf{apply}(M, M) \mid (\lambda x{:}M)M \mid (\Pi x{:}M)M$$

We will denote by EXP the set of syntactic closed expressions. We make a distinction between free, or real variables, or parameters, written $\xi, \zeta, \ldots$, and the bound, or apparent, variables, written $x, y, z, \ldots$ If M is an expression, ξ a parameter, and N an expression, we let $(\xi/N)M$ be the expression we get by ordinary subsitution of N to ξ in M. If M is an expression, x a bound variable, and N any expression, we will denote by $M[N]$ the expression $[x = N]M$, which behaves like an ordinary substitution except that $[x = N]((\lambda y{:}A)M) = (\lambda y{:}A)M$ and $[x = N]((\Pi y{:}A)M) = (\Pi y{:}A)M$ if $y = x$. We denote by PAR the set of parameters, which is supposed to be infinite. We don't assume that terms are considered up to α-conversion. This is crucial if we want to describe really an actual implementation. This will be possible by an indexing over finite sets of parameters and later by an indexing over contexts.

Given a finite subset $I \subset$ PAR, we denote by EXP(I) the set of expressions whose free variables belong to I. If $\xi \in$ PAR does not belong to I, we denote by I, ξ the set $I \cup \{\xi\}$.

The rules of Type Theory are presented in the appendix. They describe inductively when a judgement J holds in a context Γ. There are four possible forms of judgement, that are A _set_, $A = B$, $a \in A$ and $a = b \in A$.

Let us define an order relation between context by $\Gamma \subseteq \Gamma_1$ iff any $\xi \in A$ in Γ is also in Γ_1. A direct inductive argument shows that if a judgement holds in Γ, and $\Gamma \subseteq \Gamma_1$, then the same judgement holds also in Γ_1. From now on, we will consider contexts as "possible worlds" in a Kripke-like manner. This is a convenient way of making precise the notion of parameters "available at a given moment of time" (see [5] for another example of this method).

Lemma 1.1 If a judgement J holds in a context $\Gamma_1, \xi : A, \Gamma_2$, and $M \in A$ in the context Γ_1, then $(\xi/M)J$ holds in the context $\Gamma_1, (\xi/M)\Gamma_2$. If B set in the context $\Gamma_1, \xi : A, \Gamma_2$ and $M_1 = M_2 \in A$ in the context Γ_1 then $(\xi/M_1)B = (\xi/M_2)B$ in the context $\Gamma_1, (\xi/M_1)\Gamma_2$. If $N \in B$ in the context $\Gamma_1, \xi : A, \Gamma_2$ and $M_1 = M_2 \in A$ in the context Γ_1 then $(\xi/M_1)N = (\xi/M_2)N \in (\xi/M_1)B$ in the context $\Gamma_1, (\xi/M_1)\Gamma_2$.

This is directly proved by induction.

In this approach, substitution is a meta-operation on terms. Another possible formulation of Type Theory is to take substitution as an explicit term forming operation.

Once the substitution lemma is proved, it is direct to prove that if $A = B$ holds in Γ, then both A set and B set holds in Γ, and that if $M = N \in A$ holds in Γ, then both $M \in A$ and $N \in A$ holds in Γ.

Since we have chosen a "Russell-like" formulation of universes (see Martin-Löf 84 [9] for an explanation of this terminology), there are some lemmas to be proved about equality judgements between sets.

Lemma 1.2 The following properties hold:

1. if $A = B$ and $A \in U$ or $B \in U$, then both A, B are of type U and $A = B \in U$,

2. if $A = B$, then either A, B are both U, or $A = B \in U$ or A is $(\Pi x{:}A_0)A_1$, B is $(\Pi y{:}B_0)B_1$, and $A_0 = B_0$, $A_1[\xi] = B_1[\xi]$ $[\xi \in A_0]$,

3. $U \in U$ is not derivable,

4. if A set and A is not U or a product, then we have $A \in U$,

5. if $A = U$ $[\Gamma]$, or $U = A$ $[\Gamma]$, then A is U,

6. if $M \in A$ $[\Gamma]$ and M is a product, A is U.

Proof: The first claim is proved directly by induction. The second claim is proved using the first. The last four claims are proved by a direct induction or case analysis. ∎

One property that does not seem directly provable is strengthening, which says that if a judgement J holds in the context $\Gamma_1, \xi : A, \Gamma_2$ and ξ does not occur in Γ_2 and J, then J holds in Γ_1, Γ_2. This property will be a consequence of our main proposition 1.1. Strengthening will be essential in proving closure by η-reduction, and the equivalence between the present formulation of Type Theory and a formulation where conversion is defined at the level of raw terms.

Because of this, it is essential to formulate the rule Π-equality 2, which expresses the rule of η-conversion, as the equality $f = (\lambda x{:}A)\mathsf{apply}(f, x) \in (\Pi x : A)B$, if $f \in (\Pi x : A)B$. Indeed, it does not seem possible to prove directly that if $(\lambda x{:}A)\mathsf{apply}(f, x) \in (\Pi x{:}A)B$ holds and x does not appear free in f, then f is typable in the empty context.

Another property that does not seem directly provable is closure by β-reduction. This closure property is a consequence of the fact that Π is one-to-one.

About the correctness and completeness proof

We want to stress two features of this proof. The first is that we work with a type system where equality between sets or between terms is a judgement. We have thus four kinds of judgement, namely A *set*, $A = B$, $a \in A$ and $a = b \in A$. This is to be contrasted with a presentation of type theory where equality is defined at the level of raw terms, and there are only two judgements, namely A *set*, and $a \in A$. This last version was the first one chosen by Martin-Löf, see for instance Martin-Löf 72 [8], and the first version appears in Martin-Löf 84 [9], or Harper 87 [6]. It is not at all clear that these two presentations are equivalent, even in the case where there is only β-conversion. Actually, when we work with the equality as judgement version of type theory, and we define the computation of the head-normal form $M \Rightarrow c$ in an untyped way, it is not clear that if A *set* and $A \Rightarrow B$, then $A = B$, or even B *set*, and that if $a \in A$ and $a \Rightarrow b$, then $a = b \in A$. A key lemma in proving this appears to be that Π is one-to-one, that is, if $(\Pi x{:}A_1)B_1 = (\Pi y{:}A_2)B_2$, then $A_1 = A_2$ and $B_1[\xi] = B_2[\xi]$ $[\xi \in A_1]$. This will be a corollary of proposition prop:main, as well as the equivalence between the two formulations of type theory.

The second is that our proof will be a syntactic reflection of the semantical proof of consistency described in Martin-Löf 84. What we are doing here is thus very close to the interpretation presented in Smith 84 [13], but for a non-extensional theory. To each set A, we will associate one predicate Φ_A defined on syntactic expressions, and one equivalence relation Δ_A on the set of expressions that satisfy Φ_A. We will show then that if $M \in A$, then $\Phi_A(M)$ and if $M = N \in A$, then $\Delta_A(M, N)$. We will also show that if $\Phi_A(M)$ then M is normalisable, and if $\Delta_A(M, N)$ then M, N have a common β, η reduct. As corollary of the correctness proof of the algorithm, we will get the normalisation and the Church-Rosser property.

We can thus see our proof as a generalisation of the usual computability method, as in Martin-Löf 72. In this generalisation, one defines inductively a predicate and one equivalence relation on the set defined by this predicate, instead of defining only one predicate.

2 Weak head-normal form

We will say that a term is **canonical** if, and only if, it is U or an abstraction or a product.

The notion of weak head-normal form is given by its operational semantics.

$$\xi \Rightarrow \xi$$

$$U \Rightarrow U$$

$$(\lambda x{:}A)M \Rightarrow (\lambda x{:}A)M$$

$$(\Pi x{:}A)M \Rightarrow (\Pi x{:}A)M$$

$$\frac{M \Rightarrow (\lambda x{:}A)M_1 \quad M_1[N] \Rightarrow P}{\mathsf{apply}(M, N) \Rightarrow P}$$

$$\frac{M \Rightarrow M_1}{\mathsf{apply}(M, N) \Rightarrow \mathsf{apply}(M_1, N)} \quad M_1 \text{ not canonical}$$

We say that M has a **weak head-normal form** N iff $M \Rightarrow N$. M_1 and M_2 are **weakly equivalent**, notation $M_1 \simeq M_2$ iff M_1 and M_2 have identical weak head-normal forms. A term is **simple** iff it has a weak head-normal form which is not canonical. Notice that a weak head-normal form that is not canonical is either a parameter, or of the form $\mathsf{apply}(N, M)$ where N is a weak head-normal form that is not canonical.

It is important to notice the difference between the relation $M_1 \simeq M_2$ and Kleene equality, which would be defined as: if M_1 (resp. M_2) has a weak head-normal form, then so has M_2 (resp. M_1) and they are identical. With the present definition, $M_1 \simeq M_2$ implies that both M_1 and M_2 have a weak head-normal form.

Lemma 1.3 The following facts hold:

1. a given term has at most one weak head-normal form,

2. if $M \in \mathsf{EXP}(I)$ and $M \Rightarrow N$, then $N \in \mathsf{EXP}(I)$,

3. If $\mathsf{apply}(M, N)$ has a weak head-normal form, then so does M,

4. if $M_1 \simeq M_2$, and $\mathsf{apply}(M_1, N)$ has a weak head-normal form, then $\mathsf{apply}(M_1, N) \simeq \mathsf{apply}(M_2, N)$.

Remark: The first claim says that the algorithm described by the relation $\Rightarrow$ is deterministic. The last claim is false in general if $\mathsf{apply}(M_1, N)$ has no weak head-normal form. For instance, with $\Delta = (\lambda x{:}U)\mathsf{apply}(x, x)$, we have that $\Delta \simeq \Delta$, but not that $\mathsf{apply}(\Delta, \Delta) \simeq \mathsf{apply}(\Delta, \Delta)$.

3   An algorithm for β, η-conversion

The algorithm

We define recursively when two terms M_1 and M_2 are "equivalent", notation $M_1 \Leftrightarrow M_2$. This will be defined between closed expressions, and we need to consider also the relation $M_1 \Leftrightarrow M_2 \; [I]$, I finite subset of PAR, $M_1, M_2 \in \mathsf{EXP}(I)$. A consequence of the indexing by a finite set of parameters (and, later, of the use of contexts as Kripke world) is that we don't have to assume anything about α-conversion. The indexing by a finite set of parameters follows also the actual implementation of the algorithm, where we keep track of the real variables used so far in order to create a fresh variable.

$M \Leftrightarrow N \; [I]$ if, and only if, M has a weak head-normal form M_0, N has a weak head-normal form N_0 and the pair (M_0, N_0) is of one of the following form:

- (ξ, ξ),

- (U, U),

- $((\lambda x{:}A_1)M_1, (\lambda y{:}A_2)N_1)$ and $M_1[\xi] \Leftrightarrow N_1[\xi]$ $[I, \xi]$,

- $((\Pi x{:}M_1)M_2, (\Pi y{:}N_1)N_2)$ with $M_1 \Leftrightarrow N_1$ $[I]$ and $M_2[\xi] \Leftrightarrow N_2[\xi]$ $[I, \xi]$,

- $(\mathsf{apply}(M_1, M_2), \mathsf{apply}(N_1, N_2))$ with $M_1 \Leftrightarrow N_1$ $[I]$ and $M_2 \Leftrightarrow N_2$ $[I]$,

- $((\lambda x{:}A)T, N_0)$ with $T[\xi] \Leftrightarrow \mathsf{apply}(N_0, \xi)$ $[I, \xi]$, where N_0 is not canonical,

- $(M_0, (\lambda x{:}A)T)$ with $\mathsf{apply}(M_0, \xi) \Leftrightarrow T[\xi]$ $[I, \xi]$, where M_0 is not canonical.

It can be shown that the choice of the "generic parameter" ξ such that ξ does not belong to I is irrelevant (there exists such a ξ because PAR is infinite). From this remark, we see that if $M_1 \Leftrightarrow M_2$ $[I]$ and $I \subseteq I_1$, then $M_1 \Leftrightarrow M_2$ $[I_1]$.

One of the goal of the paper is to show that, if M, N are two syntactic expressions that are sets, or are terms of the same type, then M, N are convertible iff $M \Leftrightarrow N$.

It is clear from this definition that $\Leftrightarrow$ is symmetric. Furthermore, if $M_1 \simeq M_2$ and $M_2 \Leftrightarrow N$, then $M_1 \Leftrightarrow N$.

Notice that the algorithm described by $\Leftrightarrow$ "forgets" the type of the abstractions. Intuitively, this is because $M \Leftrightarrow N$ is considered only if it is known already that M, N set or $M, N \in A$. This is also essential for the next two lemmas.

Lemma 1.4 If $M_1, M_2 \in \mathsf{EXP}(I)$ verify $\mathsf{apply}(M_1, \xi) \Leftrightarrow \mathsf{apply}(M_2, \xi)$ $[I, \xi]$, then $M_1 \Leftrightarrow M_2$ $[I]$. If $a \Leftrightarrow b$ $[I]$, and a, b are simple, then $\mathsf{apply}(a, M) \Leftrightarrow \mathsf{apply}(b, M)$ $[I_1]$ for any $I \subseteq I_1$, $M \in \mathsf{EXP}(I_1)$.

Proof: We suppose that $M_1, M_2 \in \mathsf{EXP}(I)$ verify $\mathsf{apply}(M_1, \xi) \Leftrightarrow \mathsf{apply}(M_2, \xi)$ $[I, \xi]$. Then, both $\mathsf{apply}(M_1, \xi)$ and $\mathsf{apply}(M_2, \xi)$ have a weak head-normal form. It follows by lemma 1.3 that both M_1, M_2 have a weak head-normal form, that are abstraction or non-canonical. There are then four cases that can be checked directly. For instance, if $M_1 \Rightarrow (\lambda x{:}A)T$ and $M_2 \Rightarrow M_0$, M_0 not canonical, $\mathsf{apply}(M_1, \xi) \Leftrightarrow \mathsf{apply}(M_2, \xi)$ $[I, \xi]$ is equivalent to $T[\xi] \Leftrightarrow \mathsf{apply}(M_0, \xi)$ from which $M_1 \Leftrightarrow M_2$ follows.

The other part is direct. ∎

Lemma 1.5 $\Leftrightarrow$ is a partial equivalence relation, i.e. is symmetric and transitive.

Proof: By induction on the proof that $M_1 \Leftrightarrow M_2$, we show that if $M_2 \Leftrightarrow M_3$, then $M_1 \Leftrightarrow M_3$. ■

Normalisable terms

We define inductively a predicate Norm on the set of syntactic expressions. It will be a family of predicates Norm(M) [I] defined on EXP(I) such that Norm(M) [I] and $I \subseteq I_1$ implies Norm(M) [I_1]. We say that Norm(M) [I], or that $M \in$ EXP(I) is **normalisable** iff $M \Rightarrow M_0$ and M_0 is of the form:

- ξ,

- U,

- $(\lambda x{:}M_1)M_2$ and Norm(M_1) [I], Norm($M_2[\xi]$) [I,ξ],

- $(\Pi x{:}M_1)M_2$ and Norm(M_1) [I], Norm($M_2[\xi]$) [I,ξ],

- apply(M_1, M_2) and Norm(M_1) [I], Norm(M_2) [I].

Notice that given a proof of Norm(M_1), Norm(M_2) [I], we can decide whether or not $M_1 \Leftrightarrow M_2$ [I], that is, $\Leftrightarrow$ is a decidable relation on the set of normalisable terms. Notice also that if Norm(M) [I], then $M \Leftrightarrow M$ [I]. The relation Bisim is the equivalence relation on $\{M \in$ EXP $\mid$ Norm(M)$\}$ which is the restriction of $\Leftrightarrow$ on this set.

4   Computability relation

Contexts as Kripke possible world

We have four inductively defined relations on the set of syntactic expressions that correspond to the four judgement of type theory. They are described in the appendix. If Γ is a context, and I the finite set of parameters that occur in Γ, we will write EXP(Γ), $M_1 \Leftrightarrow M_2$ [Γ] and Norm(M) [Γ] respectively for EXP(I), $M_1 \Leftrightarrow M_2$ [I] and Norm(M) [I].

We recall that we have defined an order relation between context by $\Gamma \subseteq \Gamma_1$ iff if $\xi \in A$ is in Γ, then it is also in Γ_1. A direct inductive argument shows that if a judgement holds in Γ, and $\Gamma \subseteq \Gamma_1$, then the same judgement holds also in Γ_1. From now on, we will consider contexts as "possible worlds" in a Kripke-like manner. This is a convenient way of making precise the notion of parameters "available at a given moment of time" (see [5] for another example of this method).

From now on, we take the convention that any statement or proof is, even if it is not stated explcitely, relativised to an arbitrary context.

For instance, a set X is now a family $X(\Gamma)$ of sets such that $X(\Gamma_1) \subseteq X(\Gamma_2)$ if $\Gamma_1 \subseteq \Gamma_2$. We will denote also by $x \in X$ $[\Gamma]$ the fact that x belongs to $X(\Gamma)$, and we will say in this case that x belongs to X **at level** Γ. A predicate φ on X is a now a proposition $\varphi(x)$ $[\Gamma]$ depending on a context Γ and on $x \in X(\Gamma)$, which is increasing in the context Γ, that is such that $\varphi(x)$ $[\Gamma]$ and $\Gamma \subseteq \Gamma_1$ implies $\varphi(x)$ $[\Gamma_1]$. There is a similar definition for relations. An example of such a set is the set of expressions. A predicate on this set is the predicate Norm, and a binary relation on this set is $\Leftrightarrow$.

Let φ_1, φ_2 be two predicates on EXP. Following the rules of Kripke semantics, we say that $\varphi_1(x)$ implies $\varphi_2(x)$ at level Γ iff for all $\Gamma_0 \supseteq \Gamma$, $\varphi_1(x)$ $[\Gamma_0]$ implies that $\varphi_2(x)$ $[\Gamma_0]$.

We let $X(\Gamma)$ be the set of pairs (ψ, δ) where ψ is a predicate on EXP at level Γ and δ an equivalence relation on $\{M \in \text{EXP} \mid \psi(M)\}$ at level Γ. The equality on $X(\Gamma)$ is $(\varphi_1, \delta_1) = (\varphi_2, \delta_2)$ $[\Gamma]$ iff $\varphi_1(M) \equiv \varphi_2(M)$ and $\delta_1(M, N) \equiv \delta_2(M, N)$ at level Γ (where $\equiv$ denotes logical equivalence).

Definition of the computability relation

If A *set*, let us say that a pair $(\Phi, \Delta) \in X$ is a **computability relation on** A iff the following conditions are satisfied:

1. $\Phi(a)$ implies $a \in A$,

2. $\Delta(a, b)$ implies $a = b \in A$,

3. $a \in A$, a simple and Norm(a) imply $\Phi(a)$,

4. $a = b \in A$, a, b simple and Bisim(a, b) imply $\Delta(a, b)$,

5. if $\Phi(a)$ then Norm(a),

6. if $\Delta(a, b)$ then $a \Leftrightarrow b$,

7. if $\Phi(a)$, $a = u \in A$, $a \simeq u$, then $\Phi(u)$,

8. if $\Delta(a, b)$, $u = a \in A$, $u \simeq a$, $b = v \in A$, $b \simeq v$, then $\Delta(u, v)$.

We are going to define a predicate Ψ on EXP. Intuitively, $\Psi(A)$ means that A is a "well-formed" set. We will have that $\Psi(A)$ implies A *set*. For A

such that $\Psi(A)$, we will define $\Theta_A = (\Phi_A, \Delta_A) \in X$ computability relation on A.

We first define Φ_U. Actually we define simultaneously Φ_U such that $\Phi_U(A)$ implies $A \in U$, and for A such that $\Phi_U(A)$ we define $\theta_A = (\varphi_A, \delta_A) \in X$ computability relation on A.

We say that $\Phi_U(A)$ [Γ] iff $A \in U$ [Γ] and

- either A is simple, in which case we ask $\mathsf{Norm}(A)$ and we define $\varphi_A(M)$ [Γ_1], for $\Gamma_1 \supseteq \Gamma$, by $M \in A$, $\mathsf{Norm}(M)$ at level Γ_1 and $\delta_A(M_1, M_2)$ is $M_1 = M_2 \in A$ & $M_1 \Leftrightarrow M_2$ at level Γ_1,

- or $A \Rightarrow (\Pi x{:}A_0)A_1$, in which case we ask

  1. $A = (\Pi x{:}A_0)A_1 \in U$,
  2. $\Phi_U(A_0)$,
  3. $\varphi_{A_0}(a)$ implies $\Phi_U(A_1[a])$,
  4. $\delta_{A_0}(a, b)$ implies $\theta_{A_1[a]} = \theta_{A_1[b]}$.

These last conditions are stated at level Γ.

In this case, we define $\varphi_A(M)$ [Γ_1] for $\Gamma_1 \supseteq \Gamma$ by $M \in A$ and

  – $\varphi_{A_0}(a)$ implies $\varphi_{A_1[a]}(\mathsf{apply}(M, a))$,
  – $\delta_{A_0}(a, b)$ implies $\delta_{A_1[a]}(\mathsf{apply}(M, a), \mathsf{apply}(M, b))$,
  – if $M \Rightarrow (\lambda y{:}B_0)T$, then $\mathsf{Norm}(B_0)$.

$\delta_A(M_1, M_2)$ is the equivalence relation on $\{M \in \mathsf{EXP} \mid \varphi_A(M)\}$ defined by

$$M_1 = M_2 \in A \ \& \ [\varphi_{A_0}(a) \Rightarrow \delta_{A_1[a]}(\mathsf{apply}(M_1, a), \mathsf{apply}(M_2, a))].$$

These last definitions are stated at level Γ_1.

Remark: A priori, it is not clear that if $A \in U$, and $A \Rightarrow B$, then A is simple or B is a product. It will follow from the fact that Π is one-to-one that A is simple or B is a product, that $B \in U$, and that $A = B$.

Let us explicit the definition of $\varphi_A(M)$ [Γ_1] in the case where $A \Rightarrow (\Pi x{:}A_0)A_1$. It means first that the judgement $M \in A$ holds in the context Γ_1. Next, if $\Gamma_1 \subseteq \Gamma_2$, then $\varphi_{A_0}(a)$ [Γ_2] implies $\varphi_{A_1}(\mathsf{apply}(M, a))$ [Γ_2] and

$\delta_{A_0}(a, b)$ [Γ_2] implies $\delta_{A_1[a]}(\mathsf{apply}(M, a), \mathsf{apply}(M, b))$ [Γ_2]. Finally, if $M \Rightarrow (\lambda y{:}B_0)T$ [Γ_1] then $\mathsf{Norm}(B_0)$ [Γ_1].

Notice that if follows directly from this definition that $\Phi_U(A)$, $A = B \in U$, and $A \simeq B$ imply $\Phi_U(B)$ and $\theta_A = \theta_B$.

There is a problem a priori in such an inductive definition, because of the fact that the predicate Φ_U that is defined has negative occurences. A discussion on this difficulty is postponed to the next section. This discussion will justify also the following induction principle. Let P be a predicate on EXP. Suppose that if A is simple, then $\Phi_U(A)$ implies $P(A)$, and that if $\Phi_U(A)$, $A \Rightarrow (\Pi x{:}A_0)A_1$, $A = (\Pi x{:}A_0)A_1 \in U$, $P(A_0)$, $\varphi_{A_0}(a) \Rightarrow P(A_1[a])$, then $P(A)$. Then, we can conclude that, for all A, $\Phi_U(A)$ implies $P(A)$.

Lemma 1.6 If $\Phi_U(A)$, then $\mathsf{Norm}(A)$ and $\theta_A = (\varphi_A, \delta_A)$ is a computability relation on A.

Proof: Remark that this entails that if $\Phi_U(A)$, then $\varphi_A(\xi)$ [$\xi \in A$], because ξ is simple and normalisable.

Consider the property $P(A)$ that $\Phi_U(A)$ and

1. $\mathsf{Norm}(A)$,

2. $a \in A$, a simple and $\mathsf{Norm}(a)$ imply $\varphi_A(a)$,

3. $a = b \in A$, a, b simple and $\mathsf{Bisim}(a, b)$ imply $\delta_A(a, b)$,

4. if $\varphi_A(a)$ then $\mathsf{Norm}(a)$,

5. if $\delta_A(a, b)$ then $a \Leftrightarrow b$,

6. if $\varphi_A(a)$, $a = u \in A$, $a \simeq u$, then $\varphi_A(u)$,

7. if $\delta_A(a, b)$, $u = a \in A$, $u \simeq a$, $b = v \in A$, $b \simeq v$, then $\delta_A(u, v)$.

By definition of Φ_U, $P(A)$ if A is simple and $\Phi_U(A)$.

Next, suppose $\Phi_U(A)$, $A \Rightarrow (\Pi x{:}A_0)A_1$, $A = (\Pi x{:}A_0)A_1 \in U$, $P(A_0)$, and $\varphi_{A_0}(a)$ implies $P(A_1[a])$.

Notice first that, by induction hypothesis, $\varphi_{A_0}(\xi)$ [$\xi \in A_0$], since ξ is simple and normalisable of type A_0 at level $\xi \in A_0$.

Since $\Phi_U(A)$, we have $\Phi_U(A_1[\xi])$ [$\xi \in A_0$] and hence, $\mathsf{Norm}(A_1[\xi])$ [$\xi \in A_0$] by induction hypothesis. We have also $\mathsf{Norm}(A_0)$ by induction hypothesis, and hence $\mathsf{Norm}(A)$.

Let $M \in A$ be simple and normalisable. For any a such that $\varphi_{A_0}(a)$, we have that apply(M, a) is simple and normalisable, because M is simple and a normalisable, and hence by induction hypothesis, $\varphi_{A_1[a]}(\text{apply}(M, a))$. For any a, b such that $\delta_{A_0}(a, b)$, we have that apply(M, a) and apply(M, b) are simple and that Bisim$(\text{apply}(M, a), \text{apply}(M, b))$, because Bisim$(a, b)$ and M is simple. Hence, by induction hypothesis, $\delta_{A_1[a]}(\text{apply}(M, a), \text{apply}(M, b))$. This shows that $\varphi_A(M)$ holds.

In the same way, we can show that if $M, N \in A$, M, N are simple and Bisim(M, N), then $\delta_A(M, N)$, using lemma 1.4.

If $\varphi_A(M)$, then we have $\varphi_{A_1[\xi]}(\text{apply}(M, \xi))$, because $\varphi_{A_0}(\xi)$ $[\xi \in A_0]$. Hence Norm$(\text{apply}(M, \xi))$ at level $\xi \in A_0$. This implies that M is simple or has a weak head-normal form which is an abstraction. If M is simple, then Norm$(\text{apply}(M, \xi))$ implies Norm(M). If $M \Rightarrow (\lambda y{:}B_0)T$, then Norm$(B_0)$. This, together with Norm$(\text{apply}(M, \xi))$, implies that M is normalisable.

If $\delta_A(M, N)$, then we have $\delta_{A_1[\xi]}(\text{apply}(M, \xi), \text{apply}(N, \xi))$, because we have $\varphi_{A_0}(\xi)$ $[\xi \in A_0]$. Hence apply$(M, \xi) \Leftrightarrow \text{apply}(N, \xi)$ at level $\xi \in A_0$ by induction hypothesis. We deduce $M \Leftrightarrow N$ by lemma 1.4.

Next, suppose that $a \in A$, $\varphi_A(a)$, $a = u \in A$, and $a \simeq u$ and we have to show that $\varphi_A(u)$ holds. We have $u \in A$ since $a = u \in A$. If $M \in A_0$ and $\varphi_{A_0}(M)$, then we have to show that $\varphi_{A_1[M]}(\text{apply}(u, M))$ holds. We have $\varphi_{A_1[M]}(\text{apply}(a, M))$ because $\varphi_A(a)$. Furthermore apply$(a, M) = \text{apply}(u, M) \in A_1[M]$. By lemma 1.8, we have that apply(a, M) is normalisable and hence has a weak head-normal form. By lemma 1.3, we have apply$(a, M) \simeq \text{apply}(u, M)$. By induction hypothesis, the lemma holds for $A_1[M]$. Hence $\varphi_{A_1[M]}(\text{apply}(u, M))$. Furthermore, if $u \Rightarrow (\lambda x{:}B_0)T$, then Norm$(B_0)$ because $u \simeq a$ and $\varphi_A(a)$. The proof of the last claim is similar.

■

Notice the essential use of contexts as Kripke worlds in this reasoning.

We define the equivalence relation Δ_U on the set of expressions that satisfies Φ_U by: $\Delta_U(A, B)$ iff $A = B \in U$, $\theta_A = \theta_B$, $A \Leftrightarrow B$ and if $A \Rightarrow (\Pi x{:}A_0)A_1$, $B \Rightarrow (\Pi y{:}B_0)B_1$ then $A_0 = A_1$ and $B_0[\xi] = B_1[\xi]$ $[\xi \in A_0]$.

Lemma 1.7 (Φ_U, Δ_U) is a computability relation on U.

We can now define $\Psi(A)$, and for A such that $\Psi(A)$, the predicate Φ_A and the equivalence relation Δ_A. We say that $\Psi(A)$ $[\Gamma]$ iff A set $[\Gamma]$ and

- either A is U, we have already defined Φ_U and Δ_U,

- or $A \in U$ $[\Gamma]$ and $\Phi_U(A)$ $[\Gamma]$, in which case we take Θ_A to be θ_A,

- or A is $(\Pi x{:}A_0)A_1$, in which case we ask

  - $\Psi(A_0)$,
  - $\Phi_{A_0}(a)$ implies $\Psi(A_1[a])$,
  - $\Delta_{A_0}(a, b)$ implies $\Theta_{A_1[a]} = \Theta_{A_1[b]}$.

These last conditions are stated at level Γ.

In this case, we define $\Phi_A(M)\ [\Gamma_1]$ for $\Gamma_1 \supseteq \Gamma$ by $M \in A$ and

  - $\Phi_{A_0}(a)$ implies $\Phi_{A_1[a]}(\mathsf{apply}(M, a))$,
  - $\Delta_{A_0}(a, b)$ implies $\Delta_{A_1[a]}(\mathsf{apply}(M, a), \mathsf{apply}(M, b))$,
  - if $M \Rightarrow (\lambda y{:}B_0)T$, then $\mathsf{Norm}(B_0)$.

$\Delta_A(M_1, M_2)$ is the equivalence relation on $\{M \in \mathsf{EXP} \mid \varphi_A(M)\}$ defined by

$$M_1 = M_2 \in A\ \&\ [\Phi_{A_0}(a) \Rightarrow \Delta_{A_1[a]}(\mathsf{apply}(M_1, a), \mathsf{apply}(M_2, a))].$$

These last definitions are stated at level Γ_1.

Notice that this definition is a priori ambiguous, since we can have both $A \in U$, and A is $(\Pi x{:}A_0)A_1$. But in this case, we have also $A_0 \in U$, and $A_1[\xi] \in U\ [\xi \in A_0]$, and we can show inductively on the proof of $A \in U$ that both cases give the same definition. This ambiguity does not appear if we use a formulation "à la Tarski" of universes, as in Martin-Löf 84 [9], or if we restrict the proof to LF, where there is a syntactic distinction between types and kinds.

Lemma 1.8 If $\Psi(A)$, then $\mathsf{Norm}(A)$ and $\Theta_A = (\Phi_A, \Delta_A)$ is a computability relation on A.

Proof: The argument is the same as the one for Φ_U given above, and is by induction on the proof that $\Psi(A)$. We use furthermore the fact that the statement holds for U, using lemma 1.7 and 1.6. ∎

Justification of this definition

The inductive definitions of Ψ, and of Φ_U are of the following form: we define simultaneously both a predicate φ on the set EXP, and a function on $\{M \in \mathsf{EXP} \mid \varphi(M)\}$. For Φ_U for instance, we define simultaneously the predicate Φ_U and $\theta_A \in X$ defined for $A \in \{M \in \mathsf{EXP} \mid \Phi_U(M)\}$. We have to convince ourselves that the above definition is correct. We will show how to reduce this kind of definition to the existence of a least fixed-point of a monotone operator on a complete lattice.

For a first such reduction, consider the set Y of pairs (φ, f) where φ is a predicate on EXP and f a function from $\{M \in \text{EXP} \mid \varphi(M)\}$ to X. Notice first that Y is a complete lattice for the ordering $(\varphi_1, f_1) \leq (\varphi_2, f_2)$ defined by $\varphi_1(M) \Rightarrow \varphi_2(M)$ and, if $\varphi_1(M)$, then $f_1(M) = f_2(M)$. Notice next that the definition of Φ_U can be seen as a monotone operator from Y to Y. This is essentially the justification implicit in Martin-Löf 72 [8] which is explained in another framework in Aczel 77 [1].

For a second reduction, more set-theoretical in nature, we consider $A \longmapsto (\varphi_A, \delta_A)$ as a functional relation R between EXP and X, that is a relation R on $\text{EXP} \times X$ such that, for any $M \in \text{EXP}$, there exists at most one $x \in X$ such that $R(M, x)$. Notice first that the definition of Φ_U can be seen as a monotone operator on the set of relation between EXP and X. This is a complete lattice for the inclusion. Notice next that the least fixed-point of this operator is a functional relation. We define then Φ_U to be the domain of this functional relation, that is the set of $M \in \text{EXP}$ such that there exists $x \in X$ such that $R(M, x)$. This reduction appears in Allen 87 [2], and was pointed out to the author by S. Hayashi.

Of course, we have now to show that a monotone function on a complete lattice has a least fixed-point, at least in these particular cases. It is well-known how to do it using an impredicative definition (this is Tarski fixed-point theorem). One may wonder if there exist more basic reductions. One alternative is even to admit the existence of Φ_U and the induction principle over it as a new axiom. We will limit ourselves here to have indicated these two possible reductions to the existence of a fixed-point of a monotone function on a complete lattice.

5   Completeness of the algorithm

We define first inductively when a "type-checking" context $\Gamma = \xi_1 \in A_1, \ldots, \xi_n \in A_n$ is valid, and when it is valid, when a substitution, written $(\xi_1/a_1) \ldots (\xi_n/a_n)$, fits this context at level Γ_0, and when two such substitutions $(\xi_1/a_1) \ldots (\xi_n/a_n)$ and $(\xi_1/b_1) \ldots (\xi_n/b_n)$ are considered to be equal at level Γ_0.

If $\Gamma = \xi \in A$, then Γ is valid iff $\Psi(A)$. Furthermore (ξ/a) fits Γ at level Γ_0 iff $\Phi_A(a)\ [\Gamma_0]$ and $(\xi/a), (\xi/b)$ are equal iff $\Delta_A(a, b)\ [\Gamma_0]$.

Next, if Γ is valid, if A set $[\Gamma]$, and $\Psi(\sigma A)$ for any σ that fits Γ at level Γ_0, and $\Theta_{\sigma_1 A} = \Theta_{\sigma_2 A}$ $[\Gamma_0]$ whenever σ_1 and σ_2 are equal, then $\Gamma, \xi \in A$ is valid. Furthermore, $\sigma(\xi/a)$ fits $\Gamma, \xi \in A$ at level Γ_0 iff $\Phi_{\sigma A}(a)$ $[\Gamma_0]$, and $\sigma_1(\xi/a_1), \sigma_2(\xi/a_2)$ are equal iff σ_1, σ_2 are equal and $\Delta_{\sigma_1 A}(a_1, a_2)$ $[\Gamma_0]$.

Proposition 1.1 If A *set*, then $\Psi(A)$. If $A = B$, then $\Psi(A), \Psi(B), \Theta_A = \Theta_B$. If $a \in A$, then $\Psi(A)$ and $\Phi_A(a)$. Finally, if $a = b \in A$, then $\Psi(A)$ and $\Delta_A(a, b)$.

Proof: More generally, we prove inductively that if Γ is a valid context, σ a substitution that fits Γ at level Γ_0, and σ_1, σ_2 two equal substitutions that fit Γ at level Γ_0, then

- if A *set* $[\Gamma]$, then, at level Γ_0, $\Psi(\sigma A)$, and $\Psi(\sigma_1 A), \Psi(\sigma_2 A)$, and $\Theta_{\sigma_1 A} = \Theta_{\sigma_2 A}$,

- if $A = B$ $[\Gamma]$, then, at level Γ_0, $\Psi(\sigma A)$, $\Psi(\sigma B)$ and $\Theta_{\sigma A} = \Theta_{\sigma B}$,

- if $a \in A$ $[\Gamma]$, then, at level Γ_0, $\Psi(\sigma A)$, $\Phi_{\sigma A}(\sigma a)$, and $\Theta_{\sigma_1 A} = \Theta_{\sigma_2 A}$, $\Delta_{\sigma_1 A}(\sigma_1 a, \sigma_2 a)$,

- if $a = b \in A$ $[\Gamma]$, then, at level Γ_0 $\Psi(\sigma A)$, $\Theta_{\sigma_1 A} = \Theta_{\sigma_2 A}$, and $\Delta_{\sigma A}(\sigma a, \sigma b)$.

This is proved by induction together with the fact that any context is valid. Lemma 1.8 handles the rules of β-conversion and the rule of η-conversion.

Let us show for instance how is handled the rule Π-equality 2. To simplify the notations, we suppose the context empty. We have then $\Psi((\Pi x: A)B), \Phi_{(\Pi x A)B}(f)$, and we want to show $\Phi_{(\Pi x A)B}((\lambda x : A)\mathsf{apply}(f, x))$ and $\Delta_{(\Pi x A)B}(f, (\lambda x:A)\mathsf{apply}(f, x))$. By the definition of Ψ, we have that $\Psi(A)$, that $\Phi_A(a)$ implies $\Psi(B[a])$, and $\Delta_A(a, b)$ implies $\Theta_{B[a]} = \Theta_{B[b]}$, $\Phi_A(a)$ implies $\Phi_{B[a]}(\mathsf{apply}(f, a))$ and $\Delta_A(a, b)$ implies $\Delta_{B[a]}(\mathsf{apply}(f, a), \mathsf{apply}(f, b))$. Let us assume $\Phi_A(a)$ and show that $\Phi_{B[a]}(\mathsf{apply}((\lambda x : A)\mathsf{apply}(f, x), a))$. This follows from $\Phi_{B[a]}(\mathsf{apply}(f, a))$ and lemma 1.8. Since $\mathsf{Norm}(A)$ because $\Psi(A)$ and by lemma 1.8, we have $\Phi_{(\Pi x A)B}((\lambda x:A)\mathsf{apply}(f, x))$. In the same way, if $\Delta_A(a, b)$, then we have $\Delta_{B[a]}(\mathsf{apply}((\lambda x:A)\mathsf{apply}(f, x), a), \mathsf{apply}((\lambda x: A)\mathsf{apply}(f, x), b))$ follows from $\Delta_{B[a]}(\mathsf{apply}(f, a), \mathsf{apply}(f, b))$ and lemma 1.8.

∎

In particular, if $M = N$, or $M = N \in A$, then $M \Leftrightarrow N$ and this expresses the completeness of our algorithm for testing conversion of terms.

6   Correctness of the algorithm

A first application is the fact that Π is one-to-one.

Proposition 1.2 If $(\Pi x{:}A_0)A_1 = (\Pi y{:}B_0)B_1$, then $A_0 = B_0$ and $A_1[\xi] = B_1[\xi]$ $[\xi \in A_0]$.

Proof: We use lemma 1.2. The result is clear in the case of Π-formation 2. And if $(\Pi x{:}A_0)A_1 = (\Pi y{:}B_0)B_1 \in U$, then $\Delta_U((\Pi x{:}A_0)A_1, (\Pi y{:}B_0)B_1)$ by proposition 1.1, hence the result. ∎

The rest of this section collects direct consequences of the fact that Π is one-to-one.

Corollary 1.1 If $M \in A_1$, $M \in A_2$, then $A_1 = A_2$.

Proof: By induction on M using proposition 1.2. ∎

Lemma 1.9 If $(\lambda x{:}A_1)b \in (\Pi y{:}A_2)B$, then $A_1 = A_2$ and $b[\xi] \in B[\xi]$ $[\xi \in A_1]$.

Proof: We have $(\lambda x : A_1)b \in (\Pi x : A_1)B_1$, with $b[\xi] \in B_1[\xi]$ $[\xi \in A_1]$ and $(\Pi x : A_1)B_1 = (\Pi y{:}A_2)B$. By proposition 1.2, we get $A_1 = A_2$ and $B_1[\xi] = B[\xi]$ $[\xi \in A_1]$, hence he result. ∎

Lemma 1.10 If A *set* and $A \Rightarrow B$, then B *set* and $A = B$. If $a \in A$, and $a \Rightarrow b$, then $b \in A$ and $a = b \in A$.

Proof: We show by induction on $M \Rightarrow N$, that if $M \Rightarrow N$ then if M *set*, then N *set* and $M = N$, and if $M \in A$, then $N \in A$ and $M = N \in A$.

Let us show the case where M is $\mathsf{apply}(M_1, N_1)$, $M_1 \Rightarrow (\lambda x : A_2)M_2$ and $M_2[N_1] \Rightarrow N$. We have $M_1 \in (\Pi x : A_1)B_1$, $N_1 \in A_1$. By induction hypothesis, $(\lambda x{:}A_2)M_2 \in (\Pi x{:}A_1)B_1$ and $M_1 = (\lambda x{:}A_2)M_2 \in (\Pi x{:}A_1)B_1$. By lemma 1.9, $A_1 = A_2$ and $M_2[\xi] \in B_1[\xi]$ $[\xi \in A_1]$. We deduce that $M_2[N_1] \in B_1[N_1]$. By induction hypothesis, $N \in B_1[N_1]$ and $M_2[N_1] = N \in B_1[N_1]$. But we have $\mathsf{apply}(M_1, N_1) = \mathsf{apply}((\lambda x{:}A_2)M_2, N_1) \in B_1[N_1]$ by Π-elimination 2, and $\mathsf{apply}((\lambda x : A_2)M_2, N_1) = M_2[N_1] \in B_1[N_1]$ by Π-equality 1. ∎

This lemma can be expressed as the statement of the subject-reduction for β-reduction.

The next proposition states the correctness of the algorithm corresponding to the relation $\Leftrightarrow$. This is only stated in the empty context, but the relativised version to amy context holds as well.

Proposition 1.3 If A set, B set, and $A \Leftrightarrow B$ then $A = B$. Similarly, if $a \in A$, $b \in A$ and $a \Leftrightarrow b$, then $a = b \in A$. Furthermore, if $a \Leftrightarrow b$, $a \in A$, $b \in B$, and a, b are simple, then $A = B$, and $a = b \in A$.

Proof: We use essentially lemma 1.10 and lemma 1.2. We prove simultaneously by induction on $M \Leftrightarrow N$ that if $M \Leftrightarrow N$, then if M, N set then $M = N$, if $M, N \in A$ then $M = N \in A$, and if M, N are simple and $M \in A, N \in B$, then $A = B$ and $M = N \in A$.

Let us consider for instance the case where $M \Rightarrow \mathsf{apply}(M_1, M_2)$ and $N \Rightarrow \mathsf{apply}(N_1, N_2)$ and $M_1 \Leftrightarrow M_2$, $N_1 \Leftrightarrow N_2$. We have that M, N are simple. If $M \in A$, $N \in B$, then we have $M_1 \in (\Pi x{:}C)A_1$, $M_2 \in C$, $N_1 \in (\Pi y{:}D)B_1$, $N_2 \in D$ and $A_1[M_2] = A$, $B_1[N_2] = B$. This follows from lemma 1.10. Since M_1, N_1 are simple, we can apply the induction hypothesis and we get that $(\Pi x : C)A_1 = (\Pi y : D)B_1$, and $M_1 = N_1 \in (\Pi x : C)A_1$. By proposition 1.2, this implies $C = D$ and $A_1[\xi] = B_1[\xi]$ $[\xi \in C]$. We have then $M_2, N_2 \in C$. By induction hypothesis, this implies $M_2 = N_2 \in C$. We then get that $\mathsf{apply}(M_1, M_2) = \mathsf{apply}(N_1, N_2) \in A_1[M_2]$, and $A = A_1[M_2] = B_1[N_2] = B$. ∎

Corollary 1.2 If A, B set and $A = B$ $[\Gamma]$, then $A = B$. If $M, N \in A$ and $M = N \in A$ $[\Gamma]$, then $M = N \in A$.

Proof: By proposition 1.1 and proposition 1.3. ∎

The relativised version of this corollary says that the equational theory at level Γ_1 is a conservative extension of the one at level $\Gamma \subseteq \Gamma_1$.

7 Equivalence with another formulation of Type Theory

Lemma 1.11 If M set then M has a β-normal form M_0 such that $M = M_0$. If $M \in A$, then M has a β-normal form M_0 such that $M = M_0 \in A$.

Proof: We have Norm(M) if M *set* or $M \in A$ by proposition 1.1. We prove next by induction on the proof that Norm(M) using lemma 1.10 that if Norm(M), then if M *set* then M has a normal form M_0 such that $M = M_0$, and if $M \in A$ then M has a normal form M_0 such that $M = M_0 \in A$. ∎

Let us say that two expressions M, N are confluent if they can be reduced to a same term by β, η-reductions.

Proposition 1.4 If $M = N$, or $M = N \in A$, then M, N are confluent.

Proof: We define the size $s(M)$ of a term M as the number of symbols in M. We prove by induction on $s(M) + s(N)$ that if $M \Leftrightarrow N$, M, N in β-normal form then if M, N *set* then M, N are confluent, if $M = N \in A$ then M, N are confluent, and finally, if M, N are simple and $M \in A, N \in B$, then $A = B$ and M, N are confluent.

Let us treat only two cases. Let us suppose that M is $(\lambda x{:}P)M_1$ and N is $(\lambda y{:}Q)N_1$, and $M_1[\xi] \Leftrightarrow N_1[\xi]$, and $M = N \in A$. We have then $M_1[\xi] \in B_1[\xi]$ $[\xi \in P]$ and $N_1[\xi] \in C_1[\xi]$ $[\xi \in Q]$ with $A = (\Pi x{:}P)B_1 = (\Pi y{:}Q)C_1$. By proposition 1.2, we have $P = Q$, and $B_1[\xi] = C_1[\xi]$ $[\xi \in P]$, and thus $M_1[\xi] = N_1[\xi] \in B_1[\xi]$ $[\xi \in P]$. By induction hypothesis, we have that $M_1[\xi]$ and $N_1[\xi]$ are confluent. Furthermore, $P = Q$ implies $P \Leftrightarrow Q$ by proposition 1.1. By induction hypothesis, P and Q are confluent. Hence, M and N are confluent.

If M is simple, and N is $(\lambda x{:}T)N_1$, and $M = N \in A$, then we have $A = (\Pi x{:}T)B$ with $N_1[\xi] \in B[\xi]$ $[\xi \in T]$. We have then apply$(M, \xi) = N_1[\xi] \in B[\xi]$ $[\xi \in T]$. By induction hypothesis, using the fact that $s(\text{apply}(M, \xi)) + s(N_1[\xi]) < s(M) + s(N)$, we get that apply$(M, \xi)$ and $N_1[\xi]$ are confluent. Hence, M and N are confluent.

We can then apply proposition 1.1, and lemma 1.11. ∎

Lemma 1.12 If A *set* and $A = (\Pi x{:}B_0)B_1$ $[\Gamma]$, then $A = (\Pi x{:}A_0)A_1$ with $A_0 = B_0$ $[\Gamma]$ and $A_1[\xi] = B_1[\xi]$ $[\Gamma, \xi \in A_0]$.

Proof: This is clear if $A = (\Pi x{:}B_0)B_1$ $[\Gamma]$ can be derived by Π-formation 2. If $A = (\Pi x{:}B_0)B_1 \in U$ $[\Gamma]$, then $\Delta_U(A, (\Pi x{:}B_0)B_1)$ at level Γ, and so $A \Rightarrow (\Pi x{:}A_0)A_1$, and at level Γ, $A = (\Pi x{:}A_0)A_1 \in U$, $A_0 = A_1 \in U$, $B_0[\xi] = B_1[\xi] \in U$ $[\xi \in A_0]$. By lemma 1.10, we get actually t hat $A = (\Pi x{:}A_0)A_1$ in the empty context. ∎

Lemma 1.13 If A set $[\Gamma_1, \xi : B, \Gamma_2]$ and ξ does not appear in Γ_2 and A, then A set $[\Gamma_1, \Gamma_2]$. If $M \in A$ $[\Gamma_1, \xi : B, \Gamma_2]$ and ξ does not appear in Γ_2 and M, then there exists A' set $[\Gamma_1, \Gamma_2]$ such that $M \in A'$ $[\Gamma_1, \Gamma_2]$ and $A = A'$ $[\Gamma_1, \xi : B, \Gamma_2]$.

Proof: By induction, using lemma 1.12 and corollary 1.2. ∎

Corollary 1.3 If the judgement J holds in the context $\Gamma_1, \xi : A, \Gamma_2$ and ξ does not appear in Γ_2 and J, then J holds in Γ_1, Γ_2.

Notice that this lemma does not hold in extensional Type Theory (like the one of Martin-Löf 84 [9]).

Lemma 1.14 The subject reduction property holds for η-reduction.

Proof: This means that, if $(\lambda x : A)\mathsf{apply}(f, x) \in C$ and x is not free in f, then $f = (\lambda x{:}A)\mathsf{apply}(f, x) \in C$.

Indeed, we have $C = (\Pi x{:}A)B$, with $\mathsf{apply}(f, \xi) \in B[\xi]$ $[\xi \in A]$. Hence, at level $\xi \in A$, the type of f is a product $(\Pi x{:}A_1)B_1$ and we have that $A = A_1$, and $B_1[\xi] = B[\xi]$. By lemma 1.13 and lemma 1.12, we deduce that $f \in (\Pi x{:}A_2)B_2$ in the empty context, with, at level $\xi \in A$, $A_1 = A_2$ and $B_2[\zeta] = B_1[\zeta]$ $[\zeta \in A_2]$. This means $A_1 = A_2$ $[\xi \in A]$ and $B_1[\zeta] = B_2[\zeta]$ $[\xi \in A, \zeta \in A_2]$.

This implies $B_2[\xi] = B[\xi]$ $[\xi \in A]$. By corollary 1.2, we have also $A_2 = A$ in the empty context. Hence, $(\Pi x{:}A)B = (\Pi x{:}A_2)B_2$ and f is of type $(\Pi x{:}A)B = C$. By the rule of Π-equality 2, and by the rule of Set equality, we get $f = (\lambda x{:}A)\mathsf{apply}(f, x) \in C$. ∎

Proposition 1.5 If A, B set and A, B are confluent, then $A = B$.

It is now clear the "conversion-as-judgements" version of type theory is equivalent to the version where conversion is defined at the level of raw terms, like for the usual presentation of LF [6] or in [8]. Indeed, one can see a priori that if a judgement holds for the "conversion-as-judgment" version, it holds for the other version. Proposition 1.5 shows the converse.

One can also deduce the decidability of type-checking, following an usual argument (see for instance [5]).

Conclusion

We tried to present a direct, semantically motivated, proof of the correctness and completness of an algorithm that tests conversion in type theory. Our proof can be seen as an expression of one possible semantics of type theory. It applies also to Edinburgh LF. It may be interesting to apply it for the case of set theory expressed in Martin-Löf's logical framework.

Acknowledgement and related works

In [7], D. Howe proves the fact that Π is one-to-one for NuPrl and extensional Type Theory.

In [12], A. Salvesen proves that Π is one-to-one and the Church-Rosser property for the version of LF where "conversion defined on raw terms".

The problem of conversion of terms in presence of η-conversion is also studied in [4].

In [11], the idea of contexts as Kripke worlds is used for giving a constructive version of the notion of possible worlds.

I want to thank Catarina Svensson for pointing out to me that the equivalence between the two formulations of Type Theory was a non-trivial property. Thanks also to Bengt Nordström, Jan Smith, Lena Magnusson and Anne Salvesen for interesting discussions on this topic. Finally, I want to thank Per Martin-Löf for his remarks on a previous version of this paper.

1   The Rules.

General rules.

Context formation

$$\frac{A \; set}{\xi \in A \; context}$$

$$\frac{\Gamma \; context}{\xi \in A \; [\Gamma]}$$

Where $\xi \in A$ in Γ.

$$\frac{\Gamma \; context \qquad A \; set \; [\Gamma]}{\Gamma, \xi \in A \; context}$$

Where ξ not in Γ.

The rules below are also valid when relativised to an arbitrary context. The restriction on the parameter ξ is that it is "generic" w.r.t. the conclusion of the rule, i.e. does not appear in this conclusion. It can be proved that its choice is irrelevant.

Reflexivity

$$\frac{a \in A}{a = a \in A} \qquad \frac{A \; set}{A = A}$$

Symmetry

$$\frac{a = b \in A}{b = a \in A} \qquad \frac{A = B}{B = A}$$

Transitivity

$$\frac{a = b \in A \qquad b = c \in A}{a = c \in A} \qquad \frac{A = B \qquad B = C}{A = C}$$

Set equality

$$\frac{a \in A \qquad A = B}{a \in B} \qquad \frac{a = b \in A \qquad A = B}{a = b \in B}$$

Cartesian Product of a Family of Sets.

Π – formation 1

$$\frac{A \; set \qquad B[\xi] \; set \; [\xi \in A]}{(\Pi x{:}A)B \; set}$$

Π – formation 2

$$\frac{A = C \qquad B[\xi] = D[\xi] \; [\xi \in A]}{(\Pi x{:}A)B = (\Pi y{:}C)D}$$

Π – introduction 1

$$\frac{b[\xi] \in B[\xi] \; [\xi \in A]}{(\lambda x{:}A)b \in (\Pi x{:}A)B}$$

II – introduction 2

$$\frac{A_1 = A_2 \quad b_1[\xi] = b_2[\xi] \in B[\xi] \; [\xi \in A_1]}{(\lambda x{:}A_1)b_1 = (\lambda x{:}A_2)b_2 \in (\Pi x{:}A_1)B}$$

II – elimination 1

$$\frac{f \in \Pi(A,B) \qquad a \in A}{\text{apply}(f,a) \in B[a]}$$

II – elimination 2

$$\frac{\begin{array}{l} f = g \in (\Pi x{:}A)B \\ a = b \in A \end{array}}{\text{apply}(f,a) = \text{apply}(g,b) \in B[a]}$$

II – equality 1

$$\frac{\begin{array}{l} b[\xi] \in B[\xi] \; [\xi \in A] \\ a \in A \end{array}}{\text{apply}((\lambda x{:}A)b, a) = b[a] \in B[a]}$$

II – equality 2

$$\frac{f \in (\Pi x{:}A)B}{f = (\lambda x{:}A)\text{apply}(f, x) \in (\Pi x{:}A)B}$$

The Set of Small Sets.

U – formation:

$$\text{U set}$$

U – introduction 1:

$$\frac{A \in \text{U} \qquad B[\xi] \in \text{U} \; [\xi \in A]}{(\Pi x{:}A)B \in \text{U}}$$

U – introduction 2:

$$\frac{A = C \in \text{U} \qquad B[\xi] = D[\xi] \in \text{U} \; [\xi \in A]}{(\Pi x{:}A)B = (\Pi y{:}C)D \in \text{U}}$$

Set – formation 1

$$\frac{A \in U}{A \ set}$$

Set – formation 2

$$\frac{A = B \in U}{A = B}$$

Bibliography

[1] Aczel. P. (1979), Frege structures and the notions of propositions, truth, and set in: Barwise, J., Keisler, H.J., and Kunene, K. (eds), *Logic Colloquium 77*, North-Holland, Amsterdam.

[2] Allen. S. (1987), A Non Type-Theoretic Semantics for Type-Theoretic Language, Ph. D. Thesis, Cornell U.

[3] Beeson M.J. (1984), *Foundations of Constructive Mathematics*, Springer-Verlag, Berlin.

[4] Breazu-Tannen V., Gallier J. (1989), Polymorphic rewriting conserves algebraic strong normalisation and confluence, Proceedings of ICALP, Stresa.

[5] Coquand Th., Gallier J. (1990), A Proof of Strong Normalisation Using a Kripke-Like Interpretation, Draft, in the proceeding of the first workshop on Logical Framework.

[6] Harper. R. (1988), An Equational Formulation of LF, LFCR Report Series, ECS-LFCS-88-67, Edinburgh.

[7] Howe. D. (1989), Equality In Lazy Computation Systems, in the proceedings of the fourth Logic in Computer Science.

[8] Martin-Löf. P. (1972), An Intuitionistic Theory of Types, Unpublished manuscript.

[9] Martin-Löf. P. (1984), *Intuitionistic Type Theory*, Studies in Proof Theory, Lecture Notes, Bibliopolis.

[10] Nordström B., Petersson K., Smith. J. M. (1990), *Programming in Martin-Löf Type Theory*, Oxford Science Publications, Clarendon Press, Oxford.

[11] Ranta. A. (1988), Constructing possible worlds, Mimeographed, University of Stockholm, to appear in Theoria.

[12] Salvesen. A. (1989), The Church-Rosser Theorem for LF with beta,eta-reductions, Draft.

[13] Smith. J. (1984), An Interpretation of Martin-Löf's Type Theory in a Type-Free Theory of Propositions, *Journal of Symbolic Logic*, Vol. 49, no. 3, 730 - 753.

[14] Statman. R. (1983), λ-definable functionals and β, η-conversion, *Arch. Math. Logic 23*, 21 - 26.

Inductive sets and families in Martin-Löf's type theory and their set-theoretic semantics

PETER DYBJER
Department of Computer Sciences
Chalmers University of Technology and University of Göteborg
S-412 96 Göteborg, Sweden

Abstract

Martin-Löf's type theory is presented in several steps. The kernel is a dependently typed λ-calculus. Then there are schemata for inductive sets and families of sets and for primitive recursive functions and families of functions. Finally, there are set formers (generic polymorphism) and universes. At each step syntax, inference rules, and set-theoretic semantics are given.

1 Introduction

Usually Martin-Löf's type theory is presented as a closed system with rules for a fixed collection of set formers including Π, Σ, $+$, Eq, N_n, N, W, and U_n. But it is often pointed out that the system is in principle open to extension: we may introduce new sets when there is a need for them.

---

*This is a slightly modified version of a paper with the same title which appeared in the Proceedings of the First Workshop on Logical Frameworks, Antibes, May 1990. Editors G. Huet and G. Plotkin. Pages 213-230. This research was partly supported by ESPRIT Basic Research Action "Logical Frameworks" and Styrelsen för Teknisk Utveckling.

The principle is that a set is by definition inductively generated - it is defined by its introduction rules, which are rules for generating its elem ents. The elimination rule is determined by the introduction rules and expresses definition by primitive recursion on the way the elements of the set are generated. (Normally the term *primitive recursive* refers to number-theoretic functions. But it makes sense to use this term generally for the kind of recursion you have in Martin-Löf's type theory, since it is recursion on the way the elements of a set are generated. This includes primitive recursive functionals and transfinite recursion on well-orderings. An alternative term would be *structural recursion* in analogy with *structural induction*.)

Backhouse [3] et.al. [4] exhibited a schema for *inductive sets* which delimits a class of definitions admissible in Martin-Löf's type theory, which includes all the standard operations for forming small sets except the equality set. This schema extends Schroeder-Heister's schema for the logical constants [19, 20] to the type-theoretic case, where proof objects are explicitly represented in the theory.

Coquand and Paulin [6] and Dybjer [8] extended Backhouse's schema to incorporate *inductive families* and thus also *inductive predicates*. (Coquand and Paulin [6] presented their schema as an extension of impredicative higher order logic and the calculus of constructions, but the formal pattern is much the same as the one in Dybjer [8].) An inductive family of sets P is defined by giving rules for generating index-element pairs $\langle i, a \rangle$ such that $a : P(i)$, just as an inductive set P is defined by giving rules for generating elements a such that $a : P$.

As an example consider the finite sets N_n. In Martin-Löf's presentations [12, 13, 14] this is a countable external sequence of sets. We could make this into an internal sequence by putting $N_n = N'(n)$, where N' is a family of sets indexed by the internal natural numbers $n : N$. N' can then be defined by primitive *recursion*:

$$N'(0) = \emptyset,$$
$$N'(s(a)) = 1 + N'(a).$$

(Formally, one needs universes to define a family of sets by recursion.) But an alternative is to define N' by *induction*. We have the following introduction rules:

$$\frac{a : N}{0'(a) : N'(s(a))}, \qquad \frac{a : N \qquad b : N'(a)}{s'(a, b) : N'(s(a))}.$$

There is a form of primitive recursion associated with this kind of definition. For example we can define a function i which for $n : N$ injects $N'(n)$ into

N by

$$i(s(a), 0'(a)) = 0 : N \quad (a : N),$$
$$i(s(a), s'(a, b)) = s(i(a, b)) : N \quad (a : N, b : N'(a)).$$

Inductive families become inductive predicates under the propositons-as-sets principle. An example is the equality relation $Eq(A)$ on a set A which is a standard set former of Martin-Löf's type theory. It is defined as the least reflexive relation, that is, by the introduction rule

$$\frac{a : A}{Eq(A)(a, a)}.$$

Another example is the predicate *Even* on natural numbers. It has the following introduction rules:

$$Even(0), \quad \frac{a : N \quad Even(a)}{Even(s(s(a)))}.$$

In both cases I have followed the practice of suppressing elements which are thought of as proof objects. Also note that the family N' becomes 'nonzero' when thought of as a predicate, and that its second introduction rule becomes redundant if we only care about truth (inhabitation).

Other examples of inductive families (and predicates) can be found in Dybjer [8, 9], Coquand and Paulin [6], Pfenning and Paulin-Mohring [17], Hedberg [10], and Szasz [22].

The schema covers all the standard operations for forming small sets including the equality set. It also subsumes Martin-Löf's schema for inductive predicates in predicate logic [11].

In this paper I give a somewhat different presentation of the schema than in Dybjer [8].

One difference is that definitions of functions by primitive recursion are presented schematically too (much like in Martin-Löf [12]) rather than by the usual kind of elimination rules.

I also separate the presentation of the process of inductive generation of sets and families from the process of introducing parameters. For example, A and B are parameters in $\Sigma x : A.B[x], A + B, Eq(A)$, and $Wx : A.B[x]$. Another name for this feature is *generic polymorphism*. But a parameter need not be a set or a family. It can also be an element as in Christine Paulin's definition of the equality relation: in addition to the set A, one of the elements $a : A$ is fixed, and a unary predicate $Eq'(A, a)$ is defined by the introduction rule

$$Eq'(A, a)(a).$$

Also, as usual, a definition of a primitive recursive function may depend on parameters. For example, the addition function $+(a)(b)$ can be defined by defining a unary function $+(a)$, which depends on the parameter a, by primitive recursion over N.

Moreover, I present a version of type theory without a logical framework and without an underlying theory of expressions (like in Martin-Löf's presentations of type theory before and including the book [14]).

I also show how to interpret type theory, with the schema, in classical set theory. This gives a useful interpretation, compare Troelstra [23, page 2]: 'The simplest interpretation of ML_0 is in terms of a hierarchy within classical set theory, where Π, Σ, etc, correspond to the formation of cartesian products, disjoint unions etc. as already indicated above; function, i.e., elements of cartesian products are regarded as equal if for each argument their values are equal, etc.' This interpretation is 'non-intended' in the sense that it is not the interpretation described by Martin-Löf [14], whereby basic concepts, such as judgement, set, proposition, element, equality, etc. are explained intuitively. The intention is that these explanations will make the inference rules of type theory intuitively evident. But there is a similarity between the set-theoretic interpretation and the intended one: the formation rules receive their meaning from the introduction rules and the elimination rules receive their meaning from the equality (or computation) rules.

Salvesen [18] presented details of a set-theoretic interpretation of type theory without a general schema for inductive definitions. Well-orderings and the first universe were interpreted as inductively defined sets obtained by iterations of κ-continuous operators.

Coquand and Paulin [6] proposed to give a set-theoretic interpretation of their schema for *inductive sets* by (i) translating the introduction rules defining a set to a strictly positive set operator in type theory; (ii) introducing rules for fixed points of such set operators in type theory and showing that the corresponding rules of the schema can be derived; (iii) interpreting type-theoretic strictly positive operators as κ-continuous functors on the category of sets, where card $\kappa < \aleph_\omega$ in the theory without universes. (This interpretation does of course not extend to the full system of the calculus of constructions extended with inductive types. Having a set-theoretic model is one of the properties which distinguishes predicative from impredicative type theory.)

In this paper I use Aczel's [1] notion of rule set rather than continuous functors. It is really only a variation, since a rule set generates a continuous operator. But it allows a direct concrete translation of the type-theoretic introduction rules to set-theoretic rule sets and generalizes the concrete construction of the term algebra T_Σ on a first order signature Σ.

I also interpret *inductive families.*

I would also like to mention that Aczel [2] has shown how to interpret certain inductive sets, such as the well-orderings of type theory, in a *constructive set theory* (which itself can be interpreted in Martin-Löf's type theory). Does it follow that the whole of Martin-Löf's type theory can be interpreted in this constructive set theory? (Universes are not discussed in Aczel's paper, however.)

Type theory is presented in the following steps.

- The dependently typed λ-calculus (section 2). This is like the simply typed λ-calculus with Π instead of →. It consists essentially of the general rules and the rules for Π in Martin-Löf [13, 14].

- Schema for inductive sets (section 3). This part of the schema is closely related to the well-orderings.

- Schema for primitive (structural) recursive functions (section 4).

- Schema for inductive families (section 5). This generalizes the schema for inductive sets. The simpler case is presented separately for the purpose of the presentation only.

- Schema for primitive recursive families of functions (section 6). This generalizes the schema for primitive recursive functions.

- Set formers (generic polymorphism) are discussed in section 7. There the possibilty of internalizing the schema is discussed too.

- Universes (section 8).

At each step I first give syntax, then inference rules, and finally a set-theoretic interpretation.

I do not discuss simultaneous induction and recursion here; see instead Dybjer [8].

The type theory considered here is the *intensional, monomorphic* (has unicity of type) version of Martin-Löf 1986 (see Nordström, Petersson, and Smith [15]) but formulated without a logical framework. Note however, that we can interpret η-conversion on the level of sets, and the rule

$$\frac{Eq(A)(a,b)}{a = b : A},$$

which relates definitional and propositional equality and causes equality to be extensional (see section 5). Note also that the interpretation allows polymorphic constructors, but not polymorphic recursive functions (section 7). Thus we have almost, but not quite, got a model of the *extensional, polymorphic* version of type theory of Martin-Löf 1979 [13, 14].

2 The dependently typed λ-calculus

We use ordinary notation, but omit mentioning variable restrictions, etc.

Expressions

Set expressions:

$$A \quad ::= \quad \Pi x : A_0.A_1[x].$$

Element expressions:

$$a \quad ::= \quad x \mid \lambda x : A.a[x] \mid a_1(a_0).$$

Context expressions:

$$\Gamma \quad ::= \quad \epsilon \mid \Gamma, x : A.$$

Judgement expressions:

$$J \quad ::= \quad \Gamma \ context \mid \Gamma \vdash A \ set \mid \Gamma \vdash a : A \mid \Gamma \vdash A = A' \mid \Gamma \vdash a = a' : A.$$

Inference rules

Some premises are omitted.

General rules:

$$\epsilon \ context \qquad \frac{\Gamma \ context \qquad \Gamma \vdash A \ set}{\Gamma, x : A \ context}$$

$$\frac{\Gamma \vdash A \ set}{\Gamma \vdash A = A} \qquad \frac{\Gamma \vdash a : A}{\Gamma \vdash a = a : A}$$

$$\frac{\Gamma \vdash A = A'}{\Gamma \vdash A' = A} \qquad \frac{\Gamma \vdash a = a' : A}{\Gamma \vdash a' = a : A}$$

$$\frac{\Gamma \vdash A = A' \qquad \Gamma \vdash A' = A''}{\Gamma \vdash A = A''} \qquad \frac{\Gamma \vdash a = a' : A \qquad \Gamma \vdash a' = a'' : A}{\Gamma \vdash a = a'' : A}$$

$$\frac{\Gamma \vdash A = A' \qquad \Gamma \vdash a : A}{\Gamma \vdash a : A'} \qquad \frac{\Gamma \vdash A = A' \qquad \Gamma \vdash a = a' : A}{\Gamma \vdash a = a' : A'}$$

$$\frac{\Gamma \vdash A \ set}{\Gamma, x : A \vdash x : A}$$

$$\frac{\Gamma \vdash A_0 \ set \qquad \Gamma \vdash A_1 \ set}{\Gamma, x : A_0 \vdash A_1 \ set} \qquad \frac{\Gamma \vdash A_0 \ set \qquad \Gamma \vdash A_1 = A_1'}{\Gamma, x : A_0 \vdash A_1 = A_1'}$$

$$\frac{\Gamma \vdash A_0 \ set \quad \Gamma \vdash a : A_1}{\Gamma, x : A_0 \vdash a : A_1} \qquad \frac{\Gamma \vdash A_0 \ set \quad \Gamma \vdash a = a' : A_1}{\Gamma, x : A_0 \vdash a = a' : A_1}$$

Rules for the cartesian product of a family of sets:

$$\frac{\Gamma \vdash A_0 \ set \quad \Gamma, x : A_0 \vdash A_1[x] \ set}{\Gamma \vdash \Pi x : A_0.A_1[x] \ set}$$

$$\frac{\Gamma \vdash A_0 = A_0' \quad \Gamma, x : A_0 \vdash A_1[x] = A_1'[x]}{\Gamma \vdash \Pi x : A_0.A_1[x] = \Pi x : A_0'.A_1'[x]}$$

$$\frac{\Gamma, x : A_0 \vdash a[x] : A_1}{\Gamma \vdash \lambda x : A_0.a[x] : \Pi x : A_0.A_1[x]}$$

$$\frac{\Gamma, x : A_0 \vdash a[x] = a'[x] : A_1}{\Gamma \vdash \lambda x : A_0.a[x] = \lambda x : A_0.a'[x] : \Pi x : A_0.A_1[x]}$$

$$\frac{\Gamma \vdash a_1 : \Pi x : A_0.A_1[x] \quad \Gamma \vdash a_0 : A_0}{\Gamma \vdash a_1(a_0) : A_1[a_0]}$$

$$\frac{\Gamma \vdash a_1 = a_1' : \Pi x : A_0.A_1[x] \quad \Gamma \vdash a_0 = a_0' : A_0}{\Gamma \vdash a_1(a_0) = a_1'(a_0') : A_1[a_0]}$$

$$\frac{\Gamma, x : A_0 \vdash a_1[x] : A_1[x] \quad \Gamma \vdash a_0 : A_0}{\Gamma \vdash (\lambda x : A_0.a_1[x])(a_0) = a_1[a_0] : A_1[a_0]}$$

The present formulation of type theory is intended to conform with Martin-Löf's intensional version of 1986 except that we do not use a level of *logical types* (a *logical framework*). In intensional type theory η-conversion is valid on the level of types but not on the level of sets. Π is inductively defined by the single introduction rule for λ, and η does not follow from the equality rule relating λ and the selector *funsplit*. Here I take Π as primitive, but if it is to conform with the inductively defined Π, then η ought not to be included.

Interpretation of expressions

The basic idea is to interpret a type-theoretic concept as the corresponding set-theoretic concept, which usually has the same name. So a (type-theoretic) set is interpreted as a (set-theoretic) set, an element of a set as an element of a set, (definitional) equality as (extensional) equality, (type-theoretic) cartesian product as (set-theoretic) cartesian product, function as function graph, etc. A context is interpreted as a set of assignments.

Let $[a]\rho$ be the denotation of the expression a under the assignment ρ. This assigns a set to each variable in a finite list of variables which includes all variables which are free in a. Let $\emptyset$ be the empty assignment and let ρ_x^u abbreviate $\rho \cup \{\langle x, u \rangle\}$. Let also $[\![a]\!]$ abbreviate $[\![a]\!]\emptyset$.

The interpretation function is partial. Partiality is introduced in the interpretation of application. But the interpretation of a derivable judgement will be defined and true.

The method with a partial interpretation function has also been used by Streicher for a categorical interpretation of the calculus of constructions [21].

Interpretation of set expressions:

$$[\![\Pi x : A_0.A_1[x]]\!]\rho \quad = \quad \prod_{u \in [\![A_0]\!]\rho} [\![A_1[x]]\!]\rho_x^u.$$

This is defined iff $[\![A_0]\!]\rho$ is defined and $[\![A_1[x]]\!]\rho_x^u$ is defined whenever $u \in [\![A_0]\!]\rho$.

Interpretation of element expressions:

$$[\![x]\!]\rho \quad = \quad \rho(x).$$

This is always defined.

$$[\![\lambda x : A.a[x]]\!]\rho \quad = \quad \{\langle u, [\![a[x]]\!]\rho_x^u \rangle | u \in [\![A]\!]\rho\}.$$

This is defined iff $[\![A]\!]\rho$ is defined and $[\![a[x]]\!]\rho_x^u$ is defined whenever $u \in [\![A]\!]\rho$.

$$[\![a_1(a_0)]\!]\rho \quad = \quad ([\![a_1]\!]\rho)([\![a_0]\!]\rho).$$

This is defined iff $[\![a_1]\!]\rho$ and $[\![a_0]\!]\rho$ are defined, and $[\![a_1]\!]\rho$ is a function the domain of which contains $[\![a_0]\!]\rho$. (Observe that it is possible to interpret polymorphic application in set theory. This is not the case for interpretations of type theory in general, compare Streicher [21].)

Interpretation of context expressions:

$$[\![\epsilon]\!] \quad = \quad \{\emptyset\}.$$

This is always defined.

$$[\![\Gamma, x : A]\!] \quad = \quad \{\rho_x^u | \rho \in [\![\Gamma]\!] \wedge u \in [\![A]\!]\rho\}.$$

This is defined iff $[\![\Gamma]\!]$ is defined and $[\![A]\!]\rho$ is defined whenever $\rho \in [\![\Gamma]\!]$.

Interpretation of judgement expressions:

$$[\![\Gamma \ context]\!] \quad \text{iff} \quad [\![\Gamma]\!] \text{ is a set of assignments.}$$

This is defined iff $[\Gamma]$ is defined.

$$[\Gamma \vdash A \; set] \quad \text{iff} \quad [A]\rho \text{ is a set whenever } \rho \in [\Gamma].$$

This is defined iff $[\Gamma]$ is defined and if $[A]\rho$ is defined whenever $\rho \in [\Gamma]$.

$$[\Gamma \vdash a : A] \quad \text{iff} \quad [a]\rho \in [A]\rho \text{ whenever } \rho \in [\Gamma].$$

This is defined iff $[\Gamma]$ is defined and if $[a]\rho$ and $[A]\rho$ are defined whenever $\rho \in [\Gamma]$.

$$[\Gamma \vdash A = A'] \quad \text{iff} \quad [A]\rho = [A']\rho \text{ whenever } \rho \in [\Gamma].$$

This is defined iff $[\Gamma]$ is defined and if $[A]\rho$ and $[A']\rho$ are defined whenever $\rho \in [\Gamma]$.

$$[\Gamma \vdash a = a' : A] \quad \text{iff} \quad [a]\rho = [a']\rho \wedge [a]\rho \in [A]\rho \text{ whenever } \rho \in [\Gamma].$$

This is defined iff $[\Gamma]$ is defined and if $[a]\rho$, $[a']\rho$, and $[A]\rho$ are defined whenever $\rho \in [\Gamma]$.

Soundness of the inference rules

Checking the soundness of the inference rules means checking that the interpretation of the conclusion of a rule is defined and true whenever the interpretation of the premises are defined and true.

It is quite straightforward to check the soundness of all the inference rules. As an illustration we show the soundness of the rule of application. The premises are interpreted as

$$[a_1]\rho \in \prod_{u \in [A_0]\rho} [A_1[x]]\rho_x^u \text{ whenever } \rho \in [\Gamma]$$

and

$$[a_0]\rho \in [A_0]\rho \text{ whenever } \rho \in [\Gamma].$$

From this we conclude that

$$([a_1]\rho)([a_0]\rho) \in [A_1[x]]\rho_x^{[a_0]\rho} \text{ whenever } \rho \in [\Gamma],$$

and hence the conclusion of the rule follows, since

$$[A_1[x]]\rho_x^{[a_0]\rho} = [A_1[a_0]]\rho$$

follows from a substitution lemma which holds for the interpretation.

Telescopes

In the description of the schema below we shall frequently refer to sequences of dependent sets, to sequences (tuples) of elements, and to sequences of typings of elements. De Bruijn has introduced the term *telescope* for such sequences of dependent sets [5]. Telescopes can also be viewed as obtained by iterating the Σ-construction. They are similar to contexts; they are contexts treated as objects.

It is intended that the reader view the terms telescope, tuple, etc., and certain associated notations as abbreviations and reduce them to formal notions of type theory in a way to be suggested below. (The description is not complete, and sometimes the notation needs to be interpreted with some good will in order to make sense.)

The new notation is explained as follows:

- *As* telescope means that

  A_1 set,

  $A_2[x_1]$ set $(x_1 : A_1)$,

  $\vdots$,

  $A_n[x_1, \ldots, x_{n-1}]$ set $(x_1 : A_1, \ldots, x_{n-1} : A_{n-1})$;

- *As* = *As'* means that

  $A_1 = A_1$,

  $A_2[x_1] = A_2[x_1] \ (x_1 : A_1)$,

  $\vdots$,

  $A_n[x_1, \ldots, x_{n-1}] = A'_n[x_1, \ldots, x_{n-1}] \ (x_1 : A_1, \ldots, x_{n-1} : A_{n-1})$;

- *as* :: *As* means that

  $a_1 : A_1$,

  $a_2 : A_2[a_1]$,

  $\vdots$,

  $a_n : A_n[a_1, \ldots, a_{n-1}]$;

- *as* = *as'* :: *As* means that

  $a_1 = a'_1 : A_1$,

  $a_2 = a'_2 : A_2[a_1]$,

$$\vdots,$$
$$a_n = a'_n : A_n[a_1, \ldots, a_{n-1}].$$

We also write $f(as)$ for $f(a_1, \ldots, a_n)$, $f(as, bs)$ for $f(a_1, \ldots, a_n, b_1, \ldots, b_m)$, etc.

An alternative approach would be to extend type theory with *formal* notions of telescopes and tuples. In addition to the standard forms of judgement we would have the new forms As is a telescope; $As = As'$; $as :: As$; $as = as' :: As$. As other forms of judgement these judgements would be made under assumptions. We would then have suitable rules for forming telescopes and tuples. Furthermore, if we have telescopes, a context can be viewed as a single assumption $xs :: As$. Compare also the discussion in section 7 on internalization of the schema.

The set-theoretic semantics can be extended to telescopes and tuples. When we write $us \in [\![As]\!]$, we understand that us is a tuple $\langle u_1, \ldots, u_n \rangle$ such that $u_1 \in [\![A_1]\!], \ldots, u_n \in [\![A_n[x_1, \ldots, x_{n-1}]]\!]_{x_1 \ldots x_{n-1}}^{u_1 \ldots u_{n-1}}$.

We also use index notation such as $(a_k)_k$, $(A_k)_k$, and $(a_k : A_k)_k$ to stand for $a_1, \ldots, a_n$, $A_1, \ldots, A_n$, and $a_1 : A_1, \ldots, a_n : A_n$ respectively. This will be used, for example, to talk about *non-dependent* telescopes of the form $(A_k)_k$.

3   Schema for inductive sets

We have now presented the syntax and rules of the dependently typed λ-calculus. This theory, call it T_0, can be extended successively to obtain a sequence of theories $T_1, T_2, \ldots$.

There are two kinds of extensions.

The first kind is when T_{n+1} is obtained from $T = T_n$ by adding formation and introduction rules for a new set former P (see section 3, 5, and 7).

The second kind is when T_{n+1} is obtained from $T = T_n$ by adding a new function constant f, which is defined by primitive recursion on some set (or family) and is specified by its type and its computation rules (see section 4, 6, and 7). In this way we get schematic elimination and equality rules.

We first treat the simple case without parameters and inductive families.

Expressions

Set expressions:

$$A ::= P.$$

Element expressions
$$a ::= intro_i(as, (b_k)_k).$$

Inference rules

(J abbreviates $\Gamma \vdash J$.)
Formation rules:
$$P \ set,$$
$$P = P.$$

The *i*th *introduction rules*:
$$\frac{as :: Gs_i \qquad (b_k : Hs_{ik}[as] \to P)_k}{intro_i(as, (b_k)_k) : P},$$

$$\frac{as = as' :: Gs_i \qquad (b_k = b'_k : Hs_{ik}[as] \to P)_k}{intro_i(as, (b_k)_k) = intro_i(as', (b'_k)_k) : P},$$

where

- Gs_i is a telescope relative to T;

- $Hs_{ik}[xs]$ is a telescope relative to T in the context $xs :: Gs_i$ for each k.

Note the similarity between the schematic introduction rule and the introduction rule for well-orderings $Wx : G.H[x]$. The latter is obtained by letting $i = 1$, $Gs_i = G$, $k = 1$ and $Hs_{11}[x] = H[x]$. Compare also section 7.

Inductive sets in set theory

We shall use Aczel's [1] set-theoretic notion of rule set to interpret the introduction rules for a new set former. The set defined inductively by a rule set is the least set closed under all rules in the rule set.

A *rule* on a base set U in Aczel's sense is a pair of sets $\langle u, v \rangle$, often written
$$\frac{u}{v},$$
such that $u \subseteq U$ and $v \in U$.

Let Φ be a set of rules on U.

A set w is Φ-*closed* if
$$\frac{u}{v} \in \Phi \wedge u \subseteq w \supset v \in w.$$

There is a least Φ-closed set
$$\mathcal{I}(\Phi) = \bigcap \{w \subseteq U | w \ \Phi\text{-}closed\},$$
the set inductively defined by Φ.

Interpretation of expressions

Interpretation of set expressions:

$$[P]\rho \;=\; \mathcal{I}(\Phi_P),$$

where

$$\Phi_P = \bigcup_i \{ \frac{\bigcup_k \operatorname{ran} v_k}{\langle n_{intro_i}, us, (v_k)_k\rangle} \,|\, us \in [Gs_i], (v_k \in [Hs_{ik}[xs]]^{us}_{xs} \to U)_k \},$$

where $n_{intro_i} \in \omega$ is a code for the constructor *intro$_i$*, and $U = V_\alpha$, the set of sets generated before stage α in the cumulative hierarchy, where α is chosen so that Φ_P is a rule set on U. This induces the following requirements on the ordinal α:

- V_α is closed under tupling, that is, α is a limit ordinal;

- $\omega \subseteq V_\alpha$, that is, $\omega \le \alpha$;

- $[Gs_i] \subseteq V_\alpha$ for all i;

- $[Hs_{ik}[xs]]^{us}_{xs} \to V_\alpha \subseteq V_\alpha$ for all $us \in [Gs_i]$ and all ik. This can be achieved if $[Hs_{ik}[xs]]^{us}_{xs} \subseteq V_\alpha$ and if $\operatorname{card} [Hs_{ik}[xs]]^{us}_{xs} < \operatorname{card} \alpha$ for all $us \in [Gs_i]$ and all ik. Because assume that $v_k \in [Hs_{ik}[xs]]^{us}_{xs} \to V_\alpha$. Then for each $ws \in [Hs_{ik}[xs]]^{us}_{xs}$ we have $\langle ws, v_k(ws)\rangle \in V_{\beta_{ws}}$ for some ordinal $\beta_{ws} < \alpha$. Let $\beta = \sup_{ws \in [Hs_{ik}[xs]]^{us}_{xs}} \beta_{ws} < \alpha$. Hence, $v_k = \{\langle ws, v_k(ws)\rangle \,|\, ws \in [Hs_{ik}[xs]]^{us}_{xs}\} \subseteq V_\beta$. So $v_k \in V_\alpha$.

$\mathcal{I}(\Phi_P)$ is independent of the choice of a particular α which satisfies these requirements. Because let Φ_P and Φ'_P be defined using $\alpha < \alpha'$ respectively. Then the Φ_P-closed subsets of V_α are the same as the Φ'_P-closed subsets of V_α.

If the theory T does not include universes, then we can choose α such that $\operatorname{card} \alpha < \aleph_\omega$ (assuming $\aleph_{\alpha+1} = 2^{\aleph_\alpha}$).

Interpretation of element expressions:

$$[intro_i(as, (b_k)_k)]\rho \;=\; \langle n_{intro_i}, [as]\rho, ([b_k]\rho)_k\rangle.$$

Soundness of the inference rules

Formation rule. We have already shown that $[P]\rho$ is a set.

The introduction rule is sound because assume that $us \in [Gs_i]\rho$, whenever $\rho \in [\Gamma]$, and $v_k \in [Hs_{ik}[xs]]\rho^{us}_{xs} \to [P]$, whenever $\rho \in [\Gamma]$, for all k. Then it follows that $\bigcup_k \operatorname{ran} v_k \subseteq [P]$ and hence since $[P]$ is Φ_P-closed $\langle n_{intro_i}, us, (v_k)_k\rangle \in [P]$.

Logical consistency

Absurdity ($\perp$) is identified with the distinguished empty set defined by the empty list of introduction rules. We get that $[\![\perp]\!] = \emptyset$, so we cannot have $a : \perp$, since this entails $[\![a]\!] \in \emptyset$. Hence the set-theoretic interpretation shows the logical consistency of Martin-Löf's type theory.

Excluded middle

The disjunction $A \vee B$ of two propositions A and B is identified with the disjoint union $A + B$ of the corresponding sets and is defined by the two introduction rules

$$\frac{a : A}{inl(a) : A \vee B}, \qquad \frac{b : B}{inr(b) : A \vee B}.$$

Under the given interpretation type-theoretic disjoint union is interpreted as set-theoretic disjoint union. So $A \vee \neg A$, which is defined as $A \vee (A \to \perp)$, is interpreted as the disjoint union of $[\![A]\!]$ and $[\![A]\!] \to \emptyset$. This set is always nonempty in classical set theory. So the truth of excluded middle in type theory under the set-theoretic interpretation is a consequence of excluded middle in classical set theory.

4 Primitive recursive functions

Functions can be defined by recursion on the way the elements of P are generated (primitive or structural recursion). Here we give a schema for such definitions rather than a single elimination rule.

Syntax

$$a ::= f.$$

Inference rules

Elimination rules:

$$f : \Pi z : P.C[z],$$
$$f = f : \Pi z : P.C[z].$$

The *i*th *equality rules*:

$$\frac{as :: Gs_i \qquad (b_k : Hs_{ik}[as] \to P)_k}{f(intro_i(as, (b_k)_k))},$$
$$= d_i(as, (b_k, \lambda zs :: Hs_{ik}[as].f(b_k(zs)))_k)$$
$$: C[intro_i(as, (b_k)_k)]$$

where

- $C[z]$ is a set in the context $z : P$;

-

$$d_i \quad : \quad \Pi xs :: Gs_i.$$
$$(\Pi y_k : (Hs_{ik}[xs] \to P).$$
$$\Pi y'_k : (\Pi zs :: Hs_{ik}[xs].C[y_k(zs)]))_k.$$
$$C[intro_i(xs, (y_k)_k)].$$

Primitive recursive functions in set theory

A rule set Φ is *deterministic* if

$$\frac{u}{v} \in \Phi \wedge \frac{u'}{v} \in \Phi \supset u = u'.$$

If Φ is deterministic, functions on $\mathcal{I}(\Phi)$ can be defined by recursion on the way the elements in $\mathcal{I}(\Phi)$ are generated.

Interpretation of expressions

Since Φ_P is deterministic, type-theoretic primitive recursion can be interpreted as set-theoretic primitive recursion on $\mathcal{I}(\Phi_P)$. Let

$$[\![f]\!]\rho \quad = \quad \mathcal{I}(\Psi_f),$$

where

$$\Psi_f \quad = \quad \bigcup_i \{ \frac{\bigcup_k \{\langle v_k(ws), v'_k(ws)\rangle | ws \in [\![Hs_{ik}[xs]]\!]^{us}_{xs}\}}{\langle\langle n_{intro_i}, us, (v_k)_k\rangle, [\![d_i]\!](us, (v_k, v'_k)_k)\rangle} |$$
$$us \in [\![Gs_i]\!],$$
$$(v_k \in [\![Hs_{ik}[xs]]\!]^{us}_{xs} \to [\![P]\!],$$
$$v'_k \in \prod_{ws \in [\![Hs_{ik}[xs]]\!]^{us}_{xs}} [\![C[y_k(zs)]]\!]^{ws\,v_k}_{zs\,y_k})_k \}.$$

Ψ_f is a rule set on $\sum_{w \in [\![P]\!]} [\![C[z]]\!]^w_z$. This is easily proved by Φ_P-induction since the pairs in $\mathcal{I}(\Psi_f)$ are generated in parallel with the elements of $\mathcal{I}(\Phi_P)$ and since the requirements on d_i ensure that the second component is in $[\![C[z]]\!]^w_z$.

Soundness of the inference rules

Since Φ_P is deterministic Ψ_f defines a function on $[P]$. Hence

$$[f]\rho \in \prod_{w \in [P]\rho} [\![C[z]]\!]\rho_z^w \, ,$$

and the elimination rule is validated.

To prove the soundness of the equality rules we need to prove three things: two memberships and an equality. The memberships are immediate. The equality is a direct consequence of the definition of Ψ_f.

5 Inductive families

We now treat the more general case of inductively defined families of sets.

Expressions

Set expressions:

$$A ::= P(is).$$

Element expressions

$$a ::= intro_i(as, (b_k)_k).$$

Inference rules

Formation rules:

$$\frac{is :: Is}{P(is) \ set} \, ,$$

$$\frac{is :: Is}{P(is) = P(is)} \, ,$$

where

- *Is* is a telescope relative to T.

The *i*th *introduction rules:*

$$\frac{as :: Gs_i \qquad (b_k : \Pi zs :: Hs_{ik}[as].P(qs_{ik}[as, zs]))_k}{intro_i(as, (b_k)_k) : P(ps_i[as])} \, ,$$

$$\frac{as = as' :: Gs_i \qquad (b_k = b'_k : \Pi zs :: Hs_{ik}[as].P(qs_{ik}[as, zs]))_k}{intro_i(as, (b_k)_k) = intro_i(as', (b'_k)_k) : P(ps_i[as])} \, ,$$

where

- Gs_i is a telescope relative to T;

- $Hs_{ik}[xs]$ is a telescope relative to T in the context $xs :: Gs_i$ for each k;

- $qs_{ik}[xs, zs] :: Is$ relative to T in the context $xs :: Gs_i, zs :: Hs_{ik}[xs]$ for each k;

- $ps_i[xs] :: Is$ relative to T in the context $xs :: Gs_i$.

Inductive families in set theory

Let I and U be sets and let Φ be a rule set on $I \times U$. Then Φ inductively defines a family $\mathcal{IF}(\Phi)$ of sets in U over I by

$$\mathcal{IF}(\Phi)(i) = \{u \in U \,|\, \langle i, u \rangle \in \mathcal{I}(\Phi)\}$$

for each $i \in I$.

Interpretation of expressions

Interpretation of set expressions:

$$[\![P(is)]\!]\rho \;=\; \mathcal{IF}(\Phi_P)([\![is]\!]\rho),$$

where

$$\Phi_P \;=\; \bigcup_i \{ \frac{\bigcup_k \{\langle [\![qs_{ik}[xs, zs]]\!]^{us\;ws}_{xs\;zs}, v_k(ws)\rangle \,|\, ws \in [\![Hs_{ik}[xs]]\!]^{us}_{xs}\}}{\langle [\![ps_i[xs]]\!]^{us}_{xs}, \langle n_{intro_i}, us, (v_k)_k \rangle \rangle} \;|$$
$$us \in [\![Gs_i]\!],$$
$$(v_k \in [\![Hs_{ik}[xs]]\!]^{us}_{xs} \to U)_k \},$$

where U is chosen so that Φ_P is a rule set on $[\![Is]\!] \times U$. Such a $U = V_\alpha$ is found in a similar way to the case for inductive sets above.

Interpretation of element expressions:

$$[\![intro_i(as, (b_k)_k)]\!]\rho \;=\; \langle |intro_i|, [\![as]\!]\rho, ([\![b_k]\!]\rho)_k \rangle.$$

Soundness of the inference rules

Formation rule. This is sound since $\mathcal{IF}(\Phi_P)$ is a family of sets over $[\![Is]\!]$. The introduction rule is sound because assume that

$$us \in [\![Gs_i]\!]\rho$$

and

$$v_k \in \prod_{ws \in [Hs_{ik}[xs]]\rho_{xs}^{us}} [P(qs_{ik}[xs, zs])]\rho_{xs\,zs}^{us\,ws},$$

whenever $\rho \in [\Gamma]$, for all k. Then it follows that for each $ws \in [Hs_{ik}[xs]]\rho_{xs}^{us}$ we have

$$\langle [qs_{ik}[xs, zs]]\rho_{xs\,zs}^{us\,ws}, v_k(ws) \rangle \in \mathcal{I}(\Phi_P).$$

Hence, by Φ_P-closedness

$$\langle [ps_i[xs]]\rho_{xs}^{us}, \langle n_{intro_i}, us, (v_k)_k \rangle \rangle \in \mathcal{I}(\Phi_P)$$

and thus

$$\langle n_{intro_i}, us, (v_k)_k \rangle \in [P(ps_i[xs])]\rho_{xs}^{us}.$$

Propositional equality

As mentioned in the introduction, the equality relation Eq is an inductive predicate. If $a, b : A$, then $[Eq(A)(a,b)]$ is inhabited iff $[a] = [b]$. So the special equality rule

$$\frac{Eq(A)(a,b)}{a = b : A}$$

of extensional type theory is valid under the interpretation. The same fact holds if Paulin's equality Eq' is used instead of Eq.

6　Primitive recursive families of functions

We give a schema for functions which are defined by recursion on the way the elements of $P(is)$ are generated. This generalizes the schema in section 4. Note that we have a kind of simultaneous recursion: an element of $P(ps_i[as])$ is generated from the elements of $(P(qs_{ik}[as, zs]))_k$.

Syntax

$$a ::= f(is)$$

Inference rules

Elimination rule:

$$\frac{is :: Is}{f(is) : \Pi z : P(is).C[z]},$$

$$\frac{is = is' :: Is}{f(is) = f(is') : \Pi z : P(is).C[z]}.$$

The ith equality rule:

$$\frac{as :: Gs_i \qquad (b_k : \Pi zs :: Hs_{ik}[as].P(qs_{ik}[as, zs]))_k}{\begin{aligned} & f(ps_i[as])(intro_i(as, (b_k)_k)) \\ = \ & d_i(as, (b_k, (\lambda zs :: Hs_{ik}[as].f(qs_{ik}[as, zs])(b_k(zs))))_k) \\ : \ & C[ps_i[as], intro_i(as, (b_k)_k)] \end{aligned}},$$

where

- $C[xs, z]$ is a set in the context $xs :: Is, z : P(xs)$;

-

$$\begin{aligned} d_i \ : \ & \Pi xs :: Gs_i. \\ & (\Pi y_k : (\Pi zs :: Hs_{ik}[xs].P(qs_{ik}[xs, zs])). \\ & \Pi y_k' : (\Pi zs :: Hs_{ik}[xs].C[qs_{ik}[xs, zs], y_k(zs)]))_k. \\ & C[ps_i[xs], intro_i(xs, (y_k)_k)]. \end{aligned}$$

Primitive recursive families of functions in set theory

The rule set Φ_P is still deterministic. As a consequence we could define functions on the pairs $\langle is, c \rangle$ in $\mathcal{I}(\Phi_P)$. But we want curried versions instead. Such functions can be defined as inductive families of set-theoretic functions.

Interpretation of expressions

Let

$$[f(is)]\rho \ = \ \mathcal{IF}(\Psi_f)([is]\rho),$$

where

$$\Psi_f \ = \ \bigcup_i \{ \frac{\bigcup_k \{ \langle [qs_{ik}[xs, zs]]_{xs\,zs}^{us\,ws}, \langle v_k(ws), v_k'(ws) \rangle \rangle \mid ws \in [Hs_{ik}[xs]]_{xs}^{us} \}}{\langle [ps_i[xs]]_{xs}^{us}, \langle \langle n_{intro_i}, us, (v_k)_k \rangle, [d_i](us, (v_k, v_k')_k) \rangle \rangle} \mid$$

$$us \in [Gs_i],$$

$$(v_k \in \prod_{ws \in [Hs_{ik}[xs]]_{xs}^{us}} [P(qs_{ik}[xs, zs])]_{xs\,zs}^{us\,ws},$$

$$v_k' \in \prod_{ws \in [Hs_{ik}[xs]]_{xs}^{us}} [C[qs_{ik}[xs, zs], y_k(zs)]]_{xs\,zs\,y_k}^{us\,ws\,v_k})_k \}.$$

Ψ_f is a rule set on $\sum_{us \in [Is]} \sum_{w \in [P(xs)]_{xs}^{us}} [C[xs, z]]_{xs\,z}^{us\,w}$.

Soundness of inference rules

Omitted.

7 Polymorphism

Generic set formers and parameters

So far we have presented a completely monomorphic version of type theory similar to the type theory presented in Martin-Löf [12]. (Martin-Löf also introduced a new constant P for each instance of $\Pi x : A_0.A_1[x]$ and a new constant f for each instance of $\lambda x : A.a[x]$. Thereby bound variables were avoided altogether.) But it is important both for convenience and expressiv eness to introduce *parameters* in the inductive and the primitive recursive definitions. (We distinguish *generic set formers*, the arguments of which are called parameters, and *inductive families of sets*, the arguments of which are called *indices*.) A parameter can be either a set (or family) or an element (or function); some examples were given in the introduction.

The set-theoretic interpretation extends directly to the case with parameters.

Typical ambiguity

The set-theoretic interpretation given above is polymorphic (introduces typical ambiguity) in the constructors but not in the recursive functions. This is because the denotation of $intro_i(as, (b_k)_k)$ does not depend on the denotations of Gs_i, and $Hs_{ik}[xs]$, and (in the case of families) Is, whereas the denotation of f depends on the denotations of Gs_i, $Hs_{ik}[xs]$, and d_i, and (in the case of families) Is, $ps_i[xs]$, and $qs_{ik}[xs, zs]$.

Internalization

I have presented an open theory, that is, a theory which can be extended whenever there is a need for it. But the schema precisely determines what an admissible extension of a given theory T is, and hence the schema defines a collection of theories obtainable by such extensions.

Is it possible to turn this external schema into an internal construction? Consider first the case of *inductive sets*. Each set P is determined by a list (indexed by i) of pairs of telescopes Gs_i and lists (indexed by k) of telescopes Hs_{ik}. It is tempting to write something like

$$P = \mathcal{W}((xs :: Gs_i, (Hs_{ik}[xs])_k)_i)$$

and

$$f = T((xs :: Gs_i, (Hs_{ik}[xs])_k, d_i)_i),$$

because of the similarity between the schema for inductive sets and primitive recursive functions on the one hand and the rules for the well-orderings on the other. We could then put

$$Wx : A_0.A_1[x] = W(((x : A_0), ((A_1[x])))),$$

since the well-orderings is the special case where all lists and telescopes have length 1. Other standard set formers would be defined by

$$
\begin{aligned}
\bot &= W(()), \\
\top &= W(((), ())), \\
N &= W(((), ()); ((), (()))), \\
\mathcal{O} &= W(((), ()); ((), (())); ((), ((N)))), \\
A_0 + A_1 &= W((((A_0), ()); ((A_1), ()))), \\
A_0 \times A_1 &= W((((A_0; A_1), ()))), \\
\Sigma x : A_0.A_1[x] &= W((((x : A_0; A_1[x]), ()))).
\end{aligned}
$$

However, there are no formal means in type theory for introducing W and T, not even in the theory of logical types (Martin-Löf's logical framework). It seems that we would need to extend this framework with certain formal notions of telescope and non-dependent list.

Also note that we need the extra generality provided by the schema as compared with the well-orderings, since we consider *intensional* type theory. In *extensional* type theory on the other hand, we can use well-orderings for representing inductive sets. But this representation uses non-trivial codings and assumes some basic set formers, such as $\bot$, $\top$, $+$, and Σ, in addition to Π, which is needed for the schema too. This representation is described in Dybjer [7], where it is also explained why it does not work for intensional type theory.

For *inductive families* we could similarly try to write

$$P = W\mathcal{F}(Is, (xs :: Gs_i, (zs :: Hs_{ik}[xs], qs_{ik}[xs, zs])_k, ps_i[xs])_i)$$

and

$$f = T\mathcal{F}(Is, (xs :: Gs_i, (zs :: Hs_{ik}[xs], qs_{ik}[xs, zs])_k, ps_i[xs], d_i)_i).$$

This does not resemble any standard set former, even though the first three arguments have a similar function to the first three arguments of Petersson's and Synek's trees [16].

Some set formers written in terms of $\mathcal{WF}$:

$$Eq(A) \;=\; \mathcal{WF}((A;A),((x:A),(),(x;x))),$$
$$Eq'(A,a) \;=\; \mathcal{WF}((A),((),(),(a))).$$

8 Universes

For each theory T we can define a universe U_0, which is the *set* (of codes) of the sets introduced in T. Since it is a set it is inductively defined by its introduction rules, but these introduction rules do not follow the schema given above.

Expressions and inference rules

We assume a countable sequence $U_0, U_1, U_2, \ldots$ and formulate rules for universes á la Russell [14].
  Formation rules:

$$U_n \; set,$$
$$U_n = U_n.$$

Introduction rules:

$$U_m : U_n,$$
$$U_m = U_m : U_n$$

if $m < n$, and

$$\frac{\Gamma \vdash A_0 : U_n \qquad \Gamma, x : A_0 \vdash A_1[x] : U_n}{\Gamma \vdash \Pi x : A_0.A_1[x] : U_n},$$

$$\frac{\Gamma \vdash A_0 = A_0' : U_n \qquad \Gamma, x : A_0 \vdash A_1[x] = A_1'[x] : U_n}{\Gamma \vdash \Pi x : A_0.A_1[x] = \Pi x : A_0'.A_1'[x] : U_n}.$$

Elimination rules:

$$\frac{A : U_n}{A \; set},$$

$$\frac{A = A' : U_n}{A = A'}.$$

These rules extend the dependently typed λ-calculus with universes (getting the theory T_0^U) and are independent of the particular set formers introduced later. As in the case without universes we may extend T_0^U to obtain a sequence of theories $T_1^U, T_2^U, \ldots$. When extending $T = T_n^U$ to

T_{n+1}^U by adding a new set former P or a new function constant f we may use the rules for universes to justify that the Gs_i, $Hs_{ik}[xs]$, etc. are sets.

$$\frac{is :: Is}{P(is) : U_n}$$

If P depends on parameters which themselves are sets (or families) and thus appear as premises in the formation rule, then similar premises, stating that the parameters are in U_n, appear in the corresponding universe introduction rule.

Alternatively, if we had the internal set former $\mathcal{WF}$ for inductive families, then we could reflect its formation rule as an introduction rule for universes.

Set-theoretic interpretation

A natural interpretation of the sequence of type-theoretic universes is a sequence of set-theoretic universes.

But this interpretation does not reflect the fact that a universe is a set in type theory, and thus inductively generated by its introduction rules. In particular the universe elimination rule is not interpreted. (This rule is usually omitted, since it depends on the particular set formers introduced.)

We could try to interpret a universe as a set inductively generated by its introduction rules by associating a rule set in the sense of Aczel, as we did for other sets. This is similar to Salvesen's interpretation of universes [18]. But the universe elimination rule would still not be interpreted, since extensionally equal sets in the universe, which are not necessarily definitionally equal, are identified.

Instead we could interpret universes á la Tarski, see Martin-Löf [14]. But then a new problem would appear: the Π-formation rule is reflected as the following introduction rule for U_0:

$$\frac{a_0 : U_0 \qquad a_1 : T_0(a_0) \to U_0}{\dot{\Pi}(a_0, a_1) : U_0},$$

where $\dot{\Pi}(a_0, a_1)$ is the code for $\Pi x : T_0(a_0).T_0(a_1(x))$ and $T_0(x)$ is the decoding function which assigns a set to an element $x : U_0$. This rule has a negative occurrence of the family $T_0(x)$, which is defined simultaneously with U_0. But this problem can be resolved since we can still define an operator ϕ, which inductively generates the family $[T_0(x)]_x^u$, where $u \in [U_0]$, and thus simultaneously its domain of definition $[U_0]$.

Assume for simplicity that we only have introduced one inductive set P without using universes and without using parameters. Let its code be

$\dot{P} : U_0$. So U_0 is inductively generated by the introduction rules for $\dot{\Pi}$ and $\dot{P}$. Let t be a function with domain $\mathrm{dom}\, t$ and define the function

$$\phi(t) \;=\; \{\langle n_{\dot{P}}, [\![P]\!]\rangle\} \;\cup$$
$$\{\langle\langle n_{\dot{\Pi}}, u_0, u_1\rangle, \prod_{x\in t(u_0)} t(u_1(x))\rangle | u_0 \in \mathrm{dom}\, t, u_1 \in t(u_0) \to \mathrm{dom}\, t\}.$$

Let ϕ^α be ϕ iterated α times on $\emptyset$. This is an increasing chain, since $\emptyset \subseteq \phi(\emptyset)$ and $t \subseteq \phi(t)$ implies $\phi(t) \subseteq \phi^2(t)$. Hence ϕ has a least fixed point $\mathcal{I}(\phi)$, and we let

$$[\![U_0]\!]\rho = \mathrm{dom}\,\mathcal{I}(\phi)$$

and

$$[\![T_0(a)]\!]\rho = (\mathcal{I}(\phi))([\![a]\!]\rho).$$

If we assume the existence of a set-theoretic universe which itself is a set, then we can show that $[\![U_0]\!]$ is a set, and that $[\![T_0(x)]\!]_x^u$ is a family of sets, where $u \in [\![U_0]\!]$. (Indeed, if $[\![P]\!]$ is an infinite set and if $[\![U_0]\!]$ is a set then it follows that $\sup_{u\in[\![U_0]\!]} \mathrm{card}\, [\![T_0(x)]\!]_x^u$ is a strongly inaccessible cardinal.) Moreover, we let

$$[\![\dot{P}]\!] = n_{\dot{P}}$$

and

$$[\![\dot{\Pi}(a_0, a_1)]\!] = \langle n_{\dot{\Pi}}, [\![a_0]\!], [\![a_1]\!]\rangle,$$

and then the two universe introduction rules are easily justified. The two properties of the decoding function also follow directly. Finally, the universe elimination rule expresses definition of functions on U_0 by primitive recursion. To interpret such a function we use the same technique as when interpreting T_0 above.

Acknowledgements. The origin of this paper is a discussion with Thierry Coquand during a visit to INRIA-Rocquencourt in March 1989, when we compared our different ways of formalizing inductive sets in type theory. I was also shown the set-theoretic interpretation described in Coquand and Paulin [6] and wondered whether it would be possible to construct a direct interpretation of the schema using Aczel's rule sets. Other people who have contributed by pointing out errors or giving useful suggestion include Susumu Hayashi, Michael Hedberg, Christine Paulin, and Thomas Streicher. I also had interesting discussions with Lars Hallnäs and Viggo Stoltenberg-Hansen, who argued that it be worth-while to investigate what set-theoretic principles are needed for the interpretation and told me about the relevance of admissible sets. Finally, I am very grateful to an anonymous referee who read the paper carefully and suggested numerous improvements.

Bibliography

[1] Aczel, P. (1977). An introduction to inductive definitions, in *Handbook of Mathematical Logic*, ed. J. Barwise (North Holland), 739–782.

[2] Aczel, P. (1986). The type theoretic interpretation of constructive set theory: inductive definitions, in *Logic, Methodology and Philosophy of Science VII* (Elsevier Science Publishers B.V.), 17–49.

[3] Backhouse, R. (1986). On the meaning and construction of the rules in Martin-Löf's theory of types. Report CS 8606, University of Groningen, Department of Mathematics and Computing Science. Also in *Proceedings of the Workshop on General Logic, Edinburgh, February 1987*, report ECS-LFCS-88-52, Department of Computer Science, University of Edinburgh.

[4] Backhouse, R., Chisholm, P., Malcolm, G., and Saaman, E. (1989). Do-it-yourself type theory (part 1), *Formal Aspects of Computing* 1, 19–84.

[5] de Bruijn, N.G. (1980). A survey of the project AUTOMATH, in *To H.B. Curry: Essays on Combinatory Logic, Lambda Calculus and Formalism*, eds. J.P. Seldin and J.R. Hindley (Academic Press), 579–606.

[6] Coquand, T. and Paulin, C. (1990). Inductively defined types, preliminary version, in *LNCS 417, COLOG '88, International Conference on Computer Logic* (Springer-Verlag) 50–66.

[7] Dybjer, P. (1988). Inductively defined sets in Martin-Löf's set theory, in *Proceedings of the Workshop on General Logic, Edinburgh, February 1987*, report ECS-LFCS-88-52, Department of Computer Science, University of Edinburgh.

[8] Dybjer, P. (1989). An inversion principle for Martin-Löf's type theory, in *Proceedings of the Workshop on Programming Logic, Båstad, Re-*

port 54, Programming Methodology Group, University of Göteborg and Chalmers University of Technology, 177–190.

[9] Dybjer, P. (1990). Comparing integrated and external logics of functional programs, *Science of Computer Programming* 14, 59–79.

[10] Hedberg, M. (1991). Normalizing the associative law - an experiment with Martin-Löf's type theory, *Formal Aspects of Computing*, to appear.

[11] Martin-Löf, P. (1971). Hauptsatz for the intuitionistic theory of iterated inductive definitions, in *Proceedings of the Second Scandinavian Logic Symposium*, ed. J.E. Fenstad (North-Holland), 179–216.

[12] Martin-Löf, P. (1975). An intuitionistic theory of types: Predicative part, in *Logic Colloquium '73* (North-Holland), 73–118.

[13] Martin-Löf, P. (1982). Constructive mathematics and computer programming, in *Logic Methodology and Philosophy of Science, VI, 1979* (North-Holland), 153–175.

[14] Martin-Löf, P. (1984). *Intuitionistic Type Theory*. (Bibliopolis, Napoli).

[15] Nordström, B., Petersson, K., and Smith, J.M. (1990). *Programming in Martin-Löf's Type Theory: an Introduction* (Oxford University Press).

[16] Petersson, K. and Synek, D. (1989). A set constructor for inductive sets in Martin-Löf's type theory, in *LNCS 389, Category Theory and Computer Science*, ed. D. Pitt et. al, (Springer-Verlag), 128–140.

[17] Pfenning, F. and Paulin-Mohring, C. (1989). Inductively defined types in the calculus of constructions, in *LNCS 442, Mathematical Foundations of Program Semantics, 5th International Conference*, eds. M. Main, A. Melton, M. Mislove, D. Schmidt (Springer-Verlag), 209–228.

[18] Salvesen, A.B. (1984). Typeteori - en studie. University of Oslo Cand. Scient. thesis.

[19] Schroeder-Heister, P. (1984). A natural extension of natural deduction. *Journal of Symbolic Logic*, 49(4).

[20] Schroeder-Heister, P. (1985). Judgements of higher levels and standardized rules for logical constants in Martin-Löf's theory of logic. Unpublished paper.

[21] Streicher, T. (1988). Correctness and Completeness of a Categorical Semantics of the Calculus of Constructions. Universität Passau Ph.D. thesis.

[22] Szasz, N. (1991). A machine checked proof that Ackermann's function is not primitive recursive, Chalmers Universtity of Technology Licentiate thesis, to appear.

[23] Troelstra, A.S. (1987). On the syntax of Martin-Löf's type theories. *Theoretical Computer Science*, 511–26.

PROOFS AND COMPUTATION

Proof-search in the λΠ-calculus

David Pym
University of Edinburgh
Scotland, U.K.

Lincoln Wallen
University of Oxford
England, U.K.

We formulate a system for proof-search in the λΠ-calculus by exploiting a cut-elimination theorem and a subformula property. We modify this system to support the use of unification and prove that the modification reduces the search space uniformly. A permutation theorem is then exploited to reduce the search space further and a notion of *intrinsic well-typing* is introduced to ensure an adequate computational basis for proof-search.

1 Introduction

We present a series of proof systems for the λΠ-calculus: a theory of *first-order dependent function types* [7], [18], [11]. The systems are complete, but differ substantially as bases for algorithmic proof-search.

The first system, called **N**, is a natural deduction formulation of the λΠ-calculus. This system is also known as the type system of the (Edinburgh) Logical Framework or LF [11]. The main judgement of **N** is the typing assertion: $\Gamma \vdash M{:}A$, meaning that the term M has type A given the type assignments for free variables and constants recorded in Γ. This relation is decidable. A typical rule of **N** is the elimination rule for the dependent function type constructor, Π:

$$\Pi E \quad \frac{\Gamma \vdash M : (\Pi x{:}A.B) \quad \Gamma \vdash N : A}{\Gamma \vdash MN : B[N/x]}$$

where $B[N/x]$ denotes capture-avoiding substitution of N for free occurrences of x in B.[1]

In Section 3 we formulate a sound and complete Gentzen-style sequent calculus **G** and use a cut-elimination result for **G** to obtain a system for the semi-decidable relation of *inhabitation:* $\Gamma \Rightarrow A$, with the meaning $(\exists M)(\Gamma \vdash M{:}A)$. This system, called **L**, forms a foundation for proof-search in the λΠ-calculus since the judgements of **L** assert the *existence* of proofs of the judgements of **N** (as in the case of first-order logic [23]).

---

[1]Readers unfamiliar with dependent types should read the construction $\Pi x{:}A.B$ as a (typed) universal quantifier such as $\forall x{:}A.B$; x is the bound variable, ranging over the type A, which may occur free in the term B.

A typical rule of **L** is the Π-left rule, the counterpart of the Π-elimination rule of **N**:

$$\Pi l \quad \frac{\Gamma, z{:}B[N/x] \Rightarrow C}{\Gamma \Rightarrow C}$$

(a) $w : (\Pi x{:}A.B) \in \Gamma$
(b) $z \notin \mathrm{Dom}(\Gamma)$ (1)
(c) **G**\cut proves $\Gamma \vdash N{:}A$.

L is almost *logicistic*, in the sense of Gentzen, but there remains one localized appeal to an external notion, that notion being the system **G**\cut (*i.e.*, **G** without the cut rule) in side condition (c) of the rule above. Indeed, with respect to the Π-type structure of terms in the language, **L** has a *subformula property* [10]. As a consequence, if the inference rules are used as *reduction operators* from conclusion to premisses then **L** induces a search space Sp(**L**) of derivations of a given sequent. A formalization of this notion of search space can be found in Section 4. Notice that if the Π*l* rule is used as a reduction, the choice of term N to use in the premiss is unconstrained by the conclusion of the rule. The sub*formula* property of the Π-types does not extend to a full sub*term* property (*cf.* the quantifier rules of the predicate calculus). The *axiom* sequent (or *closure* condition for the reduction system) is:

$$\Gamma, z{:}A, \Gamma' \Rightarrow A$$

i.e., the conclusion occurs as the type of a declaration in the context.

In Section 4 we formulate the system **U** which is is obtained from **L** by removing the appeal to **G**\cut in the Π*l* rule. The Π*l* rule of **U** is thus:

$$\Pi l \quad \frac{\Gamma, z{:}B[\alpha/x] \Rightarrow C}{\Gamma \Rightarrow C}$$

(a) $w : (\Pi x{:}A.B) \in \Gamma$ (2)
(b) $z \notin \mathrm{Dom}(\Gamma)$.

This rule introduces an *indeterminate* into the proof, denoted here by α. Indeterminates are distinct from the usual *eigenvariables* that appear in derivations.

A leaf $\Gamma \Rightarrow A$ of a **U**-derivation may be *closed* by an *instantiation:* a mapping from indeterminates to terms, such that for at least one declaration $z : B \in \Gamma$ we have $B\sigma \equiv A\sigma$. (Here $B\sigma$ denotes the image of B under the mapping σ etc.) The calculation of instantiations can be performed by a *unification algorithm* for the language. A suitable algorithm has been developed by the first author [24] based on a standard algorithm for simple type theory [14]. A similar algorithm has been developed, independently, by Elliott [8], [9].

A **U**-proof is a pair $\langle \psi, \sigma \rangle$ consisting of a **U**-derivation ψ and an instantiation σ such that $\psi\sigma$ (the image of ψ under σ) is an **L**-proof. Not every instantiation that closes all the leaves of a given U-derivation will yield an L-proof when so applied. It is sufficient to check that the instantiation can be *well-typed* in the derivation to ensure that the result is an L-proof. If Γ is the context and A the type of the indeterminate α when introduced into the U-derivation, the well-typing condition for α amounts to:

$$\Gamma\sigma \vdash \alpha\sigma : A\sigma$$

ensuring that side condition (c) of the Π*l* rule of L (1)—the condition omitted from the Π*l* rule of U (2)—is nevertheless satisfied in $\psi\sigma$. The unconstrained choice of term in the Π*l* rule of L is replaced by a highly constrained choice in U.[2] Since instantiations are only calculated by unifying declarations in the leaves of proofs to force the leaves to close, all such instantiations considered are *minimal* in a sense made precise in Section 4. It is then easy to prove that the search space Sp(U) induced by U is a subspace of Sp(L), but which nevertheless contains representatives for all L-proofs. This wholesale reduction in the search space is analogous to that obtained by Robinson in the context of the predicate calculus [26].

The well-typing of an instantiation depends on the structure of the derivation from which it is calculated. If it fails to be well-typed in that derivation it may be well-typed in some permutation of the derivation, since rule applications (or reductions) can sometimes be permuted whilst leaving the endsequent (*i.e.*, root) of the derivation and its leaves unchanged. The degree to which this can be done is summarized in the form of a *Permutation Theorem*, in the sense of Kleene [15] and Curry [6], and underlies the material of Sections 5 and 6.

In the final refinement of the paper, the well-typing condition on the instantiation in the notion of U-proof $\langle \psi, \sigma \rangle$ is weakened to require only that there exist a legal permutation of ψ, say ψ^*, in which the instantiation is well-typed; *i.e.*, $\psi^*\sigma$ is an L-proof. Of course the crucial computational question is whether the existence of at least one suitable ψ^*, given ψ and σ, can be determined as the search progresses. We show in Section 6 that this is indeed the case using a *reduction ordering:* a notion which was introduced by Bibel [4] for classical connectives and extended by the second author in [29] to various non-classical connectives.[3] In effect we consider

---

[2] The inference system that corresponds to the calculation of instantiations by unification does indeed have a *subterm property*. The soundness and completeness result for U is a form of *Herbrand Theorem* for the theory. The unification algorithm searches amongst the terms of a "Herbrand universe" defined by each leaf sequent. This aspect is not explored in detail in this paper, see [24].

[3] The condition is equivalent to an enhanced "occurs-check" in the unification algorithm if a suitable notion of *Skolem function* were introduced. The suitable notion is *not* the obvious one that the reader might suppose from experience of classical

two derivations to be equivalent with respect to a given instantiation if they are permutation variants of each other. The reduction ordering ensures that there is always at least one derivation in the equivalence class in which the instantiation is well-typed.

The reader may find it helpful to refer back to the overview given above to identify the motivation for various technicalities below.

This paper extends an earlier paper [25] in that we discuss the proof-theoretic foundation of the sequent calculus L and in that we provide a preliminary analysis of the notion of *search space* which allows us to prove certain *containment* results. We also provide a proof of the *Permutation Theorem* for the λΠ-calculus and provide examples to illustrate the important definitions.

2   λΠ-calculus: a theory of dependent function types

The λΠ-calculus is a language with entities on three levels: *objects, types and families of types,* and *kinds*. Objects are classified by types, types and families of types by kinds. The distinguished kind Type classifies the types; the other kinds classify functions f which yield a type $f(x_1)\ldots(x_n)$ when applied to objects $x_1, \ldots, x_n$ of certain types determined by the kind of f. Any function definable in the system has a type as domain, while its range can either be a type, if it is an object, or a kind, if it is a family of types. The λΠ-calculus is therefore predicative.

The theory we shall deal with is a formal system for deriving assertions of one of the following shapes:

$\vdash \Sigma$ sig Σ is a signature

$\vdash_\Sigma \Gamma$ context Γ is a context

$\Gamma \vdash_\Sigma K$ kind K is a kind

$\Gamma \vdash_\Sigma A : K$ A has kind K

$\Gamma \vdash_\Sigma M : A$ M has type A

where the syntax is specified by the following grammar:

$$\Sigma \quad ::= \quad \langle\rangle \mid \Sigma, c : K \mid \Sigma, c : A$$
$$\Gamma \quad ::= \quad \langle\rangle \mid \Gamma, x : A$$
$$K \quad ::= \quad \text{Type} \mid \Pi x : A.K$$
$$A \quad ::= \quad c \mid \Pi x : A.B \mid \lambda x : A.B \mid AM$$
$$M \quad ::= \quad c \mid x \mid \lambda x : A.M \mid MN$$

quantifiers, not least because the logic under investigation here is intuitionistic. In general, the theoretical diversion via Skolemization is unnecessary and can be difficult to justify semantically, even in simple type theory (*cf.* [19]). Our approach follows Herbrand's Theorem (which is finitary) rather than the Skolem-Herbrand-Gödel Theorem (which is not).

We let M and N range over expressions for objects, A and B for types and families of types, K for kinds, x and y over variables, and c over constants. We refer to the collection of variables declared in a context Γ as $\text{Dom}(\Gamma)$. We assume α-conversion throughout. The inference rules of the λΠ-calculus appear in Table 1. We shall refer to this system as **N** to emphasize that it is a system of natural deduction.

A summary of the major metatheorems pertaining to **N** and its reduction properties are given by Theorem 2.1, [11], [27], [12], [2].

THEOREM 2.1 (THE BASIC METATHEORY OF THE λΠ-CALCULUS) *Let* X *range over basic assertions of the form* $A{:}K$ *and* $M{:}A$. *We write* **N** *proves* $\Gamma \vdash_\Sigma X$ *to denote the provability of the assertion* $\Gamma \vdash_\Sigma X$ *in the system* **N**.

1. *Thinning is an admissible rule: if* **N** *proves* $\Gamma \vdash_\Sigma X$ *and* **N** *proves* $\vdash_{\Sigma,\Sigma'} \Gamma, \Gamma'$ *context, then* **N** *proves* $\Gamma, \Gamma' \vdash_{\Sigma,\Sigma'} X$.

2. *Transitivity is an admissible rule: if* **N** *proves* $\Gamma \vdash_\Sigma M{:}A$ *and* **N** *proves* $\Gamma, x : A, \Delta \vdash_\Sigma X$, *then* **N** *proves* $\Gamma, \Delta[M/x] \vdash_\Sigma X[M/x]$.

3. *Uniqueness of types and kinds: if* **N** *proves* $\Gamma \vdash_\Sigma M{:}A$ *and* **N** *proves* $\Gamma \vdash_\Sigma M{:}A'$, *then* $A =_{\beta\eta} A'$, *and similarly for kinds.*

4. *Subject reduction: if* **N** *proves* $\Gamma \vdash_\Sigma M{:}A$ *and* $M \to^*_{\beta\eta} M'$, *then* **N** *proves* $\Gamma \vdash_\Sigma M'{:}A$, *and similarly for types.*

5. *All well-typed terms are strongly normalizing.*

6. *All well-typed terms are Church-Rosser.*

7. *Each of the five relations defined by the inference system of Table 1 is decidable, as is the property of being well-typed.*

8. *Predicativity: if* **N** *proves* $\Gamma \vdash_\Sigma M : A$ *then the type-free* λ-*term obtained by erasing all type information from* M *can be typed in the Curry type assignment system.*

9. *Strengthening is an admissible rule: if* **N** *proves* $\Gamma, x{:}A, \Gamma' \vdash_\Sigma X$ *and if* $x \notin \text{FV}(\Gamma') \cup \text{FV}(X)$ *then* **N** *proves* $\Gamma, \Gamma' \vdash_\Sigma X$.

A term is said to be *well-typed in a signature and context* if it can be shown to either be a kind, have a kind, or have a type in that signature and context. A term is *well-typed* if it is well-typed in some signature and context. The notion of $\beta\eta$-reduction, written $\to_{\beta\eta}$, can be defined both at the level of objects and at the level of types and families of types in the obvious way, for details see [12]. $M =_{\beta\eta} N$ iff $M \to^*_{\beta\eta} P$ and $N \to^*_{\beta\eta} P$

for some term P, where * denotes reflexive and transitive closure. For simplicity we shall write $\to_{\beta\eta}$ for $\to_{\beta\eta}^*$.

We stress that all five of the forms of assertion defined by the inference fules of Table 1 are decidable. We also stress that N is a system of first-order types in the following sense: the Π-type formation rule has the form:

$$\frac{\Gamma \vdash_\Sigma A:\text{Type} \quad \Gamma, x:A \vdash_\Sigma B:\text{Type}}{\Gamma \vdash_\Sigma \Pi x:A.B : \text{Type}} ;$$

both A and B must be of kind Type (see also Rule 11 of Table 1). There are no variables of kind Type and consequently there are no higher-order types (of kind Type).

The $\lambda\Pi$-calculus may be conservatively extended with non-dependent function types, $A \to B$, denoting $\Pi x:A.B$ whenever x does not occur free in B. Similarly, we can write $A \to K$, for $\Pi x:A.K$ when x does not occur free in K. This extension is particularly valuable from the point of view of proof-search in the Gentzen-style system defined below, in that it allows us to separate out the propositional part of the logic from the quantificational part: the former gains a full analysis *within* the system while the latter (Πl), as we have seen, requires external notions. Henceforth we shall use N to denote the system with explicit $\to$ constructions; *i.e.*, the rules of Table 2 are added to those of Table 1. The basic metatheoretic properties of Theorem 2.1 hold for this extended syntax.

In a more general setting, the $\lambda\Pi$-calculus is related to the logic $\lambda\mathbf{P}$ of Barendregt's cube, Barendregt *et al.* [3]. The principal differences are that (i) in the $\lambda\Pi$-calculus the signature is distinguished as an initial segment of the context in which all kind-declarations must occur and from which discharge is not permitted, and (ii) in the $\lambda\Pi$-calculus the η-rule is admitted. The presence of the η-rule increases the difficulty of the proof of Theorem 2.1, in particular the proof of the Church–Rosser property (Part 6) [27].

3   A metacalculus for N.

The inference rules of the system N represent a linearized natural deduction presentation of the $\lambda\Pi$-calculus. The system is said to be:

- *Linearized* because the hypotheses are recorded in the context;

- *Natural deduction* because of the form of the application rules — they correspond to the implication-elimination rule of natural deduction formulations of intuitionistic logic [10], [23], [13].

Valid Signature

$$\frac{}{\vdash \langle\rangle \ \text{sig}} \tag{3}$$

$$\frac{\vdash \Sigma \ \text{sig} \quad \vdash_\Sigma K \ \text{kind} \quad c \notin \text{Dom}(\Sigma)}{\vdash \Sigma, c : K \ \text{sig}} \tag{4}$$

$$\frac{\vdash \Sigma \ \text{sig} \quad \vdash_\Sigma A: \text{Type} \quad c \notin \text{Dom}(\Sigma)}{\vdash \Sigma, c : A \ \text{sig}} \tag{5}$$

Valid Context

$$\frac{\vdash \Sigma \ \text{sig}}{\vdash_\Sigma \langle\rangle \ \text{context}} \tag{6}$$

$$\frac{\vdash_\Sigma \Gamma \ \text{context} \quad \Gamma \vdash_\Sigma A: \text{Type} \quad x \notin \text{Dom}(\Gamma)}{\vdash_\Sigma \Gamma, x : A \ \text{context}} \tag{7}$$

Valid Kinds

$$\frac{\vdash_\Sigma \Gamma \ \text{context}}{\Gamma \vdash_\Sigma \text{Type} \ \text{kind}} \tag{8}$$

$$\frac{\Gamma \vdash_\Sigma A: \text{Type} \quad \Gamma, x : A \vdash_\Sigma K \ \text{kind}}{\Gamma \vdash_\Sigma \Pi x : A.K \ \text{kind}} \tag{9}$$

Valid Elements of a Kind

$$\frac{\vdash_\Sigma \Gamma \ \text{context} \quad c : K \in \Sigma}{\Gamma \vdash_\Sigma c: K} \tag{10}$$

$$\frac{\Gamma \vdash_\Sigma A: \text{Type} \quad \Gamma, x : A \vdash_\Sigma B: \text{Type}}{\Gamma \vdash_\Sigma \Pi x : A.B: \text{Type}} \tag{11}$$

$$\frac{\Gamma \vdash_\Sigma A: \text{Type} \quad \Gamma, x : A \vdash_\Sigma B: K}{\Gamma \vdash_\Sigma \lambda x : A.B: \Pi x : A.K} \tag{12}$$

$$\frac{\Gamma \vdash_\Sigma B: \Pi x : A.K \quad \Gamma \vdash_\Sigma N: A}{\Gamma \vdash_\Sigma BN: K[N/x]} \tag{13}$$

$$\frac{\Gamma \vdash_\Sigma A: K \quad \Gamma \vdash_\Sigma K' \ \text{kind} \quad K =_{\beta\eta} K'}{\Gamma \vdash_\Sigma A: K'} \tag{14}$$

Valid Elements of a Type

$$\frac{\vdash_\Sigma \Gamma \ \text{context} \quad c : A \in \Sigma}{\Gamma \vdash_\Sigma c: A} \tag{15}$$

$$\frac{\vdash_\Sigma \Gamma \ \text{context} \quad x : A \in \Gamma}{\Gamma \vdash_\Sigma x: A} \tag{16}$$

$$\Pi I \quad \frac{\Gamma \vdash_\Sigma A: \text{Type} \quad \Gamma, x : A \vdash_\Sigma M: B}{\Gamma \vdash_\Sigma \lambda x : A.M: \Pi x : A.B} \tag{17}$$

$$\Pi E \quad \frac{\Gamma \vdash_\Sigma M: \Pi x : A.B \quad \Gamma \vdash_\Sigma N: A}{\Gamma \vdash_\Sigma MN: B[N/x]} \tag{18}$$

$$\frac{\Gamma \vdash_\Sigma M: A \quad \Gamma \vdash_\Sigma A': \text{Type} \quad A =_{\beta\eta} A'}{\Gamma \vdash_\Sigma M: A'} \tag{19}$$

Table 1

Valid Kinds

$$\frac{\Gamma \vdash_\Sigma A : \text{Type} \quad \Gamma, x{:}A \vdash_\Sigma K \text{ kind} \quad x \notin \text{FV}(K)}{\Gamma \vdash_\Sigma A \to K \text{ kind}} \tag{20}$$

Valid Elements of a Kind

$$\frac{\Gamma \vdash_\Sigma A : \text{Type} \quad \Gamma, x{:}A \vdash_\Sigma B{:}K \quad x \notin \text{FV}(K)}{\Gamma \vdash_\Sigma \lambda x{:}A . B : A \to K} \tag{21}$$

$$\frac{\Gamma \vdash_\Sigma B{:}A \to K \quad \Gamma \vdash_\Sigma N{:}A}{\Gamma \vdash_\Sigma BN : K} \tag{22}$$

$$\frac{\Gamma \vdash_\Sigma A : \text{Type} \quad \Gamma, x{:}A \vdash_\Sigma B : \text{Type} \quad x \notin \text{FV}(B)}{\Gamma \vdash_\Sigma A \to B : \text{Type}} \tag{23}$$

Valid Elements of a Type

$$\to \text{I} \quad \frac{\Gamma \vdash_\Sigma A : \text{Type} \quad \Gamma, x{:}A \vdash_\Sigma M{:}B \quad x \notin \text{FV}(B)}{\Gamma \vdash_\Sigma \lambda x{:}A . M : A \to B} \tag{24}$$

$$\to \text{E} \quad \frac{\Gamma \vdash_\Sigma M{:}A \to B \quad \Gamma \vdash_\Sigma N : !A}{\Gamma \vdash_\Sigma MN : B} \tag{25}$$

Table 2

In this section we introduce a system **G** for the λΠ-calculus in the style of Gentzen's sequent calculus LJ [10]. Via the formulae-as-types isomorphism between natural deduction proofs in intuitionistic propositional logic and the terms of the simply-typed lambda calculus [13], **G** provides a basis for a metacalculus for calculating the *normal* proofs of **N**.

In the setting of the formulae-as-types isomorphism, the →E rule of the system **N**:

$$\to \text{E} \quad \frac{\Gamma \vdash_\Sigma M : A \to B \quad \Gamma \vdash_\Sigma N{:}A}{\Gamma \vdash_\Sigma MN{:}B}$$

corresponds to the sequent calculus rule:

$$\supset \text{E} \quad \frac{\Gamma \vdash \phi \supset \psi \quad \Gamma \vdash \phi}{\Gamma \vdash \psi}$$

of intuitionistic propositional logic (in the obvious notation). In the system **G** the →E rule is replaced by the → *l* rule:

$$\to l \quad \frac{@{:}A \to B \in \Sigma \cup \Gamma \quad \Gamma \vdash_\Sigma N{:}A \quad \Gamma, y{:}B \vdash_\Sigma M{:}D}{\Gamma \vdash_\Sigma M[@N/y]{:}D}$$

for $y \notin FV(D)$, which says that given some constant or variable $@ : A \to B \in \Sigma \cup \Gamma$, some object N of type A in the context Γ, then given an object M which inhabits the type D in the context $\Gamma, y{:}B$, the rule $\to l$ constructs an object $M[@N/y]$ which inhabits the type D in the context Γ. Under the formulae-as-types isomorphism, the corresponding sequent calculus rule of intuitionistic propositional logic is

$$\frac{\Gamma \vdash \phi \quad \psi, \Delta \vdash \gamma}{\phi \supset \psi, \Gamma, \Delta \vdash \gamma}$$

see [13], Section 5.

In a similar way, the ΠE rule of the system $\mathbf{N}$:

$$\Pi E \ \frac{\Gamma \vdash_\Sigma M : \Pi x{:}A \,.\, B \quad \Gamma \vdash_\Sigma N{:}A}{\Gamma \vdash_\Sigma MN{:}B[N/x]},$$

is replaced in the system $\mathbf{G}$ by the Πl rule:

$$\Pi l \ \frac{@ {:} \Pi x{:}A.B \in \Sigma \cup \Gamma \quad \Gamma \vdash_\Sigma N{:}A \quad B[N/x] =_{\beta\eta} C \quad \Gamma, y{:}C \vdash_\Sigma M{:}D}{\Gamma \vdash_\Sigma M[@N/y]{:}D},$$

for $y \notin FV(D)$, which is understood in a manner similar to the $\to l$ rule.

Extension of the formulae-as-types correspondence to universal quantifiers and dependent types in the setting of *Generalized Type Systems* is reported in the work of Barendregt [3]. This work is due variously to Berardi, Terlouw, Geuvers and Barendsen. The extension of this correspondence to Gentzen-style Generalized Type Systems and sequent calculi is under investigation (*cf.* Martin-Löf [17]).

The system $\mathbf{G}$ includes the cut rule:

$$\frac{\Gamma, x{:}A \vdash_\Sigma X \quad \Gamma \vdash_\Sigma N{:}A}{\Gamma \vdash_\Sigma X[N/x]}.$$

$\mathbf{G}$ is relatively sound and complete with respect to $\mathbf{N}$.

PROPOSITION 3.1 (SOUNDNESS AND COMPLETENESS)

> $\mathbf{G}$ proves $\Gamma \vdash_\Sigma M{:}A$ *iff* $\mathbf{N}$ proves $\Gamma \vdash_\Sigma M{:}A$.

A cut-elimination theorem can also be obtained; that is $\mathbf{G}\backslash$cut is relatively complete with respect to $\mathbf{N}$ provided we work with inhabiting objects in β-normal form.

THEOREM 3.2 (CUT-ELIMINATION) *Let* $\mathbf{G}\backslash$cut *be the system* $\mathbf{G}$ *without the cut rule and let* M *and* A *be* β*-normal forms. Then*

> $\mathbf{G}\backslash$cut *proves* $\Gamma \vdash_\Sigma M{:}A$ *iff* $\mathbf{N}$ *proves* $\Gamma \vdash_\Sigma M{:}A$.

While this might seem surprising at first sight (as we might expect completeness for *all* inhabiting objects by analogy with usual completeness of systems without cut) it actually corresponds to the fact that in such systems we do not get completeness for proofs, but rather that every proof in the system with cut *which is in normal form* corresponds to a proof in the system without cut. Indeed, the proof of the completeness of the system without cut may be considered to be analogous to that given by Prawitz [23] for proofs in normal form. To see this observe that the rules of **G** without the cut rule are such that only β-normal forms can be derived from β-normal forms. Note however that the cut rule is able to derive terms that are not β-normal forms from β-normal forms because the cut-term N might be a λ-abstraction.

The reader is referred to [24] for the proofs of Proposition 3.1 and Theorem 3.2. Where no confusion can arise, we omit "**N** proves", "**G** proves". "**G**\cut proves", *etc.*.

For proof-search we are not interested in the decidable typing assertions $\Gamma \vdash_\Sigma M{:}A$, in which the object M encodes the proof of the assertion, but rather in semi-decidable inhabitation assertions of the form $\Gamma \Rightarrow_\Sigma A$, which is to be read as "A is inhabited relative to the context Γ and signature Σ". Here, a proof remains to be calculated, and may not exist. This leads us to the following definition of sequent:

DEFINITION 3.3 (Sequent) A *sequent* is a triple $\langle \Sigma, \Gamma, A \rangle$, written $\Gamma \Rightarrow_\Sigma A$, where Σ is a signature, Γ a context and A a type (family). The intended interpretation of the sequent is the (meta)assertion:

$$(\exists M) \quad \textbf{N} \text{ proves } \Gamma \vdash_\Sigma M{:}A. \qquad \square$$

There are two candidates for a calculus for manipulating such sequents. The first is obtained from the natural deduction system **N** by deleting inhabiting objects. This gives rise to a Π-elimination rule of the form:

$$\Pi\text{E} \quad \frac{\Gamma \Rightarrow_\Sigma \Pi x{:}A \,.\, B}{\Gamma \Rightarrow_\Sigma B[N/x]} \qquad \text{(a) } \textbf{N} \text{ proves } \Gamma \vdash_\Sigma N{:}A$$

which is similar to the usual natural deduction rule for quantifiers. The fact that the type A in the premiss is not a subformula of the conclusion means that a proof procedure based on such a calculus would have to invent the type.

The second candidate is obtained from the sequent calculus **G**\cut by deleting inhabiting objects. This gives rise to a Πl rule of the form:

$$\Pi l \quad \frac{\Gamma, y{:}D \Rightarrow_\Sigma C}{\Gamma \Rightarrow_\Sigma C}$$

(a) @: $\Pi x{:}A.B \in \Sigma \cup \Gamma$
(b) $y \notin \mathrm{Dom}(\Gamma)$
(c) **G**\cut proves $\Gamma \vdash_\Sigma N{:}A$
(d) $B[N/x] \to_{\beta\eta} D$

This rule is preferable to the elimination rule for proof-search because it restricts the non-determinism to the choice of object M, and such choices may be calculated by unification. Thus we define a semi-logicistic calculus **L** for deriving sequents as follows:

DEFINITION 3.4 (The system **L**)

$Ax1 \qquad \Gamma, x{:}A, \Gamma' \Rightarrow_\Sigma A$

$Ax2 \qquad \Gamma \Rightarrow_{\Sigma, c:A, \Sigma'} A$

$$\to r \quad \frac{\Gamma, x{:}A \Rightarrow_\Sigma B}{\Gamma \Rightarrow_\Sigma A \to B} \qquad \text{(a) } x \notin \mathrm{Dom}(\Gamma)$$

$$\Pi r \quad \frac{\Gamma, x{:}A \Rightarrow_\Sigma B}{\Gamma \Rightarrow_\Sigma \Pi x{:}A.B} \qquad \text{(a) } x \notin \mathrm{Dom}(\Gamma)$$

$$\to l \quad \frac{\Gamma \Rightarrow_\Sigma A \qquad \Gamma, y{:}B \Rightarrow_\Sigma C}{\Gamma \Rightarrow_E C}$$

(a) @: $A \to B \in \Sigma \cup \Gamma$
(b) $y \notin \mathrm{Dom}(\Gamma)$

$$\Pi l \quad \frac{\Gamma, y{:}D \Rightarrow_\Sigma C}{\Gamma \Rightarrow_\Sigma C}$$

(a) @: $\Pi x{:}A.B \in \Sigma \cup \Gamma$
(b) $y \notin \mathrm{Dom}(\Gamma)$
(c) **G**\cut proves $\Gamma \vdash_\Sigma M{:}A$
(d) $B[N/x] \to_{\beta\eta} D$

Here $B[N/x]$ denotes capture-avoiding substitution of N for x, and the conditions $x, y \notin \mathrm{Dom}(\Gamma)$ mean that x and y do not label any declaration in the context Γ. For simplicity and efficiency, we work exclusively with $\beta\eta$-normal forms, and for such terms syntactic identity ($\equiv$) is taken up to α-congruence (change of bound variable). As usual we refer to the variable x of the Πr rule as the *eigenvariable* of the inference. We can ensure that in any derivation eigenvariables occur only in sequents above the inference at which they are introduced. Both distinguished occurrences of A are said to be the *principal formula* of the $Ax1$ and $Ax2$ rules. $A \to B$ is the principal formula of the $\to r$ and $\to l$ rules and $\Pi x{:}A.B$ is the principal formula of the Πr and Πl rules. A and B are the *side formulae* of the $\rightarrow r$ and Πr rules, and A and $B[N/x]$ are the side formulae of the Πl rule. A, B and C are the side formulae of the $\rightarrow l$ rule. @ is the *principal atom* in the $\rightarrow l$ and Πl rules. **L**-*derivations* are trees of sequents regulated by the operational rules, and **L**-*proofs* are derivations whose leaves are axioms. □

In this paper, we restrict our attention to inhabitation assertions for types of kind Type.[4]

DEFINITION 3.5 (Well-formed sequent) A sequent $\Gamma \Rightarrow_\Sigma A$ is said to be *well-formed* just in case **G**\cut proves $\Gamma \vdash_\Sigma A$: Type. □

From Theorem 2.1 we have:

PROPOSITION 3.6 *The well-formedness problem for sequents is decidable.*

For proof-search derivations are constructed from the root, or *endsequent*, toward the leaves in the spirit of Kleene [16] and systems of tableaux [28] (see Section 4). In support of this usage we have the following result:

PROPOSITION 3.7 (PYM, 1990) *For well-formed sequents* $\Gamma \Rightarrow_\Sigma A$,

$$\textbf{L} \text{ proves } \Gamma \Rightarrow_\Sigma A \quad \textit{iff} \quad (\exists M) \quad \textbf{G}\backslash\text{cut proves } \Gamma \vdash_\Sigma M{:}A. \quad \square$$

We revert to the system **G**\cut to decide if the endsequent is well-formed. If so, **L** may be used to prove inhabitation of A with respect to the context Γ. Moreover the inhabiting object M is obtained as the extract-object of the **L**-proof $\Gamma \Rightarrow_\Sigma A$, constructed by replacing the inhabiting objects in the proof, starting with the constants and variables at the leaves, in the manner of the system **G**\cut, *q.v.* [24]. **L** is not fully logicistic since an appeal is still made to **G**\cut for each application of the Πl rule (third side condition).

4   Unification and search

In this section we introduce a new calculus **U** which allows unification to be used to calculate terms for use with Πl inferences. The calculation is constrained by the propositional structure of the derivation in such a way that only terms that are *relevant* to the formation of a proof (rather than a mere derivation) are considered (*cf.* [26]). The search space of **U** is then shown to be a proper subspace of the search space of **L** containing

---

[4]This is a very natural restriction for the use made of the $\lambda\Pi$-calculus in the (Edinburgh) Logical Framework, *q.v.* [24].

representatives for all proofs in the latter. U-based search is therefore a *complete* and *uniform* improvement over L-based search.

We introduce a new syntactic class of variables called *indeterminates*, denoted by lowercase Greek letters α, β, *etc.*, and extend the syntactic category of objects to include them thus:

$$Objects \quad M \quad ::= \quad c \mid \alpha \mid x \mid \lambda x{:}A.M \mid MN.$$

Notice that indeterminates cannot appear λ-bound. By virtue of this extension, entities of all syntactic classes may now contain indeterminates as subterms. When we wish to emphasize that a syntactic entity does not contain any indeterminates we shall refer to it as being *ground*.

We define U by dropping the axiom schemata of L and modifying the Πl rule as follows:

DEFINITION 4.1 (U-derivation) The rules of U consist of the $\to r$, $\to l$ and Πr rules of L, together with the rule

$$\Pi l \quad \frac{\Gamma, z{:}B[\alpha/x] \Rightarrow_\Sigma C}{\Gamma \Rightarrow_\Sigma C} \qquad \begin{array}{l} \text{(a)} \ @ : \Pi x{:}A.B \in \Sigma \cup \Gamma \\ \text{(b)} \ z \notin \mathrm{Dom}(\Gamma). \end{array}$$

U-*derivations* are trees regulated by the above rules such that the sequent at the root of the tree is well-formed. In applications of the Πl rule we call Γ the *typing context* of α and A the *type* of α. We shall use $\mathrm{Ind}(\psi)$ and $\mathrm{Eig}(\psi)$ to denote the indeterminates and eigenvariables respectively of a derivation ψ. □

Indeterminates are, in a certain sense, bound within derivations like eigenvariables: their exact identity is irrelevant since each one may be indexed by the unique Πl inference that gives rise to it in a derivation. In the sequel we shall take identity of U-derivations up to change in such indeterminates (*cf.* pure variable proofs). Notice that we have not yet defined U-*proofs* since there are no axiom schemata. U thus consists of four operational rules; the Πl rule no longer contains an external appeal to G\cut or a choice of term, but is otherwise identical to the Πl rule of L.

EXAMPLE 4.2 Figure 1 contains an example of a U-derivation. □

DEFINITION 4.3 (Instantiation) An *instantiation* for a derivation ψ is a mapping from $\mathrm{Ind}(\psi)$ to *ground* objects. The (capture-avoiding) extension of instantiations to all of the constructs of the language is defined in the obvious way.[5] □

---

[5]Formally, we must ensure that any new variables generated during unification (*q.v.* [14], [24]) are distinct from the eigenvariables and indeterminates of the derivation.

$$\cfrac{\Gamma,p{:}-,r{:}D(\alpha) \Rightarrow_\Sigma D(a) \quad \cfrac{\cfrac{\cfrac{\Gamma,p{:}-,y{:}B(\alpha),s{:}E,q{:}C(\beta) \Rightarrow_\Sigma C(y)}{\Gamma,p{:}-,y{:}B(\alpha),s{:}E \Rightarrow_\Sigma C(y)}}{\Gamma,p{:}-,y{:}B(\alpha) \Rightarrow_\Sigma E \to C(y)}}{\Gamma,p{:}- \Rightarrow_\Sigma (\Pi y{:}B(\alpha).(E \to C(y)))}}{\cfrac{\Gamma,p{:}(\Pi y{:}B(\alpha).(E \to C(y))) \to D(\alpha) \Rightarrow_\Sigma D(a)}{\Gamma \Rightarrow_\Sigma D(a)}}$$

$$
\begin{aligned}
&\Pi l_2\\
&\to r\\
&\Pi r\\
&\to l\\
&\Pi l_1
\end{aligned}
$$

$\Sigma = A{:}\mathrm{Type},a{:}A,B{:}A \to \mathrm{Type},b{:}B(a),C{:}B(a) \to \mathrm{Type},D{:}A \to \mathrm{Type},E{:}\mathrm{Type}$
$\Gamma = u{:}\Pi x{:}A.((\Pi y{:}B(x).(E \to C(y))) \to D(x)), \quad v{:}\Pi z{:}B(a).C(z)$

Typing context for α: Γ
Typing context for β: $\Gamma,p{:}(\Pi y{:}B(\alpha).(E \to C(y))) \to D(\alpha),y{:}B(\alpha),s{:}E$

Indeterminates: $\mathrm{Ind}(D1) = \{\alpha,\beta\}$
Eigenvariables: $\mathrm{Eig}(D1) = \{y\}$

Figure 1: U-derivation D1.

The following notion compensates for the absence of axiom schemata in **U**.

DEFINITION 4.4 (Closure) A sequent $\Gamma \Rightarrow_\Sigma A$ is said to be *closed under* an instantiation σ just in case $B\sigma \equiv A\sigma$ for some declaration $@{:}B \in \Sigma \cup \Gamma$. A U-derivation is said to be *closed under* σ just in case all of its leaf sequents are closed under σ. (Again, we work exclusively with $\beta\eta$-normal forms.) □

We are interested in instantiations that are *well-typed* in the following sense.

DEFINITION 4.5 (Well-typing) An instantiation σ is said to be *well-typed* in a given U-derivation just in case for every indeterminate α of the derivation, with typing context Γ and type A, we have:
$$\mathbf{G}\backslash\text{cut} \quad \text{proves} \quad \Gamma\sigma \vdash_\Sigma \alpha\sigma{:}A\sigma. \quad □$$

LEMMA 4.6 *If σ is a well-typed instantiation for U-derivation ψ with domain $\mathrm{Ind}(\psi)$, then $\psi\sigma$ is an L-derivation.*

PROOF. By induction on the structure of U-derivations. The well-typing condition ensures that the image under σ of each instance of a Πl rule of **U** in ψ satisfies the side conditions on the Πl rule of **L**. The remaining operational rules are common to the two systems. □

We are now in a position to define a notion of proof for **U**.

DEFINITION 4.7 (U-proof) A U-*proof* is a pair $\langle \psi, \sigma \rangle$, where ψ is a U-derivation and σ an instantiation with domain $\mathrm{Ind}(\psi)$, such that (1) ψ is closed under σ, and (2) σ is well-typed in ψ. □

THEOREM 4.8 *If* $\langle \psi, \sigma \rangle$ *is a* U-*proof,* $\psi\sigma$ *is an* L-*proof.*

PROOF. By the lemma above $\psi\sigma$ is an **L**-derivation; closure ensures that the leaves of $\psi\sigma$ are **L**-axioms.

We remark that it is immediate that an **L**-proof gives rise to a unique **U**-proof (up to change in indeterminates): this is the converse of Theorem 4.8.

EXAMPLE 4.9 The mappings $\theta_1 = \{\alpha \mapsto a, \beta \mapsto y\}$ and $\theta_2 = \{\alpha \mapsto a, \beta \mapsto b\}$ are instantiations for derivation (D1) of Figure 1. Both are well-typed since (for $i = 1, 2$) $\Gamma\theta_i \vdash_{\Sigma} \alpha\theta_i{:}A$ and $(\Gamma, p{:}-, y{:}B(\alpha), s{:}E)\theta_i \vdash_{\Sigma} \beta\theta_i{:}B(\alpha)\theta_i$. θ_1 closes the derivation whereas θ_2 does n ot. Consequently $\langle D1, \theta_1 \rangle$ is a **U**-proof, $\langle D1, \theta_2 \rangle$ is not. □

We can use a unification algorithm to calculate instantiations when a putative leaf has been reached, then check the well-typing condition using **G**\cut. In this way the propositional structure of the **U**-derivation constrains the search for terms used at Πl inferences. The reader should note that the structure of the type of an atom, $@ : A \in \Sigma \cup \Gamma$, is fixed by the (well- formed) endsequent and that this structure cannot be altered by subsequent instantiations of indeterminates: *i.e.*, the outermost connective of A, and of all of its sub*formulae*, is unchanged under the instantiation of indeterminates.

We now develop a simple argument that this use of **U** constitutes a uniform improvement over the standard use of **L** for proof search. The argument is relative to an arbitrary well-formed sequent $\Gamma \Rightarrow_{\Sigma} A$. Let Der(**L**) (resp. Der(**U**)) denote the (r.e.) set of **L**-derivations (resp. **U**-derivations) of the given sequent. There is a natural ordering $\sqsubseteq_L$ (resp. $\sqsubseteq_U$) on Der(**L**) (resp. on Der(**U**)) induced by the obvious notion of *subderivation*.

Searching for a proof of $\Gamma \Rightarrow_{\Sigma} A$ using **L** consists of *reducing* derivations one step at a time: *i.e.*, matching the leaf of a derivation with the conclusion of a rule in **L** and forming a new derivation with the premisses of the rule as new leaves. The original derivation is thus a subderivation of the new one.

DEFINITION 4.10 (Search space of **L**) The *search space* of **L**, denoted by Sp(**L**), is the ordered set $\langle \mathrm{Der}(\mathbf{L}), \sqsubseteq_L \rangle$. □

Sp(**L**) may of course be viewed as a directed graph, the nodes being derivations and the arcs indicating one-step reductions.

Theorem 4.8 and its converse allow us to express the search space of **L** in terms of **U**-derivations and instantiations in preparation for comparison with the search space of **U**. Let D be the set of pairs $\langle \psi, \sigma \rangle$ such that (1) $\psi \in \mathrm{Der}(\mathbf{U})$, (2) σ is well-typed in ψ and (3) $\mathrm{Dom}(\sigma) = \mathrm{Ind}(\psi)$. Define $\sqsubseteq$ on $D \times D$ by: $\langle \psi, \sigma \rangle \sqsubseteq \langle \phi, \tau \rangle$ iff $\psi \sqsubseteq_{\mathbf{U}} \phi$ and $\sigma = \tau \upharpoonright \mathrm{Ind}(\psi)$.

PROPOSITION 4.11 $\langle D, \sqsubseteq \rangle \cong \langle \mathrm{Der}(\mathbf{L}), \sqsubseteq_{\mathbf{L}} \rangle$.

PROOF. Define a mapping from $\langle D, \sqsubseteq \rangle$ to $\langle \mathrm{Der}(\mathbf{L}), \sqsubseteq_{\mathbf{L}} \rangle$ by $\langle \psi, \sigma \rangle \mapsto \psi\sigma$. Theorem 4.8 and its converse ensure that this mapping is an isomorphism of the carrier sets, and it is easy to check that it preserves the order. □

At this point we could define the search space of **U** to be those pairs $\langle \psi, \sigma \rangle \in D$ such that ψ is closed under σ. Such a definition would yield the desired containment relation between the search spaces of the two calculi. However, we postpone the definition and develop a finer analysis of the structure of **U**-search.

DEFINITION 4.12 (Relevance) Let $\langle \psi, \sigma \rangle \in D$, $\alpha \in \mathrm{Dom}(\sigma) = \mathrm{Ind}(\psi)$ and $\tau = \sigma \upharpoonright \mathrm{Dom}(\sigma) \backslash \{\alpha\}$. Let x be the eigenvariable introduced by the Πl reduction that introduced α. Finally, let ϕ be the derivation obtained from ψ by deleting the Πl reduction that introduced α.

(i) The component of σ, $\alpha \mapsto t$, is said to be *directly relevant* to $\langle \psi, \sigma \rangle$ if the number of closed leaves in $\psi\tau$ is strictly less than the number in $\psi\sigma$.

(ii) $\alpha \mapsto t$ is said to be *indirectly relevant* to $\langle \psi, \sigma \rangle$ if either (1) there is some $\beta \in \mathrm{Dom}(\tau)$, directly or indirectly relevant to $\langle \psi, \tau \rangle$, that is *not* well-typed in $\langle \phi, \tau \rangle$; or (2) x is either free in some type in ψ, or a principal atom in ψ.

(iii) The indeterminate α is said to be *relevant* if either it is directly relevant or it is indirectly relevant, and is said to be *irrelevant* if it is neither. □

Informally, $\alpha \in \mathrm{Dom}(\sigma)$ is relevant if either it or its associated eigenvariable contributes to either the closing a leaf of ψ, either directly via closure, or indirectly by contributing to the well-typing of a directly relevant component, or to the construction of ψ via an $\to l$ or a Πl rule.

DEFINITION 4.13 (Minimality) $\langle \psi, \sigma \rangle \in D$ is said to be *propositionally minimal* just in case every $\alpha \in \mathrm{Dom}(\sigma)$ is relevant. □

EXAMPLE 4.14 Both components of θ_1 are directly relevant in $\langle D1, \theta_1 \rangle$. α is also indirectly relevant. α is directly relevant in θ_2, but β is irrelevant. θ_1 is therefore minimal, whereas θ_2 is not. □

While it is not true that every L-proof, seen as an element $\langle \psi, \sigma \rangle \in D$, has σ minimal, we have:

LEMMA 4.15 *If* $\langle \psi, \sigma \rangle \in D$ *and if* $\psi\sigma$ *is an* L-*proof, there is some* ϕ *such that* $\left\langle \phi, \sigma \upharpoonright \mathrm{Ind}(\phi) \right\rangle$ *is propositionally minimal.*

PROOF. Let $\langle \psi, \sigma \rangle$ be an L-proof that is not propositionally minimal. This arises because there is a leaf sequent of ψ in which there is an irrelevant indeterminate α. This indeterminate is introduced to ψ by a Πl reduction which also introduces an eigenvariable x to ψ. Since α is irrelevant, x does not contribute either to the closure of ψ or to its construction (as the principal atom of a left rule). Furthermore, α does not contribute to the closure of ψ. Therefore we can delete from ψ the Πl reduction that introduced α and x to obtain a derivation χ which is closed under the instantiation $\tau = \sigma \upharpoonright \mathrm{Ind}(\chi)$ and is such that $\langle \chi, \tau \rangle \in D$. By deleting the Πl reductions associated with all such irrelevant indeterminates, and by restricting σ to the remaining indeterminates, we obtain a (closed) propositionally minimal $\left\langle \phi, \sigma \upharpoonright \mathrm{Ind}(\phi) \right\rangle \in D$, as required. □

DEFINITION 4.16 (Search space of U) The *search space* of U, denoted $\mathrm{Sp}(\mathbf{U})$, is the set of propositionally minimal pairs $\langle \psi, \sigma \rangle \in D$ such that ψ is closed under σ, ordered by $\sqsubseteq$. □

Indeed, the space $\mathrm{Sp}(\mathbf{U})$ is now the quotient of the space $\mathrm{Sp}(\mathbf{L})$ by both closure and propositional minimality. In particular:

THEOREM 4.17 $\mathrm{Sp}(\mathbf{U}) \subset \mathrm{Sp}(\mathbf{L})$. *Moreover,* $\mathrm{Sp}(\mathbf{U})$ *contains representatives for all* L-*proofs.*

PROOF. By definition and Lemma 4.15. □

We should like to think that the search for a proof using U consists of reducing derivations one step at a time, as in L, but with the modified Πl rule and the calculation via unification of instantiations that close leaves. The above analysis of $\mathrm{Sp}(\mathbf{U})$ is inadequate in that the definition of the search space of U really fails to capture this intuition. The development of an adequate analysis of these notions constitutes a current (and substantial) research project and is related to the possibilities for incremental search afforded by the notion of intrinsic well-typing developed in the sequel (see Section 6).

$$
\cfrac{
\cfrac{
\cfrac{
\Gamma, p\!:\!-,\, r\!:\!D(\alpha) \Rightarrow_\Sigma D(a) \quad
\cfrac{
\cfrac{
\cfrac{
\Gamma, p\!:\!-,\, q\!:\!C(\beta),\, y\!:\!B(\alpha),\, s\!:\!E \Rightarrow_\Sigma C(y)
}{
\Gamma, p\!:\!-,\, q\!:\!C(\beta),\, y\!:\!B(\alpha) \Rightarrow_\Sigma E \to C(y)
}
}{
\Gamma, p\!:\!-,\, q\!:\!C(\beta) \Rightarrow_\Sigma (\Pi y\!:\!B(\alpha).(E \to C(y)))
}
}{}
}{
\Gamma, p\!:\!(\Pi y\!:\!B(\alpha).(E \to C(y))) \to D(\alpha),\, q\!:\!C(\beta) \Rightarrow_\Sigma D(a)
}
}{
\Gamma, p\!:\!(\Pi y\!:\!B(\alpha).(E \to C(y))) \to D(\alpha) \Rightarrow_\Sigma D(a)
}
}{
\Gamma \Rightarrow_\Sigma D(a)
}
$$

with labels: cline2 − 2, $\to r$, Πr, $\to l$, Πl_2, Πl_1

$\Sigma = A\!:\!\text{Type}, a\!:\!A, B\!:\!A \to \text{Type}, b\!:\!B(a), C\!:\!B(a) \to \text{Type}, D\!:\!A \to \text{Type}, E\!:\!\text{Type}$

$\Gamma = u\!:\!\Pi x\!:\!A.((\Pi y\!:\!B(x).(E \to C(y))) \to D(x)),\quad v\!:\!\Pi z\!:\!B(a).C(z)$

Typing context for α: Γ
Typing context for β: $\Gamma, p\!:\!(\Pi y\!:\!B(\alpha).(E \to C(y))) \to D(\alpha)$

Indeterminates: $\text{Ind}(D2) = \{\alpha, \beta\}$
Eigenvariables: $\text{Eig}(D2) = \{y\}$

Figure 2: U-derivation D2.

5   Permutability of inferences and proof-search

The typing contexts of the indeterminates in a U-derivation depend on the structure of the derivation. For example, the U-derivation (D2) shown in Figure 2 is another derivation of the same endsequent as derived by (D1) (Figure 1). (D1) and (D2) differ in the order in which inference rules are applied.

The instantiation $\theta = \theta_1 = \{\alpha \mapsto a, \beta \mapsto y\}$ closes both derivations, but whereas θ is well-typed in (D1), it is not well-typed in (D2) since

$$\Gamma, p\!:\!(\Pi y\!:\!B(\alpha).(E \to C(y))) \to D(\alpha) \not\vdash_\Sigma y\!:\!B(a).$$

Our final refinement is to alter the notion of U-proof so that existence of $\langle D2, \theta \rangle$ is sufficient to infer the existence of $\langle D1, \theta \rangle$, and hence to soundly terminate the search with success. That is, we investigate conditions under which rule instances may be *permuted* whilst leaving the endsequent and leaves of the derivation essentially unchanged. Implicitly we are defining an equivalence relation on derivations such that $\langle D2, \theta \rangle$ and $\langle D1, \theta \rangle$ are in the same equivalence class. The search strategy need construct *at most* one derivation from each class; the search being terminated if *at least* one member of the class is a proof.

The reader should be wary of supposing that the above problem can be overcome simply by defining a normal form for derivations in which inferences on the right are grouped as close to the root of the derivation as possible — in reduction terms: right reductions being preferred over left reductions.[6] Whilst this normal form certainly quotients the set of derivations, we obtain below (implicitly) a *stronger* equality on derivations and hence gain a smaller quotient space. Notice that both (D1) and (D2) are in this normal form. The relative order of Π*l* inferences is in fact important.[7]

Let ψ be a U-derivation of a given endsequent and let $\mathcal{F}_\psi$ denote the collection of inferences that comprise ψ. We use $\mathcal{F}_\psi(\Xi) \subseteq \mathcal{F}_\psi$ to denote the inferences of a given type Ξ, for Ξ one of the following: $\to l$, $\to r$, Π*l* or Π*r*. Let σ be an instantiation for ψ.

DEFINITION 5.1 The following binary relations are defined on $\mathcal{F}_\psi$:

(i) $R <_\psi R'$ iff a side formula of R is the principal formula of R' [8];

(ii) $R \ll_\psi R'$ iff R occurs below R' in ψ;

(iii) $R \sqsubset_\sigma R'$ iff the indeterminate or eigenvariable introduced by R is a free variable of $\alpha\sigma$, where α is the indeterminate introduced by R'. □

EXAMPLE 5.2 Consider the derivations (D1) and (D2) of Figures 1 and 2.

(i) We have
$$\mathcal{F}_1 = \mathcal{F}_2 = \{\Pi l_1, \Pi l_2, \Pi r, \to r, \to l\}.$$

Notice that an inference in a derivation is determined by its form (Π*l*, *etc.*) and its principal formula occurrence in the derivation. We have numbered the Π*l* inferences in each derivation to distinguish them. The above identification is useful here since (D1) arises from a permutation of the inferences of (D2). It will always be clear which derivation we have in mind when we refer to Π*l*₁ *etc.*.

(ii) Next, we have

$$<_1 \; = \; <_2 \; = \; < \; = \; \{(\Pi l_1, \to l), (\to l, \Pi r), (\Pi r, \to r)\}.$$

---

[6]Such a strategy is complete, in that it allows a proof to be found for any provable sequent, and finds proofs whose extract-objects (*q.v.* Note 8) are long $\beta\eta$-normal forms, see [24].

[7]Recall that in the LF, left Πs are used to encode *both* the universal *and* existential quantifiers of encoded logics [11].

[8]More accurately: iff a side formula of R is a "descendent" of the principal formula of R; we distinguish the "occurrences" of a formula in a derivation [16].

This should be expected from the subformula property of the system **U** given that $\mathcal{F}_1 = \mathcal{F}_2$.

$$\ll_1 \;=\; \{(\Pi l_1, \to l),(\to l, \Pi r),(\Pi r, \to r),(\to r, \Pi l_2)\}^+$$
$$\ll_2 \;=\; \{(\Pi l_1, \Pi l_2),(\Pi l_2, \to l),(\to l, \Pi r),(\Pi r, \to r)\}^+,$$

where $+$ indicates transitive closure. These orderings are just the tree orderings on the derivations.

(iii) Finally, we have

$$\sqsubset_\theta \;=\; \{(\Pi r, \Pi l_2)\}.$$

□

$\ll_\psi$ decomposes into sixteen subrelations: $\ll_\psi^{\Xi,\Omega} \subseteq \mathcal{F}_\psi(\Xi) \times \mathcal{F}_\psi(\Omega)$ for Ξ, Ω amongst $\to l$, $\to r$, Πl and Πr. $\ll_\psi$ and its subrelations are called the *skeletal orderings* of the derivation ψ. Notice also that $<_\psi$ is a subrelation of $\ll_\psi$.

DEFINITION 5.3 (Reduction ordering) The *reduction ordering* induced by a **U**-derivation ψ and a instantiation σ is defined by:

$$\lhd_{\psi,\sigma} \;=_{\mathrm{def}}\; (<_\psi \cup \prec_\psi \cup \sqsubset_\sigma)^+,$$

where the relation $\prec_\psi$ is defined by:

$$\prec_\psi \;=_{\mathrm{def}}\; \ll_\psi \setminus \bigcup_{\Xi \in \mathcal{F}_\psi} (\ll_\psi^{\Pi l,\Xi} \cup \ll_\psi^{\Xi,\Pi l}).$$

□

EXAMPLE 5.4 We have that

$$\bigcup_{\Xi \in \mathcal{F}_1} \ll_1^{\Pi l,\Xi} \;=\; \{(\Pi l_1, \Pi l_2),(\Pi l_1, \; rightarrowl),(\Pi l_1, \Pi r),(\Pi l_1, \to r)\}$$

$$\bigcup_{\Xi \in \mathcal{F}_2} \ll_2^{\Xi,\Pi l} \;=\; \{(\Pi l_1, \Pi l_2)\}.$$

We leave it to the reader to verify that, as expected,

$$\bigcup_{\Xi \in \mathcal{F}_1} \left(\ll_1^{\Pi l,\Xi} \;\cup\; \ll_1^{\Xi,\Pi l} \right) \;=\; \bigcup_{\Xi \in \mathcal{F}_2} \left(\ll_2^{\Pi l,\Xi} \;\cup\; \ll_2^{\Xi,\Pi l} \right),$$

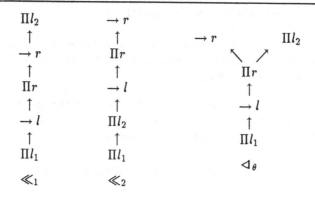

Figure 3: $\ll_i$ and $\lhd_\theta$ as DAGs for $\langle Di, \theta \rangle$, i=1,2.

$$\prec_1 = \prec_2 = \prec \;\; = \;\; \{(\to l, \Pi r),(\Pi r, \to r)\}^+$$

and

$$\lhd_{1,\theta} = \lhd_{2,\theta} = \lhd_\theta \;\; = \;\; (< \cup \prec \cup \sqsubset_\theta)^+$$
$$= \;\; \{(\Pi l_1, \to l),(\to l, \Pi r),(\Pi r, \to r),(\Pi r, \Pi l_2)\}^+.$$

Reduction and skeletal orderings can be pictured as DAGs as in Figure 3
$\square$

The presence of a relation in $\lhd_{\psi,\sigma}$ indicates that that relationship between specific inferences may not be altered by permutation. Consequently, the definition of $\prec_\psi$ fixes the relative positions of all rule applications in ψ *except* Πl rule applications (since they are removed from $\ll_\psi$ to form $\prec_\psi$).

DEFINITION 5.5 (i) (Compatibility) A derivation is said to be *compatible* with an instantiation just in case the reduction ordering induced is irreflexive.

(ii) (Degree) The *degree* of a compatible derivation is the number of pairs of inferences in the derivation whose skeletal order is inconsistent with the reduction ordering. That is, $\langle R, R' \rangle$ for which both $R \ll_\psi R'$ (R is below R' in ψ) and $R' \lhd_{\psi,\sigma} R$. If a derivation is compatible with an instantiation with degree n, we say it is *n-compatible*. $\square$

EXAMPLE 5.6 From the DAGs in Figure 3 it is easy to see that (D1) is 0-compatible and (D2) 2-compatible with $\lhd_\theta$. In the latter case the Πl_2 inference is below two inferences which precede it in $\lhd_\theta$. $\square$

THEOREM 5.7 (PERMUTATION THEOREM)

If ψ is compatible with σ, then there is a 0-compatible U-derivation ψ^* of the same endsequent. Moreover, if ψ is closed under σ, so is ψ^*. We say that ψ^* is a *permutation* of ψ.

PROOF. By induction on the degree of ψ. We interchange Πl inferences with other inferences to reduce the degree. One must check that the leaves of the permuted derivation contain the same declarations (though in a different order).

In order to simplify the presentation of the argument we distinguish two cases:

1. In which we consider the exchange of the Πl rule with the binary rule $\rightarrow l$;

2. In which we consider the exchange of the Πl rule with each of the unary rules $\rightarrow r$, Πr and Πl itself.

The first case divides into two subcases (we give the details of just one case). Suppose that R' is $\rightarrow l$ and R is Πl. Here we must assume tha t the Πl occurs on one of the branches of the proof, and then add an instance of Πl with the same indeterminate to the other branch immediately above the $\rightarrow l$. This addition introduces no new inconsistencies and preserves closure. If we did not introduce this copy of the inference, the reordering of these two rules would introduce many new inconsistencies, thereby destroying our inductive argument. Consequently, we may assume that, locally, the original derivation tree is of the form:

$$\frac{\dfrac{\Gamma, x:C(\alpha) \Rightarrow_\Sigma D}{\Gamma \Rightarrow_\Sigma D} \quad \dfrac{\Gamma, y:E, x:C(\alpha) \Rightarrow_\Sigma A}{\Gamma, y:E \Rightarrow_\Sigma A}}{\Gamma \Rightarrow_\Sigma A} \, ,$$

where there is some $@ : D \rightarrow E \in \Sigma \cup \Gamma$ and some $@' : \Pi z : B \cdot C(z) \in \Sigma \cup \Gamma$. (The substitution ordering, $\sqsubset_\sigma$, ensures that $@' \neq y$.) Locally, the reordered derivation is of the form:

$$\frac{\dfrac{\Gamma, x:C(\alpha) \Rightarrow_\Sigma D \quad \Gamma, x:C(\alpha), y:E \Rightarrow_\Sigma D}{\Gamma, x:C(\alpha) \Rightarrow_\Sigma A}}{\Gamma \Rightarrow_\Sigma A} \, .$$

We must show that if each branch of the original derivation leads to a closed leaf under σ, then each branch of the reordered derivation leads to a closed leaf under σ. It is immediate that this holds for the left hand branch of the derivation, since the reordering leaves the bottom, left hand sequent unchanged. As for the right hand branch, we note that the components of the context of the bottom, right hand sequent are altered only in order. Therefore the right hand branch of the reordered derivation is closed under σ. Since $\sqsubseteq_\sigma$ is a subrelation of $\lhd_{\psi,\sigma}$ and because $\lhd_{\psi,\sigma}$ is irreflexive, y is not a subterm of $C(\alpha)$. Therefore the reordering of the context is consistent with the reordered derivation and the degree of the reordered derivation is one less than that of the original derivation.

The exchange of Πl with the unary operators divides into five subcases (we give the details of the proof in just one case). Suppose that R' is Πl and R is Πl. Locally, the original derivation is of the form:

$$\frac{\dfrac{\Gamma, x:C(\alpha), y:D(\beta) \Rightarrow_\Sigma A}{\Gamma, x:C(\alpha) \Rightarrow_\Sigma A}}{\Gamma \Rightarrow_\Sigma A},$$

for suitable instances of Πl. Locally, the reordered derivation, which has degree one less than that of the original derivation, is of the form:

$$\frac{\dfrac{\Gamma, y:D(\beta), x:C(\alpha) \Rightarrow_\Sigma A}{\Gamma, y:D(\beta) \Rightarrow_\Sigma A}}{\Gamma \Rightarrow_\Sigma A}.$$

Once again we note that the components of the bottom sequent have altered only in order, so that if the original derivation is closed under σ, then so is the reordered derivation. Since $\sqsubseteq_\sigma$ is a subrelation of $\lhd_{\psi,\sigma}$ and because $\lhd_{\psi,\sigma}$ is irreflexive, x is not a subterm of $D(\beta)$. Therefore the reordering of the context is consistent with the reordered derivation and the degree of the reordered derivation is one less than that of the original derivation.

This completes the proof. $\square$

We have as a corollary to the construction performed in the proof of the Permutation Theorem:

COROLLARY 5.8 $\lhd_{\psi^*,\sigma} = \lhd_{\psi,\sigma}$.

PROOF. The only relationships changed in the permutation are those excluded from $\lhd_{\psi,\sigma}$. $\square$

We have already verified this for our example derivations.

The following lemma shows that the 0-compatibility of a derivation and instantiation is a necessary condition for the well-typing of the latter in the former.

LEMMA 5.9 *If* σ *is well-typed in* ψ, ψ *is 0-compatible with* σ.

PROOF. An inconsistency between the skeletal ordering of ψ and the reduction ordering arises from an inconsistency between $\sqsubset_\sigma$ and the skeletal ordering. Since $\sqsubset_\sigma \subseteq \mathcal{F}_\psi(\Xi) \times \mathcal{F}_\psi(\Pi l)$, it must arise from a Πl inference, introducing α say, being nearer the root of the derivation than a Πl or Πr inference that gives rise to a variable, v say, free in $\alpha\sigma$. But then v cannot be declared in the typing context of α since it is introduced above α, and therefore σ is not well-typed, contradicting our hypothesis. Therefore there can be no inconsistencies and ψ is 0-compatible with σ. $\square$

6   Incremental search

From a computational point of view testing for compatibility is a simple matter given a derivation and an instantiation: it is an acyclicity check in a directed graph. Compatibility is not, however, a *sufficient* test for well-typing. The Permutation Theorem gives us the existence of 0-compatible derivations in which we might test for well-typing of the instantiation incrementally (*i.e.*, as it is found) but this involves repeatedly constructing permutations using the constructive proof of the theorem. This is inelegant and computationally expensive.

Another alternative would be to ignore well-typing until a closed, compatible derivation and instantiation have been found, and then use the Permutation Theorem once and check well-typing. We reject this option on the grounds that typing constraints reduce the search space of the unification algorithm drastically.

We develop instead a computationally tractable test on a derivation and instantiation that, if passed, guarantees the well-typing of the instantiation in all 0-compatible permutations of the derivation. Our ability to define such a notion is a corollary of the strong normalization result for $\lambda\Pi$-calculus [11] with its attendant subformula property, just as the results obtained in [4] and [29] for other logics rely on metatheorems of this sort.

Henceforth we treat contexts as ordered structures or DAGs rather than sequences since the dependencies between declarations form such an order. Consequently the implicit union, denoted above by a comma, such as in "$\Gamma, x{:}A$", should be understood as an order preserving union of the order (DAG) Γ and the singleton order $x{:}A$. The latter will be higher in the resulting order than the declarations of the free variables in A, and incomparable with the other maximal elements of Γ. This assumption simplifies our discussion.

The following notions are introduced for a U-derivation ψ of a well-formed endsequent. Let $V(\psi) = \text{Ind}(\psi) \cup \text{Eig}(\psi)$. We use u, v, w possibly subscripted to denote elements of $V(\psi)$ and refer to them simply as "variables". Let $T(v)$ denote the typing expression for the variable v in ψ.

DEFINITION 6.1 (Intrinsic typing context) The *intrinsic typing context*, $I(v)$, for each variable $v \in V(\psi)$, is defined inductively on the structure of the endsequent as follows:

$$I(v) \quad =_{\text{def}} \quad \biguplus_{w \in \text{FV}(T(v))} (I(w), w{:}T(w)),$$

where $\biguplus$ denotes order-preserving union of orders. □

$I(v)$ is well-defined since the endsequent is well-formed. Indeed, we have:

LEMMA 6.2 $I(v) \vdash_\Sigma T(v)$: Type.

PROOF. By construction and the well-formedness of the endsequent. □

EXAMPLE 6.3 For our example derivations of Figures 1 and 2 we have $V(D1) = V(D2) = \{\alpha, y, \beta\}$. Moreover, since both derivations have the same endsequent we have for both:

$$
\begin{aligned}
T(\alpha) &= A, & \text{FV}(T(\alpha)) &= \emptyset, & I(\alpha) &= \emptyset; \\
T(\beta) &= B(a), & \text{FV}(T(y)) &= \{\alpha\}, & I(y) &= \alpha{:}A; \\
T(\beta) &= A, & \text{FV}(T(\beta)) &= \emptyset, & I(\beta) &= \emptyset.
\end{aligned}
$$

Consequently,

$$
\begin{aligned}
I(\alpha) \vdash_\Sigma T(\alpha)\text{: Type} &= \vdash_\Sigma A\text{: Type}; \\
I(y) \vdash_\Sigma T(y)\text{: Type} &= \alpha{:}A \vdash_\Sigma B(\alpha)\text{: Type}; \\
I(\beta) \vdash_\Sigma T(\beta)\text{: Type} &= \vdash_\Sigma B(a)\text{: Type}.
\end{aligned}
$$

□

Let ψ be compatible with the ground instantiation σ. We give an inductive definition of the intrinsic typing context, $I_\sigma(v)$, and type, $T_\sigma(v)$, of a variable v of ψ under a compatible instantiation σ. The induction is on the (well-founded) reduction ordering $(\lhd_{\psi,\sigma})$ over the domain of σ.

DEFINITION 6.4 $(I_\sigma(v)$ and $T_\sigma(v))$ Base. For all $v \in V(\psi)$, define $I_\epsilon(v) = I(v)$ and $T_\epsilon(v) = T(v)$. (ϵ is the empty instantiation.)

Step. Given $v \in V(\psi)$, we assume that we have defined $I_\sigma(w)$ and $T_\sigma(w)$ for all $w \in V(\psi)$ such that $w \lhd_{\psi,\sigma} v$ (Inductive Hypothesis). Define

$$
D_0(v) = \begin{cases}
I_\epsilon(v) \vdash_\Sigma T_\epsilon(v)\text{:Type}, & v \in \text{Eig}(\psi); \\
I_\epsilon(v), \biguplus_{w \in \text{FV}(v\sigma)}(I_\sigma(w), w{:}T_\sigma(w)) \vdash_\Sigma T_\epsilon(v)\text{:Type}, & v \subset n\text{Ind}(\psi).
\end{cases}
$$

Now, let $\alpha_1, \alpha_2, \ldots, \alpha_n$ be an enumeration of those indeterminates declared in the context of $D_0(v)$ such that if $\alpha_i \lhd_{\psi,\sigma} \alpha_j$ then $i < j$. By definition of $\lhd_{\psi,\sigma}$ and $I(v)$, we have $\alpha_i \lhd_{\psi,\sigma} v$ for $1 \leq i < n + 1$. Define

$$D_{k+1}(v) \;=\; \text{CUT}\,(I_\sigma(\alpha_k) \vdash_\Sigma \alpha_k \sigma{:}T_\sigma(pha_k) \;\;,\;\; D_k(v)), \qquad 0 \leq k < n.$$

If $D_n(v)$ is the assertion: $\Delta \vdash_\Sigma C{:}\text{Type}$, then define

$$I_\sigma(v) \;=_{\text{def}}\; \Delta$$
$$T_\sigma(v) \;=_{\text{def}}\; C. \qquad \square$$

The "CUT" operation in the above definition is the admissible rule of transitivity (see Theorem 2.1). That is, $D_{k+1}(v)$ is defined in terms of $D_k(v)$ by the following inference figure:

$$\frac{I_\sigma(\alpha_k) \vdash_\Sigma \alpha_k \sigma{:}T_\sigma(\alpha_k) \qquad D_k(v)}{D_{k+1}(v)} \; \text{CUT}.$$

The cut rule is being used to effect substitution of the values (under σ) of indeterminates throughout the judgement starting from the "uninstantiated" intrinsic typing context and type. The definition is well-formed since the context of the left premiss of each cut is a subcontext of the right premiss. (This follows from the construction of $I(v)$.) The cut above then serves to eliminate the declaration $\alpha_k{:}T_\sigma(\alpha_k)$ from the context of $D_k(v)$, replacing α_k by $\alpha_k \sigma$ throughout the rest of the assertion.

The enumeration taken is irrelevant since independent cuts commute. Consider

$$\frac{I_\sigma(u_2) \vdash_\Sigma u_2\sigma{:}T_\sigma(u_2) \qquad \dfrac{I_\sigma(u_1) \vdash_\Sigma u_1\sigma{:}T_\sigma(u_1) \qquad D_k(v)}{D_{k+1}(v)}}{D_{k+2}(v)}$$

and

$$\frac{I_\sigma(u_1) \vdash_\Sigma u_1\sigma{:}T_\sigma(u_1) \qquad \dfrac{I_\sigma(u_2) \vdash_\Sigma u_2\sigma{:}T_\sigma(u_2) \qquad D'_k(v)}{D'_{k+1}(v)}}{D'_{k+2}(v)}.$$

In the first derivation $\alpha_k = u_1$ and $\alpha_{k+1} = u_2$. In the second, $\alpha_k = u_2$ and $\alpha_{k+1} = u_1$. If u_1 and u_2 are assumed independent (*i.e.*, unrelated via $\lhd_{\psi,\sigma}$), we have $u_i \notin \text{Dom}(I_\sigma(u_j))$, $i \neq j$. Hence substitution of the value $u_1\sigma$ for u_1 does not interfere with substitution of the value $u_2\sigma$ for u_2, and $D_{k+2} = D'_{k+2}$.

EXAMPLE 6.5 Recall, from our examples, that $\theta = \{\alpha \mapsto a, \beta \mapsto y\}$ and that $\alpha \lhd_\theta y \lhd_\theta \beta$. $FV(\alpha\theta) = \emptyset$, so

$$D_0(\alpha) = I_\epsilon(\alpha) \vdash_\Sigma T_\epsilon(\alpha): \text{Type} = \vdash_\Sigma A: \text{Type}.$$

Thus, $I_\theta(\alpha) = \emptyset$ and $T_\theta(\alpha) = A$. For y we have

$$D_0(y) = I_\epsilon(y) \vdash_\Sigma T_\epsilon(y): \text{Type} = \alpha{:}A \vdash_\Sigma B(\alpha): \text{Type}.$$

$D_1(y)$ is defined by the inference figure:

$$\frac{I_\theta(\alpha) \vdash_\Sigma \alpha\theta{:}T_\theta(\alpha) \quad D_0(y)}{D_1(y)} = \frac{\vdash_\Sigma a{:}A \quad \alpha{:}A \vdash_\Sigma B(\alpha): \text{Type}}{\vdash_\Sigma B(a): \text{Type}}.$$

Consequently, $I_\theta(y) = \emptyset$ and $T_\theta(y) = B(a)$. $FV(\beta\theta) = \{y\}$, so

$$\begin{aligned} D_0(\beta) &= I_\epsilon(\beta) \vdash_\Sigma T_\epsilon(\beta): \text{Type} \\ &= I_\theta(y), y{:}T_\theta(y) \vdash_\Sigma B(a): \text{Type} \\ &= y{:}B(a) \vdash_\Sigma B(a): \text{Type}. \end{aligned}$$

Consequently, $I_\theta(\beta) = y{:}B(a)$ and $T_\theta(\beta) = B(a)$. $\quad\square$

We can now state the desired well-typing condition for σ in ψ.

DEFINITION 6.6 (Intrinsic well-typing) σ is said to be *intrinsically well-typed* in ψ just in case for all indeterminates α of ψ, we have:
$$I_\sigma(\alpha) \vdash_\Sigma \alpha\sigma{:}T_\sigma(\alpha). \quad\square$$

The importance of the definition is summarized by:

PROPOSITION 6.7 *If σ is intrinsically well-typed in ψ, then it is intrinsically well-typed in all compatible permutations of ψ. In particular it is well-typed in 0-compatible permutations.*

PROOF. Reference to the definition will show that the intrinsic well-typing of σ in ψ does not depend on the Πl structure of ψ. (In fact we deliberately forbade such dependence by our definition of $\lhd_{\psi,\sigma}$.) Hence the conditions are unaffected by permutations allowed by the reduction ordering $\lhd_{\psi,\sigma}$, which is itself unaltered by permutation (Corollary 5.8). For a 0-compatible permutation ψ^* of ψ, the intrinsic typing context for a variable is a subcontext of the typing context in $\psi^*\sigma$. Since "Thinning" is admissible (Theorem 2.1), σ is well-typed in ψ^*. $\quad\square$

In a similar vein, we state without proof the following:

PROPOSITION 6.8 *If σ is well-typed in a 0-compatible derivation ψ, it is intrinsically well-typed in ψ.*   □

EXAMPLE 6.9 Following through with our example we note that

$$I_\theta(\alpha) \vdash_\Sigma \alpha\theta{:}T_\theta(\alpha) \;=\; \vdash_\Sigma a{:}A$$
$$I_\theta(\beta) \vdash_\Sigma \beta\theta{:}T_\theta(\beta) \;=\; y{:}B(a) \vdash_\Sigma y{:}B(a).$$

Hence θ is intrinsically well-typed in (D1) and, most importantly, also in (D2).   □

We can now (re)define a computationally acceptable notion of U-proof that takes advantage of the Permutation Theorem.

DEFINITION 6.10 (U-proof) A **U-***proof* is a pair $\langle \psi, \sigma \rangle$, where ψ is a U-derivation and σ an instantiation with domain $\mathrm{Ind}(\psi)$, such that (1) ψ is closed under σ; (2) ψ is compatible with σ, and (3) σ is intrinsically well-typed in ψ.   □

This definition should be compared with Definition 4.7.

THEOREM 6.11 *For well-formed sequents* $\Gamma \Rightarrow_\Sigma A$,

$$\textbf{U} \text{ proves } \Gamma \Rightarrow_\Sigma A \qquad \textit{iff} \qquad \textbf{L} \text{ proves } \Gamma \Rightarrow_\Sigma A.$$

PROOF. (Only if.) Suppose $\langle \psi, \sigma \rangle$ is a U-proof of $\Gamma \Rightarrow_\Sigma A$. The Permutability Theorem gives us a permutation ψ^* of ψ, closed under (hypothesis 1), and compatible with (hypothesis 2), the instantiation σ. Hypothesis (3), via Proposition 6.7, ensures that σ is well-typed in ψ^*. Hence $\psi^*\sigma$ is an L-proof.

(If.) Let $\langle \psi, \sigma \rangle$ be such that $\psi\sigma$ is an L-proof of $\Gamma \Rightarrow_\Sigma A$. By definition ψ is closed under σ and σ is well-typed in ψ. Compatibility follows from Lemma 5.9, and intrinsic well-typing from Proposition 6.8.   □

7 Conclusions

Instantiations can be generated by a unification algorithm acting on putative axiom sequents. They can first be checked for compatibility (occurs-check) and then for intrinsic well-typing. The incremental nature of intrinsic typing means that the typing information can be used to constrain the unification algorithm. Newly calculated values for previously uninstantiated indeterminates may be used to eliminate those indeterminates from the typing contexts of the remaining ones. No permutations need be calculated. Note however that if we permit unification to calculate non-ground instantiations then we must modify the constructions of Section 6 to permit the inclusion of further proof-search.

We have been somewhat cautious in this development and allowed only Π*l* rules to migrate. As a consequence the basic structure of a derivation is largely fixed. The next step is to remove the ordering constraints induced by the propositional structure of the logic, perhaps using unification here as was done in [29] for first-order intuitionistic logic. The final result would be a *matrix method* in the style of Bibel [4] or Andrews [1].

Closure instantiations are calculated by unification. In general, the instantiations calculated by the unification algorithm introduce new variables (*i.e.*, variables that are not present in the original context) to the derivation[9]. However, we require only those substitutions which are well-typed instantiations (under some reordering), and so for a a given U-derivation ψ we accept (for further analysis) just those substitutions σ which do not introduce new variables. The unification algorithm of [24] is *sound* and *complete* for the calculation of such instantiations, subject to further proof-search.

We have considered ground endsequents and ground instantiations explicitly. The extension of U to non-ground endsequents is straightforward but involved. A non-ground sequent together with a *typing constraint* T for its indeterminates is considered to stand for the set of its well-formed ground instances. (The typing constraint consists of intrinsic typing contexts and types for each indeterminate occuring in the endsequent, ensuring that the mutual dependencies do not render any extension of the initial reduction ordering cyclic.) This determines a set $S(T)$ of ground *answer instantiations*. Any non-ground instantiation calculated from a U-proof $\langle \psi, \sigma \rangle$ of the sequent determines a set of ground well-typed *extensions* $S_\psi(T)$.

We consider non-ground endsequents because they have an interesting logic programming interpretation. A sequent $\Gamma \Rightarrow_\Sigma A$ may be interpreted as a *logic program* in the following sense: Σ determines a language, Γ a list of *program clauses* and A a *query* written in the language Σ. Indeterminates correspond to *program variables* or *logic variables*; these correspond to the logical variables of the programming language Prolog [5]. The whole sequent represents a request to compute an instantiation σ for the indeterminates of the sequent such that σ renders the sequent $\Gamma\sigma \Rightarrow_\Sigma A\sigma$ L-provable. We are exploiting the fact that the underlying lambda calculus of the λΠ-calculus encodes a computation of type A; *i.e.*, a term M for which $\Gamma \vdash_\Sigma M{:}A$ is provable. A full discussion of this notion of logic programming, including both operational (as presented here) and model-

---

[9]Indeed, this is true of the basic algorithm for the simply-typed λ-calculus of [14]

theoretic semantics, may be found in [24] and in a forthcoming paper by the authors, where we also discuss the application of our techniques to a form of *resolution rule* which generalizes Paulson's higher-order resolution [21] to the $\lambda\Pi$-calculus. A notion of logic programming for the LF which is similar to the λProlog language of Miller and Nadathur [20] has been implemented in the Elf system by Pfenning [22].

Acknowledgements. The authors are grateful to Alan Bundy, Robert Harper, Furio Honsell, Gérard Huet, Gordon Plotkin, Randy Pollack, Anne Salvesen and the referees for helpful suggestions and comments.

References

[1]   Andrews, P.B. Theorem-proving via general matings. *J. Assoc. Comp. Mach.* **28**(2) pp. 193–214, 1981.

[2]   Avron, A., Honsell, F., Mason, I. Using Typed Lambda Calculus to Implement Formal Systems on a Machine. University of Edinburgh report ECS-LFCS-87-31, 1987.

[3]   Barendregt, H. Introduction to Generalized Type Systems. *Proc. 3rd Italian Conference on Theoretical Computer Science.* World Scientific Publishing Co., Singapore, 1989.

[4]   Bibel, W. Computationally Improved Versions of Herbrand's Theorem. In J. Stern, editor, Proc. of the Herbrand Symposium, *Logic Colloquium '81*, pp. 11-28, North-Holland, 1982.

[5]   Clocksin, W.F., Mellish, C.S. Programming in Prolog, Springer-Verlag, 1984.

[6]   Curry, H.B. The permutability of rules in the classical inferential calculus. *J. Symbolic Logic* **17**, pp. 245– 248 , 1952.

[7]   van Daalen, D.T., The language theory of AUTOMATH. Ph.Dthesis, Technical University of Eindhoven, The Netherlands, 1980.

[8]   Elliott, C. Higher-order Unification with Dependent Function Types. *Proc. 3rd International Conference on Rewriting Techniques and Applications*, Chapel Hill NC, 1989. Springer-Verlag Lecture Notes in Computer Science 355, N. Dershowitz Ed., pp. 121–136.

[9]   Elliott, C. Extensions and Applications of Higher-order Unification. Ph.D thesis, Carnegie-Mellon University, 1990. Available as report CMU-CS-90-134.

[10] Gentzen, G. Untersuchungen über das logische Schliessen, *Mathematische Zeitschrift* **39** (1934) pp. 176–210, 405- 431.

[11] Harper, R., Honsell, F., Plotkin, G. A Framework for Defining Logics. *Proc. Second Annual Symposium on Logic in Computer Science,* pp. 194–204. IEEE, 1987.

[12] Harper, R., Honsell, F., Plotkin, G. A Framework for Defining Logics. To appear in *J. Assoc. Comp. Mach..*

[13] Howard, W.A. The formulae-as-types notion of construction. In: To H.B. Curry: Essays on Combinatory Logic, Lambda Calculus and Formalism (editors J.P. Seldin & J.R. Hindley). Academic Press, 1980.

[14] Huet, G. A Unification Algorithm for Typed λ-calculus. *Theor. Comp. Sci.* **1**(1975) pp. 27–57.

[15] Kleene, S.C. Permutability of inferences in Gentzen's calculi *LK* and *LJ. Memoirs of the American Mathematical Society* **10**, pp. 1– 26, 1952.

[16] Kleene, S.C. Mathematical logic. Wiley and Sons, 1968.

[17] Martin-Löf, P. On the meanings of the logical constants and the justifications of the logical laws. Technical Report 2, Scuola di Specializziazione in Logica Matematica, Dipartimento di Matematica, Università di Siena, 1985.

[18] Meyer, A., Reinhold, M. 'Type' is not a type: preliminary report. *Proc. 13th ACM Symposium on the Principles of Programming Languages,* 1986.

[19] Miller, D. Proofs in higher-order logic. Ph.D thesis, Carnegie-Mellon University, Pittsburgh, USA, 1983. Available as report MS-CIS-83-37, University of Pennsylvania, 1983.

[20] Miller, D., Nadathur, G. Higher-order Logic Programming. Report MS-CIS-86-17, University of Pennsylvania, 1986.

[21] Paulson, L. Natural Deduction Proof as Higher-order Resolution. *J. Logic Programming* **3**, pp. 237–258, 1986.

[22] Pfenning, F. Elf: a language for logic definition and verifed metaprogramming. *Proc. Fourth Annual Symposium on Logic in Computer Science,* pp. 98-105. IEEE, 1989.

[23] Prawitz, D. Natural Deduction: A Proof-theoretical Study. Almqvist & Wiksell, Stockholm, 1965.

[24]   Pym, D.J. Proofs, Search and Computation in General Logic. Ph.D thesis. University of Edinburgh, 1990. Available as report CST-69-90, Department of Computer Science, University of Edinburgh, 1990. (Also published as LFCS report ECS-LFCS-90-125.)

[25]   Pym, D.J., Wallen, L.A. Investigations into Proof-search in a System of First-order Dependent Function Types. *Proc. 10th International Conference on Automated Deduction.* Kaiserslautern, FRG, July 1990. Lecture Notes in Artificial Intelligence 449, pp. 236–250, Springer-Verlag, 1990.

[26]   Robinson, J. A machine-oriented logic based on the resolution principle. *J. Assoc. Comp. Mach.* **12**, pp. 23–41, 1965.

[27]   Salvesen, A. Personal Communication. University of Edinburgh, 1990.

[28]   Smullyan, R.M. First-order logic. *Ergebnisse der Mathematik*, Volume **43**, Springer Verlag, 1968.

[29]   Wallen, L.A. Automated deduction in non-classical logics. MIT Press, 1989.

Finding Computational Content in Classical Proofs

Robert Constable and Chet Murthy
Cornell University

1 Summary

We illustrate the effectiveness of proof transformations which expose the computational content of classical proofs even in cases where it is not apparent. We state without proof a theorem that these transformations apply to proofs in a fragment of type theory and discuss their implementation in Nuprl. We end with a discussion of the applications to Higman's lemma [13, 21, 10] by the second author using the implemented system.

2 Introduction: Computational content

Informal practice

Sometimes we express computational ideas *directly* as when we say $2 + 2$ reduces to 4 or when we specify an algorithm for solving a problem: "use Euclid's GCD (greatest common divisor) algorithm to reduce this fraction." At other times we refer only indirectly to a method of computation, as in the following form of Euclid's proof that there are infinitely many primes:

For every natural number n there is a prime p greater than n. To prove this, notice first that every number m has a least prime factor; to find it, just try dividing it by $2, 3, \cdots, m$ and take the first divisor. In particular $n! + 1$ has a least prime factor. Call it p. Clearly p cannot be any number between 2 and n since none of those divide $n! + 1$ evenly. Therefore $p > n$. **QED**

This proof implicitly provides an algorithm to find a prime greater than n. Namely, divide $n! + 1$ by all numbers from 2 to $n! + 1$ and return the first divisor. The proof guarantees that this divisor will be greater than n and prime. We can "see" this algorithm in the proof, and thus we say that the proof has *computational content*.

In day-to-day mathematics people use a variety of schemes to keep track of computational content. There is no single or systematic way. People use phrases like "reduce b to b'" or "apply algorithm f." They also tend to use phrases like "this proof is constructive" or "the proof shows us how to compute." It is also sensible to say "we treat all of the concepts constructively." To understand the last phrasing notice that it is not possible to tell from the usual statement of a theorem alone whether its proofs must be constructive (or whether any proof is). To see this consider the statement:

There are two irrational numbers, a and b such that a^b is rational.

Classical Proof: Consider $\sqrt{2}^{\sqrt{2}}$; it is either rational or not. If it is, then take $a = \sqrt{2}$ and $b = \sqrt{2}$. Otherwise, take $a = \sqrt{2}^{\sqrt{2}}$ and $b = \sqrt{2}$, then $a^b = \left(\sqrt{2}^{\sqrt{2}}\right)^{\sqrt{2}} = \sqrt{2}^2 = 2$.

This proof does not allow us to compute the first 10 digits of a since there is no way, *given in the proof*, to tell whether $a = \sqrt{2}$ or $a = \sqrt{2}^{\sqrt{2}}$. The statement of the theorem does not tell whether a constructive proof is required, in contrast to the following form, which does:

We can exhibit two algorithms A and B for computing irrational numbers, a and b respectively, such that a^b is rational. Here is a proof which suffices for both theorems. Take $a = \sqrt{2}$ and $b = 2 \cdot \log_2(3)$. Notice that there are algorithms A and B to compute these numbers. We leave it as an exercise to show that both these numbers follow from the existence of unique prime factorizations.

Often when we say "there exists an object b having property P" we really mean that we can explicitly exhibit an algorithm for computing b. This use of language is so common that to convey computational ideas we can just say that "there exists" is meant constructively. Another example of how language is used to convey computational intention is this.

Let us show: At least one of $(e + \pi)$ or $(e * \pi)$ is transcendental. Suppose not, then both are algebraic. So the coefficients of

$(x-\pi)(x-e) = x^2 - (e+\pi)*x + (e*\pi)$ are algebraic. But then according to the theorem that the field of all algebraic numbers is algebraically complete, all the roots are algebraic. But this contradicts the fact that e and π are both transcendental.

The use of "or" in this case does not tell us that we can decide which disjunct is true. But when we say every number n is even or odd, we notice that we can decide which. It is also common to say "for all x, $P(x)$ or $Q(x)$," when we mean that we can decide for any x whether it is $P(x)$ or $Q(x)$ that is true. Again, sometimes a proof will tell us that, as in the case of the proof:

> For all natural numbers n, n is prime or n is composite. We can prove this by testing whether n is prime.

This proof shows us how to decide the *or*. So another way to convey computational content is to indicate that *or* is to be interpreted in a constructive sense.

Systematic accounting

There have been various attempts to keep track of computational ideas systematically. The constructive or intuitionistic use of language is one of the oldest and most throughly studied. Another way is to explicitly use algorithms to define functions and limit assertions to equalities between them, as in Skolem's account of arithmetic [27]. There are formal languages in which programs are explicitly used to express algorithms. Another way is to introduce a double set of concepts, say function and computable function, classical and constructive logical operators, and so forth. This leads to a highly redundant language, so there have been efforts to reduce the duplication, which have resulted in certain epistemic logics [25, 17].

The approach of using an Intuitionistic or constructive core language has been extensively studied by philosophers, logicians, mathematicians and computer scientists for most of this century. Many deep and beautiful results about this method are now known, and they are being applied extensively in computer science (already since the late 60's). The applications are to the design of programming languages [24, 2], to programming methodology [19, 4], to program verification and formal methods [5, 4], and to automated reasoning [23]. This paper discusses further applications, in particular to foundational issues about the nature of computation and to problems in the semantics of functional programming languages. We believe that this "constructive language" approach to accounting for computational content has so far been the most direct approach, although for historical reasons going back to the highly emotional debates between Brouwer and Hilbert, the approach seems a bit "controversial." Moreover, there are strong connections to issues in the philosophy of mathematics which are still unresolved and some people are loath to appear to be taking a stand on issues about which they have little concern or knowledge. It is fair to say that many scientists have used these concepts and results without regard for the philosophical issues. This paper takes no philosophical stand. We try to continue the tradition of using the techniques of constructive logic to shed light on fundamental *scientific issues*.

Constructive language

A natural starting place to understand the systematic use of constructive language is with the notion of *existence*. As far back as the ancient Greeks the notion of existence in mathematics was identified with the concept of a construction (by ruler or compass). The constructive interpretation of the quantifier $\exists x \in T.P$, meaning that there is an object of type T such that property P holds of it, is that we can construct the object in T, call it t, and know that P is true when x refers to t. I.e., P with some description of t substituted for x is true. The computational interpretation here is clear, if we think of a description of t as an algorithm for building the object. Under this interpretation, a key step in understanding constructive language is knowing how to describe the objects in a type. Before we can be specific about existential statements, we must make some commitments about what ways we allow for describing objects. Looking to simple examples like the natural numbers for guidance, we see that there are irreducible descriptions, such as 0, and compound ones, such as $0 + 0$. Following Martin-Löf [19], we adopt the notion that our language of descriptions will be based on the idea that some are *canonical*, such as 0, and some are not, such as $0 + 0$. The key principle about noncanonical descriptions is that they can be *computed* to canonical ones. This is a precise version of the notion that a description tells us how to build the object because the canonical name is a direct description of the object.

Once we have settled on a computational interpretation of existence, we then want to make sure that the other quantifiers and logical operations preserve it. This forces us to interpret "P or Q" as meaning that we know which of P or Q is true, since we can build a noncanonical description of an object a based on a case analysis. e.g., in (1.2) below, the computation of a forces (1.1) to be computational also:

$$\sqrt{2}^{\sqrt{2}} \text{ is rational or not } \sqrt{2}^{\sqrt{2}} \text{ is rational,} \tag{1.1}$$

$$\text{if } \sqrt{2}^{\sqrt{2}} \text{ is rational take } a = \sqrt{2} \text{ else take } a = \sqrt{2}^{\sqrt{2}}. \tag{1.2}$$

Another important feature we would like in our computational understanding of language is that when we assert

for all x of type S there is a y of type T such that P

(symbolized as $\forall x \in S.\exists y \in T.P$), we mean that there is an algorithm to compute a function from S to T which produces the witness object in T given any object s of S. This suggests that we interpret the universal quantifier $\forall x \in S.P$ as asserting that there is an algorithm taking any object of type S and producing a proof of P.

The simplest statements are built out of terms (the statements themselves can be construed as terms). There is no computational content to a meaningful irreducible, such as 0 or a. But for compound terms, such as $2 + 2$ or $3 + 1$, we might say that the computational content is the set of all computations or reductions of the term. So the exact meaning depends on how the term is built (e.g., how $+$ is defined.)

The atomic statements we consider have the form $P(a_1; \cdots; a_n)$, for a_i terms, and P an operator. Associated with each atomic statement is a computation or set of computations. We take these to be the computational content. For example, the computation associated with the statement $4 = 2 + 2$ is a justification from the axioms of $+$. Compound statements are formed from $\forall, \exists, \lor, \land, \Rightarrow$ with their computations being naturally defined in terms of the computations of the relevant subsidiary statements. Thus, the computations of $a = b \Rightarrow b = a$ are the computations which transform computations of $a = b$ into computations of $b = a$. The computations of $\exists x \in T.P$ are those which compute a t in T and a computation of P where t has been substituted for x.

Seeing computational content

One advantage of constructive language is that it allows us to see computational content directly; we can read it off from a proof of a theorem stated constructively. In fact, constructive proofs are so transparent that we can just see the content and extract it automatically. As an example, consider the theorem

Theorem 0.1 *root:* $\forall n \in \mathbb{N}.\exists r \in \mathbb{N}.r^2 \leq n \leq (r + 1)^2$

Proof: Let n be given in $\mathbb{N}$, by *induction* on n show $\exists r.\ r^2 \leq m \& n < (r+1)^2$.

Base: Choose $r = 0$, use simple arithmetic.

Ind: Assume h : $\exists r.\ r^2 \leq n \& n < (r+1)^2$ using hyp h, choose r_0
$\quad d : (r_0 + 1)^2 \leq (n+1) \vee (n+1) \leq (r_0 + 1)^2$ by arithmetic.
$\quad$ Show $\exists r.\ r^2 \leq (n+1) \& (n+1) < (r_0+1)^2$ by *or elimination* on d
$\quad$ If $(r_0 + 1)^2 \leq (n+1)$ then $r = (r_0 + 1)$, use arithmetic
$\quad$ If $(n+1) < (r_0 + 1)^2$ then $r = r_0$, use arithmetic
$\quad$ **QED**

∎

The computational content of this proof in the Nuprl language [3] is given by the function:

$\lambda n.\ ind(n; < 0, arith >;$
$\qquad u.\lambda h.\ spread(h :\ r_0, isroot.$
$\qquad\qquad seq(arith : disjunct.$
$\qquad\qquad\quad decide(disjunct;$
$\qquad\qquad\qquad lesseq.(r_0 + 1, arith);$
$\qquad\qquad\qquad qtr\ .(r_0, arith))))$

This can be extracted automatically from the proof. It is an algorithm which computes an integer square root and a proof that the number computed is a root.

We can see computational content in classical proofs as well. Consider the following nonconstructive proof that a root exists (nonconstructive because it proceeds by contradiction).

Theorem 0.2 $\forall n \in \mathbb{N}.\exists r \in \mathbb{N}.r^2 \leq n \& n < (r+1)^2$

Proof: ("Classical"):
Given any $n \in \mathbb{N}$,
Assume $\forall r \in \mathbb{N}.r^2 > n \vee (r+1)^2 \leq n$

Let $\quad G = \{r : \mathbb{N} | r^2 > n\}$
$\qquad S = \{r : \mathbb{N} | (r+1)^2 \leq n\}$

Note $\quad$ 1. $S \cap G = $ void
$\qquad\quad$ 2. S's elements are smaller than G's

Let $\quad r_0 > n$ be the least element of G
$\ *\quad r_0^2 > n$ by definition of G

** $r_0 - 1 \in S$ since r_0 is least

$(r_0 - 1 + 1)^2 \leq n$ by def of S

$r_0^2 \leq n$

∎

Intuitively, we would expect that the small modifications we made to the first proof to arrive at the second could not destroy the obvious computation inherent in the former. Moreover, we can "see" that the second proof ought to yield an algorithm, and if we are careful, we can see that the algorithm is really the same as that found in the first proof. So we would wonder if there is a way in which we can extract computational content from classical proofs such as the latter, and from more opaque classical proofs. The answer is "yes," and indeed much more can be done. First, there are various (more or less) tortuous methods [11, 15, 26], e.g. Gödel's Dialectica interpretation, which suffice. But in 1978 H. Friedman [9] drastically simplified the method. We will examine these techniques in the next section.

3 Extracting computations by translation : the A-translation

The A-translation is a short name for the method that H. Friedman [9] used to simplify and extend G. Kreisel's theorem that any classical proof of $\exists x \in \mathsf{N}.P$, where P is decidable, can be transformed into a constructive proof of the same statement. This result is itself effective, and an implementation of it would enable us to extract content from certain classical proofs, such as Theorem 0.2, by transforming them in this way and then extracting content from the resulting constructive proof. The usual presentation of this method involves two steps, first translating the classical language into a constructive one, then massaging the transation so as to bring out the content. The first step is due to Gödel.

Gödel translations

In 1932 Gödel showed how to interpret classical language into constructive. The key ideas are to notice that one way to understand the classical meaning of *or* is to say that P *or* Q means that we cannot imagine any other possibility; that is we cannot say that both $\neg(P)$ and $\neg(Q)$. So P *or* Q could be read as $\neg(\neg(P) \wedge \neg(Q))$. The key to understanding the classical use of the existential quantifier is to say that $\exists x \in T.P$ means it cannot be the case that for all x in T, $\neg(P)$ holds. If we use the symbols $\otimes$ and $\exists\!\!\!\ominus$ for the classical disjunction and existential quantifier respectively, then the translations are:

$$(A\&B)^\circ = A^\circ\&B^\circ \qquad (A \Rightarrow B)^\circ = A^\circ \Rightarrow B^\circ$$
$$\forall x.B^\circ = \forall x.\ B^\circ \qquad (A\otimes B)^\circ = \neg(\neg A^\circ\ \&\ \neg B^\circ)$$
$$(\exists x.B)^\circ = \neg\forall x.\ \neg B^\circ \qquad atomic^\circ = atomic$$
$$\bot^\circ = \bot$$

Note: $\neg B = (B \Rightarrow \bot)$
where $\bot$ denotes the false proposition

Example: $(P\otimes\neg(P))^\circ = \neg(\neg(P)\ \&\ \neg\neg(P))$, for P atomic

Figure 1.1: **Gödel Transformation**

$$P\otimes Q \equiv \neg((\neg(P) \wedge \neg(Q)))$$
$$\exists x \in T.P \equiv \neg(\forall x \in T.\neg(P)).$$

Classically these are laws relating the operations mentioned, but constructively they are definitions of new operators. Applying these definitions to a classical statement results in a constructive one that explains the classical statement in computational terms. Gödel defined a complete embedding of classical arithmetic into constructive arithmetic, showin in Figure 1.1.

Theorem 0.3 (Gödel) *If F is provable in classical arithmetic from Γ, written $\Gamma \vdash_{PA} F$, then F° is provable in constructive arithmetic from Γ°, written $\Gamma^\circ \vdash_{HA} F^\circ$.*

Corollary 0.1 *If $\vdash_{PA} \exists x \in \mathsf{N}.\phi(x)$, where $\phi(x)$ is decidable, then $\vdash_{HA} \neg\neg(\exists x \in \mathsf{N}.\phi(x))$.*

Friedman's A-translation

In 1978 Friedman [9] gave a new syntactic proof that one could automatically transform classical proofs of Σ^0_1 sentences (existential sentences where the body is decidable) into constructive proofs. This proof was in two steps, the first consisting of the just-defined double-negation translation. The second step can be defined in numerous ways, depending upon the exact kind of source and destination logics we wish to consider. We define it as Friedman did, and then a simplification, originally due to Leivant [16], which makes the task of A-translation essentially effortless.

The purpose of A-translation is to transform a Gödel-translated proof of a Σ^0_1 sentence back into a proof of the original sentence. Let $\Gamma \vdash_T G$ mean that there exists a proof of G under the assumptions Γ in theory T.

Definition 0.1 (A-Translation) *The A-translation of a proposition ϕ is accomplished by simultaneously disjoining every atomic formula of ϕ with the proposition A, and is written ϕ^A.*

For example, $(a = b \wedge b = c)^A \equiv (a = b \vee A) \wedge (b = c \vee A)$. We can prove the following theorem:

Theorem 0.4 (Friedman) *If $\Gamma \vdash_{HA} F$ then $\Gamma^A \vdash_{HA} F^A$ for any A.*

Consider now a classical proof

$$x : \mathsf{N} \vdash_{PA} \exists y \in \mathsf{N}.\Phi(x, y),$$

and let $A \equiv \exists y \in \mathsf{N}.\Phi(x, y)$. The Gödel-translation theorem lets us construct

$$x : \mathsf{N} \vdash_{HA} \neg\neg(\exists y \in \mathsf{N}.\Phi(x, y))$$

(again, $\Phi(x, y)$ is decidable) from which, by A-translation, we get:

$$x : \mathsf{N} \vdash_{HA} ((\exists y \in \mathsf{N}.\Phi(x, y)^A) \Rightarrow A) \Rightarrow A, \qquad (1.3)$$

where, as we said, A is the original goal. Now, when Φ is decidable, $\Phi(x, y)^A \Leftrightarrow (\Phi(x, y) \vee A)$. It is trivial to show

$$x : \mathsf{N} \vdash_{HA} (\exists y \in \mathsf{N}.(\Phi(x, y) \vee A)) \Rightarrow A$$

when $A = \exists y \in \mathsf{N}.\Phi(x, y)$, and we can thus easily show

$$x : \mathsf{N} \vdash_{HA} (\exists y \in \mathsf{N}.\Phi(x, y)^A) \Rightarrow A, \qquad (1.4)$$

(which we refer to as "Friedman's top-level trick".) Putting together Figures 1.3 and 1.4, we get

$$x : \mathsf{N} \vdash_{HA} \exists y \in \mathsf{N}.\Phi(x, y).$$

While this passage from the double-negated proof to the A-translated, double-negated proof looks quite complicated, what's really going on is that we first translate the double-negated proof from a constructive logic into a minimal logic, and then replace every instance of $\bot$ with A. Thus, if we were already in a minimal logic, we would not have to do the first step, and we could just replace every $\bot$ with A. In any case, regardless of what version of the A-translation we use, we can prove

Theorem 0.5 (Friedman) *Given a classical proof*

$$x : \mathsf{N} \vdash_{PA} \exists y \in \mathsf{N}.\Phi(x, y),$$

where Φ is decidable, we can construct a constructive proof of the same, $x : \mathsf{N} \vdash_{HA} \exists y \in \mathsf{N}.\Phi(x, y)$, via double-negation translation, followed by A-translation, followed by the top-level trick.

It follows trivially that the same holds for all Π_2^0 sentences provable in PA.

In the following development of the translation of a particular simple argument, we assume that the target logic of the double-negation translation is minimal. Hence, the A-translation simply replaces $\perp$ in the double-negated proof with A. Since the logic is minimal, this replacement operation does not perturb the proof, and so the double-negated proof is still a valid proof of the A-translated sentence.

Let's say that again. If we assume that double-negation translation leaves us in a minimal logic, then a proof of a double-negated sentence is *also* a proof of any A-translation of that sentence. This means that A-translation is really just a "name change", which does nothing of real importance; whereas double-negation translation does all the real work of extracting computations. So we focus upon the effect of double-negation translation, to see how it extracts computational content.

4   Hidden constructions

One advantage of the A-translation method is that it can help to uncover constructions that are difficult to see. We will illustrate this idea with a very simple example. A-translation has also been employed by C. Murthy [20] to obtain a computation (albeit a grossly infeasible one) from a classical proof of Higman's Lemma [10]. The following simple example is enough to illustrate several important concepts.

Let $\mathsf{N} \equiv \{0, 1, 2, \cdots\}$. Consider a function $f : \mathsf{N} \to \mathsf{N}$ whose values are all either 0 or 1. Call such a function *binary*. Here is a trivial fact about binary functions whose proof we will call **pf1**.

For all $f : \mathsf{N} \to \mathsf{N}$ which are *binary*, there exist $i, j \in \mathsf{N}$, $i < j$ such that $f(i) = f(j)$. Here is a classical proof. Either there are infinitely many 0's in the range of f (abbreviated $Zeros(f)$) or not. If not, then there are infinitely many 1's ($Ones(f)$). In the first case, choose i, j to be two distinct numbers on which f is 0. In the other case, choose i, j to be distinct numbers on which f is 1.

This is a highly nonconstructive proof. Indeed it is quite difficult to see any construction in it at all. But there are quite trivial constructive proofs such as the following which we call **pf2**.

> Consider $f(0), f(1), f(2)$. If $f(0) = f(1)$ then $i = 0, j = 1$. If $f(0) \neq f(1)$, then if $f(0) = f(2)$ take $i = 0, j = 2$. If $f(0) \neq f(2)$, then it must be that $f(1) = f(2)$ since f is *binary*, so take $i = 1, j = 2$.

This proof is very constructive, and we see that the extracted algorithm is just

```
if f(0) = f(1)
then i := 0, j := 1
else if f(0) = f(2)
     then i := 0, j := 2
     else i := 1, j := 2
```

It is interesting that the A-translation of **pf1** does not produce the same algorithm as that obtained from **pf2**. We see the difference below.

We now examine some of the key steps in a more rigorous treatment of the first proof, **pf1**. We will try to outline just enough of the argument that the hidden construction becomes visible. First some definitions. We write $Ones(f)$ to mean that there are infinitely many 1's in the range of f, similarly for $Zeros(f)$. The classical definitions are:

$$Ones(f) \equiv \forall i \in \mathsf{N}.\exists j \in \mathsf{N}.i < j \wedge f(j) = 1$$
$$Zeros(f) \equiv \forall i \in \mathsf{N}.\exists j \in \mathsf{N}.i < j \wedge f(j) = 0.$$

A key lemma is that there are either infinitely many ones or infinitely many zeros. It is expressed as:

$$\forall f \in \mathsf{N} \to \mathsf{N}.binary(f) \Rightarrow Ones(f) \otimes Zeros(f).$$

When Gödel-translated this is

$$\forall f \in \mathsf{N} \to \mathsf{N}.binary(f) \Rightarrow \neg(\neg(Ones(f)) \wedge \neg(Zeros(f)))$$

which is

$$\forall f \in \mathsf{N} \to \mathsf{N}.binary(f) \Rightarrow ((Ones(f) \Rightarrow \bot) \wedge (Zeros(f) \Rightarrow \bot)) \Rightarrow \bot.$$

The informal classical proof employs the fact that either $Ones(f)$ or $\neg(Ones(f))$. If $\neg(Ones(f))$, then there is some point x_0 such that for $y > x_0$, $f(y) = 0$. This means that $Zeros(f)$. Let us look at the proof more

Show:$\forall f \in N \to N.binary(f) \Rightarrow ((Ones(f) \Rightarrow \perp) \wedge (Zeros(f) \Rightarrow \perp)) \Rightarrow \perp$

Proof.   assume $f : N \to N$, $binary(f)$,

$Ones(f) \Rightarrow \perp$, $Zeros(f) \Rightarrow \perp$

"there is an x beyond which no values are 1's"

This corresponds to trying elimination on $Ones(f) \Rightarrow \perp$ to get $\perp$.

Show $\forall x \in N. \neg\neg(\exists y \in N.x < y \wedge f(y) = 1)$

Proof. arb $x : N$, show $(\exists y \in N.(x < y \wedge f(y) = 1) \Rightarrow \perp) \Rightarrow \perp$

$a1$:assume $\exists y \in N.(x < y \wedge f(y) = 1) \Rightarrow \perp$

(this is equivalent to $\forall y \in (x < y \Rightarrow f(y) \neq 1)$., beyond x all

values are 0)

plan to get $\perp$ by elim on $Zeros(f) \Rightarrow \perp$

show $Zeros(f)$, i.e. $\forall z \in N. \neg\neg(\exists y \in N.z < y \wedge f(y) = 0)$

Proof. arb $z : N$ show $(\exists y \in N.(z < y \wedge f(y) = 0) \Rightarrow \perp) \Rightarrow \perp$

$a2$: assume $\exists y \in N.(z < y \wedge f(y) = 0) \to \perp$

(now know from $a1$, $a2$ that can't have f be either 0 or 1, get $\perp$)

let $w = max(z,x) + 1$

$d : f(w) = 0 \vee f(w) = 1$ by binary (f)

show $\perp$ by cases on d above

if $f(w) = 0$ then $z < w \wedge f(w) = 0$ so

$\exists y \in N.(z < y \wedge f(y) = 0)$

$\perp$ by elim on $a2$

if $f(w) = 1$ then $x < w \wedge f(w) = 1$ so

$\exists y \in N.(x < y \wedge f(y) = 1)$

$\perp$ by elim on $a1$

$\perp$

Qed so Zeros(f)

$\perp$ by elim on $\neg(Zeros(f))$

Qed Ones(f)

$\perp$ by elim on $\neg(Ones(f))$

QED

Figure 1.2: Constructive proof of **L0**

Show: $Zeros(f) \Rightarrow G$
Proof. a1: assume $\forall x(\exists y(x < y \land f(y) = 0)) \rightarrow \bot) \rightarrow \bot$
    show $(\exists i, j \ F \rightarrow \bot) \rightarrow \bot$
    a2: assume $(\exists i, j \ . \ F \rightarrow \bot)$, show $\bot$
        could try to show $\exists i, j \ . \ F$ and use $\rightarrow$ elim, but that is too direct, we need
        to use $Zeros(f)$
    a3: $(\exists y(0 < y \land f(y) = 0) \rightarrow \bot) \rightarrow \bot$ by allel a1, on 0
        show $\exists y(0 < y \ \& \ f(y) = 0) \rightarrow \bot$ for $\rightarrow$ elim on a3
        assume $\exists y.(0 < y \land f(y) = 0)$ to show $\bot$
        choose y_0 where $0 < y_0 \land f(y_0) = 0$
        a4: $(\exists y(y_0 < y \ \& \ f(y) = 0)) \rightarrow \bot) \rightarrow \bot$ by allel a1 on y_0
            show $\exists y(y_0 < y \land f(y) = 0) \rightarrow \bot$ for $\rightarrow$ elim on a4
            a5: assume $\exists y(y_0 < y \land f(y) = 0), show \bot$
                choose y_1 where $y_0 < y_1 \land f(y_1) = 0$.

            $\exists F$ by $\exists$ intro y_0, y_1
    $\bot$ by elim a2 (showing $\bot$ at a5)
    $\bot$ by elim a4
    $\bot$ by elim a3 (showing $\bot$ at a2)
QED

Figure 1.3: Constructive proof of **L2**

carefully. We give a constructive proof of the Gödel-translated sentence, **L0**, in Figure 1.2. The other two key steps are to show that $Ones(f)$ and $Zeros(f)$ each imply the goal.

Let $F \equiv i < j \land f(i) = f(j)$, and $\exists F \equiv \exists i, j \in \mathsf{N}.F$ and the double-negation translation of this is the classical goal $G \equiv \neg\neg(\exists F)$. We must prove the two lemmas:

$$\textbf{L1} \quad : \quad Ones(f) \Rightarrow G \quad \text{and}$$
$$\textbf{L2} \quad : \quad Zeros(f) \Rightarrow G.$$

A proof of **L2** is given in Figure 1.3. For brevity we have omitted the types on quantifiers, and we put these proofs together in figure 1.4, to yield

$$\forall f \in \mathsf{N} \rightarrow \mathsf{N}.binary(f) \Rightarrow \neg\neg(\exists F)$$

As we said before, we assume that this proof of $\neg\neg(\exists F)$ is in a minimal logic; hence, we can automatically generate, for any A, a proof of

$$x : \mathsf{N}, binary(f) \vdash_{HA} (\exists F \Rightarrow A) \Rightarrow A,$$

Theorem 0.6 $\forall f \in N \to N.binary(f) \Rightarrow \neg\neg(\exists F):$

Proof. assume $f : N \to N$, $b : binary(f)$, show $\neg\neg(\exists F)$
  a1: assume $\neg(\exists F)$, show $\perp$
  a2:$\neg(\neg(Zeros(f)) \wedge \neg(Ones(f)))$
    by lemma **L0**, with parameters f, b
  $\perp$ by *function elimination* on a2
    show $\neg(Zeros(f)) \wedge \neg(Ones(f))$ by *and introduction*
    show $\neg(Zeros(f))$
      a3: assume $Zeros(f)$, show $\perp$
      $h{:}\neg\neg(\exists F)$ by lemma **L1** with parameter a3
      $\perp$ by elim h on a1
    $\neg(Zeros(f))$
    show $\neg(Ones(f))$
      a4: assume $Ones(f)$, show $\perp$
      $h{:}\neg\neg(\exists F)$ by lemma **L2** with parameter a4
      $\perp$ by elim h on a1
    $\neg(Ones(f))$
    $\neg(Zeros(f)) \wedge \neg(Ones(f))$
  $\perp$
QED

Figure 1.4: Putting it together

and from this, by Friedman's top-level trick, a proof of

$$x : \mathsf{N}, binary(f) \vdash_{HA} \exists i, j \in \mathsf{N}.i < j \wedge f(i) = f(j).$$

5 Mechanizing the translations in Nuprl

The work presented in preceding sections came out of a two-year long project to understand the meaning of Friedman's translations. As part of this project, we implemented Friedman's metatheorem as a proof transformation procedure that translated proofs in a classical variant of Nuprl into proofs in constructive Nuprl. Unfortunately, we cannot implement Friedman's metatheorem for all of Nuprl; that is, the *entire* Nuprl type theory, with the addition of the axiom of excluded middle, is not a suitable candidate for Friedman's translation. In fact, we arrive at a counter-example (the translated axiom of choice) which demonstrates that we must discard, in a sense, the propositions-as-types principle in order to define a translatable logic. In the following, we spell out restrictions on Nuprl which yield a theory Nuprl°, which *can* be translated.

Having spelled out the subtheory of Nuprl which, when made classical, is translatable, we will briefly discuss the mechanized implementation of the "binary" theorem, and then discuss parts of the translated, extracted computation. Finally, we describe some results that came out of this project. They are described in detail in the second author's thesis [20].

Effective translation

The problem in translating a constructive type theory such as Nuprl is that Nuprl is not really a constructive *logic*. Consider that in a "standard" logic, a proposition is not something which we may quantify over. Rather, we must first "comprehend" it into a set or a type, and then quantify over that. In a type theory, there is no such comprehension, or rather, every proposition is automatically comprehended into a set. But in a classical logic suitable for translation, we should not be able to directly comprehend a classically proven proposition into a type, since we could then apply the axiom of choice to extract a function out of a classically proven ∀ − ∃ statement. We will show that this pattern of reasoning is not in general translatable.

Said another way, a classical proof of a proposition resembles a guarantee that we can never construct a counter-example to the proposition. There is often no means given to construct evidence for the proposition, and so we should not be able to quantify over inhabitants of the proposition, but only reason from the fact that the proposition is inhabited. This conforms well with the classical notion that a proposition is simply proven; the proofs of a proposition are indistinguishable, since they are noncomputational. Likewise, we should always be able to reason that if $P \Leftrightarrow Q$, then $\Phi(P) \Leftrightarrow \Phi(Q)$, where P, Q are propositions, and Φ is a predicate on propositions. This means that proposition constructors must bi-implicatively respect bi-implication.

These ideas can be made precise by defining a theory much like Nuprl, called Nuprl°, such that proofs in Classical Nuprl° can always be translated back into Nuprl°. We define a trivial mapping from Nuprl° to Nuprl (an erasing of certain annotations) that finishes the job. A Nuprl° proof is one that satisfies the following:

- Every proposition in every sequent must be statically well-formed. That is, the well-formedness of a proposition should not depend upon the truth (inhabitation) of some other proposition. Some examples of this problem come up in uses of the "set" type, which is used in Nuprl to hide computational content.

- Every proposition constructor should respect $\Leftrightarrow$, as explained before. This restriction is simple to enforce, and it comes about because we wish to enforce the "logical" nature of our language.

- the "proposition-hood" of a term must be syntactically decidable; that is, we must be able to statically decide whether a given term in a given sequent is a proposition or not, and no term which is a proposition in one sequent can be a data-value, or data-type, in another sequent (e.g. a parent sequent or subsidiary sequent). We enforce this condition by annotating every term (and every subterm) with either a P (for proposition) or a D (for data), and verifying that certain compatibility conditions hold between adjacent sequents in proof trees.

With these three conditions, we can show that, for a suitable subset of the type constructors of the Nuprl type theory (e.g., Π-types, Σ-types, universes, higher-order predicates and data, integers, lists, etc,) the Classical Nuprl° theory, with excluded middle, is translatable automatically into constructive Nuprl°. We can then embed Nuprl° back into Nuprl by simply erasing the annotations. Hence, we have a set of sufficient conditions for the success of the translation in Nuprl.

One wonders if these restrictions are really relevant; if these restrictions actually exclude pathological cases of proofs which are intrinsically not translatable, and include important cases of proofs which we must translate. The second part of this question is easily answered: our translation effort, which succeeded in translating Higman's Lemma, attests to the tractability of doing mathematics within this fragment of Nuprl. To answer the first part of the question, we showed that, for a particular formalization of the axiom of choice, which is trivially provable in Nuprl, its double-negation translation is not provable in Nuprl. It can be written thus:

$$\forall x \in Dom.\exists y \in Rng.\Phi(x,y) \Rightarrow \exists f \in Dom \rightarrow Rng.\forall x \in Dom.\Phi(x, f(x)),$$

and its proof in Nuprl is $\lambda\, h.\langle\lambda\, x.h(x).1,\ \lambda\, x.h(x).2\rangle$. We can think of this as a function which, given an input function, stands as a proof of $\forall x \in Dom.\exists y \in Rng.\Phi(x,y)$, *splits* the input function into the two parts, the first of which computes values in Rng, and the second part of which witnesses the correctness of the first part.

But this proof assigns a name, h, to the proof of

$$\forall x \in Dom.\exists y \in Rng.\Phi(x,y),$$

which we expressly forbade in our conditions above. For this $\forall\exists$ sentence is an object of proof, hence a proposition, and to assign a name to the proofs (inhabitants) of a proposition is to quantify over it, which, again, is forbidden in our fragment of Nuprl. The double-negation translation of this axiom is equivalent to the following sentence (where Φ is double-negated):

$$\forall x \in Dom.\neg\neg(\exists y \in Rng.\Phi(x,y)) \Rightarrow \neg\neg(\forall x \in Dom.\exists y \in Rng.\Phi(x,y)),$$

and we showed that this sentence is not true in the standard model of Nuprl [1]. Thus, we cannot use the axiom of choice to construct functions by induction in our classical proofs. Instead, we must formalize functions as binary relations for which certain existence and uniqueness predicates hold. Using such a formulation, we can then do almost all of the reasoning we wish to about functions, paying only a small price in terms of cumbersomeness of the logic.

We have not yet discussed the A-translation, nor have we discussed the actual implementation of our proof translations. However, the actual implementation details follow rather straightforwardly from the restrictions on the forms of proofs, and the A-translation follows likewise. The difficult part is restricting the Nuprl logic to make translation possible at all. In the end, though, we prove

Theorem 0.7 (Conservative Extension for Nuprl⁰) *Given a proof in Classical Nuprl⁰ of a* Π_2^0 *statement, we can construct a proof in (constructive) Nuprl⁰ of the same statement.*

Proof: In [20].

```
\f.int_eq(f(1);0;
     int_eq(f(2);0;
          <1,<2,axiom>>;
          int_eq(f(3);0;
               <1,<3,axiom>>;
               <2,<3,axiom>>));
     int_eq(f(2);0;
          int_eq(f(3);0;
               <2,<3,axiom>>;
               int_eq(f(4);0;
                    <2,<4,axiom>>;
                    <3,<4,axiom>>));
          <1,<2,axiom>>))
```

Figure 1.5: The extracted binary computation

A formalization of the binary theorem

We formalized the binary theorem in Nuprl, giving it a classical proof essentially identical to the proof described earlier in this paper. The sentence actually proven was:

$$\forall f \in \mathsf{N} \to \{0,1\}. \exists i,j \in \mathsf{N}. i < j \land f(i) = f(j).$$

As described before, we proved $Ones(f) \otimes Zeros(f)$, and from this we concluded the actual goal. We then employed an automatic double-negation/A-translation tactic, which converted the proof to a constructive one, from which we extracted and executed the computational content. This program yielded the same numeric answers as the program derived earlier. We list in Figure 1.5 the computation that was extracted from this scheme, after normalization and trivial compression, and in Figure 1.6 a pseudo-code version of this program. Note that, as we said before, this strategy requires the first *four* terms of f.

We formalized a version of Nash-Williams' [10] "minimal bad sequence" proof of Higman's Lemma in Nuprl, and translated it using the same apparatus that we developed for the binary theorem, extracting constructive content in the same way. This program was approximately 12 megabytes in size, which made it infeasible to run the program on any nontrivial inputs. Later, we formalized another classical argument, in the same vein as Higman's Lemma, and from which we extracted a program of 19 megabytes in size. We were dismayed by the sizes of the extracted programs, but, as we shall discuss in the next section, this is purely a matter of the exact translation implementation (which was quite inefficient), and not an intrinsic problem with double-negation/A-translation.

```
if f(1)=0 then
  if f(2)=0 then
    <1,2>
  else if f(3)=0 then
    <1,3>
  else
    <2,3>
else if f(2)=0 then
  if f(3)=0 then
    <2,3>
  else if f(4)=0 then
    <2,4>
  else
    <3,4>
else
  <1,2>
```

Figure 1.6: The pseudo-code binary computation

6   The algorithmic content of classical proofs

We have outlined herein a general method of extracting algorithms from classical proofs of Π_2^0 sentences. However, as should be clear, the form of the algorithm extracted from a classical proof via translation is oftentimes difficult to read, understand, and relate to the original classical proof. Thus one wonders if one could extract a correct algorithm directly from the classical proof. In our work on this problem, we build on the work of Griffin [12], who discovered and verified a consistent typing for the operator "control" [7] (written C) in the simply-typed lambda-calculus. Based on his work, we have shown that there is an intimate relation between the proof translations (Kuroda [6, 18], Kolmogorov [14], etc) and continuation-passing-style translation, and that one can in fact extract sensible, meaningful algorithms directly from classical proofs. We can summarize our findings as follows:

Theorem 0.8 *Friedman's method (double-negation/A-translation) is exactly a continuation-passing-style [8, 22] compilation of the extracted "classical witness" from a proof in a classical theory (say, Peano Arithmetic).*

We have learned that many of the different double-negation translations can be understood in terms of their effect upon programs, and not just in terms of their effect upon proofs. To wit, we have shown that several different double-negation translations in fact fix the order of evaluation of expressions in a functional language, thus providing an explanation of various eager and lazy computation schemes in terms of each other, and hence in a single functional language.

Theorem 0.9

- *A particular modified Kolmogorov double-negation translation fixes a call-by-name evaluation order on functional program expressions.*

- *A modified Kuroda translation fixes an eager (call-by-value) evaluation order on functional programs.*

- *a further modification of the Kolmogorov translation makes pairing an eager operation, and allows either by-value or by-name lambda-application.*

These discoveries show that classical proofs have algorithmic content, and that this algorithmic content is made explicit by the double-negation/ A-translations. They show that the proof-translation method of double-negation/A-translation is isomorphic to the program translation method of continuation-passing-style (CPS) translation, and that classical proofs can be interpreted as nonfunctional programs (enriched with a the nonlocal control operator "control") [7]. They provide a rational, *algorithmic* foundation for Friedman's translation method, based on its effect on computations, and upon programs. That is, in a manner which is not characterized by effects upon proofs and sequents, but rather on a "semantic" basis (characterized by effects on programs and program fragments).

With this knowledge, we can evaluate the classical proof of the binary theorem directly, by assigning the operator C to be the algorithmic content of the rule of double-negation elimination. Moreover, we can utilize results of Plotkin [22] to define more efficient double-negation translations than the one which we originally chose, with the knowledge that these more efficient translations are every bit as powerful as the original ones, and, in addition, produce extensionally equivalent programs.

Acknowledgements

We wish to acknowledge Gabriel Stolzenberg, for his inspiration in opening this area of inquiry, his painstaking proofreading of this work, and his sage advice. Thanks are also due to Tim Griffin, who discussed these issues at length with us. We also wish to acknowledge the referees. This research could not have been conducted without the generous support of the National Science Foundation and the Office of Naval Research, under the auspices of Ralph Wachter, under grants CCR-8616552 and N00014-88-K-0409.

Bibliography

[1] Allen, S.F. (1987). A non-type theoretic definition of Martin-Löf's types. in *Proceedings of the Second Annual Symposium on Logic in Computer Science*, pages 215–221. IEEE.

[2] Burstall, R. and Lampson, B. (1984). A kernel language for abstract data types and modules. in *Semantics of Data Types, International Symposium, Sophia-Antipolis, France*, eds. G. Kahn, D. MacQueen, and G. Plotkin, volume 173 of *Lecture Notes in Computer Science*, Berlin. Springer-Verlag.

[3] Constable, R. (1985). The semantics of evidence. Technical Report TR 85–684, Cornell University, Department of Computer Science, Ithaca, New York.

[4] Constable, et al. (1986). *Implementing Mathematics with the Nuprl Proof Development System.* Prentice-Hall, Englewood Cliffs, New Jersey.

[5] Coquand, T. and Huet, G. (1985). Constructions: A higher order proof system for mechanizing mathematics. in *EUROCAL '85: European Conference on Computer Algebra*, ed. B. Buchberger, pages 151–184. Springer-Verlag.

[6] Dalen, D. and Troelstra, A. (1989). *Constructivism in Mathematics.* North-Holland.

[7] Felleisen, M., Friedman, D., Kohlbecker, E., and Duba, E. (1986). Reasoning with continuations. in *Proceedings of the First Annual Symposium on Logic in Computer Science*, pages 131–141.

[8] Fischer, M. (1972). Lambda-calculus schemata. in *Proceedings of the ACM Conference on Proving Assertions about Programs*, volume 7 of *Sigplan Notices*, pages 104–109.

[9] Friedman, H.. (1978). Classically and intuitionistically provably recursive functions. in *Higher Set Theory*, ed. Scott, D. S. and Muller, G. H., volume 699 of *Lecture Notes in Mathematics*, pages 21–28. Springer-Verlag.

[10] Gallier, J. (1987). What's so special about Kruskal's Theorem and the ordinal Γ_0. Technical Report MS-CIS-87-27, University of Pennsylvania, Philadelphia, PA.

[11] Girard, J-Y. (1987). *Proof Theory and Logical Complexity, vol. 1.* Bibliopolis, Napoli.

[12] Griffin, T. (1990). A formulae-as-types notion of control. in *Conference Record of the Seventeenth Annual ACM Symposium on Principles of Programming Languages*.

[13] Higman, G. (1952). Ordering by divisibility in abstract algebras. in *Proc. London Math. Soc.*, volume 2, pages 236–366.

[14] Kolmogorov, A. (1967). On the principle of the excluded middle. in *From Frege to Gödel: A Source Book in Mathematical Logic, 1879-1931*, ed. J. van Heijenoort, pages 414–437. Harvard University Press, Cambridge, Massachusetts.

[15] Kreisel, G. (1958). Mathematical significance of consistency proofs. *Journal Of Symbolic Logic*, 23:155–182.

[16] Leivant, D. (1985). Syntactic translations and provably recursive functions. *Journal Of Symbolic Logic*, 50(3):682–688.

[17] Lifschitz, V. (1982). Constructive assertions in an extension of classical mathematics. *Journal Of Symbolic Logic*, 47:359–387.

[18] Luckhardt, H. (1973). *Extensional Godel functional interpretation; a consistency proof of classical analysis*, volume 306 of *Lecture Notes in Mathematics*, pages 41–49. Springer-Verlag.

[19] Martin-Löf, P. (1982). Constructive mathematics and computer programming. in *Sixth International Congress for Logic, Methodology, and Philosophy of Science*, pages 153–175, Amsterdam. North Holland.

[20] Murthy, C. (1963). *Extracting Constructive Content from Classical Proofs*. PhD thesis, Cornell University, Department of Computer Science.

[21] Nash-Williams, C. (1963). On well-quasi-ordering finite trees. in *Proc. Cambridge Phil. Soc.*, volume 59, pages 833–835.

[22] Plotkin, G. (1975). Call-by-name, call-by-value, and the λ-calculus. *Theoretical Computer Science*, pages 125–159.

[23] Pollack, R. (1989). The theory of LEGO. Unpublished draft.

[24] Reynolds, J. (1974). Towards a theory of type structure. in *Proc. Colloque sur la Programmation, Lecture Notes in Computer Science 19*, pages 408–23. NY:Springer-Verlag.

[25] Shapiro, S. (1985). *Epistemic and Intuitionistic Arithmetic*, pages 11–46. North-Holland.

[26] Troelstra, A., editor. (1973) *Metamathematical Investigation of Intuitionistic Arithmetic and Analysis*, volume 344 of *Lecture Notes in Mathematics*. Springer-Verlag.

[27] van Heijenoort, J., editor. (1967) *From Frege to Gödel: A Source Book in Mathematical Logic, 1879-1931*. Harvard University Press, Cambridge, Massachusetts.

LOGICAL ISSUES

Models of partial inductive definitions

LARS HALLNÄS
Department of Computer Sciences
Chalmers University of Technology and University of Göteborg
412 96 Göteborg, Sweden

1 Introduction

The notion of a partial inductive definition comes from [4] where an attempt is made to give an interpretation of a class of possible non monotone inductive definitions allowing for partially defined objects. The idea was to give an elementary *logical* interpretation and leave the true complexity of the definition to the question whether an object is well defined or not with respect to the given definition. This interpretation is given in terms of a sequent calculus generated in a uniform manner from definitions D where $\Gamma \vdash_D A$ intuitively is to be understood as A follows from Γ on basis of the definition D. $\vdash_D$ describes so to speak the *logic* of D and is basically used to describe the property defined by D in terms of

$$\{a \mid \vdash_D a\}$$

The purpose of this note is to formulate a slightly different type of interpretation of the partial inductive definitions. The type of interpretation we have in mind here focus perhaps more on structural properties of the definitions themselves than the logical interpretation in terms of $\vdash_D$ which more focus on definability issues, i.e. the property defined by D etc. A basic starting point here is the fact that the structure of a partial inductive

This research has been carried out as a part of ESPRIT Basic Research Action "Logical Frameworks". It has been supported by STU (Swedish National Board for Technical Development).

definition D is reflected in computational properties of derivations in a natural deduction system $N(D)$ that can be obtained from the logic $\vdash_D$. This can for example be expressed in a Curry-Howard interpretation of partial inductive definitions as type systems for λ-terms which gives an interpretation of simply typed λ-calculus with abstract data types (see [2, 4]). To illustrate this point consider the following simple example:
We have the definitions

$$D_1 \{a = \top \qquad D_2 \{a = a \to a$$

where we may read $\top$ as *true* and $\to$ as *implication*. In terms of the logical interpretation D_1 and D_2 are the same, but if we consider computational aspects of the derivations they give rise to, then they are indeed very different. D_1 is computationally trivial while D_2 gives us non normalisable derivations. This distinction between D_1 and D_2 is an *intensional* distinction, i.e. we focus on the definitions as the primary objects rather than the properties they define. We would like to formulate such a distinction as a structural distinction between definitions on the basis of a general enough notion of structure. In what follows we will try to outline an attempt to isolate basic *structural* aspects of a computational analysis of the derivations in $N(D)$ for a given definition D. We will formulate this using a general notion of a model for a partial inductive definition and in the particular model construction given here as the main example of such models we will try to express all basic notions in terms of the structure or logic of simple and well understood definitions and thus avoid contingent syntactic issues of derivations and λ-terms as far as possible. The long term goal here is to find tools for analysing intensional phenomenon of computable functions in terms of the structure of the definitions that presents them.

The paper is organised as follows: In section 2 we will review basic notions from [4] concerning partial inductive definitions including the *logical* interpretation given there. In section 3 we will introduce and discuss the notion of model considered in this note. Section 4 gives a particular type of models of the partial inductive definitions as the main example here, models which are closely connected with a Curry-Howard interpretation of the partial inductive definitions as type systems for λ-terms with abstract data types. The final section 5 relates the models given in section 4 and the logical interpretation from [4].

2   Partial inductive definitions

Let U be a set - our universe of discourse. Objects in a given universe of discourse U will be called *atoms* and denoted by $a, b, c, \ldots$. We think of a *definition* over U as a set of equations $a = A$, *definitional clauses*, in which atoms are defined in terms of certain conditions. A definition D defines a certain property $Def(D) \subseteq U$ and the basic principle here is of course that $a \in Def(D)$ iff there is a condition A *defining* a in D such that A is true. In what follows we will consider a particular class of conditions built up from atoms using constants for *truth*, *falsity* and what intuitively correspond to *conjunction* and *implication*.

Conditions, definitional clauses and definitions

Conditions (over U)

- $\top$ is a condition,

- $\bot$ is a condition,

- Each atom is a condition,

- If C_i is a condition for $i \in I$, then $(C_i)_{i \in I}$ is a condition,

- If C and C' are conditions, then $C \to C'$ is a condition.

The index set I can be any given set, so these conditions correspond *syntactically* to formulas in infinitary propositional logic over a given set U of propositional variables.

Conditions will be denoted by $A, B, C, \ldots$. Let $Cond(U)$ stand for the collection of conditions over U and $\Gamma, \Sigma, \ldots$ stand for finite sets of conditions over a given universe U.

Definitional clauses (over U)

A definitional *clause* (over U) is an equation $a = A$, where a is an atom in U and A a condition (over U).

Definitions (over U)

A *definition* (over U) is a set (system) of definitional clauses (over U). We will use $D, D', \ldots$ to denote such definitions. The reference to U will be omitted in all cases where the particular universe of discourse is clear from context. Let $Dom(D) = \{a \mid \exists (a = A) \in D\}$.

Let $\hat{D} = D \cup \{a = \bot \mid a \notin Dom(D)\}$. The intuition is that if a is not defined in D, that is $a \notin Dom(D)$, then a is so to speak *false by definition*. For technical reasons we then add the clause $a = \bot$. The *definiens* of an atom a, $D(a)$, (relative to given definition D) is then the following set of conditions

$$D(a) = \{A \mid (a = A) \in \hat{D}\}.$$

Local D-consequence

Below we will interpret definitions D in terms of a notion of *consequence local to* D. This notion of consequence is local to D in the sense that its definition depends on D. We will consider relations $\Gamma \vdash C$. Such a relation will be called a *condition relation* if it has the following closure properties:

$$(\top) \qquad\qquad\qquad \Gamma \vdash \top$$

$$(\bot) \qquad\qquad\qquad \Gamma, \bot \vdash C$$

$$(\vdash ()) \qquad\qquad\qquad \frac{\Gamma \vdash C_i \quad (i \in I)}{\Gamma \vdash (C_i)_{i \in I}}$$

$$(() \vdash) \qquad\qquad\qquad \frac{\Gamma, C_i \vdash C}{\Gamma, (C_i)_{i \in I} \vdash C} \quad (i \in I)$$

where Γ, C_i is short for $\Gamma \cup \{C_i\}$.

$$(\vdash \to) \qquad\qquad\qquad \frac{\Gamma, C \vdash C'}{\Gamma \vdash C \to C'}$$

$$(\to \vdash) \qquad\qquad\qquad \frac{\Gamma \vdash C \quad \Gamma, C' \vdash C''}{\Gamma, C \to C' \vdash C''}$$

A condition relation $\vdash$ satisfying the following additional closure conditions will be called *D-closed*:

$$(\vdash D) \qquad\qquad\qquad \frac{\Gamma \vdash A}{\Gamma \vdash a} \quad (A \in D(a))$$

$$(D \vdash) \qquad\qquad\qquad \frac{\Gamma, A \vdash C \quad (A \in D(a))}{\Gamma, a \vdash C}$$

Now let $\vdash_D$ be the smallest D-closed condition relation $\vdash$ such that $\Gamma, a \vdash a$ holds for all a and Γ.
Let

$$Def(D) = \{a \mid \vdash_D a\}$$

$$\overline{Def(D)} = \{a \mid a \vdash_D \bot\}$$

$$Cov(D) = \{C \mid \vdash_D C\}$$

$$\overline{Cov(D)} = \{C \mid C \vdash_D \bot\}$$

$Def(D)$ is the property over U defined by D and $\overline{Def(D)}$ is the internal (intensional) complement which is equal to the external (extensional) complement $U - Def(D)$ only when D is strong enough. The *cover* of a definition $Cov(D)$ contains all conditions true in the local logic $\vdash_D$ and thus so to speak covers the reasoning needed to prove that atoms a are in $Def(D)$. We clearly have

$$a \in Def(D) \text{ iff } D(a) \cap Cov(D) \text{ is non empty.}$$

In what follows we let $D + D'$ denote set union and $D - D'$ set difference. We will al so use the notation $D \oplus D'$ to denote the definition $D + \{(a = A) \in D' \mid a \notin Dom(D)\}$. If $X \subset U$ we identify X with the definition $\{x = \top \mid x \in X\}$. It is clear that $x \in X$ iff $x \in Def(X)$ and $x \in U - X$ iff $x \in \overline{Def(X)}$.

Let $X \subset U$. We may think of conditions over U as formulas in infinitary propositional logic over U and X as an interpretation such that $X \models a$ iff $a \in X$. Then $X \models A$ is defined in the usual manner by recursion on A. Given a partial inductive definition D the associated operator $\Phi_D : P(U) \to P(U)$ is then de fined as follows

$$\Phi_D(X) = \{a \mid \exists (a = A) \in D \text{ such that } X \text{ models } A\}$$

Definitions D that does not contain any $\to$-constructions in the conditions used correspond to Aczel's interpretation of monotone inductive definitions in terms of *rule sets* in [1] and it is clear that in this case $Def(D)$ is the least fixpoint of the operator Φ_D. We have in general that if Φ_D has a fixpoint X, then $Def(D) \subset X$ (see [4]). It is clear that if we consider definitions using $\to$ constructions in conditions, then the partial inductive definitions generates also non monotone operators Φ_D.

We call partial inductive definitions using only conditions without the $\rightarrow$-construction *simple definitions*. When we speak about simple definitions and conditions in connections with such definitions in what follows this means that we just consider conditions built up from atoms using the $\top, \bot, (C_i)_{i \in I}$ constructions.

The sequent calculus defining $\vdash_D$ gives us in the present interpretation the logic of D. Given a partial inductive definition D we may associate with D a system of natural deduction $N(D)$ that will give us a natural notion of a derivation in the logic of D. Derivations are as usual built up from assumptions using a collection of rules of inference:

$$\top \quad \text{(axiom)}$$

$$\frac{\bot}{C} \quad (\bot E)$$

$$\frac{C_i \quad (i \in I)}{(C_i)_{i \in I}} \quad (()I)$$

$$\frac{(C_i)_{i \in I}}{C_i} \quad (()E)$$

$$\frac{B[A]}{A \rightarrow B} \quad (\rightarrow I)$$

$$\frac{A \rightarrow B \quad A}{B} \quad (\rightarrow E)$$

$$\frac{A}{a} \quad (A \in D(a)) \quad (DI)$$

$$\frac{a \quad C[A] \quad (A \in D(a))}{C} \quad (DE)$$

where $[A]$ as usual indicates that assumptions A may be discharged at the inference of $A \rightarrow B$ and C respectively. A natural notion of normalisation for derivations in $N(D)$ can be given in a uniform manner (see [4]). The interpretation $\vdash_D$ is in a sense *partial* which can be seen if we compare provability in $\vdash_D$ and derivability in $N(D)$. Consider the following definition

$$R = \{a = a \rightarrow b\}$$

The following derivation in $N(R)$ then shows that we can prove both a and $a \rightarrow b$ and thus b by $\rightarrow$-elimination.

$$[a] \quad \frac{\dfrac{[a \to b] \quad [a]}{b}}{\dfrac{b}{\dfrac{a \to b}{a}}}$$

But since $R(b) = \{\perp\}$ we cannot prove b in $\vdash_R$. R gives the structure of paradoxes like the ones by Russell and Curry in terms of an inductive definition which means that the interpretation $\vdash_R$ in a sense allows for partially defined atoms. This means here that the cut rule is not admissible in $\vdash_R$. It is also clear that the operator Φ_R associated with R cannot have any fixpoints. In $N(R)$ it is on the other hand a basic assumption that the logic of R gives a meaningful interpretation to all the atoms. The derivation of b in $N(R)$ thus gives a canonical example of a non normalisable derivation in the present context. For a further discussion of these matters see [4],[6].

3 Models

By a model of a definition D we intuitively understand an interpretation of the conditions used in D such that an atom a "is true" iff there is a $A \in D(a)$ which "is true". (Note that fixpoints of the associated operator Φ_D are not possible as candidates for models of a partial inductive definition D if we want to allow also for partially defined objects. This follows from previous discussion.) We think of an interpretation as having a certain explicit structure. The basic model condition stated below is then formulated in such a manner as to ensure that the structure of a definition will be reflected in the explicated structure of an interpretation modelling the given definition.

Since we want the model-concept here to be as general as possible we start with a very general notion of a definition:

By a *definition* in general we understand a triple $(Dom, Codom, D)$ where

(i) Dom and $Codom$ are two sets such that $Dom \subset Codom$,

(ii) D is a set of equations $a = A$ where $a \in Dom$ and $A \in Codom$.

We will also write $Dom(D)$ and $Codom(D)$ and use D to denote the triple $(Dom, Codom, D)$. Let $D(a) = \{A \mid (a = A) \in D\}$, i.e. $D : Dom \to P(Codom)$.

In case of the partial inductive definitions $Dom = U$ and $Codom = Cond(U)$ for a given universe U.

An *interpretation* of a definition $(Dom, Codom, D)$ is a triple

$$(T, M, \leq)$$

(i) $(M, \leq)$ is an ordered set (i.e. $\leq$ is a reflexive and transitive relation on M),

(ii) $T : Codom \rightarrow P(M)$.

We will use $T \ldots$ to denote interpretations. Given an interpretation T we will often write A for $T(A)$, i.e. given M and an interpretation T of $Codom$ writing A for a subset of M is short for the set $T(A)$.

To get some intuition one may think of M as a set of partial proofs, $T(A)$ as the set of partial proofs of A and $\leq$ as some canonical ordering of such proofs that reflects so to speak the semantical structure of a proof rather than some contingent syntactic structure of a particular presentation. One may also think of M as a set of stages at which certain conditions are known to be true and $\leq$ as the natural ordering of these stages. $T(A)$ is then the set of stages at which A is known to be true. This picture is of course closely related to the former through the Kripke semantics of intuitionistic logic.

Given an interpretation T we have a family of subsets of M indexed by $Codom$. The basic structure of an interpretation comes from the behavior of the ordering $\leq$ on this family. We will in what follows in particular focus on the following situation: given that we have an object p in $T(A)$ with a certain property E is there an object below (or above) p - with respect to $\leq$ - in $T(B)$ with the same property? These properties will here be represented by maps restricting the sets $T(A)$ to certain subsets.

A *restriction* map is a function $v : P(M) \rightarrow P(M)$ such that $v(X) \subset X$. We write $X|v$ for $v(X)$.

Given that we think of A as a set of partial proofs when viewed as a subset of M trough the interpretation T, then a typical restriction is to consider the subset of total proofs(compare the distinction between derivations and closed derivations). So it is in this particular case reasonable to expect that if an interpretation of D really models D, then for a certain subclass v of the partial proofs we have that $p \in a|v$ iff there is a $q \in A|v$ for some $A \in D(a)$. Now we will use the structure of the interpretation to try to say something stronger namely that $a|v$ in a certain sense is almost equal to $\bigcup_{A \in D(a)} A|v$. We will use this as the basic criterion and say that v models or satisfies D. If we on the other hand view M as a set of stages, then restrictions can naturally be thought of as relating knowledge to different observers.

Let

$$(X, \leq) = \{q \mid \exists p \in X (p \leq q)\}$$

$$(\leq, X) = \{q \mid \exists p \in X (q \leq p)\}$$

Given an interpretation of D we say that a restriction map v *satisfies D* ($v \models D$) for the given interpretation if

$$\bigcup_{A \in D(a)} (\leq, A|v) \subset (\leq, a|v)$$

and

$$(a|v, \leq) \subset \bigcup_{A \in D(a)} (A|v, \leq)$$

Since $\leq$ is transitive this is equivalent with

$$\bigcup_{A \in D(a)} A|v \subset (\leq, a|v)$$

and

$$a|v \subset \bigcup_{A \in D(a)} (A|v, \leq)$$

Note that $(X, \leq)$ and $(\leq, X)$ are two closure operators dual to each other in a certain sense, so the situation is the following one: we have two closure operators F and G and *equality* between sets X and Y ($a|v$ and $\bigcup_{A \in D(a)} A|v$) modulo the duality between these closure operators in the sense that $F(Y) \subset F(X)$ and $G(X) \subset G(Y)$. In terms of proofs if p is a total proof of some $A \in D(a)$, then there is a total proof $q \geq p$ of a and if there is a total proof p of a, then there is a total proof $q \leq p$ of some $A \in D(a)$. In terms of stages of knowledge and an observer v we have the following: if v knows that A is true at some stage p for some $A \in D(a)$, then there is a later stage q at which v knows that a is true and if v knows that a is true at some stage p, then v must already at some earlier stage q have known that some $A \in D(a)$ is true. Let

$$Def_v(D) = \{a \mid \exists p \in a|v\}$$

$$Cov_v(D) = \{A \mid \exists p \in A|v\}$$

$Def_v(D)$ is the property defined by D in the given interpretation with respect to v and similarly $Cov_v(D)$ is the cover of D in the given interpretation with respect to v. We then have the following

Proposition 1.0.1 *If $v \models D$, then $a \in Def_v(D)$ iff $D(a) \cap Cov_v(D) \neq \emptyset$.*

Proof: Follows directly from definitions.   ∎

Here are some simple examples to further illustrate the notion $v \models D$:

(i) Let $M = \{\top, \bot\}$ and assume *Codom* is propositions build up from propositional variables (*Dom*) using conjunction and negation. The ordering of M is naturally the reflexive closure of $\bot \leq \top$. Now let $T(A)$ be the truth value of A for a given classical valuation I. Let $v(X) = X - \{\bot\}$ for $X \subset M$. Then $v \models D$ means

$$I \models a \text{ iff } I \models A \text{ for some } A \in D(a)$$

$(T, M, \leq)$ could of course be based on a more general algebra of truth values. We could also think of $(M, \leq)$ as a Kripke model where $T(A)$ is the set of points in M which forces A.

(ii) Let D be a set of closed term equations over some first order signature, typically a first order equational function definition

$$f(t_1, \ldots, t_n) = g(h_1(t_1), \ldots h_n(t_n))$$
$$\vdots$$

Given an interpretation $(T, \leq)$ we may think of $T(t)$ as a set of computations, i.e. computations of t according to some given function definition, and $p \leq q$ as p being a subcomputation of q. Assume that D is deterministic and that $v \models D$. We may think of v as the machine. If p is a computation of $f(t_1, \ldots, t_n)$ with respect to v, i.e. $p\,\mathrm{inf}(t_1, \ldots, t_n)|v$, then there is a computation q of $g(h_1(t_1), \ldots h_n(t_n))$ with respect to v which is a subcomputation of p. If p is a computation ov $g(h_1(t_1), \ldots h_n(t_n))$ with respect to v, then p is a subcomputation of a computation of q of $f(t_1, \ldots, t_n)$ with respect to v.

(iii) Consider the monotone operator Φ_D given by the definition D

$$a = \top$$
$$\{f(b) = b\}_{b \in U}$$

where $f : U \to U$.

Let $(T, \leq)$ be an interpretation. If $v \models D$, then assuming that $\top|v \neq \emptyset$ the set

$$\{a \mid T(a)|v \neq \emptyset\}$$

is a fixpoint of Φ_D. Here it is natural to think of $T(A)$ as a set of proofs of A and $p \leq q$ as p being a subproof of q.

4   The ⋆ models of partial inductive definitions

In this section we will give an example of models of the partial inductive definitions in the sense of section 3 above. The type of construction carried out here has basically its origin in the following considerations:
(i) A natural interpretation of a condition A would be in terms of derivations of A in the natural deduction calculus $N(D)$ for a given definition D. That is $T(A)$ would be the set of derivations with A as conclusion. One basic idea in natural deduction systems is that the introduction rules states the truth conditions for various forms of propositions while the elimination rules merely reflects the meaning given to propositions by the introduction rules. Note that the introduction rules for atoms in $N(D)$ correspond to the definitional clauses in D. It is thus natural to think of the ordering $\leq$, i.e. the structure, of the interpretation as given by the computation of derivations into normal form and the subderivation relation of derivations in normal form. This is closely related to the Böhm tree analysis of terms in λ-calculus. The structure of the interpretation would then somehow reflect the computational structure of the derivations in $N(D)$. There are several immediate candidates for basic restriction maps

$$c(X) = \{p \in X \mid p \text{ is a closed derivation}\}$$

$$cn(X) = \{p \in X \mid p \text{ is a normal closed derivation}\}$$

$$cnb(X) = \{p \in X \mid p \text{ is a normalisable closed derivation}\}$$

The counterexample to normalisation for the calculus $N(R)$ as was given in section 1 shows that the map c cannot be used to model partial inductive definitions in general. The type of restriction maps that we will consider below to model the definitions in a given interpretation are instead closely connected with the map cnb.
(ii) We would like to base the interpretation and the basic restriction maps on a subclass of the partial inductive definitions which contains only definitions which have a simple well understood interpretation and structure. That would mean we achieve some reduction. The interpretation in terms of $\vdash_D$ is of course simple since it is given by a monotone inductive definition without complicated side conditions, but the structure of proofs are poor and too implicit. Normalisation in $N(D)$ on the other hand involves syntactical complications in the precise description of substitution that we would like to avoid here to get a good compromise between *rich* structure and *simple* definitions. We will use ideas from [5] and roughly work with

a construction for explicit substitution understood in terms of naive substitution, i.e. replacement, and then characterise the notions of closed and open derivations (total and partial proofs) in terms of the logical properties of the simple definitions that defines the computational structure of the derivations. A lot of inspiration here comes from Prawitz' work on general proof theory [8, 9], Martin-Löf [7] and Girard [3].

Technically the interpretation of partial inductive definitions considered here is based on pairs of simple definitions. We will use such definitions as a basis for the ordering $\leq$ and the basic restriction maps.

Given a simple definition D and a condition C we define the set (D, C) of *subconditions* of C along D, i.e. subconditions modulo unfolding equations in D :

$$\overline{C \in (D, C)}$$

$$\frac{(C_i)_{i \in I} \in (D, C)}{C_i \in (D, C)} \ (i \in I)$$

$$\frac{a \in (D, C)}{A \in (D, C)} \ (A \in D(a))$$

We then let

$$a \leq_D b \ \text{iff} \ (D, a) \subset (D, b)$$

The *base* of a simple definition is its set of $\leq_D$-minimal objects.

The interpretations we consider in this section will have the following form:

We have a given set M and a mapping $T : Codom \rightarrow P(M)$ together with a tuple of simple definitions $D_1, \ldots, D_n$. One of the D_i will give the ordering of the interpretation in terms of $\leq_{D_i}$. We use the logic $\vdash_{D_i}$ of these definitions to construct basic restriction maps like

$$cl(C) = \{p \in C \mid p \text{ is closed}\}$$
$$op(C) = \{p \in C \mid p \text{ is open}\}$$

where p is *closed* if

$$p \in \bigcap_{i \leq n} Def(D_i)$$

and p is *open* if

$$p \in \bigcup_{i \le n} \overline{Def(D_i)}.$$

That p is closed should intuitively correspond to the notion of a total proof, i.e. a closed normalisable derivation.

We start with a set X -intuitively a set of undefined constants - and a mapping $i : X \to Codom$. Let $\hat{X} = \{\hat{x} \mid x \in X\}$. We think of x as an *open variable*, i.e. free for substitution, and of $\hat{x}$ as a *closed variable*, the formal dual to x. Below we give an inductive definition of $p : A$ for $A \in Codom$. Intuitively $p : A$ means that p is partial proof of A or a construction of A - syntactically speaking a derivation of A.

$$\overline{x : A} \ (i(x) = A)$$

$$\overline{\hat{x} : A} \ (i(x) = A)$$

$$\overline{\mathsf{T} : \mathsf{T}}$$

$$\frac{p : \bot}{(A, p) : A}$$

$$\frac{p : A \to B \qquad q : A}{(pq) : B}$$

$$\frac{x : A \qquad p : B}{(x.p) : A \to B}$$

$$\frac{f(i) : A_i \quad (i \in I)}{(f, I) : (A_i)_{i \in I}}$$

$$\frac{p : (A_i)_{i \in I}}{(p.i) : A_i}$$

$$\frac{i(x) = A \qquad p : A \qquad q : B}{(pxq) : B}$$

$$\frac{p : A}{(ap) : a} \ (A \in D(a))$$

$$\frac{p : a \qquad g(A) : C \ (A \in D(a)) \qquad x_A : A \ (A \in D(a))}{(p, F) : C}$$

where $F(A) = (x_A, g(A))$.

Note that (pxq) is a notation for what intuitively corresponds to explicit substitution as a construction within terms.

I prefer to think of this definition as a fundamental inductive definition in the sense of Kleene (see [1]), i.e. an inductive definition that is to be considered as basic and primitive, but there is of course no problem in coding the objects p as sets and give a precise definition of a monotone set-theoretic operator defining pairs (p, A) for $p : A$.

Now let the domain M of our interpretation be the set of p such that $p : A$ for some $A \in Codom$. It is easy to prove that if $p : A$ then A is unique. Let $T(A)$ be the set of p such that $p : A$.

We will now give two simple definitions $D_⋆$ and $D^⋆$ that will serve as basis for the basic restriction maps that we will consider and we will choose $\leq_{D^⋆}$ to order the domain M of our interpretation. These definitions are obtained from two definitions $K(D, X)$ and $L(D, X)$ as follows

$$\begin{cases} D_⋆ & = & K(D, X) - \hat{X} \\ D^⋆ & = & L(D, X) \oplus (K(D, X) - X) \end{cases}$$

$K(D, X)$ gives intuitively the subderivation structure of the objects in M while $L(D, X)$ gives the computational structure of these objects. $D_⋆$ is so to speak the *syntax* of objects that doesn't contain any closed variables and $D^⋆$ gives what roughly correspond to a Böhm tree analysis of the given objects.

Let $K(D, X)$ be the following simple definition

$$\begin{cases} \top & = & \top \\ x & = & \top \\ \hat{x} & = & \top \\ (A, p) & = & p \\ (pq) & = & (p, q) \\ (x.p) & = & p \\ (f, I) & = & (f(i))_{(i \in I)} \\ (p.i) & = & p \\ (pxq) & = & (p, q) \\ (ap) & = & p \\ (p, F) & = & (p, ((F(A))_2)_{A \in D(a)}) \end{cases}$$

In order to give the other basic definition $L(D, X)$ we first need to define the notion of an object p being in *computable form* (CF for short):

$$\overline{((x.p)q) \in CF} \qquad \overline{(pxq) \in CF}$$

$$\overline{((f,I).i) \in CF} \qquad \overline{((ap),F) \in CF}$$

$$\frac{p \in CF}{(A,p) \in CF} \qquad \frac{p \in CF}{(pq) \in CF}$$

$$\frac{p \in CF}{(p.i) \in CF} \qquad \frac{p \in CF}{(p,F) \in CF}$$

$p \in CF$ correspond to the notion of head redex in λ-calculus.
For p in CF we define $R(p)$ - a one step computation procedure -

$$\left\{ \begin{array}{rcl}
R((x.p)q) & = & (qxp) \\
R((f,I).i) & = & f(i) \\
R((ap),F) & = & (pxq) \text{ for } F(A) = (x,q) \\
R((A,p)) & = & (A,R(p)) \\
R((pq)) & = & (R(p)q) \\
R((p.i)) & = & (R(p).i) \\
R((p,F)) & = & (R(p),F)
\end{array} \right.$$

For q in CF let $R((pxq)) = (pxR(q))$. If q is not in CF the definition will depend on the form of q.

$$\left\{ \begin{array}{rcl}
R((px\mathsf{T})) & = & \mathsf{T} \\
R((pxz)) & = & z \\
R((px\hat{z})) & = & \hat{z} \\
R((pxx)) & = & (pxp) \\
R((px(A,q))) & = & (A,(pxq)) \\
R((px(qq'))) & = & ((pxq)(pxq')) \\
R((px(x.q))) & = & (x.q) \\
R((px(y.q))) & = & (y.(pxq)) \\
R((px(f,I))) & = & ((pxf),I) \\
R((px(q.i))) & = & ((pxq).i) \\
R((px(q,F))) & = & ((pxq),pxF)
\end{array} \right.$$

where

$$(pxf)(i) = px(f(i))$$

and

$$(pxF)(A) = \left\{ \begin{array}{ll}
(y,(pxr)), & \text{if } F(A) = (y,r); \\
(x,r), & \text{if } F(A) = (x,r).
\end{array} \right.$$

Note the clause $R((pxx)) = (pxp)$ which means we use a fixpoint construction in the computation of proofs. We do this to get a richer structure and a nice notion of convergence.

Now let $L(D, X)$ be the definition given by

$$\left\{ \begin{array}{rcl} \hat{x} & = & \top \; (x \in X) \\ (x.q) & = & \hat{x}xq \\ (p, F) & = & (p, (\hat{x}xq)_{(x,q) \in F(A) \& A \in D(a)}) \\ r & = & R(r) \end{array} \right.$$

where (p, F) is not in CF, $p : a$ and $r \in CF$.

x is a *true* variable in $D_\star$ and a *false* variable in $D^\star$ while $\hat{x}$ is true in $D^\star$ and false in $D_\star$. This duality is used to define the notions of closed and open objects. x is an open object since $x \vdash_{D^\star} \bot$ while $(x.x)$ is a closed object since $\top \vdash_{D_\star} (x.x)$ and $\top \vdash_{D^\star} (x.x)$. $(x.x)$ is true in $D_\star$ since x is and $(x.x)$ is true in $D^\star$ since $(x.x)$ computes to $\hat{x}$ which by definition is true in $D^\star$. Note that if p is open or closed, then p is in a certain sense a *finite* construction since this means that either p is in the inductively defined set for both $D_\star$ and $D^\star$ or in the inductively defined complement for one of them.

Let us say that a restriction map v is *closed* if

(i) $C|v$ is *convergent* with respect to $\overline{CF}$, i.e. if $p \in C|v$, then $\forall q \leq p \exists r \in \overline{CF}(r \leq q)$,

(ii) no open objects in $C|v$,

(iii) $(aq) \in a|v$ iff $q \in A|v$, for some $A \in D(a)$,

(iv) $p \in A|v$ implies $R(p) \in A|v$.

We have the following

Proposition 1.0.2 *If v is a closed restriction map, then $v \models D$.*

Proof: So we have to prove

(a) $\bigcup_{A \in D(a)} (\leq A|v) \subset (\leq, a|v)$,

(b) $(a|v, \leq) \subset \bigcup_{D(a)} (A|v, \leq)$.

(a) Assume $q \leq p$ for some $p \in A|v$ where $A \in D(a)$. Now by (iii) $(ap) \in a|v$, so $q \leq p'$ for some $p' \in a|v$.

(b) Assume $q \geq p$ for some $p \in a|v$. Let us say that an object p is in *canonical* form if p is of one of the following forms

$$\top, (aq), (x.q), (f, I).$$

Claim 1.0.1 *If p is not open, then $\vdash_{D_*} p$.*

Claim 1.0.2 *If $p \in \overline{CF}$, then p is open or in canonical form.*

Proof: By induction on $\vdash_{D_*} p$. ∎

So if $p \in \overline{CF}$, then p is (ar) for some $r \in A$ for some $A \in D(a)$. Now by (iii) we have $r \in A|v$. Now assume that $p \in CF$. Then by (i) and (iv) we know that for some $r \in \overline{CF}$ $r \leq p$ such that $r \in a|v$. r is not open, so it is in canonical form and thus $r' \leq r$ for some $r' \in A|v$ for some $A \in D(a)$. ∎

Proposition 1.0.3 *cl is a closed restriction map.*

Proof: We prove the properties (i)-(iv) given above.

(i) Assume $p \in C|cl$ and $q \leq p$. We may assume that $q \in CF$. $\vdash_{D^*} q$, so for some n $R^n(q) \in \overline{CF}$ where $\vdash_{D_*} R^n(q)$.

(ii) and (iii) both follows directly by definition.

(iv) If $p \in A|cl$, then $\vdash_{D_*} p$ and $\vdash_{D^*} p$. Clearly $\vdash_{D^*} R(p)$. $\vdash_{D_*} R(p)$ follows from the fact that R is not introducing any $\hat{x}$ into $R(p)$. Thus $R(p)$ is a closed object. By a simple induction on CF it is easy to see that $p \in A$ implies $R(p) \in A$. ∎

So we have $cl \models D$ which is the basic test here. A further analysis of cl will involve more complex restriction maps since $(\leq, C \rightarrow C'|cl)$ in general will contain open objects.

5 Logic

Let $\sigma(p) = \{x \mid x \leq p\}$, i.e. the *variable* basis of p. We can then interpret the validity of a sequent modulo a restriction map v by saying that

$$\Gamma \vdash_v A$$

holds if there is a $p \in A|v$ such that $\forall x \in \sigma(p) \exists A \in \Gamma(x \in T(A))$. Now consider the following restriction map - where WF means *wellfounded-*

$$\beta(A) = \{p \in A \mid p \in Def(D_*) \& WF((\leq, \{p\}))\}$$

That is we restrict A to true in D_* and finite in D^*. We can then prove the validity of the intended logical interpretation of the partial inductive definitions using the restriction map β given a set X containing all the variables we will have use for.

Given some $x \in A$ clearly $x \in A|\beta$. Thus x proves the sequent

$$\Gamma, A \vdash_\beta A$$

$\top$ is a closed object which thus proves the sequent

$$\Gamma \vdash_\beta \top$$

Assume $x \in \perp$, then (C, x) proves the sequent

$$\Gamma, \perp \vdash_\beta C$$

Assume $f(i)$ proves $\Gamma \vdash_\beta C_i$ for $i \in I$. Then clearly $(f, I) \in (C_i)_{i \in I}|\beta$ which thus proves the conclusion $\Gamma \vdash_\beta (C_i)_{i \in I}$. So we have

$$\frac{\Gamma \vdash_\beta C_i \quad (i \in I)}{\Gamma \vdash_\beta (C_i)_{i \ in I}}$$

Assume p proves $\Gamma, C_i \vdash_\beta C$. Then clearly $(y.ixp)$, where $y \in (C_i)_{i \in I}$, proves the conclusion $\Gamma, (C_i)_{i \in I} \vdash_\beta C$ for the proper choice of variables x, y. So we have

$$\frac{\Gamma, C_i \vdash_\beta C}{\Gamma, (C_i)_{i \in I} \vdash_\beta C} \quad (i \in I)$$

Assume p proves $\Gamma, C \vdash_\beta C'$. Assume $x \in C$ and $x \in \sigma(p)$. We have $x \notin \sigma((x.p))$. If $p \in C'|\beta$, then $(x.p) \in C \to C'|\beta$. So $(x.p)$ proves the conclusion $\Gamma \vdash_\beta C \to C'$. Thus we have

$$\frac{\Gamma, C \vdash_\beta C'}{\Gamma \vdash_\beta C \to C'}$$

Assume p proves $\Gamma \vdash_\beta C$ and that q proves $\Gamma, C' \vdash_\beta C''$. So $((yp)xq)$ proves the conclusion $\Gamma, C \to C' \vdash_\beta C''$ for the proper choice of variables $x \in C', y \in C \to C'$. So we have

$$\frac{\Gamma \vdash_\beta C \quad \Gamma, C' \vdash_\beta C''}{\Gamma, C \to C' \vdash_\beta C''}$$

Assume p proves $\Gamma \vdash_\beta A$ for some $A \in D(a)$. Then clearly (ap) proves the conclusion $\Gamma \vdash_\beta a$, so we have

$$\frac{\Gamma \vdash_\beta A}{\Gamma \vdash_\beta a} \quad (A \in D(a))$$

Assume that p_A proves $\Gamma, A \vdash_\beta C$ for $A \in D(a)$. Then given $x \in a$ (x, F) proves the conclusion where $F(A) = (z_A, p_A)$ for some chosen $z_A \in A$ in the variable base of p. So we have

$$\frac{\Gamma, A \vdash_\beta C \quad (A \in D(a))}{\Gamma, a \vdash_\beta C}$$

Acknowledgments

I thank the referees for all comments and for forcing me to rewrite this paper. Many thanks to Herbert Sander for a lot of help with LaTeX.

Bibliography

[1] Aczel, P. (1977). An introduction to inductive definitions, in *Handbook of Mathematical Logic*, ed. J. Barwise (North Holland, Amsterdam).

[2] Fredholm, D. and Serafimovski, S. (1990). Partial inductive definitions as type systems for lambda terms, in *Proceedings of the 1989 Båstad workshop in programming logic*, Department of Computer Sciences, Chalmers University of Technology.

[3] Girard, J-Y. (1987). Towards a geometry of interaction, in *Proceedings of AMS conference on categories, logic and computer science*, Boulder.

[4] Hallnäs, L. (1988). Partial inductive definitions, in: *Workshop on General Logic*, ed. A. Avron and R. Harper and F. Honsell and I. Mason and G. Plotkin, ESC-LFCS-88-52, Edinburgh. (A revised and extended version will appear in TCS.)

[5] Hallnäs, L. (1990). On the syntax of infinite objects: an extension of Martin-Löfs theory of expressions, in *Proceedings of COLOG-88*, ed. P. Martin-Löf and G. Mints, Springer Lecture Notes in Computer Science.

[6] Hallnäs, L. and Schroeder-Heister, P. (1991). A proof-theoretic approach to logic programming II, To appear in *The journal of logic and computation*.

[7] Martin-Löf, P. (1970) *Notes on constructive mathematics*, Almqvist & Wiksell, Stockholm.

[8] Prawitz, D. (1973). Towards a foundation of a general proof theory, in: *Logic, Methodology and the Philosophy of Sciences IV*, ed. P. Suppes, North Holland, Amsterdam.

[9] Prawitz, D. (1974). On the idea of a general proof theory, *Synthese* **27**.

Structural Frameworks, Substructural Logics, and the Role of Elimination Inferences

Peter Schroeder-Heister
Universität Tübingen/SNS
Biesingerstr. 10, 7400 Tübingen, Germany
e-mail: schroeder-heister@mailserv.zdv.uni-tuebingen.de

Abstract. Logical inferences are investigated within the context of structural frameworks, in which structural features of deductive systems are separated from logical ones. It is claimed that introduction and elimination inferences operate at different levels. While introduction inferences express logical rules in the genuine sense, elimination inferences are more like structural inferences. This distinction is blurred by certain features of intuitionistic logic, but becomes obvious when systems with restricted structural postulates (substructural logics) are considered.

1   The idea of a structural framework

According to Gentzen [14], in a sequent-style system of logic, we have to distinguish between structural and logical inference schemas. The latter govern the logical content of formulas whereas the former do not refer to logical form. An example of a structural inference schema is that of contraction:

$$\frac{X, A, A, Y \vdash C}{X, A, Y \vdash C} \ ,$$

an example of a logical inference schema is that of $\lor$-elimination

$$\frac{X \vdash A \lor B \quad Y, A \vdash C \quad Y, B \vdash C}{Y, X \vdash C} \ ,$$

where A,B and C denote formulas and X and Y denote lists of formulas. This distinction applies to sequent calculi with introductions on both sides of the turnstile (often referred to as "Gentzen-systems"[1]) as well as to sequent-style natural deduction with introduction and elimination inferences for logical constants only on the right side of the turnstile (as considered in Gentzen [15]). This paper deals mainly with sequent-style natural deduction with a single formula on the right of the turnstile. Only in the final section systems with introductions on the left of the turnstile are considered in connection with computational aspects of deduction. For conceptual simplicity, our investigations are restricted to propositional logic. We also do not deal here with systems with multiple formulas on the right of the turnstile nor with problems of negation.

The idea of "structural frameworks" (see [30]) is twofold: Firstly to extend the notion of structure, and secondly to treat all *logical* content of formulas by means of a database of rules.

Ad 1: The extension of structural means of expression concerns particularly the introduction of a structural implication $\rightarrow$ which is to be distinguished from logical implication $\supset$. It is to supplement structural conjunction which is already present in Gentzen in the form of the comma (to be distinguished from logical conjunction &). Another structural extension (that we are not dealing with in this paper) concerns structural generalization which is to be distinguished from (logical) universal quantification. It is implicit in Gentzen's usage of free variables. This does not mean that at the structural level we are duplicating things which are available at the logical level. Rather, these additional features increase the expressive power of the structural level so as to cover various logical systems in a philosophically plausible and technically uniform way. Apart from that, not every logical constant has a structural analogue (e.g., disjunction has not, at least not in the single-conclusion case). What one would need in a full system is structural conjunction, implication and generalization (of all types), which logically corresponds to a certain fragment of a simple theory of types. In a certain sense, our structural level corresponds to the judgemental level in Martin-Löf's theories.

Ad 2: Instead of considering various logical inference schemas we just consider a single inference schema of rule application. The rules themselves form a database, which is independent of the structural framework itself and may vary. In this way the content-independent inference machinery is separated from the variety of logical systems it may be used to incorporate. One even becomes independent from the logical character of the database:

---

[1]although Gentzen investigated natural deduction too.

the framework may be used for arbitrary databases of non-logical rules as well, which makes it useful for extensions of logic programming (see [31]). Again, the distinction between inference schemas and rules is a conceptual feature - it is not denied that rules can be replaced by certain inference schemas as in Gentzen.

An example of a structural framework for intuitionistic propositional logic can be given as follows: *Structural atoms* are formulas of propositional logic (letters: A, B, C). *Structural implications* are structural atoms or are of the form $(F{\rightarrow}G)$ for structural implications F and G (letters: F, G, H). *Structures* are lists of structural implications (letters: X, Y, Z). *Sequents* are of the form $X{\vdash}F$, *rules* are of the form $X{\Rightarrow}A$, i.e., sequents have arbitrary structural implications as succedents, whereas rules only have structural atoms as conclusions. *Structural inference schemas* are the following:

$$(Reflexivity) \quad \frac{}{F{\vdash}F} \qquad\qquad (Permutation) \quad \frac{X, F, G, Y{\vdash}H}{X, G, F, Y{\vdash}H}$$

$$(Contraction) \quad \frac{X, F, F, Y{\vdash}H}{X, F, Y{\vdash}H} \qquad (Thinning) \quad \frac{X{\vdash}H}{X, F{\vdash}H}$$

$$({\rightarrow}I) \quad \frac{X, F{\vdash}G}{X{\vdash}F{\rightarrow}G} \qquad\qquad ({\rightarrow}E) \quad \frac{X{\vdash}F \quad Y{\vdash}F{\rightarrow}G}{Y, X{\vdash}G}$$

$$({\vdash}{\Rightarrow}) \quad \frac{X_1{\vdash}F_1 \ \ldots \ X_n{\vdash}F_n}{X_1, \ldots, X_n{\vdash}A} \quad \text{if } F_1, \ldots, F_n{\Rightarrow}A \text{ is in the database}$$

The schema $({\vdash}{\Rightarrow})$ also covers the limiting case where the database rule has no premisses and the upper sequents of the inference are lacking.

The database may contain logical rules such as

$$A, B{\Rightarrow}A\&B \qquad A{\rightarrow}B{\Rightarrow}A{\supset}B$$

$$A{\Rightarrow}A{\vee}B \qquad B{\Rightarrow}A{\vee}B$$

$$\vdots$$

However, in principle this approach is not confined to logic; the database may contain extra-logical rules also. For logical elimination inferences see §3 below.

In contrast to previous descriptions based on "higher-level rules" (see [29, 30]), this paper strictly distinguishes between structural implications $F{\rightarrow}G$, which are obtained by iterating $\rightarrow$ to the left and to the right, and rules $X{\Rightarrow}A$, which have atoms as conclusions. The concept of "higher-level rules" mixed these two things up by using $\Rightarrow$ both as a sign for structural implication and as the rule arrow. It is essential for a computational interpretation of database rules that they may contain structural implications as premisses, but themselves are different from structural implications. Rules have a normative (definitional) meaning governed by $(\vdash\Rightarrow)$ (and by the dual principle (IP) discussed in §4). They *define* the "world" one is dealing with. Structural implications have a declarative (descriptive) meaning governed by $(\rightarrow I)$ and $(\rightarrow E)$. They make assumptions or assertions *about* this world (see [28] for further general remarks on that topic).

Our approach gives a natural view of logic programming, if one takes atomic formulas as atoms and considers database rules $F_1, \ldots, F_n \Rightarrow A$ as program clauses. Such a logic programming language permits structural implications in the bodies of clauses and thus extends definite Horn clause programming (see [20]).

2   Structural frameworks for substructural logics

Substructural logics are logical systems in which certain structural principles which are standard in the intuitionistic case are not available.[2] Examples are BCK-logic, in which Contraction is lacking, relevant logics, in which Thinning is dropped, linear logic, which has neither Contraction nor Thinning, or the Lambek calculus which is without Permutation and which in one of its versions does not even have associativity of antecedent formulas. The interest in such systems is increasing, partly due to applications of these logics in computer science and theoretical linguistics. For an overview see [11].

Structural frameworks corresponding to substructural logics can be developed by imposing the restrictions mentioned on the structural inference schemas and by extending the notion of a structural implication so as to incorporate these modifications. The logical principles themselves would, as before, be formulated as database rules. In what follows, frameworks for some prominent logics will be considered as examples, without any claim to completeness: the associative Lambek system and relevant systems without distribution as pure single-family systems, relevant logic with distribution as a pure two-family-system and BCK-logic and linear logic as single-family systems which in addition allow for structure-independent rule-application. Following Belnap's [3] classification, single-family and two-family-systems are based on one or two, respectively, structural associations in the antecedent of a sequent. In the single-family case, we denote it, as usual, by

---

[2]The term "substructural" was proposed by Kosta Došen.

the comma, which is understood as a multi-ary structural connective. In the two-family case we use the semicolon for the second structural connective. By "structure-independent" rule application we mean an inference schema for rule application which (unlike ($\vdash\Rightarrow$)) does not refer to a particular structural association within the antecedent of a sequent (this will become clear from the examples below). Belnap speaks of "families", since in his framework there are, for each structural association, corresponding logical conjunctions, disjunctions, negations, implications and constants. We borrow this terminology, but basically consider conjunctions and implications only. For the systems we are interested in, we need not treat the comma or the semicolon as a binary structural connective.

Pure single-family-systems: Relevant logic without distribution, Lambek calculus

Here we consider frameworks where, as in the intuitionistic case, there is exactly one way of associating structural implications to form a structure, which is denoted by the comma. A structural framework for relevant logic without distribution results from the framework for intuitionistic logic by taking away the postulate of Thinning; i.e., Permutation and Contraction are still available. So, as before antecedents of sequents may be viewed as finite sets. This system of relevant logic is investigated among other single-family systems in [8]. It is not the system of the mainstream of the relevant logic tradition, which rather favours systems in which the distribution law $A\&(B\lor C)\vdash(A\&B)\lor C$ holds. This distribution law cannot be obtained by just dropping Thinning in the structural framework. The proof-theoretically most elegant way is to consider a two-family structural framework (see §2.3 below).

In the Lambek calculus as first described in [22] none of the structural postulates of Permutation, Contraction and Thinning is available. This means, we have associativity of antecedent formulas, i.e., we can write structures as lists, but do not have any further structural postulate in the traditional sense apart from Reflexivity. In the sense of our structural frameworks we do have, of course, further postulates, namely those governing structural implications and the application of rules.[3] Due to the

---

[3] In the even weaker non-associative Lambek calculus introduced in [21] one would have to treat the comma as a binary operator, as done in the uniform treatment of various systems in [3]. Despite the fact that Contraction is lacking, we treat the Lambek calculus as a single-family system as in the original source [22]. One may of course add structure-independent rule application, yielding a system of the type of §2.3.

fact that Permutation is lacking, two structural implications are available, which are here denoted by $\overset{r}{\rightarrow}$ and $\overset{l}{\rightarrow}$, i.e., non-atomic structural implications may be of the form $F \overset{r}{\rightarrow} G$ or $F \overset{l}{\rightarrow} G$. The structural inference schemas governing $\overset{r}{\rightarrow}$ and $\overset{l}{\rightarrow}$ are the following:

$$(\overset{r}{\rightarrow}I) \ \frac{X, F \vdash G}{X \vdash F \overset{r}{\rightarrow} G} \qquad (\overset{r}{\rightarrow}E) \ \frac{X \vdash F \qquad Y \vdash F \overset{r}{\rightarrow} G}{Y, X \vdash G}$$

$$(\overset{l}{\rightarrow}I) \ \frac{F, X \vdash G}{X \vdash F \overset{l}{\rightarrow} G} \qquad (\overset{l}{\rightarrow}E) \ \frac{X \vdash F \qquad Y \vdash F \overset{l}{\rightarrow} G}{X, Y \vdash G}.$$

Based on these two structural implications, it is possible to include in the database introduction rules for Lambek's two logical implications $/$ and $\backslash$:

$$A \overset{r}{\rightarrow} B \Rightarrow B/A \qquad A \overset{l}{\rightarrow} B \Rightarrow A \backslash B \ .$$

It is obvious that the postulates of the structural framework are essential for which logical constants can be defined in the database. So it is not only the database of logical rules which makes the difference between logics, but the structural apparatus governing this database. This gives rise to criteria of logicality according to which one may distinguish between mere extensions of logical systems obtained by adding rules for further constants to an existing database and rival systems obtained by changing the structural postulates for an existing system.[4]

Pure two-family-systems: Relevant logic with distribution

In order to obtain a Gentzen-type system for relevant logics in which the distribution law $A \& (B \lor C) \vdash (A \& B) \lor C$ holds, Dunn [13] proposed to use two structural conjunctions for associating antecedent formulas: an extensional one denoted by the comma and an intensional one denoted by the semicolon, with Thinning holding for the comma but not for the semicolon.[5] To develop a structural framework based on this idea, we first introduce an additional operator $\overset{.}{\rightarrow}$ for forming structural implications. Then we distinguish between extensional and intensional structures. Every structural implication is both an extensional and an intensional structure. *Extensional structures are of the form* $(X_1, \ldots, X_n)$ for intensional structures

---

[4]This idea is closely related to Došen's [6] view of logical constants as punctuation marks, although Došen's structural apparatus is somewhat different from ours.
[5]For later applications and philosophical discussions of this approach see [3, 5, 16, 24, 26, 32].

$X_1, \ldots, X_n$, whereas *intensional structures* are of the form $(X_1; \ldots; X_n)$ for extensional structures $X_1, \ldots, X_n$. Furthermore, for $n = 0$ we have the empty extensional structure $\emptyset_e$ and the empty intensional structure $\emptyset_i$ as limiting cases. A *structure* is an extensional or an intensional structure. So extensional and intensional associations may be nested within a structure. Sequents are of the form $X \vdash F$ for structures X and structural implications F. Rules are either of the form $F_1, \ldots, F_n \Rightarrow A$ (extensional rules) or of the form $F_1; \ldots; F_n \Rightarrow A$ (intensional rules) for structural implications F_i and structural atoms A with limiting cases $\emptyset_e \Rightarrow A$ and $\emptyset_i \Rightarrow A$. When we use a notation like $X, F, (Y; Z) \vdash G$ for a sequent, the commas and semicolons in the antecedent denote either concatenation of equal-type structures or structure-forming operations, whichever is applicable.[6] Then the structural inference schemas include all schemas of the intuitionistic case as given in §1 (but now with X, F and G read as structures and structural implications in the present sense), and furthermore

$$(Permutation;) \quad \frac{X; F; G; Y \vdash H}{X; G; F; Y \vdash H} \qquad (Contraction;) \quad \frac{X; F; F; Y \vdash H}{X; F; Y \vdash H}$$

$$(\dot{\to}I) \quad \frac{X; F \vdash G}{X \vdash F \dot{\to} G} \qquad (\dot{\to}E) \quad \frac{X \vdash F \quad Y \vdash F \dot{\to} G}{Y; X \vdash G}$$

$$(\vdash\Rightarrow;) \quad \frac{X_1 \vdash F_1 \quad \ldots \quad X_n \vdash F_n}{X_1; \ldots; X_n \vdash A} \quad \text{if } F_1; \ldots; F_n \Rightarrow A \text{ is in the database}$$

Here the limiting cases for $n = 0$ of $(\vdash\Rightarrow)$ and $(\vdash\Rightarrow;)$ permit to infer $\emptyset_e \vdash A$ or $\emptyset_i \vdash A$, depending on whether an extensional or an intensional rule is applied.

This means that that we have corresponding principles for the comma with the associated structural implication $\to$ and for the semicolon with the associated structural implication $\dot{\to}$, with the exception that for the comma, but not for the semicolon, Thinning is available.

Introduction rules for logical constants of relevant logics may be the

---

[6]Therefore, if X is an extensional structure, the first and the second comma are appending F and $(Y; Z)$ to X. If X is an intensional structure, these commas form a three-element extensional structure out of X, F and $(Y; Z)$. Similarly, if Y and Z are both intensional structures, the semicolon appends the elements of Z to Y. If Y is intensional and Z extensional, the semicolon appends the extensional structure Z to Y. If both are extensional the semicolon forms a two-element intensional structure, etc. If X is an extensional structure, then $X, \emptyset_e$ is the same as X, otherwise the empty extensional structure $\emptyset_e$ is appended to X, and likewise for $X, \emptyset_i$ or $X; \emptyset_e$ or $X; \emptyset_i$.

following database rules

$$A, B \Rightarrow A\&B \qquad\qquad A \to B \Rightarrow A \supset B \qquad\qquad \emptyset_e \Rightarrow t_e$$

$$A; B \Rightarrow A \circ B \qquad\qquad A \dashrightarrow B \Rightarrow A\text{->}B \qquad\qquad \emptyset_i \Rightarrow t_i$$

to define extensional conjunction (&), implication ($\supset$) and truth (t_e) as well as intensional conjunction (fusion, $\circ$), intensional (relevant) implication (->) and intensional truth (t_i).

Systems with structure-independent rule application: BCK-logic, linear logic

In BCK-logic (see [25]) and linear logic (see [17][7]) one considers a single structure-sensitive association as in §2.1, but in addition a structure-independent schema for and-introduction:

$$\frac{X \vdash A \quad X \vdash B}{X \vdash A \wedge B}[8] .$$

In our context this corresponds to a general schema of structure-independent rule application. Besides rules $F_1, \ldots, F_n \Rightarrow A$, which are applied according to the schema ($\vdash\Rightarrow$), we consider rules of the form $F_1,, \ldots,, F_n \Rightarrow A$, with premisses divided by double commas, which are applied as follows:

$$(\vdash\Rightarrow,,) \quad \frac{X \vdash F_1 \ \ldots \ X \vdash F_n}{X \vdash A} \quad \text{if } F_1,, \ldots,, F_n \Rightarrow A \text{ is in the database.}$$

In a structural framework for BCK-logic we have the inference schemas of Reflexivity, Permutation, Thinning, ($\to I$), ($\to E$), ($\vdash\Rightarrow$) and ($\vdash\Rightarrow,,$), i.e., Contraction is lacking as compared to the intuitionistic case. In a structural

---

[7]By "linear logic" we mean what Girard calls "rudimentary linear logic", i.e., we are just considering the propositional fragment without exponentials. For a treatment of the structural features of linear logic within the framework of display logic see [4].

[8]By "structure-independent" as opposed to "structure-sensitive" we mean that the lower sequent of an inference schema does not refer to a particular way of structuring the antecedent as does a schema like

$$\frac{X \vdash A \quad Y \vdash B}{X, Y \vdash A\&B} \quad \text{or} \quad \frac{X \vdash A \quad Y \vdash B}{X; Y \vdash A \circ B} .$$

For the case of conjunction, Girard's terminology is "additive" versus "multiplicative" ([17]) or "alternative" versus "cumulative" ([18], Appendix B).

framework appropriate for linear logic Thinning is excluded in addition. In the database we can now include introduction rules for two conjunctions:

$$A, B \Rightarrow A \& B \qquad A_{,,} B \Rightarrow A \wedge B$$

As for the systems considered before, the structural framework itself is independent of what kind of rules are available in the database. There is no need for them to be logical rules.

Mixtures of $(\vdash \Rightarrow)$ and $(\vdash \Rightarrow_{,,})$ are also possible, e.g., by permitting rules such as $F_1, (F_{2,,} F_3) \Rightarrow A$ which would be applied as follows:

$$\frac{X \vdash F_1 \quad Y \vdash F_2 \quad Y \vdash F_3}{X, Y \vdash A}.$$

To avoid a possible misunderstanding: The distinction between structure-sensitive and structure-independent rule application is no particular feature of weak substructural logics, but exists for intuitionistic logic too. However, in the presence of Contraction and Thinning, these cases can be mutually reduced to each other.

One may, of course, add structure-independent rule application to a two-family system, yielding, e.g., a relevant logic with conjunctions &, ∘ and ∧. More generally, one may develop the idea of a universal structural framework that would allow to make all the distinctions mentioned so far. Such a meta-framework would have to provide facilities for defining structural postulates themselves in a uniform way. Došen's [9] idea of sequents of higher levels and of horizontalizing inference schemas into such sequents may become fruitful in that respect. This approach might also lead to a conceptually perspicuous treatment of modal logics within structural frameworks. The idea of such a general structural framework goes in a different direction than do most logical frameworks, since it comprises a whole world of systems even at the propositional level. Present-day logical frameworks normally start with problems of higher types and quantification and take the structural postulates of intuitionistic logic for granted.

3 The problem of elimination rules

So far the examples of logical rules have been only introduction rules. In the structural framework considered in §1 with unrestricted structural postulates, elimination rules can be added to the database as well. The ∨-elimination rule would read

$$(\vee E \ rule_i) \qquad A \vee B, (A \rightarrow C), (B \rightarrow C) \Rightarrow C$$

(the index i here stands for "intuitionistic"). Following the pattern of the ∨-elimination rule, in [29] the following general schema for introduction and elimination rules for an n-ary sentential operator s was proposed:

$$(sI\ rules)\quad X_1 {\Rightarrow} s(A_1,\ldots,A_n)\quad\ldots\quad X_n {\Rightarrow} s(A_1,\ldots,A_n)$$

$$(sE\ rule)\quad s(A_1,\ldots,A_n),(X_1{\rightarrow}C),\ldots,(X_n{\rightarrow}C){\Rightarrow}C\ .$$

Here the X_i stand for structures (lists of structural implications), in which only formulas built up from $A_1,\ldots,A_n$ by means of logical operators already defined occur. For example, in the case of s being implication, we have $n = 1$ and $X_1 = (A_1{\rightarrow}A_2)$; in the case of disjunction we have $n = 2$ and $X_1 = A_1$, $X_2 = A_2$; in the case of equivalence we have $n = 1$ and $X_1 = ((A_1{\rightarrow}A_2),(A_2{\rightarrow}A_1))$, etc. It can be shown that in all cases $(sE\ rule)$ is equivalent to the "standard" elimination rule. For example,

$$(\supset E)\quad A{\supset}B,((A{\rightarrow}B){\rightarrow}C){\Rightarrow}C$$

is equivalent to *modus ponens*

$$A{\supset}B, A{\Rightarrow}B\ .$$

According to this view, both introduction and elimination rules are part of the database of logical rules, the elimination rules being generated in a uniform way from the introduction rules. However, this becomes problematic when substructural logics are considered. The idea that the general schema $(sE\ rule)$ for elimination rules can be taken to be the same in all structural frameworks (see [30]) turns out to be infeasible.

We take the ∨-elimination rule ($\vee E\ rule_i$) as an example. Applying this rule is equivalent to using the following inference schema:

$$(\vee E\ schema_i)\quad \frac{X{\vdash}A{\vee}B\quad Y,A{\vdash}C\quad Z,B{\vdash}C}{X,Y,Z{\vdash}C}\ .$$

In the intuitionistic structural framework this is equivalent to

$$(\vee E\ schema)\quad \frac{X{\vdash}A{\vee}B\quad Y,A{\vdash}C\quad Y,B{\vdash}C}{Y,X{\vdash}C}\ .$$

However, in the absence of Thinning and Contraction these two schemas are not equivalent, and ($\vee E\ schema$) is more appropriate than ($\vee E\ schema_i$), since otherwise desirable results cannot be obtained. In systems without Thinning ($\vee E\ schema$) permits normalization of proofs whereas ($\vee E\ schema_i$) does not. To see that, suppose $X{\vdash}A{\vee}B$ is inferred from $X{\vdash}A$, and ($\vee E$ *schema$_i$*) is applied in the next step. Then the standard contraction of this redex yields $Y, X \vdash C$ (the conclusion of ($\vee E$ *schema*)) rather than $X, Y, Z \vdash C$ (for which Thinning would be needed). In a system without Contraction replacement of equivalent formulas becomes problematic with ($\vee E$ *schema$_i$*). For example, suppose that $Y, A \vee B \vdash C$ and $A \dashv\vdash A'$ have been proved. Then $Y, A' \vdash C$ and $Y, B \vdash C$ can be inferred, from which by ($\vee E$ *schema$_i$*) $Y, Y, A' \vee B \vdash C$ rather than $Y, A' \vee B \vdash C$ is obtained.[9].

This does not necessarily speak against elimination inferences as rules. By using the mixture of structure-sensitive and structure-independent rule application mentioned in §2.3 one may obtain the effect of ($\vee E$ *schema*) by means of the rule

$$(\vee E \ rule) \quad A \vee B, ((A \to C), (B \to C)) \Rightarrow C \ .$$

In all systems where one can treat structures as multisets, i.e., where one has Permutation, ($\vee E$ *rule*) would be appropriate.

However, in a Lambek-style system, where Permutation is lacking, or in a two-family system with the possibility of a nested structuring of antecedents, the situation becomes different. In both cases the $\vee$-elimination schema has to be formulated as

$$(\vee E \ schema') \quad \frac{X \vdash A \vee B \quad Y[A] \vdash C \quad Y[B] \vdash C}{Y[X] \vdash C} \ ,$$

where the square brackets denote the occurrence of a certain formula within a structure. This includes ($\vee E$ *schema*) as a special case. In a Lambek-style framework, due to the fact that Permutation is lacking, $Y[A] \vdash C$ does not necessarily imply $Y, A \vdash C$, so that ($\vee E$ *schema*) is strictly weaker than ($\vee E$ *schema'*). This again means that ($\vee E$ *schema'*) cannot be expressed by the database rule ($\vee E$ *rule*) (with $\to$ understood as $\overset{r}{\to}$ or $\overset{l}{\to}$). A similar argument applies to two-family-systems, since an A in a context $Y[A]$ cannot necessarily be extracted and moved out of the context. For example, a sequent $(A_1; A), A_2 \vdash C$ is not normally equivalent to some $X, A \vdash B$ or $X; A \vdash B$.

There seems to be a way out of this problem, namely by allowing structural implications and not just structural atoms to be conclusions (heads) of rules. The $\vee$-elimination rule could then be formulated as

$$(\vee E \ rule') \quad A \vee B, ((A \to F), (B \to F)) \Rightarrow F \ ,$$

---

[9]In particular, without Contraction, ($\vee E$ *schema$_i$*) does not guarantee the full uniqueness of disjunction in the sense that $X, A \vee B \vdash C$ is always equivalent to $X, A \vee^* B \vdash C$, with $\vee^*$ being a duplicate of $\vee$ with the same rules. Uniqueness is dual in a way to conservativeness, which again is related to normalization (see [10, 12]).

which has the effect of ($\lor E$ *schema'*). For example, in the two-family system of §2.3, $(A_1; A), A_2 \vdash C$ is equivalent to $A \vdash A_1 \dot\to (A_2 \to C)$. So from $X \vdash A \lor B$ and $(A_1; A), A_2 \vdash C$ and $(A_1; B), A_2 \vdash C$ we obtain $X \vdash A_1 \dot\to (A_2 \to C)$ by applying ($\lor E$ *rule'*), which is equivalent to $(A_1; X), A_2 \vdash C$. A similar example can be given for the Lambek-style system: suppose we have $X \vdash A \lor B$ and $A_1, A, A_2 \vdash C$ and $A_1, B, A_2 \vdash C$. Then we obtain $A \vdash A_1 \overset{l}{\to} (A_2 \overset{r}{\to} C)$ and $B \vdash A_1 \overset{l}{\to} (A_2 \overset{r}{\to} C)$ and thus $X \vdash A_1 \overset{l}{\to} (A_2 \overset{r}{\to} C)$ by applying ($\lor E$ *rule'*), which is equivalent to $A_1, X, A_2 \vdash C$.

In the single-conclusion case, this approach (which was followed in [30]) has a similar effect as Belnap's [3] use of an involutive structural negation in a multiple-conclusion framework, by means of which formulas can be moved arbitrarily between the two sides of a sequent. However, this runs counter to the intuitions of structural frameworks, which are to separate the structural aspects of a system from its logical (database) content. Structural implication(s) should only be governed by structural introduction and elimination principles like ($\to I$) and ($\to E$) and not by rules in the database. Structural implications in the heads of rules would put material (non-structural) content into structural implications, making structural implications logical entities.

The fact that ($\lor E$ *schema'*) and not ($\lor E$ *schema*) is the correct representation of $\lor$-elimination reveals in general, quite independently of our notion of a structural framework, a deep asymmetry betwen introduction and elimination inferences, more precisely, a difference in the notion of discharging assumptions. Whereas in ($\lor E$ *schema'*), one has to consider arbitrary embeddings of formulas in structures (denoted by square brackets), this is not the case with introduction schemas. For example, in the Lambek calculus the schema for \-introduction has to be formulated as

$$\frac{A, X \vdash B}{X \vdash A \backslash B}$$

with A at a specified (namely leftmost) place on the left side of the turnstile and *not* as

$$\frac{X[A] \vdash B}{X \vdash A \backslash B}$$

with A arbitrarily embedded in a context. Otherwise, under certain natural conditions, the structural law of Permutation could be proved by applying principles for logical implications.[10]

---

[10]This asymmetry between introduction and elimination rules will be treated in more detail in [27]. It also applies to sequent systems with more than one formula in

This is blurred in the intuitionistic system with its simple structural assumptions and also in weaker systems which can be based on multisets as assumption-structures. From the standpoint of a general structural framework, such structural assumptions are just limiting cases and cannot be taken as universal: two-family systems and systems without Permutation cannot be excluded without giving up the conceptual unity of structural frameworks with different structural assumptions. Conclusions to be drawn about structural frameworks in general therefore also apply to the intuitionistic case. This means that elimination-inferences cannot be properly treated as database rules but have to be given a different role.

4 Elimination inferences as structural inferences

If elimination inferences cannot be incorporated into the database, how else can they be treated? To formulate them in the ordinary way as inference schemas like ($\lor E$ *schema'*) and add them to the structural inference schemas would destroy the idea of a structural framework, in which the structural part is kept apart from the content (logical or other) which is put into the database.

A way out is indicated by the fact that the elimination inferences follow a general pattern. This general pattern can be formulated as

$$(sE \; schema) \quad \frac{X \vdash s(a_1, \ldots, a_n) \quad Y[X_1] \vdash C \; \ldots \; Y[X_n] \vdash C}{Y[X] \vdash C},$$

if the introduction rules for s are given by (sI *rules*). Unlike (sE *rule*), which turned out to be problematic with restricted structural postulates (at least with two-family systems and systems without Permutation), (sE *schema*) would be appropriate for all structural frameworks without structure-independent sI-rules. So we are not putting specific logical inference schemas into a structural framework, but one general schema. By further generalizing it we can even make it entirely independent of the specific form of rules for logical constants. In this way we obtain a general structural principle which applies to any database of rules, databases of logical introduction rules just being a special case.

More precisely, we formulate a general elimination or inversion principle for arbitrary structural atoms, not only for logically compound formulas. Given a database of rules, define

$$\mathbf{D}(A) := \{Z : Z \Rightarrow A \text{ is a substitution instance of a database rule}\}.$$

---

the succedent. The failure of conservativeness of the wrong implication law over the structural law of Permutation was observed by Wansing [33].

Then the general elimination schema is formulated as

$$(IP) \quad \frac{X \vdash A \quad \{Y[Z] \vdash C : Z \in \mathbf{D}(A)\}}{Y[X] \vdash C} .$$

It is obvious that in the case of logical constants with (*sI rules*) as introduction rules, (*sE schema*) is a special case of (IP). However, (IP) is general enough to be counted as a structural postulate as opposed to database rules which govern contents. This does not mean that (IP) has to be an ingredient of any structural framework. As with every structural postulate, one may discuss what happens if it is present and if it is lacking, obtaining various systems that way. In the case of logic, it represents a way of dealing uniformly with elimination inferences for systems weaker than intuitionistic logic. In the case of other databases, it represents a way of treating arbitrary rules as introduction rules for atoms, allowing to invert these rules in a certain way. This is why we call (IP) an "inversion principle"[11].

It may be noted that (IP) becomes an infinitary schema if $\mathbf{D}(A)$ is infinite. However, natural restrictions can be formulated that make $\mathbf{D}(A)$ finite when (IP) is applicable.[12] In the case of logical constants, $\mathbf{D}(A)$ is finite due to the restrictions on introduction rules (such as the one that the premisses X_i in an introduction rule $X_i \Rightarrow s(A_1, \ldots, A_n)$ should contain no formulas except $A_1, \ldots, A_n$).

When structure-independent rule application is available, as in frameworks suitable for linear or BCK logic, $\mathbf{D}(A)$ and (IP) have to be formulated in a more general way. For example, take the $\wedge$-introduction rule $A,, B \Rightarrow A \wedge B$. The elimination inferences should comprise the two schemas

$$\frac{X \vdash A \wedge B \quad Y[A] \vdash C}{Y[X] \vdash C} \qquad \frac{X \vdash A \wedge B \quad Y[B] \vdash C}{Y[X] \vdash C}$$

rather than the single one

$$\frac{X \vdash A \wedge B \quad Y[A, B] \vdash C}{Y[X] \vdash C} ,$$

which would be appropriate for the structure-sensitive conjunction &. In general, let U be of the form $(F_1, \ldots, F_n)$ or $(F_1,, \ldots,, F_n)$. Then U is

---

[11]In fact, (IP) is closely related to Lorenzen's "inversion principle" (see [23]), a relationship which cannot be spelled out here.

[12]One basically requires that $(\mathbf{D}(A))\sigma = \mathbf{D}(A\sigma)$ for any substitution σ, and therefore that (IP) is closed under substitution. For further discussion see [20]).

called a *premiss structure* (which is not a structure in the genuine sense, since the double comma is not considered a structure-forming operation that can occur on the left side of $\vdash$). A *selection function* is a function f operating on premiss-structures such that

$$f(U) = U \text{ if } U = (F_1, \ldots, F_n)$$
$$f(U) = F_i \text{ for some } i \ (1 \leq i \leq n) \text{ if } U = (F_1,, \ldots,, F_n) .$$

Then we define for each selection function f

$$\mathbf{D}^f(A) := \{f(U) : U \Rightarrow A \text{ is a substitution instance of a database rule}\}.$$

The generalized inversion principle consists of a set of schemas, one for each selection function:

$$(IP_{gen}) \quad \left\{ \frac{X \vdash A \quad \{Y[Z] \vdash C : Z \in \mathbf{D}^f(A)\}}{Y[X] \vdash C} : f \text{ selection function} \right\}.$$

Obviously, (IP) is a limiting case of (IP_{gen}), if $\mathbf{D}^f(A)$ is the same for all f, which holds if there is no structure-independent rule by means of which A can be obtained.

Computationally, the schema (IP) is not well tractable since the A in the left premiss does not occur in the conclusion. For computational purposes a sequent-style system with introductions on the left side of the turnstile is more appropriate. To obtain such a system, we replace in the structural frameworks considered the Reflexivity principle by

$$\overline{A \vdash A}$$

(which refers to structural atoms rather than arbitrary structural implications) and the $(\rightarrow E)$ principle by

$$(\rightarrow \vdash) \quad \frac{X \vdash F \quad Z, G \vdash H}{Z, (F \rightarrow G), X \vdash H} .$$

Analogous changes apply to cases where several structural implications are available. The schema (IP) is then reformulated as a schema for the introduction of an atom A on the left side of the turnstile:

$$(\Rightarrow \vdash) \quad \frac{\{Y[Z] \vdash C : Z \in \mathbf{D}(A)\}}{Y[A] \vdash C} ,$$

which in a certain sense is dual to $(\vdash \Rightarrow)$. (Here the letter C may equivalently be replaced by F, which gives more computational flexibility.) This is exactly the inference schema which is discussed in the context of logic programming in [19], [20] and [28], upon which the programming language GCLA is based ([1, 2]). In that context it was called the "D-rule" or the rule of "local reflection" and was motivated from an entirely different point of view which had nothing to do with structural postulates and restrictions thereof but with considerations concerning inductive definitions and treating databases in that way. The fact that a different approach leads to exactly the same principle confirms its conceptual significance.

The formulation of (IP) as a computationally meaningful principle for the introduction of atoms on the left side is another argument against the treatment of elimination inferences as database rules, even if this is possible as it is in the intuitionistic case. The structural atom C in these rules, which unifies with every other structural atom, excludes any computational reading. When applied according to ($\vdash\Rightarrow$), database rules produce only right-introduction inferences, whereas elimination inferences receive computational significance by formulating them as left-introduction inferences. The schema ($\Rightarrow\vdash$) carries out the idea of computationally relevant introductions of (structural) atoms on the left side of the turnstile in a uniform manner, independently of their specific logical form (if they have one at all).

The generalized version of ($\Rightarrow\vdash$) corresponding to (IP_{gen}) is the following:

$$(\Rightarrow\vdash_{gen}) \quad \left\{ \frac{\{Y[Z]\vdash C : Z \in \mathbf{D}^f(A)\}}{Y[A]\vdash C} \ : \ f \text{ selection function} \right\} .$$

It might be mentioned that for logic programming the combinatorial complexity of ($\Rightarrow\vdash_{gen}$) may lead to difficulties, although database rules are most easily understood and handled as structure-independent rules according to ($\vdash\Rightarrow_{,,}$) of §2.3. This is no problem for intuitionistic logic, where Thinning and Contraction is available, but becomes problematic when evaluation procedures for weaker systems are considered (see [31]).

The view we have arrived at is that of a structural framework which, besides the handling of structural association (of premises of rules or antecedents of sequents) and of structural implication, may include inversion principles. In the case of logically compound formulas, these inversion principles instantiate to elimination inferences. The (logical or extra-logical) content of formulas is expressed in a database of rules which, in the case of logical composition, are introduction rules in the ordinary sense.

Acknowledgements. The research reported here was supported by the Fritz Thyssen Foundation. I would like to thank Kosta Došen, Venkat Ajjanagadde and two anonymous referees for helpful comments and suggestions.

Bibliography

[1] Aronsson, M., Eriksson, L.-H., Gäredal, A., Hallnäs, L. & Olin, P. The programming language GCLA: A definitional appraoch to logic programming, *New Generation Computing*, **4** (1990), 381–404.

[2] Aronsson, M., Eriksson, L.-H., Hallnäs, L. & Kreuger, P. A survey of GCLA: A definitional approach to logic programming. In: P. Schroeder-Heister (ed.), *Extensions of Logic Programming. International Workshop, Tübingen, FRG, December 1989, Proceedings.* Springer LNCS, Vol. 475, Berlin (1991), 49–99.

[3] Belnap, N. D. Display logic. *Journal of Philosophical Logic*, **11** (1982), 375–417.

[4] Belnap, N. D. Linear logic displayed. *Notre Dame Journal of Formal Logic*, **31** (1990), 14–25.

[5] Belnap, N. D., Gupta, A. & Dunn, J. M. A consecution calculus for positive implication with necessity. *Journal of Philosophical Logic*, **9** (1980), 343–362.

[6] Došen, K. Logical constants as punctuation marks. *Notre Dame Journal of Formal Logic*, **30** (1989), 362–381.

[7] Došen, K. Modal logic as metalogic. *SNS-Berichte*, Universität Tübingen, no. 90-5, 1990. To appear in the *Proceedings of the Kleene '90 Conference* (Chaika, Bulgaria).

[8] Došen, K. Sequent systems and groupoid models. *Studia Logica*, **47** (1988), 353–385.

[9] Došen, K. Sequent-systems for modal logic. *Journal of Symbolic Logic*, **50** (1985), 149–168.

[10] Došen, K. & Schroeder-Heister, P. Conservativeness and Uniqueness. *Theoria*, **51** (1985), 159–173.

[11] Došen, K. & Schroeder-Heister, P. (Eds.) *Logics with Restricted Structural Rules: Proceedings of the Conference held in Tübingen, October 1990.* In preparation.

[12] Došen, K. & Schroeder-Heister, P. Uniqueness, definability and interpolation. *Journal of Symbolic Logic,* 53 (1988), 554–570.

[13] Dunn, M. Consecution formulation of positive R with co-tenability and t. In: Anderson, A.R. & Belnap, N.D., *Entailment: The Logic of Relevance and Necessity,* Vol. I, Princeton University Press, 1975, 381–391.

[14] Gentzen, G. Untersuchungen über das logische Schließen. *Mathematische Zeitschrift,* 39 (1935), 176–210, 405–431, English translation in: M.E. Szabo (ed.), *The Collected Papers of Gerhard Gentzen,* Amsterdam: North Holland, 1969, 68–131.

[15] Gentzen, G. Die Widerspruchsfreiheit der reinen Zahlentheorie. *Mathematische Annalen,* 112 (1935), 493–565.

[16] Giambrone, S. *Gentzen Systems and Decision Procedures for Relevant Logics.* Ph. D. thesis, ANU Canberra, 1983.

[17] Girard, J.-Y. Linear logic. *Theoretical Computer Science,* 50 (1987) 1–102.

[18] Girard, J.-Y., Lafont, Y. & Taylor, P. *Proofs and Types.* Cambridge University Press, 1989.

[19] Hallnäs, L. Generalized Horn Clauses. *SICS Research Report,* no. 86003, 1986.

[20] Hallnäs, L. & Schroeder-Heister, P. A proof-theoretic approach to logic programming. I. Clauses as rules. *Journal of Logic and Computation,* 1 (1990), 261–283; II. Programs as definitions, *ibid.,* in press.

[21] Lambek, J. On the calculus of syntactic types. In: R. Jacobson (ed.), *Proceedings of the 12th Symposium on Applied Mathematics,* AMS, Providence 1961, 166–178, 264–265.

[22] Lambek, J. The mathematics of sentence structure. *American Mathematical Monthly,* 65 (1958), 154–170.

[23] Lorenzen, P. *Einführung in die operative Logik und Mathematik.* Springer: Berlin 1955, 2nd ed. Berlin 1969.

[24] Meyer, R. K. Metacompleteness. *Notre Dame Journal of Formal Logic*, 17 (1976), 501–516.

[25] Ono, H. & Komori, Y. Logics without the contraction rule. *Journal of Symbolic Logic*, 50 (1985), 169–201.

[26] Read, S. *Relevant Logic: A Philosophical Examination of Inference*. Oxford: Basil Blackwell, 1988.

[27] Schroeder-Heister, P. An asymmetry between introduction and elimination inferences. In preparation. (Abstract presented at the 9th International Congress of Logic, Methodology and Philosophy of Science, Uppsala, August 1991).

[28] Schroeder-Heister, P. Hypothetical reasoning and definitional reflection in logic programming. In: P. Schroeder-Heister (ed.), *Extensions of Logic Programming. International Workshop, Tübingen, FRG, December 1989, Proceedings*. Springer LNCS, Vol. 475, Berlin (1991), 327–340.

[29] Schroeder-Heister, P. A natural extension of natural deduction. *Journal of Symbolic Logic*, 49 (1984), 1284–1300.

[30] Schroeder-Heister, P. *Structural Frameworks with Higher-Level Rules: Proof-Theoretic Investigations*. Habilitationsschrift. Universität Konstanz, 1987. (Abstract presented at the Workshop on General Logic, Edinburgh, February 1987).

[31] Schroeder-Heister, P. Substructural logics and logic programming. In: L.-H. Eriksson *et al.*, *Proceedings of the Second Workshop on Extensions of Logic Programming, Stockholm 1991*, Springer LNCS, Berlin 1992.

[32] Slaney, J. General logic. *Australian National University, ARP, Technical Report*, No. 4, 1988 (to appear in the *Australasian Journal of Philosophy*).

[33] Wansing, H. The adequacy problem for sequential propositional logic. *ITLI Prepublication Series*, LP-89-07, University of Amsterdam, 1989.

Printed in the United States
By Bookmasters